THE BURIAL COMPLEXES OF THE KNIGHT AND NORTON MOUNDS IN ILLINOIS AND MICHIGAN

MEMOIRS OF THE MUSEUM OF ANTHROPOLOGY
UNIVERSITY OF MICHIGAN
NUMBER 2

THE BURIAL COMPLEXES OF THE KNIGHT AND NORTON MOUNDS IN ILLINOIS AND MICHIGAN

By

JAMES B. GRIFFIN
RICHARD E. FLANDERS
PAUL F. TITTERINGTON

ANN ARBOR
1970

ISBN (print): 978-0-932206-64-0
ISBN (ebook): 978-1-951538-21-7

Browse all of our books at sites.lsa.umich.edu/archaeology-books.

Order our books from the University of Michigan Press at www.press.umich.edu.

For permissions, questions, or manuscript queries, contact Museum publications by email at umma-pubs@umich.edu or visit the Museum website at lsa.umich.edu/ummaa.

Plate 1. Dr. Paul F. Titterington

1895-1969

Paul F. Titterington was raised in Jerseyville, Illinois, the son of a physician. His profession was medicine and more particularly radiology but his avocation was archaeology. He received his undergraduate degree from the University of Missouri and his medical degree from St. Louis University Medical School. His interest in archaeology centered in the evidence of Indian occupation in the St. Louis area and in the application of x-rays to the study of pottery, other prehistoric materials and the study of prehistoric skeletal material. He was among the first to make contributions in this latter field. As the result of his own collecting, excavation, and purchases he acquired an outstanding group of materials from the St. Louis area and kept unusually good records.

Dr. Titterington associated with the professional archaeologists of the Middle West, particularly W. C. McKern of the Milwaukee Public Museum during the 1930's. When the Society for American Archaeology was formed in 1934 and 1935, Titterington was one of the non-professional archaeologists who was active in supporting its establishment. He wrote the lead article in the first number of American Antiquity on "Certain Bluff Mounds of Western Jersey County, Illinois." He made other significant contributions to American archaeology in his other publications. It is a privilege and a pleasure to be able to dedicate this report on the Knight Mound Group to him.

The Museum of Anthropology and the authors gratefully acknowledge the financial assistance of National Science Foundation Grant 346, and of the Grand Rapids Museum Foundation, for a substantial portion of the funds for publication.

CONTENTS

FIGURES

FIGURES

MAPS

PLATES

INTRODUCTION

In the presentation of the excavation of the Knight and Norton Mound Groups and in the discussion of the data recovered, various terms have been used which need definition or at least some explanation. No claim is made that these are adequate, definitive or that they will receive universal approbation. The phase names which appear below are proposed to provoke a proper demonstration of their validity or superficiality (Table 1). The term phase is thus used in approximately the meaning proposed in Willey and Phillips (1958: 22), "an archaeological unit possessing traits sufficiently characteristic to distinguish it from all other units similarly conceived, whether of the same or other cultures or civilizations, spatially limited to the order of magnitude of a locality or region and chronologically limited to a relatively brief interval of time.

The term Woodland is used in a very loose sense to refer to the data from prehistoric sites in the Eastern United States from about 1000 B.C. to the historic period by a large number of quite diverse societies that made pottery that was coiled, often cordmarked on the interior surface or otherwise paddled to complete the outer surface finish (Griffin, 1967). In the early half to two-thirds of this 2500 year period, hunting, gathering, collecting, trapping, fishing and other such activities provided most of the food supply. Throughout this same period of 2500 years there was an increasing dependence on agriculture.

Early Woodland refers to the cultural material and inferred behavior from sites from about 1000 B.C. to about 200 or 100 B.C. This period includes the introduction of pottery, mound building for burial of the dead, initial eastern agriculture, increasing use of special raw materials which become widely distributed such as copper, mica, galena, ocean shells, and other items most often recognized in association with increased emphasis on burial ceremonialism.

Middle Woodland refers to a time period from about 200 to 100 B.C., to about A.D. 300 when the cultural material from many sites in the Eastern United States shows evidence of participation in, or association with the cultural patterns of the Hopewellian complexes (Griffin, 1967; and Map 1).

Late Woodland refers to the post-Hopewellian Woodland societies that lasted up to the early historic period, particularly in the northern part of the Eastern United States and Canada.

In the Illinois Valley area, which includes the lower stream courses of the drainage of the Illinois and adjacent Mississippi rivers, a number of sites and ill-defined complexes have been identified that belong by stratigraphy, material remains, radiocarbon dates, or combinations of these, to the Early Woodland period. In the central Illinois Valley from a short distance north of Peoria to approximately Brown County, the work of University of Chicago archaeologists, and others (Cole and Deuel, 1937), introduced the term Red Ocher to apply to a primarily burial complex represented in Fulton County Mound F°11 and in the lower levels of F°14. The term Black Sand was applied to the non-Hopewellian material found in

NORTHEASTERN UNITED STATES-

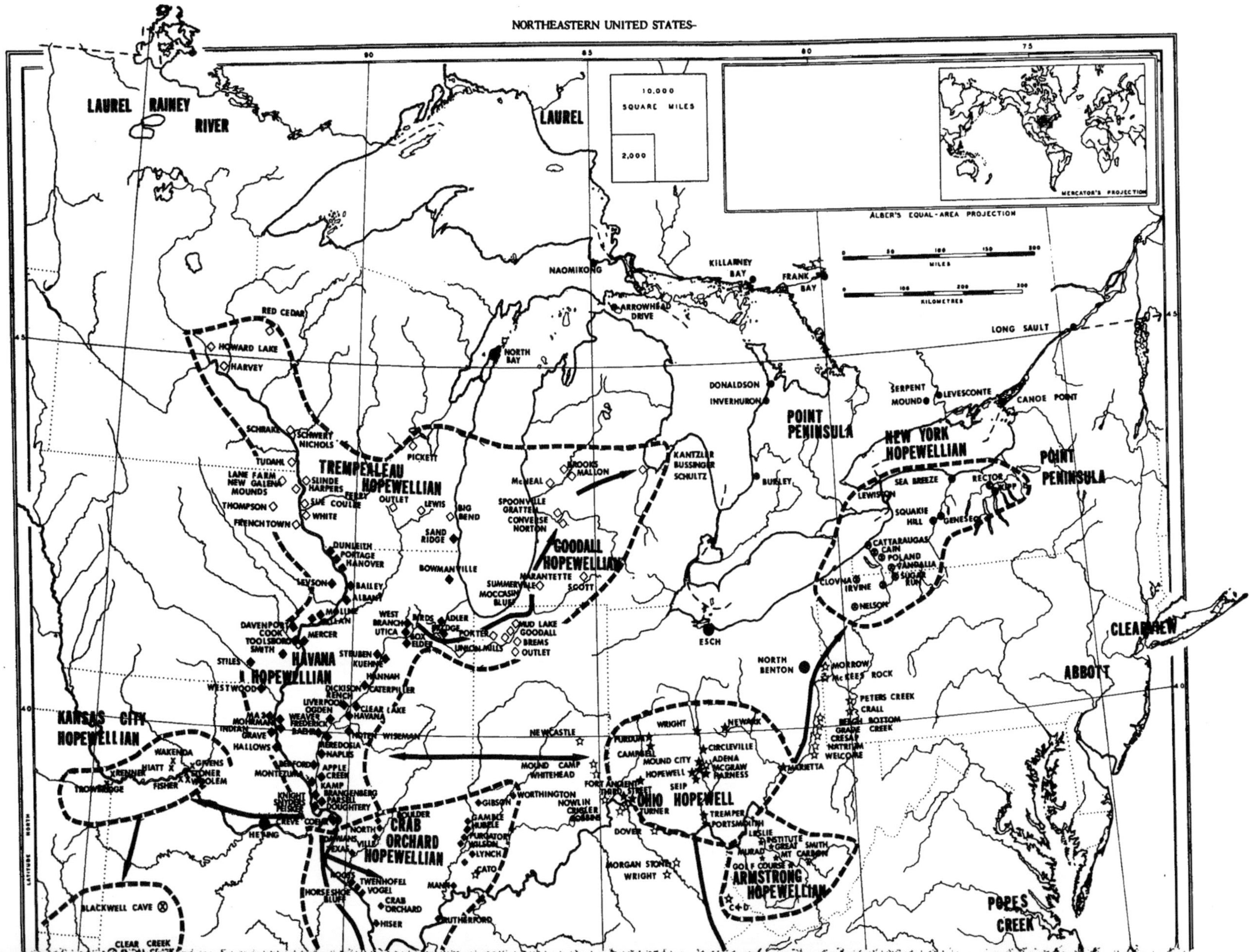

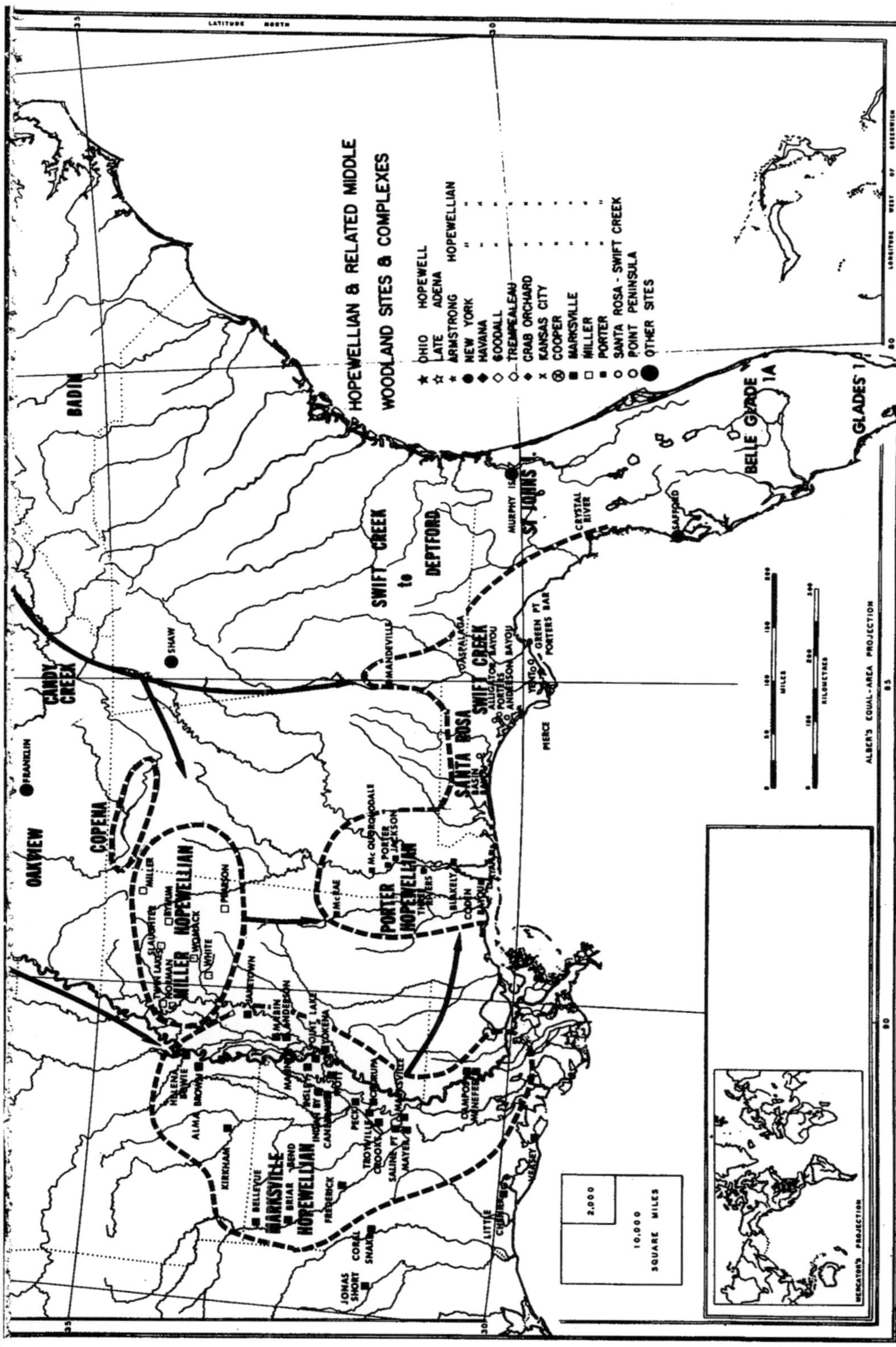

Map 1. Some Middle Woodland sites and complexes (from Griffin, 1967).

TABLE 1

PROPOSED PHASE ALIGNMENT FOR MIDDLE WOODLAND COMPLEXES IN THE ILLINOIS VALLEY

Period	Time	Lower Illinois Valley		Middle Illinois Valley		Upper Illinois Valley	
		Sites	*Phases*	*Sites*	*Phases*	*Sites*	*Phases*
Late Woodland		Apple Creek	White Hall				
	A.D. 400	Knight Mounds Woodland	Fox Creek		Weaver		?
		Knight Mound 8 Bedford Mounds 4, 9		F^{o}910			
Middle Woodland Hopewellian Complexes	200	Brangenberg Mound 2					LaPorte
		Kamp Mound 9	Pike	Steuben Mound 1, Pits C & D	Steuben		
		Bedford Mound 12 Gibson Mound 4 Gibson Mound 5		F^{v}229, House 1		Adler Mounds Utica Group 1, Mound 6	
	100	Brangenberg Mound 3		Mn^{v}15 (Early)		Utica Group 3, Mound 1	
		Klunk Mounds 1, 2, 7 Bedford Mounds 10-11	Bedford	Clear Lake Mn^{o}1 Steuben Mound 1, Pit B	Ogden	Goodall Mound 21 Porter Mound Utica Group 1, Mound 8	Utica
	A.D. 1	Bedford Mound 8 Early Macoupin Village (?)		Havana Mound 6		Utica Group 1, Mound 1	
		Snyders Pre-Hopewell Style Village	Calhoun	McDougal-Hartman Dickison Mound Havana Mound 2 Pond Village Site	Fulton		
Early Woodland	200 B.C.						
		Snyders Peisker Sub Mound 2	Peisker	F^{o}13 Liverpool Sub Mound F^{o}77	Morton		
				Liverpool Village Site F^{v}88 (Early)	Black Sand		
				F^{o}15 F^{o}11, F^{o}14 (Early)	Red Ocher		Peterson

the village under Mound F^{o}77 at the Liverpool site and in the village numbered F^{v}88. Thus, assuming that archaeological finds continue to support the concept that Red Ocher and Black Sand represent different kinds of cultural behavior of different groups, their identification as distinct "phases" of Early Woodland in the central Illinois Valley would be justified.

The term Morton complex has been in the literature for some time (Griffin, 1952*a*: 100-01) to refer primarily to a ceramic complex following Black Sand. Pottery of this complex was identified as Morton Incised and Sister Creeks Punctated from two mounds of the Morton Group, F^{o}13 and F^{o}15; Mound F^{o}54 of the Sister Creeks group which is also called the Whitnah Mound; Mound Mn^{o}1 or the Clear Lake Mound; and F^{o}35, the Dickson Camp site. The assumption is made that this complex of Morton and Sister Creeks could represent the Morton phase of late Early Woodland in the central Illinois Valley. The Neteler Stamped pottery would belong in the later Fulton phase.

In the lower Illinois Valley area from about Brown County to the town of Alton, published descriptions of comparable complexes have not appeared. According to information from Gregory Perino and Stuart Streuver, there are ceramic materials from the submound levels of the Peisker Mound 2 in Calhoun County which Streuver has suggested can be divided into an earlier Peisker phase and a later Black Sand phase (Streuver, 1968). For purposes of this paper the term Peisker phase will be used to represent both of Streuver's phases and to apply to what may be a recognizably different complex from the central Illinois Valley Black Sand phase. Perhaps that loosely defined Late Archaic group called the Titterington focus (Titterington, 1950) will be shown to have a late expression comparable to the Red Ochre phase of central Illinois (Griffin, 1968; 133-34).

In the northern Illinois Valley no coherent complex has been recognized which can be used for this Early Woodland period although some Marion Thick pottery, short stemmed projectile points, turkey tail points and other materials have been reported. The term Peterson phase can be applied to an early expression of the Early Woodland complex for the area around the southern end of Lake Michigan (Faulkner, 1960).

The Middle Woodland period is recognized by the presence of artifacts, techniques of mound construction and other cultural features identified with the Hopewell sites in Ohio. In Illinois the ceramic complex called Havana ware (the term ware is used rather loosely), is closely associated with Hopewellian mound and village sites (Griffin, 1952*a*). It is a distinctive group of ceramic features which vary considerably through time and in various regions, and this variation has been recognized for years by every competent archaeologist dealing with the problem. Cole and Deuel (1937) attempted a definition of the "Central Basin Phase" (phase in the Midwest Taxonomic method sense) by which they meant a complex later than Black Sand but not yet Hopewell. They included both the Morton ceramic complex and their 2A pottery group which is now primarily part of Havana ware. Such a distinction is not as valid a grouping as the recognition of a distinctive Morton phase and of an early expression of Havana tradition pottery which could be called the Fulton phase, because its development was first recognized in that area, and because the Pond site in Fulton County recently excavated by Howard Winters is said to belong to an occupation with early Havana pottery and without the Hopewell ware.

The group of mounds, McDougal-Hartman, Renchville and Caterpillar (Bluhm and Beeson, 1960) are placed in the Fulton phase on tenuous evidence, and hope, rather than conviction. Dickison is placed early because of the Snyders points and because the sherds in the fill of the mounds included pottery from Morton Incised to Havana Zoned Stamped. The assumption is made that the Hopewell style pottery was not yet in use.

The term Havana tradition has been adopted by archaeologists dealing with the Illinois area in an effort to recognize the distinctiveness of Illinois Valley Hopewellian complexes (Streuver, 1964; Brown, 1964). This term has only been successfully employed in describing the pottery assemblages and should be used to refer to the Havana ceramic tradition. The position taken in this paper then, is that the Fulton phase represents the period and cultural level in the central Illinois Valley associated with early forms of the Havana ceramic tradition. When all of the cultural activities of the Fulton phase are known they will constitute the activities of the early Middle Woodland period Hopewellian societies of the central Illinois Valley.

In the lower Illinois Valley region there is very little substantial evidence for such a pre-Hopewell pottery style phase. The ceramic sequence from the Snyders village site excavations of the Museum of Anthropology in 1948 and 1949 (Griffin, 1952*b*; Powell, 1957) produced ceramic evidence for an occupation with an early expression of the Havana ceramic tradition but with sufficient divergence from the central Illinois Valley to recognize a regional subtradition of Havana. The lithic component at Snyders from bottom to top is primarily Middle Woodland. With the expectation then, that a lower Illinois Valley equivalent of the Fulton phase will be recognized, the term Calhoun phase is proposed to refer to the pre-Hopewell pottery style early Middle Woodland Hopewellian complexes in the lower Illinois Valley.

There is not yet recognized a developmental sequence from the Peisker phase, Early Woodland to the Calhoun phase, as far as pottery is concerned, so that the appearance of the Havana ceramic tradition at the Snyders or other regional sites may result from the adoption of the central Illinois Valley ceramic features by the people in the lower Illinois Valley. The newly excavated Macoupin village site in Jersey County may have a Calhoun phase occupation, but it is difficult to recognize temporal variants on village sites that were occupied more or less throughout most of the Middle Woodland period.

In the upper Illinois Valley there is even less evidence of occupation during a period comparable to the proposed Fulton and Calhoun phases. None of the mounds of the Utica groups or the Adler mound can be shown to belong to this period and none of the Goodall focus mounds or village debris belong in this period. There are sherds from Plum Island (Fenner, 1963; Fig. 28, *d* and *e*), and from the Starved Rock area in the Museum of Anthropology that belong in this ceramic period. If and when this cultural expression of early Middle Woodland is recognized it can be given an appropriate baptism.

The Hopewell style pottery is a recognizable ceramic complex that can be used to mark a span of time in the Illinois Valley Middle Woodland-Hopewellian complexes. None of the excavated mounds in the central Illinois Valley area from Peoria to Beardstown have produced either whole or reconstructable Hopewell style vessels. Some part of the occupation of the Havana village Mnv15 should belong to this period as well as occupation at many other Hopewellian village sites in the area. It is almost impossible to delimit short time contemporary ceramics or other expressions of material culture from the stratigraphic pits or seriation charts based on these excavations. One of the best examples is the seriation of the Clear Lake village site by Fowler (1952, 1955) which produces general trends in ceramic change but cannot be used successfully for delineation of the associated pottery types within a phase of 100 to 200 years. The village area had been riddled with storage and refuse pits and other occupational disturbances for about one thousand years so that the "zones" are percentage zones of pottery types, not levels of sequential segregated societies. This is true of many village site situations and is one of the reasons why most emphasis on the selection of units for phases has been on mound units. Without either Hopewell style vessels or radiocarbon dates the temporal position of the excavated mounds such as that at Clear Lake (Mn°1), the Liverpool mounds, or those of the Weaver group, is difficult to determine. One burial group which can be assigned to this period was found in Pit B of Mound 1 at the Steuben site (Morse, 1963; Pl. XVII), even though other and stratigraphically later burials in Pit C and D belong to the next phase. For sentimental and/or historical reasons the term Ogden phase could be applied to the Hopewellian complexes in the central Illinois Valley that mark the appearance of the Hopewell style pottery, but before the arrival of the Baehr-Pike limestone tempered types. The dominant pottery complex of the Ogden phase remains, of course, that of the Havana ceramic tradition. A satisfactory separation of short term ceramic attributes and decorative styles is still not worked out for this tradition. The type Havana Zoned Stamped is, for example, believed to precede the appearance of the Hopewell style pottery, but it certainly continues on into both the Ogden phase and later periods.

In the lower Illinois Valley a number of mound excavations by Gregory Perino and associates have produced burials with the Hopewell style pottery and a later series of burials with Baehr style pottery. Mounds 1, 2 and 7 of the Klunk group (Perino, 1968) may be regarded as relatively early and Mounds 5, 6, 11, and 13 of the same group as relatively late. The burials in Bedford Mounds 8 and 10-11 (Streuver, 1960, and information provided by Gregory Perino), and the earlier excavated Brangenberg Mound 3 (Griffin and Morgan, 1941), may also be viewed as in this period on the basis of radiocarbon dates. This phase can be called the Bedford phase. The term is applied to lower Illinois Valley Middle Woodland societies which were in existence about the time of Christ and to about A.D. 100. Probably Snyders Mound C°114 and many of the lower Illinois Valley area Hopewellian villages would have occupations of this period. Prominent among these would be Snyders and Sconce-Schudel along the Mississippi side of Calhoun County, the early part of the Kamp village, and Blue Creek and Manker in Pike County on the west side of the Illinois River.

In the upper Illinois Valley the best representation of this time period would be Mound 1 of Utica Mound Group 1 (Griffin and Morgan, 1941; Henricksen, 1965) in a central burial area, which included a superb example of Hopewell Zoned Rocked Dentate Stamp, a Montezuma Punctated vessel and a Havana Zoned Stamped jar; and Mound 8 of Group 1 which had a Hopewell Zoned Rocked Dentate Stamp vessel with a Havanna Zoned Stamped flat-bottomed jar. The Montezuma jar and the Hopewell style vessel in Mound 8 are limestone tempered but the Hopewell style vessel in

Mound 1 is not. All three of these probably were made in the lower Illinois Valley. The term Utica phase could be used for this cultural complex associated with this horizon of the Hopewell style period of the Illinois Middle Woodland Hopewellian complexes of the upper Illinois Valley. This phase could also be applied to the earliest known Hopewellian sites in the LaPorte County, Indiana area.

The stratigraphic excavations at the Snyders site in the late 1940's indicated the gradual shift from well-made Hopewell style pottery to the ceramic varieties included in the names Baehr and Pike (Griffin, 1952*a*, and 1952*b*). The Baehr type varieties are viewed as the result of a gradual deterioration of design and skill of manufacture of vessels which occupied the same function or functions in the society as the Hopewell style vessels. This took place well after limestone had become the normal tempering ingredient in the pottery of the lower Illinois Valley. At about the same time as the gradual shift from Hopewell style varieties to the Baehr varieties, the thicker, larger jars which are much more common were also made with limestone temper and these are called Pike. Streuver's excavations in Kamp Mound 9 (Streuver, 1960) demonstrated that just before and during the construction of this major mortuary structure in northeastern Calhoun County, that the Baehr and Pike ceramics were dominant in the fictile art. This apparent shift from Havana and Hopewell type varieties took place approximately A.D. 100 to 150 in the lower Illinois Valley and seems to have been one reflection of greater cultural association of the several late Hopewellian societies in the lower Illinois Valley and immediately adjacent locales. Since the Baehr and Pike ceramic groups are essentially modified and later expressions of the Hopewell and Havana pottery the term Pike tradition is not considered appropriate if it connotes an entity comparable to the Havana ceramic tradition or that of the Hopewell tradition. However or whatever the Pike phase may be it is not an "intrusion of Pike stylistic elements into that area about the time of Christ" (Streuver, 1965; 219). Limestone pottery of Baehr and Pike varieties was transported into the central and northern Illinois Valley, to western Michigan and the Saginaw Basin and into Missouri, Iowa, and Wisconsin. Streuver has been using the term Pike to represent the cultural behavior of lower Illinois Valley societies in the latter part of the existence of Middle Woodland Hopewellian and that is what is meant here by the Pike phase.

Other mounds besides Kamp Mound 9 which are clearly in the Pike phase are Klunk Mounds 5, 6, 11 and 13; Bedford Mound 9, Brangenberg Mound 2, and the primary burials in Knight Mound 8. Much of the Knight Mound village site, the Pool village site and many others in the lower Illinois Valley had occupations during the Pike phase. This phase seems to have lasted for about 150 to 200 years to A.D. 300 to 350.

In the central Illinois Valley, pottery of the Havana ceramic tradition continued into the post-Ogden period and there were significant intrusions of Baehr and a few Pike sherds into this area. Two ceramic developments took place which can be identified and are probably sequential. The first is the Steuben Punctate type which is clearly a late expression of the Havana ceramic tradition, and the second is the gradual appearance and growth of what has been called Weaver ware (Griffin, 1952*a*). Weaver pottery is associated with very late Hopewellian complexes but it also continues and is dominant in the early Late Woodland period. Therefore, there is some justification for a Steuben phase of Late Hopewellian complexes of the central Illinois Valley which would include early Weaver ceramics. Steuben Mound 1, Pits C and D would belong in the Steuben phase, as would the later part of the Steuben village site and some part of the occupations at the Rench site near Peoria, at the Clear Lake village, and at the Weaver and Whitnah village sites. This definition does not conform to the two foci proposed by Morse (1963) for the material at the Steuben site.

In the upper Illinois Valley and eastward along the Kankakee, pottery of the Baehr-Pike types was brought in, and local pottery products were made with the same decorative features. This could be referred to as the La Porte phase after the Indiana county in which the Goodall group was located. The placement of the Adler site (Winters, 1962) in a relatively late Middle Woodland position is based on the small projectile points conforming more with the late Steuben flint complex than with the earlier Hopewellian forms. Admittedly, in the absence of any Hopewell or Baehr style pottery, Adler Mounds 3 and 5 are difficult to place in time and could perhaps belong in a time period before the appearance of Hopewell pottery at the Utica Mounds. This is another indication of our present inability to recognize the temporal placement of most of the Hopewellian culture.

It is difficult to obtain an adequate time estimate for the Goodall site near La Porte, but the sherds illustrated by Quimby (1941) which are in the Grand Rapids Public Museum do not include any clear examples of the earliest Havana tradition types, even though most of the pottery from this site is clearly part of the Havana ceramic tradition. Quimby's illustrations also include examples of Hopewell style pottery (Quimby, 1941; Pl. 15, No. 3) and examples of Baehr Brushed on his Plate 13, No. 30, and Baehr Zoned Brushed on Plate 13, Nos. 25, 26 and 27. The lobed vessel from Mound 22, discussed by Brown (1964; 115-18), is not very similar to the Havana Mound 6 vessels because of the presence on the latter vessels of the distinctive smooth upper rim band which is a marked feature of the early Havana tradition vessels in central Illinois. While there are large Snyders Corner Notched points at the Goodall site they are in a marked minority and most of the corner notched points are smaller and narrower forms. In the view adopted in this paper the Goodall site is not a single "phase" but instead, the village occupation there, and the 22 or so mounds, cover a time period from the Ogden phase of the central Illinois Valley and the Utica phase of the upper Illinois Valley up to the Steuben phase.

The post-Hopewellian societies in the Illinois Valley area may be regarded as local variants of Late Woodland. In the central Illinois Valley the Maples Mills phase was the first such recognized unit but its presumed temporal range now is thought to be about A.D. 700-900, and may represent a population movement from southern Wisconsin into the northern half of Illinois, or it may have resulted from the acceptance by Weaver potters of decorative techniques developed to the north. The term Weaver was used initially by Donald Wray (1952: 156) and regarded by him as "a period of cultural change which disrupts although it does not completely sever, the tradition of Middle Hopewell." The gradual shift from Havana tradition pottery to Weaver types is found on many of the sites with occupational evidence from the Steuben phase of Late Hopewellian to what is called here the Weaver phase of early Late Woodland. This gradual shift was first recognized by Griffin when he had the opportunity to study the extensive collection from the Clear Lake site which was sent to Ann Arbor by Mrs. Ethel Schoenbeck in 1940 to 1943, and also was reemphasized during his sorting of that collection again in the spring of 1951 along with other pottery at the Illinois State Museum. The Weaver phase then would represent post-Hopewellian populations in a time period of about A.D. 300 to 700 in the central Illinois Valley.

In the lower Illinois Valley, Dr. Paul F. Titterington, in a series of papers, beginning with the first number of American Antiquity, described the Jersey Bluff focus. The time spread now, however, is so great for this Late Woodland unit from about A.D. 300 to about A.D. 1100 that several temporal phases need to be defined. In sorting the Snyders, Knight, and other village site materials from the lower Illinois area the same difficulty of separating Late Havana tradition pottery from early Jersey Bluff was noticed as when sorting Havana ware from Weaver. In the preparation of this statement on the Knight Mound Group the interpretation that almost all of the Late Woodland burials in the Knight Mounds were early Late Woodland was inevitable. Furthermore the characteristics of the Knight Late Woodland ceramics as a group have not previously been isolated. As an admittedly temporary measure the term Fox Creek phase can be employed for the Late Woodland occupation of the extreme lower Illinois Valley and adjacent Cahokia area. The term is obtained from the small creek which flows into the Mississippi River south of the Knight Mound Group. Some of the mounds described by Titterington, such as Mound 1 near Nutwood (Titterington, 1935) belong in this phase. A recent survey of the northern American Bottoms area by P. J. Munson (1966) has proposed the recognition of a Terminal Havana unit in that area, and also an early Bluff culture occupation. These together are equivalent in concept and ceramics to what is here called the Fox Creek phase with the deletion of the Baehr-Pike pottery at Munson's sites which he recognized was probably equivalent to the Pike phase occupations.

There is difficulty in differentiating between the various ceramic groups studied by Epstein, Taylor and MacGregor and the terminology employed by Streuver and his associates in the Pike and Green County areas. Streuver (1964, 1968) has named a White Hall phase and written about its economic base (that of the Hopewellian complexes has not been published). The carry-over of some Hopewell decorative techniques and motives on White Hall pottery is quite evident. Radiocarbon determination from White Hall would suggest a beginning date of around A.D. 400 but a somewhat earlier figure for its beginning is favored here. Streuver's White Hall pottery varieties are similar to those of the Pool and Irving sites described by MacGregor (1958) and his associates. Many of them are also similar to Weaver ware varieties. Whether both a Weaver and a White Hall phase are necessary cannot now be determined for lack of either adequate Weaver or White Hall data and comparative evaluations of both.

In the upper Illinois Valley there is no known complex which has been determined to represent the early part of Late Woodland. Pottery from the Du Page drainage illustrated by Gates (1961: Fig. 4); from the Bowmanville site in Chicago by Fenner (1961: Fig. 21, *a-d;* Fig. 22, *d-g, i*); and the pottery described by Brown (1961) as the Swanson complex, may represent the unnamed phase. The Swanson complex has been attributed by Brown to the early historic period, but if so it would be a remarkable reversion to early Late Woodland ceramics. He now believes that this complex should be reevaluated.

THE KNIGHT MOUND GROUP

CALHOUN COUNTY, ILLINOIS

BY

JAMES B. GRIFFIN

RICHARD E. FLANDERS

PAUL F. TITTERINGTON

INTRODUCTION

The Knight Mound Group is located in the southeast quarter of the northwest quarter of section 10, Hamburg Township, Calhoun County, Illinois, on the bluffs immediately to the east above the flood plain of the Mississippi River and on the north side of Fox Creek. Fox Creek flows into the flood plain from the east draining a small area of the narrow upland of Calhoun County which reaches an elevation of about 750 feet. A small creek on the east side of the divide flows through Kampsville, located at the foot of the bluffs on the west side of the Illinois River. The Knight Group is about 20 miles north of the mouth of the Illinois, and about 13 miles north of the Snyders site.

The mound group is situated in a semicircular valley approximately two miles long and three-quarters of a mile wide from the Mississippi River northeast to the base of the bluff. In the north central portion of the valley about one-half mile east of the river is a low ridge about 50 feet high running parallel to the river on which there are 13 small mounds, C°1-C°13 (Pl. 2) circular to wide oval in shape. About one-half mile to the northwest of the crescent ridge is a high ridge with a tall conical mound, C°16, on its west end. Extending along the ridge to the east were Mounds C°17-26. Mounds C°14-15 were on the southern end of a high ridge about one-quarter mile northeast of the crescent ridge (Fig. 1).

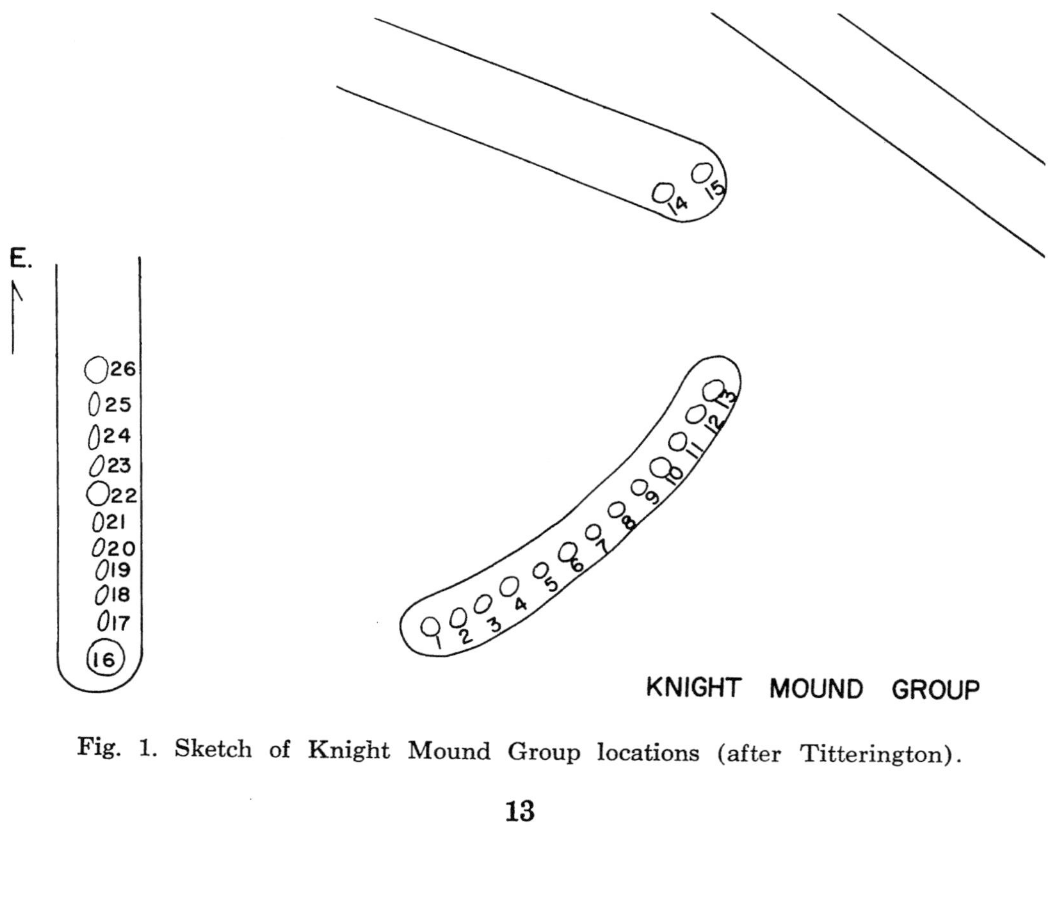

Fig. 1. Sketch of Knight Mound Group locations (after Titterington).

The village area probably occupied by the builders of the Knight Mound Group is located in the first terrace of the valley to the south and west of the mounds at an elevation of about 450 feet above sea level. Part of this village area was owned by Mrs. C. A. Knight and part by Mrs. Harry Ansell whose name was used by the University of Illinois to report on their excavations (McGregor, 1958: 202) in 1950. Village debris extends for at least one-quarter mile on the first terrace from the Ansell property south of State Highway 96 where it turns east to Kampsville. East of the primary village area and north of Route 96 there is a gradual rise to 460 to 480 feet, and in this area Griffin noticed a considerable amount of white flint chippage in April, 1948. There was no pottery in this older Archaic occupation zone.

According to the soil survey of Calhoun County the lower village area is covered by brownish yellow-gray silt loam over sand or gravel. It was developed on stream terraces. The mounds were built of soil derived from the loess deposits on the upland area. The loess called brownish yellow-gray silt loam has a sub-soil 12 to 16 inches below the surface which varies from reddish-brown to reddish-yellow (R. S. Smith, *et al.*, 1932).

Calhoun County, western Jersey County, and parts of the adjoining Green and Pike Counties are part of the Lincoln Hills section of the Ozark Plateau Province with two major rivers, the Mississippi and Illinois, and the mouths of tributary streams and the uplands. Calhoun County is long and narrow and movement of people from sites on the Mississippi side of the county to the Illinois would not have been hindered by the geography. Much of the information concerning the available and utilized food and other natural resources that are applicable to the prehistoric people of the lower Illinois River Valley are also applicable to the societies in the adjacent Mississippi Valley. The program of intensive study of the Illinois Valley now underway by Stuart Streuver of Northwestern University, will produce a better understanding of the utilization of that environment by prehistoric people. Until fairly recent times much of the produce of the Calhoun County farmers moved to market by boat or barge, not by road. It is probable that people of the Knight Mounds also moved by dugout on the two main rivers.

The temperature range is considerable, from well above 100 degrees to a maximum low of 27 degrees below zero and the rainfall from just above 20 inches to .50 inches a year. The area is on the northeastern border of the oak-hickory region of the temperate deciduous forest biome as described by Shelford (1963) which had as two important members deer and turkey. In addition, the rich floral and faunal resources of the Illinois and Mississippi rivers and their swamps, marshes, and ox-bow or cut-off lakes were major sources of food and the raw material for tools. The proximity of Calhoun County to the flood plain, which provided resting and feeding areas for migratory birds, was another favorable factor in the selection of prehistoric village locations.

The varied limestone formations with many exposures along the major streams and tributaries provided extensive chert formations for weapons and implements (Rubey, 1952). It was not necessary to go very far to acquire such raw material and most of the implements in the Knight mounds and village are probably from sources within a short distance. Definitive studies have not yet been made to accurately identify sources of lithic materials, with the exception of obsidian (Griffin, Gordus and Wright, 1969), so that statements on this matter in this volume are at present only speculations.

About 1900 a local school teacher is

known to have dug rather extensively into the tops of all the larger mounds of the group but there is also the possibility of other earlier or later excavations. Mr. Walter Wadlow of Alton, Illinois obtained the right to excavate the mounds from Mr. C. A. Knight the landowner, early in the 1940's. The mounds were excavated over a period of years by Walter Wadlow, Mr. Wadlow's father, Mr. M. L. Gibson of Alton, Illinois, Dr. Paul Titterington of St. Louis and others. Most of the provenience data, the excavation photographs, much of the description and many of the photographs of specimens are from Dr. Titterington's notebooks and negatives which he presented to the Museum of Anthropology. He also donated to the Museum most of the artifacts from the excavations. A few of the specimens such as the platform pipes were obtained by Gray LaDassor of St. Louis and are now, fortunately, in the collections of the Gilcrease Institute in Tulsa, Oklahoma.

A number of individuals have studied the Knight collection. Preceding the brief publication on the Knight figurines which are now in the Milwaukee Public Museum (McKern, Titterington and Griffin, 1945), J. B. Griffin made a detailed description of the pottery vessels in September, 1943, at Titterington's home. The descriptions with some modifications have been incorporated in this paper. On April, 1951, Edward Scully made extensive notes of the non-ceramic material which was of considerable value in subsequent studies. Richard E. Flanders utilized much of the above data in his presentation of the Knight material which formed a part of his Ph.D. thesis (Flanders, 1965). In this study he also benefited from the work on the Illinois area Hopewellian lithic complexes by Mrs. Anta Montet-White who was associated with the Museum of Anthropology from 1958 to 1965. Donald Janzen, Nancy Wilson, Bruce D. Smith and Lewis H. Larson, Jr., have also assisted in the study of the Knight Group. Richard Wilkinson has studied the skeletal material from the Knight Group that is now in the Office of Anthropology of the Smithsonian Institution as the result of Dr. Titterington's association with T. Dale Stewart.

Part of the financial support for the preparation of this report on the Knight Mound Group was provided by the Wenner-Gren Foundation in 1950 and 1951 when it was known as The Viking Fund. This grant was made to the Museum of Anthropology for the Central Mississippi Valley Archaeological Survey.

The data presented in this paper on the Knight Mound group are a record of burial customs and associated materials at one locality in northwestern Calhoun County, Illinois. The record is decidedly incomplete due to the varied circumstances of the excavation and preservation of the material. It is believed that this record has value for assessments of cultural activities during part of the prehistoric occupation of the area.

The village site on the Knight-Ansell property has not been excavated except in terms of a number of pits which produced ceramic material ranging from Middle Woodland to Mississippi complexes, with what we are calling early Bluff pottery as the dominant material in the areas excavated by the University of Illinois personnel (Taylor, 1958: 193-208). The absence of Hopewell style pottery types is striking, as is the absence of pottery types which could be Early Havana. The same statement can be made about the ceramic collection from the Knight site in the Museum of Anthropology obtained from a number of individuals over the past 25 years. The lithic collection from the Knight village site at the Museum of Anthropology has been studied by Dr. Anta M. White and it is noteworthy in the absence of true

Snyders Corner Notched forms and the representation of Norton, Gibson, and Steuben forms (White, 1968: 137-43). The Knight Village belongs primarily in the Pike phase of Late Middle Woodland, and the Fox Creek phase of Late Woodland.

MOUND C°1

Mound 1 is the northernmost of the 13 mounds on the low ridge and is an oval 50 feet by 25 feet with the long axis northwest by southeast (Fig. 2). The height

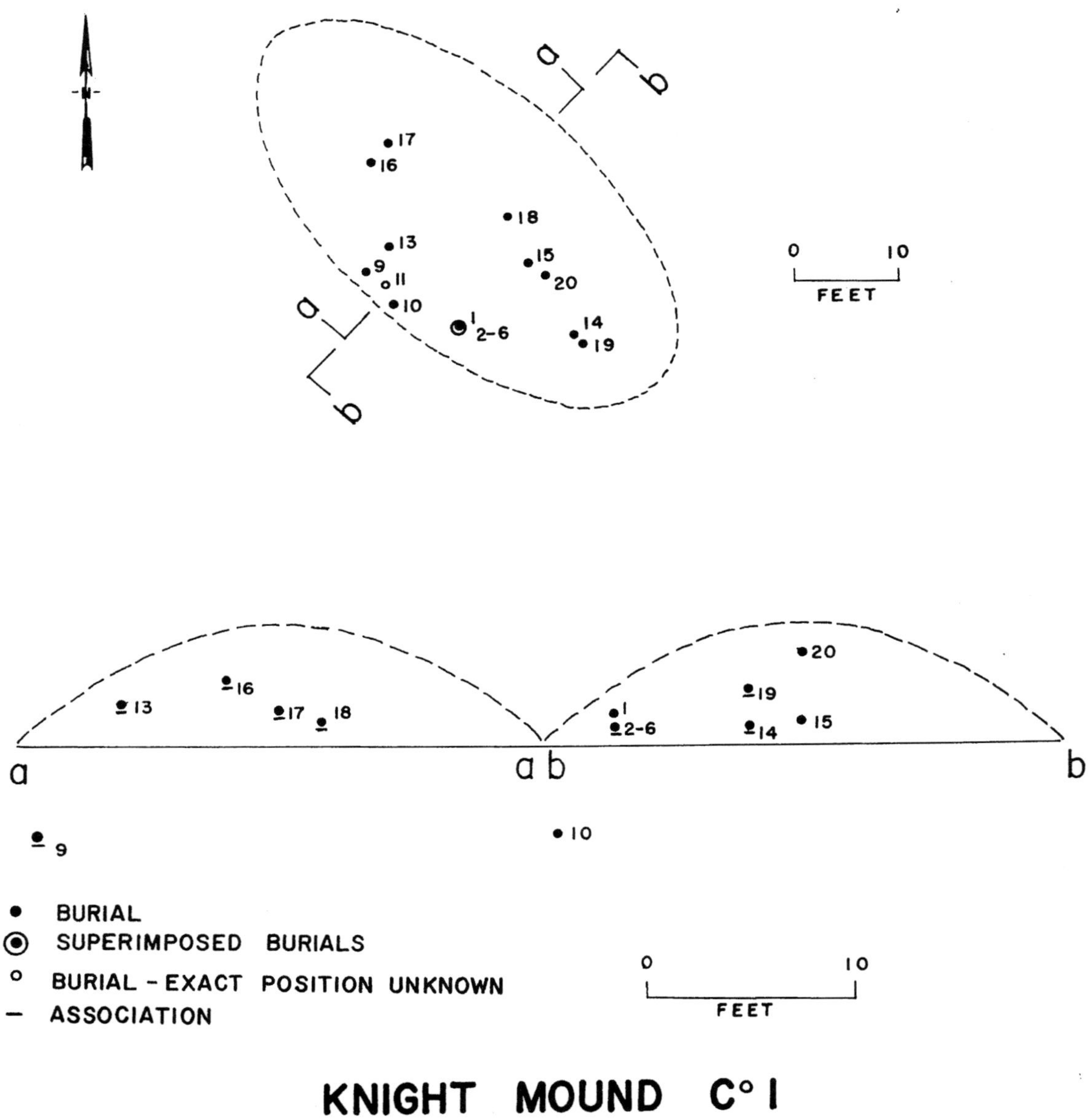

Fig. 2. Diagram of burial locations in Knight Mound C°-1 according to Dr. P. F. Titterington. Length of mound about 50 ft.

of the mound was not mentioned but can be inferred to be at least six feet by the depth of the burials given in the notes. Excavation was started on May 27, 1945, and finished on August 12, 1945. The area including Mounds C°1 and C°2 is reported as having been completely excavated and a 15-foot-wide tench was excavated in the area to the north of Mound C°1 to establish the limits of the cultural material.

Work was started on the west side of the mound near the south end with a 10-foot-wide trench. A secondary extended male burial, about sixty years old, C°1-1 (USSM Cat. No. 380191), was found 32 feet south of the north end of the mound and nine feet west of the long axis, one foot six inches above ground level (Pl. 3, *a* *b*). The long bones of the legs and the left innominate bone were in their normal relationships and both radii and ulnae were in the proper relation to each other but not to their corresponding humeri. The skull was inverted and the mandible was located between the femurs. This skeleton has healed fractures of the left humerus, both ulnae and a rib, and was evidently interred while partially articulated. Immediately below this burial at a depth of two feet two inches was found a mass burial (C°1-2 to -6) of five individuals, two adult females and three children, all in the flexed position and partially cremated in place according to the notes. The soil in the area immediately surrounding the burial appears dark in the photograph (Pl. 3,*a*, *b*). One tibia was saved from the cremation and a left humerus and femur, two right innominate bones, a right tibia and several small skull fragments are identifiable in the photograph. A small, crudely made Canteen Zoned Punctate vessel, C°1-7 (Pl. 4,*a*), was found on a level with the cremation and about three feet north.

This crudely decorated small vessel is 9.5 cm. high and 9 cm. wide. It has fine grit temper with some hematite inclusions that were probably in the clay. The rim and lip areas were thinned so that the narrow lip is .3 cm. wide and the rim thickness is .4 to .5 cm. About .8 cm. below the lip there is a very narrow shallow horizontal incised line. Pendant to this line are festoons or arcs of varying breadth and depth that are formed by the same type of incised line. Within the festoons are zones of very closely spaced tiny deep punctates made by a very sharp point. Some of these punctate areas are banded by another incised line and some are not. The decoration was placed on a smooth slightly polished uneven surface, with scattered brush marks. The interior surface is also uneven and the shallow depressions could be from finger impressions made while the vessel was shaped and decorated. The vessel may represent a continuation of the Hopewell Zoned Punctate concept but the execution was very poor. The exterior surface is light tan to slightly smoke blackened, which probably occurred during firing. The vessel has a rounded base.

There was a projectile point just to the west of this mass burial on the same level (Pl. 6, *b*). The projectile point (C°1-29) is a Steuben Expanded Stemmed point of pinkish-white flint with a convex base, slightly convex sides and expanding flake retouch. The point is side notched and is 6.8 cm. long, 2.9 cm. wide at the base (greatest width) and 7 mm. thick at the thickest part. The stem is 1.9 cm. wide and 1.6 cm. long.

Burial C°1-8 (USNM 380193) was that of an adult male but was so badly scattered that the type of interment cannot be determined. The skull, clavicle and part of one ulna were recovered during one excavation trip, and the legs, pelvis and lumbar spine during another. The skull shows a lesion of the frontal bone and an impaction of the lower left third molar, and the long bones show periostitis.

During the second excavation period, beginning June 24, 1945, three burials were encountered. Burial C°1-9 (Pl. 4,*b*), was a child nine to ten years old, probably male, extended on the back with the head to the east. C°1-9 was found 22 feet south of the north end of the mound and 12 feet west of the long axis at a depth of three feet two inches. The skull and mandible are displaced slightly to the left and the right arm and hand and the feet are missing, possibly as a result of excavation. The rest of the skeleton appears to be in its proper relationship and the burial appears to have been primary. Associated with the child was a broken Canteen Plain vessel, C°1-9A (Pl. 5,*a*), containing two mussel shell spoons (*Lampsilis ovata ventricosa* Barnes), one 8.3 cm. by 5.2 cm. and the other 9.8 cm. by 6.8 cm. The edges and hinges of the spoons are ground down. A handle is cut into the smaller one and both are left hand valves. There are two fragmentary turtle carapaces, one of the box turtle (*Terrapene carolina*), and one of the spotted turtle (*Clemmys gutata*), in contact with the outside of the pot, both with cut marks on the edges and interior (Pl. 5,*b*.) A long, slender bone pin, 23.9 cm. long and 8 mm. wide at the midshaft lay along the left side of the skull. The pin is cut from an elk metapodial and the original articulatory surface is worked into a hook. A bone awl or pin made from a rib of a large animal with blunt point and squared end lay in the area of the right forearm. This pin is 14.3 cm. long, 1.8 cm. wide at the base, 1.4 cm. wide at midshaft and has a flattened spatulate appearance (Pl. 6,*a*). Three copper awls were found, one under the right side of the pelvis and one in the area of each hand (Pl. 5,*b*). The awl by the right hand is 5.5 cm. long, 3 mm. thick at midshaft and round in cross section. The one by the left hand is 5.9 cm. long, 3 mm. thick and square in cross section. Neither shows evidence of having been formed from strips or sheets of copper. The third awl, the one found under the right pelvis, is 7.25 cm. long, 3 mm. thick, round in cross section and was evidently formed from a rolled or folded sheet of copper.

The Canteen Plain vessel is 13.6 cm. high. It has a lip diameter of 12 cm. and is 13 cm. at the shoulder. It has fine sparse grit temper and some fine to coarse sand. The rim and lip areas were thinned. The rim is .5 cm. thick while the lip is only .3 cm. wide. The thickness of the body wall varies from .5 to .6 cm. The vessel has a distinct shoulder with a slight inward constriction to the high, 6.3 cm. vertical rim. The exterior surface is smoothed and there are some faint indications of cordmarkings. Both surfaces are uneven. The exterior colors vary from light tan to smoke-blackened red, while the interior surface is grey to smoke blackened. The carbon discoloration was probably acquired during the firing of the vessel. The shape of this vessel is rather distinctive in its accentuated shoulder and high vertical rim. It has a rounded base.

Burial C°1-10 (USNM 380194), was that of an adult female extended on the back with the head to the northeast and was found 26 feet south of the north end of the mound and 15 feet six inches west of the long axis at a depth of four feet six inches. The left leg is crossed over the right at the ankle, and the skeleton appears to have been interred while fully articulated, suggesting a primary burial. There were no associations.

Burial C°1-11 consisted of fragments of a child's skull associated with a Canteen Cordmarked pot with a notched lip (Pl. 6,*c* and Pl. 7,*a*). The pot contained a complete turtle carapace (*Terrapene ornata*), 11.3 cm. long, 10.1 cm. wide and 3.3 cm. deep. The carapace has cut marks on the interior, the edges are ground and there is a small performation at the posterior end (Pl. 5,*b*). The condition of the burial and absence of the remainder of the skeleton was attributed to disturbance of the area by the roots of an old tree. The burial was evidently located near C°1-9 and C°1-10.

The Canteen Cordmarked vessel with burial C°1-11 is 14.5 cm. high. It has a lip diameter of 12 cm. and a body diameter of 14 cm. It has grit temper, apparently of sparse and fine grit. The lip was rounded with a thickness of 1.5 cm. before it was notched. The notches are closely spaced, and vary in width from .3 to .5 cm. There is a smoothed rim 4.2 cm. high, but the originally cordmarked surface was not fully obliterated. The body is cordmarked and some effort was made to also smooth this area. The individual cord impressions are only .1 cm. wide. The base is rounded. The exterior surface color ranges from light tan to dark grey while the interior surface is predominantly dark grey. The interior surface has shallow broad vertical impressions which we believe are the result of the use of the hand to support the vessel wall while it was being cordmarked or smoothed.

The third excavation period beginning July 1, 1945, also yielded three burials. C°1-12 was an infant burial with a small Canteen Cordmarked vessel in association (Pl. 7,*b*). This small vessel has a smoothed rim and a smoothed body. The work done to produce this surface was not completely effective in obliterating the cord impressions, which are .3 to .4 cm. apart. The temper is angular grit with sparse hematite inclusions. The height is 6.5 cm. The diameter at the lip is 6.8 cm. and the body diameter is 8.2 cm. There is a distinctive shoulder. The rim is inset and was designed to slope slightly toward the interior. The rim and lip are thinned, with a rounded lip width of 3 to 4 mm. and a rim thickness of 4 mm. The body is 5 to 6 mm. thick. The exterior surface color is light tan to grey and the interior is grey. There is a horizontal row of finger tip impressions on the interior at the shoulder. The vessel base is narrow and somewhat flattened but the vessel will not stand upright on a hard smooth surface.

C°1-13 was found 22 feet south of the north end of the mound, seven feet six inches west of the long axis and 20 inches deep and consisted of two infants extended with the heads to the north (Pl. 8,*a*). The skull fragments were situated side by side and the position of the frontal bone of one showed it to be resting on its base. The remainder of the skeletons with the exception of one femur, one humerus, two radii and one ulna, were either removed by excavation or were not included originally in the burial. This represents a secondary burial. Associated with the burial was a Canteen Plain pot (Pl. 8,*b*), with seven wide scallops around the rim, a badly preserved mussel shell spoon (*Proptera capax*) 8.1 cm. long and 7.0 cm. wide, and 72 *Olivella* shell beads situated under the chin and around the neck of one individual. This string of beads is not available for study and we do not have a photograph of it.

This Canteen Plain vessel C°1-13 (Pl. 8, *b*) is one of the most unusual from the standpoint of shape of the Canteen ware vessels excavated by Dr. Titterington and his associates. It is 11 cm. high and is ovoid so that the lip diameter is 14.5 by 16.8 cm. measured across the scallops. The body diameter is 14 by 15.6 cm. The lip is rounded and 5 mm. wide, while the rim and body thickness is 4 to 5 mm. The shoulder some 5.5 cm. below the lip is slightly accentuated. There is a slight constriction of the vessel walls above the shoulder. The rim is vertical to outflaring so as to produce the scallops. The exterior surface is well smoothed and, before its centuries of burial in the ground, probably had a low grade polish. The interior surface is, of course, not as well finished. The vessel is restored but appears to have had sparse fine grit temper. The exterior color ranges from light tan to smoky grey and the interior range is about the same. The vessel base is rounded.

Burial C°1-14 (USNM 380195) was an adult female extended on the back with the head to the north and was found 41 feet south of the north end of the mound, two feet six inches west of the long axis at a depth of four feet eight inches (Pl. 9,*a*). According to the photo the bones are all present and in their proper relationships, suggesting a primary burial. At the right hip of the skeleton was a Canteen Cordmarked pot with a pronounced conoidal base which contained a mussel shell spoon (*Lampsilis ovata ventricosa*).

The Canteen Cordmarked vessel is 20 cm. high (Pl. 9,*b*). It has a lip diameter of 14.8 cm. and a body diameter of 17.2 cm. The lip is rounded and 5 mm. wide. The rim and body thickness is 6 mm. The vessel is grit tempered, probably with the same sparse fine grit particles of the rest of the vessels from this mound. The cordmarked surface extends from the vessel base to the lip with vertical cord impressions. Below the slightly accentuated shoulder, horizontal cordmarks were paddled over the vertical impressions. The individual cords are 2 to 4 mm. wide. The shoulder line is 8.5 cm. below the lip. The shoulder area slopes inward slightly and the rim rises from it almost vertically but has a slight flare. The base is sub-conoidal. Most of the exterior body surface is grey to a dirty light brown but most of the rim and shoulder is blackened. The interior surface is greyish-black and has the shallow finger impressions, particularly in the area of the shoulder, that are thought to be the result of holding the interior while the shoulder was shaped and the vessel was paddled.

Burial C°1-15 (USNM 380196) was that of an adult male extended on the back with the head to the east and was found 33 feet south of the north end of the mound, with the head on the long axis at a depth of five feet. The skeleton was evidently interred while fully articulated and was found on the fourth trip which began July 8, 1945.

The fifth trip from August 9-12, 1945 yielded five burials. Burial C°1-16 was found 15 feet south of the north end of the mound, two feet six inches west of the long axis and two feet six inches deep and was a child six to seven years old extended on the back with the head to the northwest (Pl. 10*a*). The feet are missing from the skeleton, possibly as a result of excavation, but the rest of the bones are in their proper relationships. There were two ovate chipped unnotched points with straight bases found with this burial, one in the area of each hand (Pl. 10,*b*). The point in the right hand is 7.5 cm. long, 3.0 cm. wide at the base, 3.3 cm. wide at the greatest width (2.4 cm. below basal edge) and 1.0 cm. thick. This point is of light whitish-tan flint and shows an expanding flake retouch. The point in the left hand is 7.7 cm. long, 3.0 cm. wide at the base, 3.1 cm. wide at a point 1.5 cm. below the basal edge and 1.0 cm. thick. This point also shows expanding flake retouch and is of whitish-tan flint. The bases are thinned and the lateral edges do not show wear.

Burial C°1-17 (UMMA 380197) was that of an adult male extended on the back with the head to the east and was found 15 feet south of the north end of the mound on the long axis at a depth of four feet four inches (Pl. 11,*a*). The rib-cage has been caved-in, dislocating most of the ribs and the clavicle. The left humerus and hand are in their proper relationships but the radius and ulna have been separated and dislocated anteriorly and medially, possibly as a result of rodent activity. All other parts of the skeleton seem to be in articulatory positions. In the area of the fingers of the left hand were found two fragmentary unworked beaver incisors (*Castor canadensis*), one 4.9 cm. long and the other 5.7 cm. in length (Pl. 11,*b*).

C°1-18, (USNM 380198), was an adult male extended on the back with the head to the east and was found 28 feet six inches south of the north end of the mound, two feet east of the long axis at a depth of four feet six inches (Pl. 12,*a*). The rib cage had been caved in by ground pressure but the bones were in articulatory position, suggesting primary burial. Three small fragments of thin sheet copper were found over the left clavicle which was moderately stained (Pl. 5,*b*). The largest fragment is 3.5 cm. long and one fragment shows evidence of embossing but the form of the original artifact is unknown.

C°1-19 was that of a child seven to eight years of age, extended on the back with the head to the west (Pl. 12,*b*). The skeleton was evidently interred while fully articulated and was located 42 feet south of the north end, two feet west of the long axis at a depth of two feet eight inches. A markedly conoidal-based Canteen Cordmarked pot with a notched lip was found near the left shoulder and the skull was facing the pot (Pl. 13,*a*). An unworked left valve of a mussel shell (*Lampsilis ovata ventricosa*) 9.8 cm. long and 6.3 cm. wide was found inside the pot.

This vessel has a height of 13.3 cm. The body diameter is 12.2 by 11.5 cm. and the lip diameter is 12 by 10.5 cm. Actually all of the vessels from the mound are slightly asymetrical probably resulting in part from the weight of the earth in the mound. The temper is angular grit, with some sand and sparse hematite particles which protrude slightly on both surfaces. There is not the marked shoulder that is present on some of the vessels. The rim flares slightly in the top 2.5 cm. The lip and rim thickness is 5 mm. The lip has been notched transversely with square-edged tool impressions 3 mm. apart. The impressions are 3 mm. wide. The exterior is marked to the lip with a cordwrapped paddle, and then partially smoothed vertically on the body and horizontally on the rim. The interior rim surface has horizontal brushing or scraping marks while the body has vertical scraping marks. The exterior surface is tan to grey with firing clouds on the lower body. The interior is uniformly grey.

Burial C°1-20, an adult female partially flexed on the left side with the head to the east, was found 35 feet south of the north end of the mound with the pelvis on the long axis at a depth of one foot six inches (Pl. 13,*b*). The bones are in their proper relationships to each other and the skeleton shows an old healed vertebral compression fracture, a small amount of hypertrophic osteo-arthritis of the lumbar spine and very poor dental occlusion.

There were a number of artifacts found in the mound which were not associated with burials. Shell objects included an unmodified mussel shell (*Quadrula pustulosa*) and two mussel shell spoons (*Proptera capax*), one being (C°1-22) a right hand valve 10.6 cm. long and 7.8 cm. wide with all edges ground away, the other (C°1-21) a left hand valve 9.1 cm. long and 6.3 cm. wide with all edges ground and the hinges cut away. Neither spoon has a handle. A fragmentary *Amblema peruviana* mussel shell (C°1-23) 9.4 cm. long is perforated by a hole 2.0 cm. in diameter. Stone objects include two blades, a plano-convex scraper and two stone projectile points. One of the blades (C°1-25) is an obsidian flake 3.6 cm. long and 2.1 cm. wide with retouching along both edges and at the bulb of percussion. It is basally notched and is assigned to Type B (White, 1963: 48). The blade is No. 83 of a neutron activation study which identified the obsidian as coming from Obsidian Cliff in Yellowstone Park (Griffin, Gordus and Wright, 1969: 8). The other blade (C°1-26) is a pink and white flint flake 3.7 cm. long and 1.6 cm. wide and is unmodified. The plano-convex scraper (C°1-30) is ovoid in shape, 6.0 cm.

long and 4.5 cm. wide (Pl. 6,*a*). The surface appears to have been burned and there is a fine retouch along the edge. White (1963: 44) assigns it to Type 9 end scraper. The projectile points are designated as Steuben Expanded Stemmed or a variant of this type. One point (C°1-27) of pink flint has a straight base and slightly convex sides, is corner notched and is missing the point. It is 5.9 cm. long, 2.7 cm. wide at the base, 3.0 cm. wide at the barbs and the thickest point is 1.0 cm. (Pl. 10,*b*). One side is covered with a lime deposit. The stem is 1.4 cm. long and 1.8 cm. wide at the shoulder. The second point (C°1-28) is of white flint with a convex base and slightly convex sides. It is corner notched, 6.9 cm. long, 2.9 cm. wide at the base and 3.8 cm. wide at the barbs. The stem is 1.3 cm. long and 1.9 cm. wide, the greatest thickness is .8 cm. and the point shows expanding flake retouch.

C°1-24 is a rim sherd of Baehr or Pike Brushed, although whoever made it did not use limestone temper but instead small angular grit particles. The upper rim is 1.8 cm. wide, accentuated, and has an interior depressed channel in the lower half of the rim. In the channel there are vertical finger or thumbnail impressions spaced 4 mm. apart. The outer rim has crudely applied vertical plain rocked stamp impressions with a swing of 1.3 cm. At times the implement which made these impressions slipped into the lower rim for over 1.5 cm. The body is vertically brushed. This sherd is from a vessel of very late Hopewellian style.

COMMENTS ON MOUND C°1

Mound C°1 is a representative of burial practices of a Late Woodland population which has been called Jersey Bluff for some years. Because of the decorative features on the Canteen Zoned Punctate vessel C°1-7, and the simple Canteen jars, either cordmarked or plain, it is reasonable to suggest that this mound is early in the Late Woodland sequence. There are none of the Canteen vessels with smoothed upper rims and small nodes or lip lugs which mark the Late Woodland occupations close to the Early Mississippian period of around A.D. 1000. There are no marked stratigraphic differences in burial procedures in this mound with the possible exception of the cremated or partly burned mass bundle of C°1-2 to 6, which was at approximately the ground level, possibly in association with the Canteen Zoned Punctate vessel and a Steuben Expanded Stemmed point.

There were ten identifiable adult burials, nine of these were extended and one female was in a flexed or semi-flexed position. Two of the males had burial goods. With C°1-17 there were two beaver incisors near the left hand and with C°1-18 there were sheet copper fragments at the left clavicle. The flexed female had no recorded burial offerings. Most of the burial furniture was with infants or children and their burial position was extended. Four children had Canteen Cordmarked vessels and two had Canteen Plain vessels. Most of the vessels had one or two shell spoons either in the jar or otherwise with the burial. Child burial C°1-9 had two turtle shell cups, two long bone pins and three small copper awls, two of these awls were associated with the hands of the burial. This association of tools at the hand was also present with C°1-16 which had an ovate point or knife at each hand. The long bone pins are similar to mat needles illustrated by Skinner (1926: Pl. XVII) for the Prairie Potawatomie. Somewhat similar ones were used by other tribes of the Upper Mississippi Valley-Great Lakes area.

Twelve burials have identified burial orientation. Of the five child burials two were east-west, one of them had the skull to the east and the other skull was to the west. Two children side by side (C°1-13) were oriented north-south with the crania to the north. The fifth child was northwest-southeast with the head to the northwest. Three of the four adult males were east-west with the head to the east, and the fourth was north-south with the head to the north. One female was northeast-southwest with head to the northeast, and one was north-south with the head to the north. The flexed or partly flexed adult female buried in the upper part of the mound was east-west with the head to the east. Out of the 12 burials, five had the head to the east, six had the head to north, or almost north and one had the head to the west.

The small vessels placed in this mound have no indication of use as cooking vessels and their size is markedly smaller than the rim diameter of most of the similar pottery from village site debris. It is possible that they were made specifically for burial placement.

The most common small implements were made of mussel shell, particularly the spoons that were most often made from what is called in this report *Lampsilis ventricosa* (Barnes) which is known to clam diggers and others as the "pocketbook." There are three "species" of the Lampsilis "pocketbook" called *Lampsilis ventricosa* in the north, *Lampsilis ovata* in the central Mississippi-Ohio drainage and *Lampsilis excavata* in the south. For some years, following the identifications and beliefs of F. C. Baker it has been said that the presence of *Lampsilis ovata* in Indian sites in the Illinois and Mississippi drainage area north of the Ohio was the result of trade. The large number of *Lampsilis ovata* spoons in the Calhoun County area caused Griffin to consult again with Dr. Henry Van Der Schalie of the Museum of Zoology at the University of Michigan who is responsible for the first identification of the shells some years ago, and for the recent check made on them. It now appears likely, according to a recent paper (Cvancara, 1963), that there is a north-south cline and that in the Calhoun County area *Lampsilis ovata* and *Lampsilis ventricosa* overlap and are probably subspecies, just as *Lampsilis ovata* and *Lampsilis excavata* overlap in the southern area. If the molluscs did not know the taxonomic difference in breeding it is doubtful that the prehistoric Indians imported *Lampsilis ovata* from the Ohio drainage. This form, *Lampsilis ovata,* is found on a sand or gravel bottom from less than one to ten feet deep in a current. Another mussel, *Proptera capax* was used for spoons in Mound C°1, and it is known in the trade as the "flat pocketbook." This form occurs from a few inches to eight feet deep in flowing water on a sand or mud bottom. Both shells made good spoons either modified or unmodified because of the depth of the valves and their size. The *Amblema peruviana* may be a large river form of the related *Amblema costata* for both are rather large heavy forms and were suited for digging instruments. *Amblema peruviana* is found from three to twenty feet deep in good current and on a mud or mud/sand bottom. The other mussel in the mound, *Quadrula pustulosa,* was not modified, but was certainly out of its natural environment, for they live in water of depths from a few inches to ten feet or more, both in small streams and large rivers and on a bottom ranging from mud to sand to coarse gravel. Besides dependence on Prof. Van Der Schalie, the sections on the habitat preferences is cribbed without quotation marks from Parmalee's (1967) valuable handbook. Additional comments on mussels from these mounds to appear below are also referable to these same sources.

Kraig Adler, who identified many of the turtle specimens for us, has pointed out that the spotted turtle (*Clemmys gutata*) at the Knight site is south of its present range (Adler, 1968), and that it has not often been identified at prehistoric sites. One was found at the Steuben site in Marshall County, Illinois (Morse, 1963: 86 and Pl. XVII), associated with child Burials 39-41. This was a late Hopewell group burial associated with a shell spoon, a *Busycon perversum* shell vessel (Morse, 1963: Pl. XXIII, Fig. 3), a bone spatula awl or hairpin and a limestone tempered Hopewell Plain Rocker Stamped vessel (*ibid*: Pl. XXIII, Fig. 2). The child burials were about the same age or slightly later than two radiocarbon dates, M-378 at 1660 ±125 B.P., and M-380 with a date of 1650 ±125 B.P. These dates are very close to the one obtained from Knight Mound 8. The present distribution of the spotted turtle is in southwest Wisconsin, northeastern Illinois, northern Indiana, Michigan's lower peninsula and to the east. It hibernates on land, inhibits marshy meadows, bogs and woodland ponds in the spring, and in the summer and fall is found in moist woodland areas.

In Mound C°2 a large turtle shell cup of Blandings turtle is also south of its present range. Fragments of this turtle were found at the Pool site in nearby Pike County. This turtle was the one which provided the raw material for most of the Norton site cups. It is possible that about A.D. 250 to 300 the range of these two turtles was to the south of the present range. It is also possible, given the cultural connection of the lower Illinois Valley area to western Michigan, that these two cups were part of a gift exchange between Illinois and Michigan residents. Perhaps these turtle cups were exchanged for some of the Illinois Valley area limestone tempered Hopewellian vessels that were certainly transported into western Michigan. Turtle carapace cups are reported by Barrett (1911: 357) as tobacco trays used about the home by Wisconsin Menominee Indians.

It is possible that the Steuben points in this mound were included in the fill and belong to a slightly earlier occupation than the early Late Woodland group. It is almost certain that the obsidian specimen belonged to the Middle Woodland Hopewellian period (Griffin, *et al.*, 1969). The grit tempered Baehr or Pike Brushed rim sherd may also be from a slightly earlier period than the construction of the mound.

This mound is one that can be said to have been constructed by a group or groups still possessing some of the cultural characteristics of the late Middle Woodland Hopewellian societies but who are sufficiently removed to warrant the recognition of a distinctive pattern of behavior for which the term Fox Creek phase has been proposed in the introduction.

MOUND C°2

Mound C°2 is located directly to the south of C°1 on the low ridge in the middle of the valley. Mr. Walter Wadlow dug extensively in the mound during the summers of 1941 and 1943 and Dr. Titterington took crews of two to three men to the mound for "Sunday digs" in the fall of 1941 and 1944. No estimate of mound size is given but burial provenience data indicate a diameter of at least 60 feet and a height of about 5 feet (Fig. 3).

During the summer of 1941 Mr. Wadlow uncovered 30 to 35 burials from which seven skulls were saved (C°2-1 to -8). He had

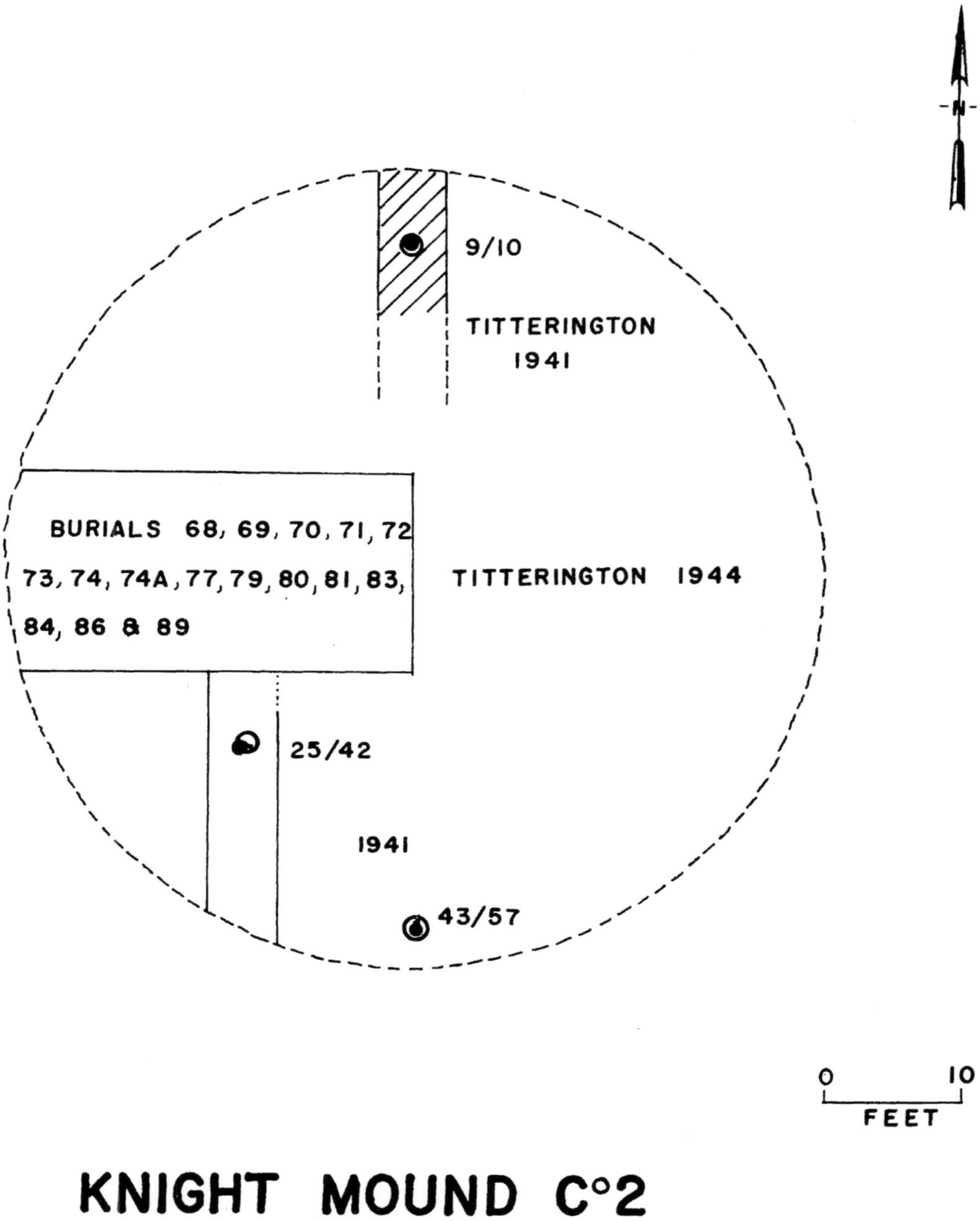

Fig. 3. Reconstruction of burial locations in Knight Mound C°2.

the impression that the burials occurred in two layers, an upper flexed layer without grave goods and a lower layer of extended burials with artifacts. Four hundred *Anculosa praerosa* shell beads (C°2-7) with one side ground down to permit stringing were found between the layers of burials (Pl. 14,*a*).

Mr. Wadlow also recovered six pots (C°2-11 to -15 and -24), the first five of which contained mussel shell spoons, a bone awl and a flat spatulate bone tool, three shell beads, an unidentified perforated object, a projectile point, a stone gorget, and several loose sherds (Pls. 17*b* and 18).

Vessel C°2-11 is a Canteen Plain jar with

a conoidal base (Pl. 14,*b*). It is 18.5 cm. high. The diameter at the lip is 13.5 by 16 cm. and the body is 16 cm. The lip thickness is 4 to 7 mm. and is unusually uneven in width, shape and height. The rim is vertical and falls directly into the body and to a rounded conoidal base. The temper is granular crushed rock with some medium to large particles largely covered over with clay on the outer and inner surfaces. The exterior surface may have been tooled with a cordwrapped paddle but the impressions are almost obliterated and the surface is roughly smoothed. The interior upper surface is horizontally scored or brushed with rather narrow shallow impressions. The exterior and interior surfaces are brownish-tan to smoke blackened.

Vessel C°2-12 is a small Canteen Plain jar with a height of 13 cm., a lip diameter of 11 by 12 cm., and a body diameter of 13 cm. (Pl. 15,*a*). It has a vertical to slightly insloping upper body and rim which are 6 mm. thick. The lip is markedly narrowed, almost to a point, and has closely spaced narrow transverse gashes on the inner and outer surfaces. The exterior surface is smoothed to burnished. The interior surface is smoothed but is uneven. The exterior surface is tan to light brown and smoke blackened while the interior surface is grey.

Vessel C°2-13 is a small Canteen Plain jar with a slightly flaring rim 3 cm. high (Pl. 15,*b*). The vessel height is 12.3 cm. It has a lip diameter of 11 cm., a rim diameter of 10.5 cm. and a body diameter of 11.3 cm. The body walls below the faint shoulder line converge to a conoidal base. The body and rim are 3 to 4 mm. thick. The lip is narrowed almost to a point and has closely spaced medium wide and medium deep transverse notches. The temper is granular with most of the particles covered by the exterior and interior smoothing process. Both interior and exterior surfaces are tan with little indication of firing discoloration.

C°2-14 is a small Canteen Cordmarked jar with a height of 13.5 cm., a lip diameter of 10.4 by 10.8 cm. and a body diameter of 11.3 by 12.2 cm. (Pl. 16,*a*). The rim is vertical and slightly narrower than the maximum diameter at the slightly accentuated shoulder. The base is conoidal. The cordwrapped paddled exterior is barklike in appearance. The cord impressions are rather large, 2 to 4 mm. wide, of loosely twisted cord, applied vertically to the rim and with a left to right downward slope on the body. The lip is uneven but mostly rounded and is 3 to 4 mm. wide, and the rim and body thickness is 4 to 5 mm. The temper is granular and the core color is black. The interior surface is blackened and the exterior is grey to smoke blackened.

Vessel C°2-15 when found had about one-fourth of the neck and rim attached to the body. The excavator, apparently with a strong interest in symmetry sawed off the rim and lost some of the resultant pieces so that the conoidal plain body is as illustrated (Pl. 16,*b*). Some modest advantage resulted from this since the tempering material is clearly identified as crushed mafic and quartzite-appearing particles which comprise about 15 to 20 per cent of the paste. These tempering particles are well smoothed-over on the exterior and interior surface. The exterior is smooth to burnished. The present body diameter at the slightly curved shoulder is 13.5 by 14.8 cm. and the body thickness is 4 to 5mm. The rim would have been 9 to 10 cm. high and has an unusual decorative pattern. On the upper outer rim there is a band of short, vertical cordwrapped stick impressions 8 to 10 mm. long extending downward from the very narrow lip. These impressions are spaced 5 mm. apart. The interior rim area of this upper band is slightly channeled and the outer surface of the decorated horizontal band protrudes slightly. Below the upper decorated band there is a smooth band 1.5 cm. wide and then a second decorated horizontal band of identical form and dimensions with interior channel and outer projection to the upper rim. Below the second cordwrapped stick band there is a plain horizontal zone with a decorative pattern composed of two horizontal rows of inverted V-shaped patterns made by very fine cordwrapped stick impressions. The paste and sections of the outer surface, particularly the rim area, has a reddish color along with greys and smoke blackened areas. The temper and color of this vessel as well as the unusual decoration suggest that it was probably an imported one.

Sherds C°2-16 to 19 from the mound (Pl. 17,*a*) include an Havana Cordmarked rim with closely spaced short cordwrapped stick impressions on the outer upper rim and a flattened insloping lip; a Canteen Cordmarked rim with shallow broad, slightly oblique cordwrapped stick impressions on the inner rim; a limestone tempered Baehr Zoned Punctate lower rim and body sherd which has vertical brush marks on it; and a Baehr Brushed body sherd.

The horizontal zoned punctate band of the Baehr Zoned Punctate rim, 1 cm. wide, is outlined by narrow, deeply incised lines which contain two horizontal rows of deeply indented trianguloid punches. This band is at the base of the rim area. Above the punctate band there is a smooth-to-polished horizontal band 2.8 cm. wide which is set apart by an upper horizontal narrow incised line.

The shell spoons are all handled right valves with the hinges cut away and all edges ground (Pl. 18). The spoons associated with vessels C°2-11 to 13 and 15, are *Lampsilis ovata ventricosa* and with vessel C°2-14 a *Proptera capax*. Dimensions of the spoons range from 8.4 cm. to 12.8 cm. long and 6.2 cm. to 7.7. cm wide. The bone awl (C°2-22) was made from the split tibiotarsal of a turkey and is 13.9 cm. long (Pl. 17,*b*). The distal end is sharply pointed and the proximal articular surface is unmodified. The flat spatulate bone tool (C°2-21), 2.4 cm. wide and 25.2 cm. long, is made from a sliver of cortex from a rib bone. All edges and the exterior surface of the artifact are ground and polished; one end is broken and reused or polished after breaking and the other end terminates in a rounded, beveled edge. The shell beads, unidentified perforated object, and gorget (C°2-20) were found around the right wrist of an undescribed burial. The three shell beads are 6 to 7 mm. in diameter and have drilled holes 4 mm. in diameter through the centers. The unidentified perforated object is 1.9 cm. long and 1.4 cm. wide, ground and polished, with a small hole drilled in one end. The two-holed bar gorget is of slate or claystone with square edges, slightly convex surfaces and convex sides and ends. It is 13.9 cm. long, 3.9 cm. wide at the middle and 3.6 cm. and 3.4 cm. wide at the ends, 8 mm. thick and with two 4 mm. holes 1.9 cm. apart in the center. The projectile point (C°2-23) has a convex base, straight sides and side notches and is 8.5 cm. long, 4.0 cm. wide at the barbs and 3.6 cm. wide at the base, 1.2 cm. thick with a stem 2.7 cm. wide and 2.1 cm. long. It is of pinkish white flint and is a late variant assigned to the Gibson Diagonal Notched type (White, 1968: 75).

Vessel C°2-24 is a Canteen Plain jar (Pl. 19,*a*) with an insploping shoulder area and a slightly outsloping rim. The lip diameter is 10.1 cm, at the base of the rim it is 11.1 cm. and the diameter across the shoulder is 13 cm. The height is 15.5 cm. The tempering material is fine grit with some quartzite inclusions. Both interior and exterior surfaces are smoothed. The lip which is only 3 mm. wide is rounded and has shallow small right to left sloping notches spaced 7 to 8 mm. apart. The rim and body are 4 mm. thick. The base is conoidal. The exterior and interior surfaces are a smoke blackened tan. This vessel was found by Walter Wadlow in the summer of 1941. It was in fragments when Dr. Titterington obtained it. Its exact position or presumed burial association is not known.

Dr. Titterington visited the site on October 12, 1941, and dug a five-foot wide pit in the north end of the mound. Burial C°2-9, found at a depth of 10 inches, was that of an adult female tightly flexed on the left side with the head to the south. The bones are in articulatory positions with only slight displacement by ground pressure. The right arm is flexed so that the right hand is located under the mandible, the left arm so that the hand lies directly in front of the face.

Burial C°2-10 (Pl. 19,*b*) was that of an adult male extended on the back with the head to the north, found in the same pit dug by Titterington at a depth of four feet. The right hand and right tibia are missing, possibly as a result of excavation. The skull is badly disintegrated, being represented only by most of the occipital and the top portions of the parietal and frontal bones. There was some displacement of the left arm but the bones are in articulatory position. There was a basal section of an antler found between the right radius and ribs of the burial. The section is cut and polished on both ends and along the shaft, the distal end is socketed and it measures 10.7 cm. in length and 2.1 cm. in diameter. The right and left halves of a dog maxilla were found beside the right ulna. The maxilla halves had been cut or ground so that the roots of the teeth and associated bone have been removed. Both halves measure 5.4 cm. long and 8 mm. thick. The left central incisor is missing and the halves were probably united when they were in use by the Indian as they were in that position when recovered (Pl. 20,*a*).

Mr. Wadlow dug a pit into the west side of the south end of the mound on August 8, 1943 and found burial C°2-25, that of an adolescent female extended on the back with the head to the west. Over the frontal bone of the skull was a Canteen Plain pottery vessel (Pl. 20,*b*) containing two worked mussel shells (*Lampsilis ovata ventricosa*, Pl. 21,*a*), one (C°2-26), a left hand valve 10.9 cm. long and 7.5 cm. wide with all edges ground and a handle cut into the edges, the other C°2-27) a right valve 10.2 cm. long by 6.9 cm. wide, all edges and the exterior surface ground. Over the left upper chest and collar bone there were ten split bone awls fashioned from the leg bone of the turkey; an unmodified blade 5.8 cm. long, 1.5 cm. wide and .4 cm. thick with discontinuous scars and "nibbled" edges on both sides, and two turkey leg bones (probably unfinished awls) with the distal articulations cut off. One of the split turkey leg bone awls is 12.5 cm. long with spur intact and pointed at the distal end. The other split turkey leg bone awls range from 8.9 cm. to 13.9 cm. in length, and are pointed on the distal end with unmodified proximal articulatory surfaces (Pl. 21,*b*).

The Canteen Plain jar associated with C°2-25 is 17.5 cm. high and has a lip diameter of 14.2 cm. The lower rim diameter is 12 cm. and that of the body is 14 cm. The lip is irregular in height, and in shape is flattened, narrowed and rounded. The rim is slightly flaring and is 4 mm. thick. The body side walls are almost vertical and the base is rounded conoidal. The tempering material is crushed rock with sparse angular inclusions. The smoothing striations on the outer surface are primarily vertical. Both interior and exterior surfaces are roughly smoothed. The interior and exterior surface color is tan with some smoke blackened areas near the base.

Burial C°2-42 was located over the lower legs and feet of C°2-25 and was that of an old adult female flexed on the left side with the head to the southwest. The skull of this burial was saved and is edentulous except for the lower left first and second bicuspids.

Burial C°2-43 was found in the extreme south end of the mound and was an adolescent female extended on the back with the head to the north. Associated with the burial in the left axillary region were six split turkey leg bone awls ranging from 11.1 cm. to 14.9 cm. in length with pointed distal ends and unmodified proximal articulatory surfaces; an awl made from part of a flat bone, 10.8 cm. long, with the basal end broken away; and seven flake knives ranging from 2.2 cm. to 4.8 cm. in length and 9 mm. to 2.3 cm. in width, one an unmodified chip and the others complete, unmodified blades (Pl. 22,*a*). None show any use chipping.

Burial C°2-57 (Pl. 22,*b*) was that of a young male extended on the back in an east-west direction and found in the extreme south end of the mound below C°2-43 at a depth of three feet six inches. The skull had been removed and was lying on the left side facing the feet in the region of the left knee. Beside the skull was a Canteen Plain pottery vessel (Pl. 23,*a*) containing two mussel shell spoons (*Lampsilis ovata ventricosa*), one left valve (C°2-58) 11.4 cm. long and 7.4 cm. wide with the hinge ground away and the edges, interior and exterior surfaces ground; the other (C°2-59) a right valve 11.9 cm. long and 7.9 cm. wide with the hinge ground away and no other modification (Pl. 23,*b*). Neither spoon has a handle and the shells are possibly matching halves.

The Canteen Plain jar C°2-57 (Pl. 23,*a*) with a height of 22 cm. is one of the largest in the mound. The lip diameter is 13 by 14.5 cm. while the lower rim is 12.5 by 14.5 cm. The body diameter is 14.5 by 15 cm. The lip is uneven in height, shape and width. It varies in thickness from 3 to 6 mm. The rim is vertical to slightly flared. There is hardly any shoulder on this vessel and the body walls are almost vertical and then contract to a conoidal base. There is sparse granular temper. The vessel is roughly smoothed on the exterior and interior. The exterior surface is tan to brown with some smoke blackened areas on the upper body and rim. Most of the interior is smoke blackened.

A trench was dug about one-third of the way through the area between Mounds 2 and 3 and a fire pit was encountered that measured four feet north and south by three feet east and west and one foot three inches thick. In the pit were scattered infant bones and an adult male skull, C°2-66. The adult skull and some other bones, evidently from the same individuals, were found beneath the burned material and showed no evidence of contact with the fire. Three large soot-covered potsherds from a partially smoothed Canteen Cordmarked vessel (C°2-64) were found in the fire pit. Several other objects were found in association with the bones (Pl. 24,*a*). These are an unworked mussell shell *Anodonta corpulenta* 13.1 cm. long, associated with the occipital bone of the infant (C°2-65); a narrow lanceolate grayish-black flint blade with a straight base, 10.6 cm. long, and a maximum width of 2.9 cm.; a stemmed scraper of Dongola flint 5.4 cm. long and a bladelet and flint chip, both of mottled pink flint, the bladelet being 5 cm. long and the chip approximately 3.8 cm. long.

In the fall of 1944 five trips were made to the mound by Dr. Titterington and a crew of two or three men. An area 30 feet long and 15 feet wide was excavated in the west side of the mound, beginning just north of the south end and extending to a point just north of the center in the area previously excavated by Wadlow. Burial C°2-68 (Pl. 24,*b*) was that of a child 12 to 14 years old and was found at a depth of three feet six inches at the edge of a previous disturbance. The skull and mandible, both humeri, scapulae, clavicles and several thoracic vertebrae with attached ribs are all that remains of the skeleton. The bones are displaced slightly but an extended position is indicated from the photograph. Twenty-eight cylindrical shell beads averaging 7 mm. in length and 6 mm. in diameter were found in the neck region (Pl. 26,*a*) and a broken Canteen Cordmarked pottery vessel was located ten inches from the right shoulder.

The Canteen Cordmarked jar with Burial C°2-68 (Pl. 25*a*) has a slightly greater lip diameter (16.5 cm.) than the height of 16 cm. The cord markings on the exterior surfaces were almost obliterated during the smoothing process but the vertical impressions of the cords are still observable. On the exterior rim there is a horizontal brushing or smoothing process but the vertical impressions of the cords are still visible. On the exterior rim there are horizontal brushing or smoothing impressions perhaps by a fiberous bundle with individual fiber (?) marks up to 2 mm. wide. These same marks are barely observable on the body exterior and interior. The body side walls gradually converge from a barely noticeable shoulder to a rounded conoidal base. The interior and exterior surfaces are brownish to smoke blackened. The lip is rounded to somewhat flattened and varies in width from 6 to 8 mm. The rim and body is 4 to 6 mm. thick. The vessel is grit tempered with angular particles which were well covered by the paste during the surface treatment of the vessel.

C°2-69 was found at a depth of 15 inches and was an adult male extended on the back with the head to the north. The bones are in articulatory position except for the lower legs and feet which are missing due to a previous disturbance. No burial offerings were recovered from this burial. C°2-70 was a young adult male extended on the back with the head to the north at a depth of three feet two inches. The lower right leg and foot are missing but the rest of the skeleton seems to be in articulartory position except for a slight displacement due to ground action. Several artifacts were found together beside the right shoulder of the individual (Pl. 25,*b*). Two turkey leg bones, 15.3 cm. and 14.1 cm. long, were unmodified except for the distal ends having been cut off. Two split turkey leg bone awls were 10.9 cm. and 8.0 cm. long with distal ends pointed, edges and surfaces ground and polished and proximal articular surfaces unmodified. There were two fragmentary turkey bone awls, one the base of an awl 5.6 cm. long and the other the point of an awl 3.1 cm. long. Thirteen blades range in length from 4.4 cm. to 2.1 cm. and in width from 2.3 cm. to 1.1 cm. All are unmodified and five are of black flint (one broken) and eight of white flint (two broken). A stone projectile point, Gibson Diagonal Notched (White, 1968) has a convex base and sides. It is 5.3 cm. long, 2.9 cm. wide at the base, 2.6 cm. wide at the barbs and the stem is 1.6 cm. long and 1.7 cm. wide. A large adult male, C°2-71, was found partially flexed and resting on the right side with the head to the southeast at a depth of one foot in the pit (Pl. 26,*b*). Burial C°2-72 was that of an adult male tightly flexed and lying on the left side with the head to the north at a depth of 16.0 inches (Pl. 27,*a*). Both of these individuals were interred while articulated and there were no associations. C°2-73 is represented by a calvarium found in the east bank of a previously dug pit. It shows some occipital deformation and was found three feet two inches deep from the surface.

C°2-74 was an adult male extended on the back with the head to the north and was found at a depth of four feet eight inches. The left shoulder and humerus and the left upper ribs had been removed by a previous excavation. Several objects were found together over the right ribs (Pl. 27,*b*). Three split turkey leg bone awls range 13.7 cm. to 12.8 cm. in length and one fragmentary awl is 4.2 cm. long. The distal ends of the awls are pointed, the edges ground and the exterior surfaces and proximal articulations are unmodified (Pl. 28,*a*). A flake knife of white flint is an unmodified waste chip from bifacial trimming and is 4.5 cm. long and 2.2 cm. wide. There was an ovate unnotched point or knife of tan flint 7.5 cm. long, 4.3 cm. wide and 1.3 cm. thick with convex base and sides. A turtle carapace (*Emydoidea blandingi*) approximately 29 cm. long and 14 cm. wide had the edges and interior surface cut and ground (Pl. 29,*a*). The Knight site is slightly south of the present range of Blandings turtle (Adler, 1968). A fragmentary bird effigy stone platform pipe was found in the area of the lower left ribs. The pipe is of claystone and the bird may possibly be some sort of hawk. There are crude horizontal incisions on the body to represent the wings. The slightly concave platform is 8.5 cm. long from the smoking end to the broken portion at the tail of the bird. The platform is 1.0 cm. thick, 2.3 cm. wide at the smoking end and 3.0 cm. wide at the center. The effigy, facing the smoking end, is 5.3 cm. long at the base and 6.5 cm. long from the "beak" to the broken portion. The interior of the bowl is 1.5 cm. in diameter and approximately 3.3 cm. deep (Pl. 29,*a*). A broken Canteen Zoned Incised pottery vessel (C°2-74, Pl. 28,*b*) and a child's tibia were found over the feet of the burial.

The Canteen Zoned Incised vessel with C°2-74 is an unusual vessel both in form and in decoration (Pl. 28,*b*). The form is somewhat suggestive of a bulbous hourglass and may represent a superimposed or vertical compound vessel. It is 17.7 cm. high. The lip diameter is 14 cm., the maximum neck construction is 12.8 cm. and the lower body is 12.8 cm. The upper body or rim is about the same diameter as the lower body. The tempering material is angular grit fragments and there are also hematite inclusions such as have been observed in other Canteen ware vessels from this group. The tempering particles are well covered on the smoothed exterior surface but some are visible on the less well smoothed interior, which has faint horizontal brush marks. The exterior surface was rubbed or smoothed after the decoration was placed on the vessel. The lip is narrowed and rounded and has closely spaced, transverse notches 5 mm. apart, across its surface. The basal thickness is 8 mm. while the body and rim are 6 mm. thick.

There is a plain horizontal band 1 cm. wide below the lip bordered by a 3 mm. wide horizontal line which is the upper border of a horizontal band about 3.5 cm. wide, which is delimited at its base by a similar horizontal incised line. Within this band there are narrow 1.5 mm. vertical incised lines spaced 1.5 cm. apart. These lines were then crossed by right to left narrow incised lines spaced 1.5 cm. apart. Below this upper band there is a plain horizontal band about 1 cm. wide which has a horizontal incised line at its base. This line forms the upper border of the next horizontal incised band which is 4 cm. high. It has a decoration of alternating incised and punctate zones. The incised zone is 9 cm. wide and has three vertical lines on each side of a crosshatched zone composed of three right to left oblique lines made over a group of three left to right slanting lines. These lines are 1 to 1.5 mm. wide as are the upper and the lower horizontal lines of this zone. The punctate zone, 10.3 cm. wide, has small circular deeply impressed punctates in an irregular pattern. The lower body has vertical incised lines extending 5.5 to 6 cm. downward from the horizontal line delimiting the incised-punctate band. These vertical lines are unevenly spaced about 8 to 10 mm. apart. Even the rounded base of this vessel did not escape the decorator of this vessel. It has narrow incised lines of the same width as those in the upper band and these were drawn at right angles across the base so as to form small squares or rectangles a little over 1 cm. wide.

Burial C°2-77 (Pl. 29,*b*) in the west central part of the mound was that of an adult male extended on the back with the head to the northeast at a depth of five feet four inches. The head is turned slightly to the left and the bones appear to be in proper relationships to each other. There was part of a Canteen Cordmarked pottery vessel immediately over the left shoulder and a worked right mussel shell valve (*Lampsilis ovata ventricosa*), 10.9 cm. long and 7.5 cm. wide with the hinge ground away, over the left clavicle of the burial (Pl. 29,*b*). Several artifacts were found between the feet of the skeleton (Pl. 30,*a*). A portion of worked antler tine is 8.4 cm. long and 1.5 cm. in diameter at the cut base with some grinding and polishing on the surface. There were two antler "drifts," one 12.5 cm. long and 2.7 cm. in diameter with both ends cut and ground and the surface polished, the other is a fragment 4.0 cm. long and 2.8 cm. in diameter with the preserved end cut and ground (Pl. 28,*a*). There were two oval hammerstones, one 8.9 cm. long, 6.0 cm. wide and 3.8 cm. thick, the other 6.5 cm. long, 5.4 cm. wide and 2.9 cm. thick, both showing battered edges. A flake knife of tan flint is 4.5 cm. long, 2.0 cm. wide, .4 cm. thick and is unmodified. There was also a standstone abrader having a pyramidal shape, 9.2 cm. high and lacking obvious grooves (Pl. 28,*a*).

The Canteen Cordmarked vessel C°2-77 with a height of 21.8 cm. is one of the largest jars in the mound (Pl. 30,*b*). It has a neck diameter of 15.5 cm. and the body diameter is 17.8 cm. The upper half to two-thirds of the outer surface has deep cordwrapped paddle impressions while the lower body and base have been smoothed, almost obliterating the cordmarkings. The interior surface is smooth. The lip is somewhat uneven in height and the width of the lip varies from 6 to 8 mm. The lip is flattened and bears some cord impressions as does the upper inner rim where the cord impressions are horizontal. The temper is sparse angular grit with some hematite particles. The color is light brown to smoke blackened on both surfaces. The rim is very slightly flared and has a thickness of 8 mm. There is a very slight constriction of the "neck" and the base is semi-conoidal.

Further excavation was carried out in the late summer and fall of 1945 in the north end of Mound C°2. Only one photograph was taken, of Burial C°2-90, but the notes contain a brief description of the features. C°2-79 and -80 are represented by a disturbed compound burial of two adults, probably males, at a depth of four feet eight inches. There were only a few bones and the position of the bodies could not be determined. Both skulls show occipital flattening. C°2-81 was a female skull found in a disturbed area at a depth of five feet. The mandible was located 27 inches northwest of the skull on the same level. C°2-83 was the calvarium of an adult, probably female. C°2-84 is represented by the frontal bone of a child in two fragments, found ten inches apart at a depth of five feet in a previously disturbed area. The two fragments of the bone are somewhat flattened and form a rather sharp ridge at the top. A small fragmentary Canteen Zoned Punctate vessel (C°2-85) was found just to the north of the skull fragments. This small jar or bowl with a markedly angular shoulder has the same type of incised lines and punctates present on jar C°2-74. They could have been made by the same tools if not by the same hand (Pl. 31,*a*). It also has an unusual decorative pattern. The vessel is only 7 cm. high, it has an estimated lip diameter of 8 cm., and a shoulder diameter of 10.2 cm. The lip is rounded to narrowed and rounded and is 3 to 4 mm. wide. The body is 5 mm. thick. The interior surface is roughly smoothed but the exterior is smooth. The interior color is quite black while the exterior is primarily tan with some smoke blackened areas on the rounded base and rim. The temper is sand and small angular grit particles.

The insloping rim 3.8 cm. high is decorated with a row of incised triangles with apex upward, which are 3.5 cm. high and 3.5 cm. wide at the base. The triangles are outlined by narrow deeply incised lines and are filled with small (3.5 mm. in diameter) annular punctates made by the end of a hollow cylinder. Below the shoulder there is a horizontal band of small curved figures, 3 cm. high, which are suggestive of the bear claw motif. They are 3 cm. high and outlined by the same kind of incised lines as on the rim, and the upper half of the "claw" has the same annular punctates. Below the punctates a small circle was incised. The basal area has an incised circular line about 4.9 cm. in diameter. From this line there are incised triangles on which the apex rises to 2.4 cm., and these triangles are filled with punctates. The apex of the triangles penetrate into the vacant spaces between the "claws." There are two small holes which penetrate the rim 8 mm. below the lip. They are 3.5 mm. in diameter and are 10 mm. apart. They are in one of the plain triangular areas pendent from the lip which are between each of the upper punctate triangles.

C°2-86 was a female cranium, a femur, two tibias and a fibula found at the bottom of a recently dug pit in the northwest edge of the mound. The long bones show periostitis. C°2-89 consisted of the maxilla and mandible of a small child with deciduous teeth and fused lower right central and lateral incisor. In addition, the notes mention a child's skull and a few other bones which were found in the north end of the mound three feet nine inches deep.

There were a number of artifacts found in Mound C°2 that were not associated with burials. From the large pit in the west side of the mound came a handled mussel shell spoon, C°2-67 (*Lampsilis ovata ventricosa*) a right valve 9.1 cm. long and 6.8 cm. wide with all edges and both surfaces ground, a flat-bottomed, straight-sided Canteen Cordmarked pottery vessel (C°2-75, Pl. 31,*b*) and a bluish-gray cone-shaped object of stone (C°2-76). This object is 4.0 cm. high and has a concave oval base 4.7 cm. by 4.3 cm. in diameter and with an 8 mm. depression. A small fragment is broken from the apex of the cone (Pl. 29,*a*).

The cup-shaped vessel C°2-75 (Pl. 31,*b*) was cordmarked over the exterior surface and subsequently smoothed. Most of the markings are vertical but on the rim area they are left to right oblique or almost horizontal. The vessel walls slope slightly outward from a flattened circular base 5 cm. in diameter. The vessel is 12 cm. high and has a lip diameter of 12.2 cm. The upper rim is curved slightly to the interior and a narrowed, almost pointed lip 3 mm. wide. The body is 5 to 6 mm. thick. The tempering material is angular grit including some quartzite particles, and there are also some very small limestone particles.

The excavation in the north end of the pit also yielded several artifacts not associated with burials. A conoidal-based Canteen Plain pottery vessel (C°2-78, Pl. 32,*a*) containing a mussell shell spoon and with a small *Busycon* (probably *carica* or *B. contrarium*) shell bowl in contact were found at a depth of four feet four inches (Pl. 32,*b*). The dimensions of the conch shell are 17.2 cm. long and 12.2 cm. wide and of the mussel shell are 8.1 cm. long and 4.7 cm. wide. (The conch shell was loaned to the Exhibit Museum in 1957 and is not now available.)

The small Canteen Plain jar, C°2-78, is only 11 cm. high and has a lip diameter of 9.3 cm. by 10 cm. It has a very slight shoulder and a short vertical rim. The lip is rounded and of uneven height and width. The interior is smoothed and the upper rim has horizontal impressions which resemble brushing. The exterior rim is crudely brushed horizontally with some of the markings being discontinuous linear incisions 5 mm. wide. The body is vertically brushed or scraped. The base is conoidal. The temper is angular grit, some sand, and some hematite particles. The body thickness is 5 to 8 mm.

A left valve, handled mussel shell spoon (C°2-82, *Lampsilis ovata ventricosa*) 11.8 cm. long and 7.3 cm. wide with all edges and both surfaces ground was found five feet two inches deep near but not directly associated with two skull fragments. A flake knife, two mussel shell hoes and a cut beaver mandible occurred at a depth ranging from three feet six inches to four feet six inches. The knife is a blade 4.3 cm. long, 1.5 cm. wide and .4 cm. thick with nibbled edges and a retouched end. Two shell digging implements one *Megalonaias gigantea* 11.0 cm. long by 10.0 cm. wide and *Amblema costata* 9.3 cm. long by 7.7 cm. wide, each have holes 1.8 cm. in diameter. The working edges show heavy use. A partial beaver mandible (*Castor canadensis*) is the left half and the only modification appears to be the removal of the incisors. Another marine shell bowl (C°2-88) in a good state of preservation was found but is not available for analysis. It was unearthed by hogs between August 7 and October 1, 1945 and was found by Dr. Titterington on top of the dirt of his excavation. According to his notes, if there were any skeletal parts in association they were eaten by hogs.

In the small area between C°1 and C°2 an extended burial of a child was found at a depth of four feet. The head was facing to the left and at the occiput there was a Canteen Cordmarked jar (Pl. 33,*a*). Around the left wrist there was a double string of 36 small copper beads and four rather rough pearl beads. There was one rather well shaped pearl bead at the right wrist. The copper beads vary slightly in size but they are 3 to 4 mm. long and 3 to 4 mm. in diameter. They are made of thin narrow strips of copper with slightly overlapping ends which must have been pounded in place over a solid cylinder such as a copper awl. The poor quality pearls were incorporated in the copper string and one of the beads is imbedded in the biconical perforation made in one of the pearls.

Jar C°2-90 (Pl. 33,*b*) is deeply marked on the rim by a cordwrapped paddle with closely spaced cords. The impressions of cords on the body are much less clear, for that area was smoothed. The vessel has a height of 15 cm., a lip diameter of 13.5 cm. and a shoulder diameter of 14 cm. The rim is slightly flaring and rises about 5 cm. above the shoulder. The lip is narrowed and rounded and has narrow deep grooves about 1 cm. apart gashed transversely or slightly obliquely across it. The body thickness is 5 mm. and the rim is 4 mm. The tempering material is angular grit with some particles up to 3 mm. in size, some sand, and some hematite inclusions. These particles are well covered on both surfaces. The color on both surfaces is light brown to grey with some smoke blackened areas around the rim.

COMMENTS ON MOUND C°2

This mound, according to Mr. Wadlow, had an upper zone of flexed burials and a lower zone of extended burials. This impression seems to be substantiated by the photographs and locations given by Dr. Titterington's notes. There is a clear difference in burial associations for most of the grave goods were with the extended burials in the lower zone. So much of the data from this mound is not available that a summary interpretation may be suspect although some observations and correlations can be made.

The two deep burials in the mound, C°2-74, -77, and the C°1-2, just outside the mound were perhaps early in the construction sequence. The adult male C°2-74 with the locally made owl (?) effigy platform pipe, lamellar flakes and turkey awls, a turtle carapace and ovate blade at a depth of four and a half feet represents an individual still possessing some of the items of Hopewellian origin. This interpretation is supported by the pottery vessel of Canteen ware, but with a zoned punctate-incised decoration regarded as a continuation of decorative concepts found in Middle Woodland ceramics in the Mississippi Valley. The compound vertical form of this jar is also regarded as another such expression. It is not clear what functional advantage would result from such a form. A similar inference of age can be made for the extended child burial C°2-90 with its copper and pearl beads which seem somewhat unusual for a pure Jersey Bluff complex. The small Canteen Zoned-Punctate vessel without depth data, but with a child burial, has a design concept which also is best attributed to a Hopewellian tradition from an earlier time.

Of the seventeen vessels in the mound, including C°2-90, eight are Canteen Plain, seven are Canteen Cordmarked and two are Canteen Zoned Punctate. Seven of the Canteen Plain vessels had one or more shell spoons in association but only a slight preference for association of vessels with males seems to be true for this group of burials. Three of the cordmarked vessels had spoons. Neither of the zoned punctate vessels were associated with spoons.

There are fourteen burials for which body position and orientation are given. Four of the burials were flexed, two males and two females. One male and one female were flexed on the left side, oriented north-south and with heads to the north. One female flexed on the left was oriented southwest-northeast with head to the southwest and one male flexed on the right was oriented southeast-northwest with head to the southeast.

There are ten extended burials of six males, and two each of females and children. Five of the males were aligned north and south with heads north while a sixth was so oriented but the placement of the head to north or south is not known. One female was oriented north-south with head north, and one was east-west with the head to the west. One extended child was north-south with head to the north. Thus 10 of the 14 burials were north-south and 9 burials had their heads to the north. It is believed that this pattern had a priority evident without need for statistical validation.

The association of lamellar flake knives with a group of split and worked bird bone awls, placed with burials, is an association which is first known in Middle Woodland burials and which continues into Jersey Bluff. The meaning of this association and the specific use or uses in the society for which these awls were made are not known.

The shell spoons were made primarily from the *Lampsilis* or *Proptera* species discussed under the summary of Mound C°1.

One *Anodonta corpulenta* shell from C°2 was probably a spoon. This shell is common in the Mississippi and its larger tributaries and in backwater areas. It has its maximum environment in quiet water of mud bottomed rivers and sloughs from three to five feet below the surface. *Amblema castata* used for one of the hoes is found in the entire Mississippi River in deep water, 3 to 20 feet deep, in good current and on a mud or mud/sand bottom. It is a heavy thick shell well-suited for hoes. Some malacologists recognize three distinct species of *Amblema* while others recognize only one species with variant forms depending on the size and depth of the river. *Megalonaias gigantea* is another large heavy shell ideally suited to function as a digging implement. It is wide spread in the Mississippi drainage in areas of low current with a coarse gravel and mud bottom.

The freshwater snail *Anculosa praerosa* was rather commonly used for necklaces and other decorative purposes primarily in post-Hopewell times in the Middle West. F. C. Baker (1941: 61) believed that this snail "must have been obtained by barter because it does not occur in the Mississippi or Illinois River near Calhoun County or the Cahokia region. It is common in the Ohio and Wabash rivers." This species is so common in these Calhoun County mounds and others of Late Hopewell and Late Woodland times in this area that it might be suggested that they were present 1500 years ago, for they are, according to Dr. Van Der Schalie a wide ranging species, and their failure to be in the Mississippi above Cairo would be difficult to explain.

The small *Busycon carica* (?) marine whelk found at a depth of four feet, four inches, with a Canteen Plain vessel, C°2-78 (Pl. 32,*b*) is another item deep in the mound which would more normally be associated with Hopewell burial activities rather than Late Woodland. This species is common in shallow water from the south shore of Cape Cod to Central east Florida. If the whelk was *Busycon contrarium* it could have come from South Carolina, around coastal Florida or along the coast of the Gulf states to Texas. This specimen certainly reached the Knight site by trade of some type, as is true of the *Cassis* sp. shells from C°8 and C°16, which will be discussed in the section on those tumuli.

The polished stone cone-shaped object, C°2-76, is a rare item for either Middle Woodland or Jersey Bluff in Illinois. Its function is not known. A similar-shaped object of crystal quartz was in Mound 17 of the Hopewell Group in Ohio (Shetrone, 1926: 275), and also in Altar 2 with the great obsidian deposit in Mound 25 (Moorehead, 1922: 137). Cones of copper and quartz were in the Tremper Mound (Mills, 1916: 210 and 219). Hemispherical cones are associated with Adena (Dragoo, 1963: 165, 173), apparently over much of its time span but none of them seem to have the projecting apex of the cone that there is on the one from C°2 or from Hopewell Mound 17 and Mound 25. Two of the same cone-shaped objects with projections appeared at the Renner site in Platte County, Missouri, near Kansas City (Wedel, 1943: 59), where they are described as being of "crystalline limestone, or calcite, of a dirty white color." One was found at the Hiatt site in Carroll County, Missouri (McKinney, 1954: 37) where it is described as "a limestone cup or cone." Another example from Missouri is from the southwestern part of the state in the drainage of the Osage River in southwestern Benton County. The object was found with Burial 2 of Mound 2 of the Fairfield Mound Group (Wood, 1967). It was with a scattered bundle burial, a cache of twelve triangular knives and an engraved shell gorget with a "cat" design. The excavator asserts that Scallorn points were also in association. However, the material from this mound could cover a considerable period of time.

The example at the greatest distance from the Ohio and Illinois concave-based cones is from the McQuorquodale Mound in Clarke County, Alabama (Wimberley and Tourtelot, 1941: 9-10), where it was associated with Burial 1 of Fill Number 1, or in the earliest burial group, which consisted of a long bone fragment, and a grooved faceted galena nodule. Other associations with the burials were a copper earspool, a triangular plate of biotite mica, a copper bead, and three two-hole rectanguloid gorgets. Only the earspool was in the early burial fill and the remainder was in the second fill. This mound is a part of a strong Middle Woodland complex in the area of Mobile Bay.

The Crooks Mound in LaSalle Parish, Louisiana, had a concave base cone (Ford and Willey, 1940: 108) without the projecting tip, but no information was given in the report as to the position in the mound, or any reference of others in the Lower Mississippi Valley. A cone with the suggestion of a tip has been recently identified as part of the ground stone industry at Poverty Point (Webb, 1968: 311). It is rare at the site but again the question may be raised as to the temporal position of the many finds at this important lower Valley site.

The construction of Knight Mound C°2 and its early burials is considered to have been initiated during the final years of the Pike phase but most of the burials were placed in this tumulus during the Fox Creek phase of Late Woodland. The time span for this shift is, of course, not known but could be approximately fifty years or less.

MOUND C°3

Mound C°3 is the third mound from the north on the low ridge in the center of the valley. No measurements were made due to a dense thicket covering the mound but it was estimated to be about 35 feet long and 20 feet wide (Fig. 4). Work was started on the mound in June, 1942. All burials in this mound were located on approximately the short axis.

Mr. Wadlow excavated a four-foot-square pit in the west side of the mound to a depth of six feet. The stratigraphy at this point showed three feet of dark yellow loess on top, two feet of red clay below this and one foot of light yellow loess on the bottom of the profile. This order was verified upon completion of the excavation when the center of the mound showed, from top to bottom, three feet six inches of dark loess and one foot of lensed black, gray and yellow dirt, traces of a white line of material (possible calcium or ash?) three feet one inch of red clay and at the bottom of the mound the light yellow loess. Mr. Wadlow also excavated a trench 12 feet long, three feet wide and five feet deep into the northwest edge of the mound, and found the same layers of dark loess, clay and light loess,

The pit in the west side of the mound was extended and enlarged by Dr. Titterington and the first burial, C°3-17, was encountered about five feet east of the west edge of the mound in the layer of red clay. It was a fully articulated adult male extended on the back with the head to the north (Pl. 34,*a*). At the top of the skull were found a rectanguloid piece of sheet mica, a bone pin, a flake knife and a Norton projectile point (Pl. 34,*b*). A second

Norton projectile point was found partially under the right side of the skull and a galena cube was underneath the skull (Pl. 35,*a*). The mica had red ocher on it and

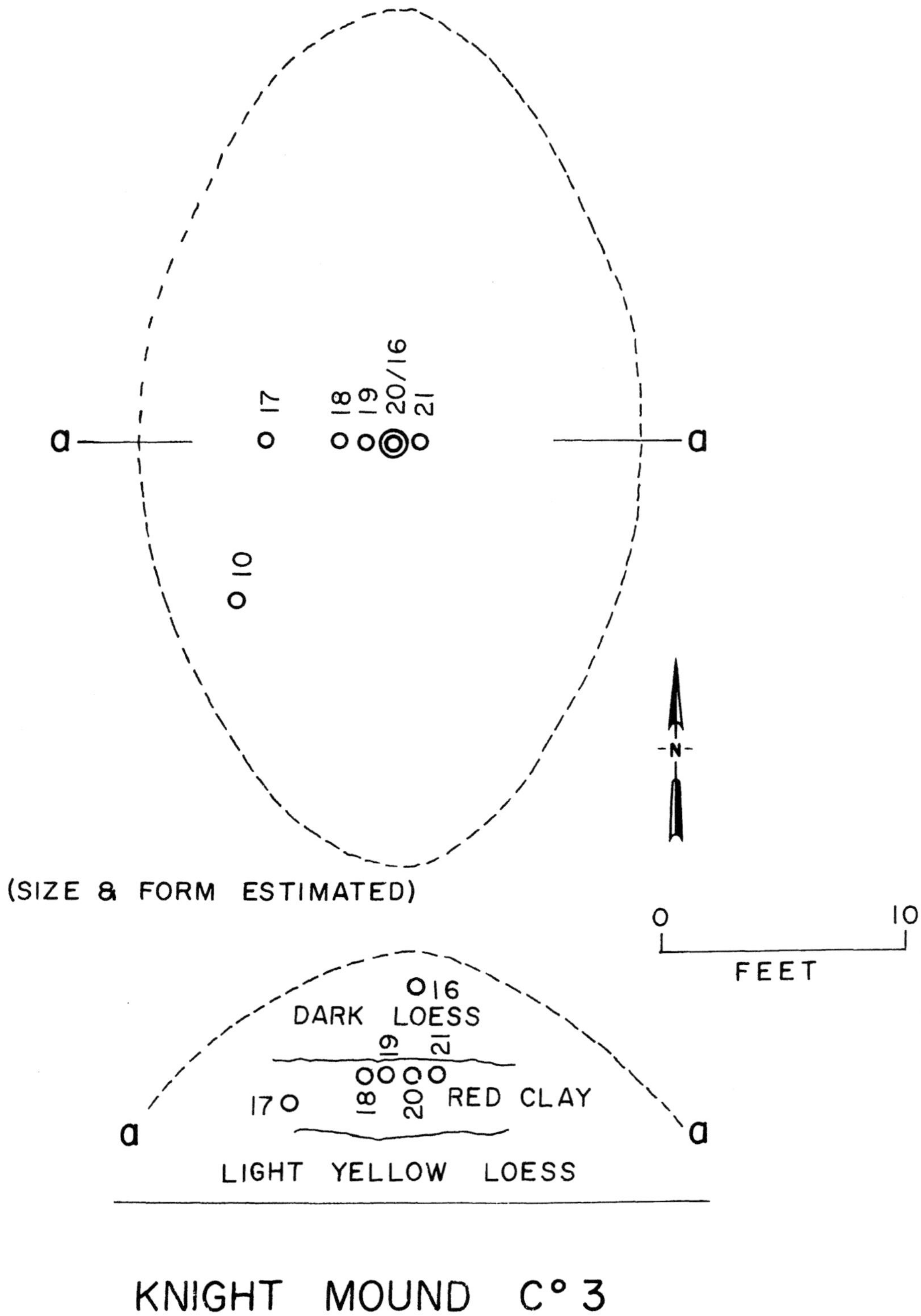

Fig. 4. Diagram of burial locations in Knight Mound C°3.

some dark stained material, possibly organic residue. The dimensions are 20.6 cm. long by 12.5 cm. wide and 3 mm. thick. The blue-gray flint Norton projectile point found at the top of the skull is 6.5 cm. long, 4.1 cm. wide at the barbs, and 2.5 cm. wide at the base and 8 mm. thick. It has a stem 1.8 cm. wide and 1.2 cm. long, convex sides, originally convex base (now broken) and corner notches. The flake knife is an unmodified blade of pink flint 6.4 cm. long, 1.1 cm. wide and .4 cm. thick with some nibbling along the edges. Both the blade and the projectile point are covered on one side with red ocher. The pin is made from an elk metapodial and is 22.7 cm. long with all edges and surfaces polished and the proximal articular surface was ground. The Norton projectile point found under the skull is of reddish-tan flint. It is 7.6 cm. long, 4.6 cm. wide at the barbs, and 2.7 cm. wide at the base, .8 cm. thick, with a stem 1.5 cm. long and 2.3 cm. wide, convex base and sides, and corner notches. Both projectile points belong to the Snyders Notched Group and are most similar to the Norton variant of this group (White, 1968: 144). The galena cube is 3.0 cm. long, 2.0 cm. wide 1.3 cm. thick and one side has a polished facet (Pl. 35,*b*).

Burials C°3-18 to -21 (Pl. 36,*a*) were encountered at a depth of about five feet near the center of the mound in the red clay layer. They are, from west to east, two adult females, a child in the early teens and an adult male, all lying close together extended on the back with the heads to the north. This mass burial is about one foot three inches higher in the mound than C°3-17. All four individuals were evidently interred while fully articulated and there were no associated artifacts.

C°3-16 (Pl. 34,*a*) was found one foot six inches deep at the center of the mound and was an adult female extended on the back with the head to the north. There was a right handled valve spoon of *Lampsilis ovata ventricosa* on the left humerus and a Canteen Plain pottery vessel (Pl. 36,*b*) over the left shoulder. This vessel was of such poor construction and firing that it had collapsed. The lip diameter is estimated at 13 cm., so that the height would have been slightly greater. The rim is 3.5 cm. high. The lip is uneven in height and rounded, to narrowed and rounded, and is from 3 to 4 mm. wide. It has granular temper. Both surfaces are smoothed and the body thickness is from 5 to 6 mm. The base was rounded conoidal.

There were a number of artifacts found by Mr. Wadlow in previous and subsequent excavations of the mound which either were not in association with a burial or occurred with burials of which there are no photographs nor descriptions. C°3-1 is assigned to a shell crescent-shaped gorget made from a conch shell (Pl. 37,*a*) and a Canteen Plain pottery vessel (Pl. 37,*b*). The gorget is 12.3 cm. wide across the horns of the crescent, 13.5 cm. wide at the greatest width and the shell is 2.8 cm. wide and 5 mm. thick. There is a small hole drilled in each horn of the crescent and the artifact has been broken and restored at the points.

The jar is 13.8 cm. high, has a lip diameter of 12.5 cm., a rim diameter of 12 cm. and is 13.2 cm. wide at the shoulder. The rim is short and vertical and the lip is uneven in height and form. It is 3 to 5 mm. wide. The vessel has grit temper with visible small quartzite and hematite particles. These are rarely visible on the smoother inner and outer surfaces. The exterior surface is well smoothed to burnished. The surface colors are tans and browns with some smoke discoloration, particularly on the outer surface.

Vessel C°3-2 is a partially reconstructed small Canteen Plain jar 10.5 cm. high and with a lip diameter slightly less than 10 cm. (Pl. 38,*a*). It has a conoidal base and a short slightly flaring rim. Both surfaces are smoothed with fine vertical striations on the outer surface. There is only a very thin greyish-tan to tan exterior and interior layer on the dark unoxidized core. The tempering is crushed rock with small particles and in low proportion to the clay. The short section of the lip available for examination is flattened and 3 mm. wide. The body is 4 mm. thick.

In September, 1942, the Museum of Anthropology received from Dr. Titterington fragments of a Baehr Zoned Brushed Incised jar excavated by Mr. Waldow. These were identified as C°3-3 (Pl. 38,*b*), and catalogued in the Museum under number 8883. This vessel has been restored and is 20.5 cm. high. It has a lip diameter of 14 cm., a diameter of 12.8 cm. at the base of the slightly flaring rim and a body diameter of 17.2 cm. The fine limestone tempering particles are almost completely leached. The interior and exterior surface color is tan to brown with some smoke blackened areas on the upper outer surface. Both surfaces were smoothed. The lip is rounded to flattened and is 4 to 5 mm. wide. It has short narrow vertical nicks on the outer lip edge spaced 4 to 6 mm. apart. There is a roughly horizontal upper rim zone from 1.3 to 1.6 cm. high bordered below by a narrow horizontal incised line. This zone is hatched with left to right oblique lines with narrow incisions from the lip to the base of the zone in one section of it, while in another section, the incised parallel oblique lines are from right to left, and in still another section there are three horizontal lines. Underneath the area of the horizontal lined upper rim zones there are small punctates at the base of the zones in a feeble recall of a good quality Hopewell Incised rim. This is the only part of the upper rim where punctates were used. At the base of the smoothed rim, there is a horizontal line of the same narrow (1 mm.), shallow appearance as the decorative technique above, and the same as was used to outline curved zones of plain surfaces from much larger areas of brushed-incised impressions on the body which extended down and on to the rounded conoidal base. Whoever made this vessel did not have a clear idea of the design or changed her mind and became confused. Perhaps she learned pottery making from both grandmothers.

C°3-4 is about half of a Canteen Incised jar (Pl. 39,*a*). It is 13 cm. high and has a lip diameter of about 12 cm. It has sparse granular grit temper. The rim is almost vertical. The lip is rounded and uneven and is from 2 to 4 mm. wide. The body is conoidal and varies in thickness from 4 mm. below the shoulder to 8 mm. at the base. The rim is 4 to 6 mm. thick. The exterior is light brown to tan and is partly smoke blackened. The interior is heavily smoke blackened and the core is dark grey to black except for a thin exterior oxidized layer. The interior and exterior surfaces are smoothed with faint vertical brushing or scraping marks on the exterior. The vessel has a carelessly applied incised design made with a fine pointed implement. There are three horizontal lines on the outer rim spaced 1.4 to 1.2 cm. apart. They were placed on top of irregularly spaced vertical lines to form squares and rectangles. The vertical lines are highly irregular in their spacing. Some of them continue on to the shoulder area while a few continue down the body almost to the base. Subsequent smoothing or handling of the vessel after the incising was done, partly obliterated some of the incised area.

Titterington gave the same number, C°3-4, to an unmodified blade of pinkish colored flint. It is 4.2 cm. long, 1.1 cm. wide and 2 mm. thick with nibbled edges and discontinuous flake scars. Presumably he had reason to think they were associated.

The people who buried a child (C°3-5)

placed at its feet a small vessel and three fragmentary and one complete split turkey leg bone awls. The complete awl is 13.5 cm. long and all specimens have ground and polished edges. Three of the awls have the proximal articular end intact and unmodified and all were probably pointed on the distal end (Pl. 39,*b*). Vessel C°3-5 is a group of sherds including one rim section and 12 body sherds. The paste, thickness and form are of a small Canteen jar with the outer surface decorated from the lip to the base with horizontal rows of plain rocker stamp impressions with a chattered appearance. The swing of the stamp is 1 cm. in vertical dimension on the slightly flaring rim and 1.5 cm. on the body. There are two horizontal rows on the rim which is 3 cm. high, and four rocker stamp rows on the body. The estimated height of the jar is 13 cm. The interior surface was smoothed with horizontal scraping impressions and the other surface was smoothed before the decoration was applied. The tempering material is grit. The exterior color is tan to light brown with blackened areas near the base. The interior is grey and the core is black. The lip is rounded and 3 mm. wide; the rim is 5 mm. thick and the lower body 8 mm. thick.

Three small sherds with the C°3-5 group belong to another small vessel which had a zoned plain rocker stamp decoration with some portion of the stamped areas outlined by a very thin, medium deep, incised line. The stamp was applied with more care and precision than the vessel just described. The granular temper and "feel" of these sherds is not that of the Hopewellian pottery but is like the Canteen ware.

The objects designated C°3-6 were also found at the feet of a child burial and consist of two stone projectile points, three mussel shells, five shell beads, a worked piece of turtle plastron and two flint bladelets (Pl. 40,*a*). One tan flint projectile point is straight sided and side notched with a slightly convex base. It is 9.8 cm. long, 3.1 cm. wide at the base, 3.3. cm. wide at the barbs and 9 mm. thick. The stem is 2.0 cm. wide and 1.3 cm. long. The other tan flint point has straight sides and a convex base, is side notched and is 8.6 cm. long, 2.7 cm. wide at the base, 3.3 cm. wide at the barbs and 1.0 cm. thick, with a stem 1.4 cm. long and 1.9 cm. wide. Both may be regarded as variants of Gibson Diagonal Notched. Two of the mussel shells were found together and are companion valves of *Plagiola lineolata*, both 6.0 cm. long and 4.5 cm. wide. The left valve has a hole 7 mm. in diameter drilled immediately below the hinge and the pointed end is battered. The right valve shows the battered end and the outer surface seems to have been covered with red ocher. The third mussel shell is a handled spoon made from a left valve of *Proptera capax* with all edges and surfaces ground. The five shell beads are globular, 8 mm. in diameter and 6 mm. long. The turtle plastron object is rectangular in shape, 11.7 cm. long and 3.1 cm. wide, with both surfaces and three edges cut and ground and the fourth edge broken along a suture. It appears to be one end of a larger object. The two white flint blades are 2.8 cm. long, 1.1 cm. wide and 1 mm. thick and 2.2 cm. long, 1.6 cm. wide and 1 mm. thick respectively, and show no modification or use marks.

A group of Canteen Plain body sherds from one vessel are identified as C°3-6. Unfortunately there are no rim sections. They have grit temper. The outer surface is well smoothed but the inner surface is less well smoothed and the small grit particles are visible on the surface. The exterior and outer surfaces are tan to smoke blackened.

C°3-7 was a burial of an adult female with the head to the east and was found less than a foot deep in the mound. At the feet of the burial was a pottery vessel (Pl. 40,*b*) containing a handled shell spoon made from a left valve of *Proptera capax*.

The spoon is ground on all edges and surfaces and is 7.2 cm. wide. Vessel C°3-7 is a Baehr Brushed rounded base jar with a channeled inner rim of the later Hopewell style jars. It has crushed limestone temper with some rather larger particles 2 to 4 mm. long. The vessel is 12.8 cm. high. The lip diameter is 11.9 by 12.5 cm. The thickened rim is 12.2 by 13 cm. wide, the lower rim 11.9 by 12.2 cm., and the greatest diameter of the body is 14.6 by 14.8 cm. The lip is 3 mm. wide and is narrowed and rounded or somewhat flattened. The rim has an upper outer collar and an interior channel. The height of the rim is uneven but averages 1.5 cm. The outer rim has horizontal shallow brushing marks which almost look like fine incising, the body has vertical striations which are irregularly spaced, narrow and shallow. The interior and exterior are smoothed and both surfaces are primarily smoke blackened. This vessel appears to have been made about the same time as the group of Baehr-style vessels in Mound C°8.

C°3-8 was assigned to a Canteen Plain pottery vessel with a notched rim and some limestone inclusions in the temper (Pl. 41,*a*). The vessel was found at the left shoulder of a child and contained a worked mussel shell and a shell gorget. The mussel shell is a right valve of *Lampsilis ventricosa,* 7.9 cm. long and 5.4 cm. wide with hinge partially cut away and the edges ground. The shell gorget is not in the collection but is seen on the left in Plate 37,*a*.

The jar is 18 cm. high, has a lip diameter of 13.5 by 14.5 cm., a lower rim diameter of 12.8 by 13 cm., and a body diameter just below the rather prominent shoulder of 14 by 14.8 cm. The outer surface had been cordmarked vertically and was subsequently smoothed, especially so on the rim area, where all of the cord impressions are obliterated. The tempering material is crushed limestone with some rather large fragments. The exterior color is tan to smoke blackened with most of the latter discoloration around the outer rim. The interior surface has the same range of color. The lip height is irregular, is narrowed 3 to 5 mm. and has deep oblique gashes across the lip which are 3 mm. wide and about the same distance apart. The rim has a slight flare.

C°3-9 was a burial of a child found 15 inches from the surface of the mound. Associated with the burial between the right hand and the right side of the pelvis were a Canteen Cordmarked pottery vessel, a shell spoon, three worked antler tines and a flake knife (Pl. 41,*b*; 42,*a*). Two of the antler tines have been cut diagonally at the base, the longer one being 10.7 cm. long with a basal diameter of 2.0 cm. and the shorter one 10.1 cm. long with a basal diameter of 1.5 cm. and with a small notch cut into the tip. The third tine is 12.9 cm. long with a 1.7 cm. basal diameter and was broken from an antler along a cut. The shell spoon is not located in the collection. The flake knife is a Type D blade (White, 1963), 6.8 cm. long, 2.1 cm. wide and 7 mm. thick with nibbled edges and retouch.

Vessel C°3-9 is a very thin-walled vessel with very sloppily applied cordwrapped paddle impressions which are criss-crossed and widely spaced (Pl. 41,*b*). The impressions are short and of tightly twisted cord. Most of the impressions on the body were covered over by smoothing the surface. The height is 16.5 cm, the lip diameter is 13 by 13.5 cm., and the shoulder is 14.3 by 14.8 cm. There is a slight inward slope to the shoulder area and the rim is slightly flared. The lip is of uneven height. It varies in width from 3 to 6 mm. and is flattened. The rim thickness is 2.5 mm. and the body varies from 3 to 5 mm.

C°3-10 was an adult female extended on the back with the head to the north and was found low in the west side of the mound at a depth of five feet. There were two pearl beads, not located in the collection, found at the wrist and five pot sherds, all representing the same Canteen Cordmarked vessel, associated with this burial.

C°3-11 was an adolescent about 15 years old with the skull sitting upright in the abdominal area but the mandible was in normal position in relation to the vertebral column. A shell spoon containing a bone awl and two chips of red flint were found under the right side of the mandible of the burial (Pl. 42,*b*). The spoon is a right handled valve of *Proptera capax* and is 9.0 cm. long and 6.5 cm. wide and the hinge cut away and the edges ground. The flint chips are unmodified blades, both 3.2 cm. long; one is 1.6 cm. wide and 6 mm. thick and the other is 1.3 cm. wide and 3 mm. thick. The larger chip has a nibbled edge and is broken, the smaller one is complete. The split bird bone awl is 9.8 cm. long, the edges are ground and the remaining portion of the proximal articular surface is unmodified. There were 29 globular shell beads averaging 7 mm. long and 8 mm. in diameter found at the right wrist and 10 *Marginella* beads averaging 1.0 cm. long found at the left wrist (Pl. 42,*b*).

C°3-12 was assigned to a shell pendant found at the head of an infant burial. The pendant is trapezoidal in shape with a single hole 3 mm. in diameter for suspension. All edges and surfaces have been ground and the pendant is 4.0 cm. long, 2.6 cm. wide at the top and 4.1 cm. wide at the bottom (Pl. 37,*a*). C°3-13 was a skull without a mandible and C°3-14 was an adult female extended on the back with the head to the northwest and showing periostitis of the tibiae, fibulae, right radius and left humerus. C°3-15 was a pair of tibiae showing periostitis.

Plate 43,*a* illustrates C°3-22 to -33 and the blade from C°3-4. C°3-22 is a mussel shell hoe, a left valve of *Fusconaia ebenus* 6.7 cm. long and 6.2 cm. wide, drilled with a 1.8 cm. hole for hefting and with the bit end worn from use. C°3-23 is an unmodified mussel shell (*Fusconaia ebenus*) 6.5 cm. long and 5.8 cm. wide with no apparent sign of use (not illustrated). C°3-24 is a Type A blade (White, 1963) with bilateral retouch 6.8 cm. long, 1.8 cm. wide and 4 mm. thick with nibbling along the edges. C°3-25 is a Type A blade with a broken tip and is 4.0 cm. long, 1.8 cm. wide and 4 mm. thick with nibbled edges. C°3-26 is an unmodified blade 4.5 cm. long, 1.8 cm. wide and 4 mm. thick with nibbled edges and discontinuous flake scars. C°3-27 is an unmodified blade, complete, 4.8 cm. long, 1.4 cm. wide and 3 mm. thick with nibbled edges. C°3-28 is a broken blade with discontinuous scars and nibbled edges, 6.0 cm. long, 2.2 cm. wide and 8 mm. thick. C°3-29 is a Type A blade with serrated bilateral retouch, a broken base and nibbled edges, 5.0 cm. long, 1.7 cm. wide and 4 mm. thick C°3-30 is a Type C blade with end retouching and nibbled edges, 4.0 cm. long, 1.1 cm. wide and 3 mm. thick.

C°3-31 is a white flint projectile point 8.9 cm. long, 4.5 cm. wide at the barbs, 1.5 cm. wide at the base and 1.3 cm. thick. It has a straight base, a straight stem 1.7 cm. wide, convex sides and a corner notch on one side and straight shoulder on the other. The stem is slightly off center and the object may be a knife or reworked point. C°3-32 is a pink flint projectile point 4.6 cm. long, 3.0 cm. wide at the barbs, 2.9 cm. wide at the base and 6 mm. thick with a straight base and sides, a stem 2.1 cm. wide and side notches. C°3-33 is an ovoid biface scraper, 6.0 cm. long, 3.5 cm. wide and 1.3 cm. thick with straight sides and ends, with one end battered. No number of specific location is assigned to two portions of dirt dauber nests.

A group of 23 sherds are from Mound C°3 (some of these are illustrated in Pl. 43,*b*.) There are five Havana Cordmarked and four Canteen Cordmarked body sherds, nine Pike Brushed body sherds and one Pike Brushed large rim with a wide, 15 cm., interior channel on the inner rim surface and vertical plain rocker stamping on the outer rim. Another Pike Brushed rim has a similar wide, 1.5 cm., channel on the inner rim, a vertical wide swing plain rocker stamp on the outer rim and a boss 1 cm. in diameter, 1.7 cm. below the lip which was produced by pressing a cylindrical tool into the inner channel. One rim is a Pike Incised type which has a thickened upper rim with a horizontal row of vertical thumbnail impressions spaced 6 mm. apart. There are four horizontal incised lines on the lower rim which were made subsequent to the vertical brushed impressions on the other surface. There is a low boss on the lower rim which was made by an annular tool 4 mm. in diameter pressed from the interior, but this area was smoothed over with clay to obliterate the opening and well smoothed before the vessel was fired. There is one Pike Plain Rocker Stamp body sherd and one Canteen Plain rim.

COMMENTS ON MOUND C°3

This mound was begun during late Hopewell times and a number of burials, C°3-17 to -21, are described as on or in a red clay layer. This is probably the lower horizon of the soil zone and it is inferred that a pit had been excavated into the zone because the mixed earth in the upper part of the mound is referred to as being "lensed" and was carried in by basket loads. The early burials were of two adult males, two adult females and one child. All of them were extended north-south burials with the heads to the north. The adult female, C°3-7, having a Baehr Brushed vessel with a shell spoon also belongs in this same cultural and temporal position. The skull of the burial is recorded as to the east and the burial position was probably extended. Only one of the Hopewellian burials, C°3-17, had much in the way of recovered burial associations.

Unfortunately there is yet no specific identification of the source or sources of Hopewellian mica and the loose identification of the Appalachian area, or North Carolina, is not as helpful in interpreting interarea contacts as is desirable. One of the Norton points is of blue-grey nodular flint probably from Union County, Illinois, which is now sometimes referred to as Gondola chert. This source was an important one for the Early and Middle Woodland populations in the Illinois Valley and nearby regions. It was not, however, of much importance during Jersey Bluff occupations in the same area. A possible source for the more common white and reddish or multicolored flint so common on Hopewellian sites in Illinois is the Crescent Quarry area in Jefferson County, Missouri, where it is found in the St. Louis division of the Lower Carboniferous limestone. There are, however, chert sources in the limestone formations of Calhoun and adjoining counties in Illinois and Missouri (Rubey, 1952: 43). Systemmatic collection and identification of the flint sources is an important phase of archaeological studies and has barely begun in most parts of the United States let alone this particular area.

Only three burials of the Jersey Bluff complex with orientation data are known from this mound. These are identified as extended adult females. Two of them were in a north-south alignment with the head to the north while the third was northwest-southeast with the head to the northwest.

The Baehr Zoned Brushed Incised vessel, C°3-3, is a classic example of the deterioration of the Hopewellian concept of zoned pottery decoration. Unfortunately, there are no associations with this vessel. It would seem to belong to about the same time period as the vessels in Mound C°8.

The same observation can be made for the Baehr Brushed vessel with C°3-7.

The Jersey Bluff ceramic complex has some important characteristics implying a short time between the late Hopewellian and early Late Woodland populations. The fragmentary vessel, C°3-5, with a child burial has crude plain rocker stamped treatment on a small Canteen form. Associated with the fragments of this vessel were a number of sherds belonging to a Canteen Zoned Plain Rocker decoration. If the excavation had been more carefully done more of this vessel would probably have been recovered. This ceramic evidence is interpreted as a continuation of previous design concepts into early Bluff times. The vessel fragments put back together as C°3-4 have in the small amount of incised decorations the possibility of a continuation of the incised-brushed treatment of the Baehr-Pike complex which is even better represented on the jar C°4-1 and in Mound C°8. Five of the vessels, or partially complete vessels, were Canteen Plain and two of them had shell spoons. One of the latter at the feet of child burial C°3-6 was associated with Gibson variant points, shell beads, and short, white flint lamellar blades. Both the points and the blades are more common in Hopewellian rather than Late Woodland times. The unusual, probably unique crescent shell gorget and the small circular notched three-hole gorget were with Canteen Plain vessels. This latter form was also found at the Fisher site in Will County, Illinois (Langford, 1927: 179). One of the circular gorgets was found with an extended child burial in the Big West Mound while a similar but larger gorget was with an adult female between pits 6 and 8. This information is from notes made by F. R. Eggan and J. B. Griffin on the Fisher collection. J. W. Griffin assigns these gorgets or pendents to his early period A at the Fisher Site (J. W. Griffin, 1946) to which he also assigned the shell tempered Fisher pottery. Another gorget of the same type was found at the Crable site in Fulton County, Illinois (Smith, 1951: Pl. V, *d'*) where it is associated with the Mississippian occupation. The extended adult female C°3-10 with a Canteen Cordmarked vessel had pearl beads in association and was one of the deepest burials. Pearl beads are more often found in a Hopewellian context than with Jersey Bluff burials. The other cordmarked vessel with child burial C°3-9 had a shell spoon, antler tines and a flake knife.

It is perhaps risky to make a judgment from the sherds recovered from Mound C°3 but the high proportion of late Hopewellian-Pike Complex examples and the Havana sherds may mean that there was relatively little Canteen pottery present in the area from which the mound fill was derived.

The early burials in the mound belong to late Pike phase while the burials with Canteen pottery may be said to be associated with the early part of Late Woodland designated in the report as the Fox Creek phase.

MOUND C°4

Mound C°4 is the fourth mound from the north on the low ridge in the center of the valley. The long axis of the mound is northwest by southeast and the mound measures 48 feet long by 38 feet wide (Fig. 5). About 1900 a local school teacher dug a pit six feet in diameter and three feet four inches deep into the top of the mound. In the bottom of this pit were scattered bones of four or five adult individuals and one stone projectile point C°4-9 (Pl. 44,*b*). The point is 7.5 cm. long with approximately 3 mm. missing from the tip, 3.3 cm. wide at the barbs and 8 mm. thick with a stem 2.2 cm. wide and 1.8 cm. long. It has an ovoid blade and convex base and belongs

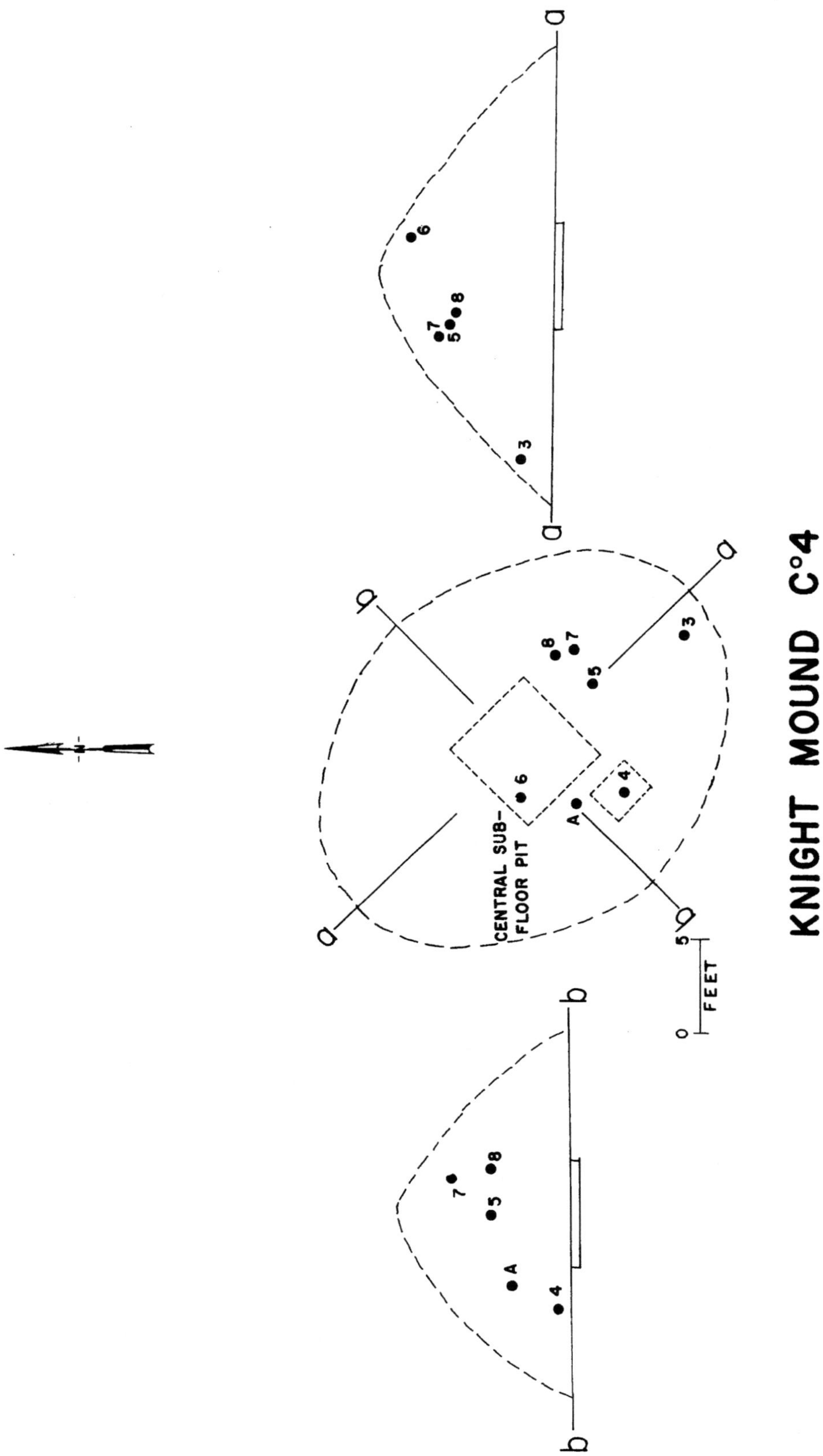

Fig. 5. Diagram of burial locations in Knight Mound C°4.

to the Knight Diagonal Notched type of the Steuben group (White, 1968).

In the fall of 1942, Mr. Walter Wadlaw's father and Mr. L. M. Gibson started in the west side of the mound about six feet from the top with an eight foot wide trench which they extended about one-fourth of the way into the mound. An adult burial was encountered at this point at a depth of four feet with an associated Canteen ware vessel with vertical and diagonal "stroked" decoration, which contained a poorly preserved worked right valve mussel shell spoon C°4-1 (Pl. 44,*a*) and a tan flint projectile point C°4-2 (Pl. 44, *b*). The point has straight sides, a straight base, parallel sided stem and flaring barbs and is 9.6 cm. long, 4.2 cm. wide at the barbs, 2.2 cm. wide at the base and 1.4 cm. thick with a stem 2.2 cm. wide and 2.0 cm. long (Marshall Barbed type, White, 1968).

Vessel C°4-1 can be dignified as Canteen Incised, but if the name is to give an idea of the character or quality of the decoration it should be called something like "Slaphappy Incised". The incised lines were made by a slightly rounded point and are from slightly less than 2 to 3 mm. wide. There are left to right oblique lines from the lip to the shoulder area and below which they are irregularly spaced and placed. Some of them were made before the vertical incisions and some were crossed by vertical lines. The vertical incisions are also on the rim area but predominate on the lower body and base. On the body there are a few upper right to lower left oblique lines. The vessel height is 12.5 cm. The lip diameter is 11.2 cm., the rim 11 cm., and the body 13.2 cm. There is a short vertical rim and a fairly pronounced shoulder. The lip is rounded to flattened, 3 to 4 mm. wide, and of uneven height. The rim is 6 mm. thick, and the body 7 mm. The vessel has a semi-conoidal base. The tempering material is granular most of which was covered during the smoothing of the surfaces. Both surfaces are tan to dark brown with some smoke blackened areas.

Wadlow and Gibson continued their excavation toward the center of the mound and removed the greater portion of the west side and southwest corner of the central pit. They also removed the greater portion of three extended burials near the center of the mound, about five feet of the west end of the three southernmost rows of limestone slabs extending over the central pit, and possible one or two complete burials from the west side of the pit.

Titterington's excavation was started at the base of the mound on the west side with a 25-foot-wide trench which passed through the center of the mound, the northern edge of the pit being five feet north of the center. A ten-foot-wide trench was also excavated from the north end of the mound to the central pit. The northwest corner of the mound could not be removed because of the presence of two trees that the owner did not want destroyed. Burial C°4-3 (Pl. 45*a*) was that of an adult male extended on the back with the head to the west and was found 44 feet south of the north end of the mound and three feet west of the long axis at a depth of five feet. All bones of the skeleton are in their proper relationships although the rib cage was caved in and the clavicles somewhat displaced by ground pressure. Three raccoon *os penii*, two pieces of mica and a beaver incisor were found immediately beside the lateral aspect of the lower left leg (Pl. 45,*b*). The raccoon penis bones are each 10 cm. long with no apparent modification. The beaver incisor is fragmentary and does not appear to have been modified. The mica sheets are roughly rectanguloid with fragmentary edges and measure 11.5 cm. by 7.2 cm. and 8.4 cm. by 8.0 cm. respectively (Pl. 46,*a*). Burial C°4-4 was represented by a five feet by four feet area of small limestone slabs and fragments of adult bones in no discernible order. It was found 28 feet south of the north end of the mound and 10 feet west of the long axis at a depth of five feet three inches. Burial C°4-5 was that of an adult male extended on the back with the head to the east and was found 34 feet south of the north end of the mound on the long axis at a depth of three feet eight inches. C°4-6 was an adult male extended on the back with the head to the west. This burial was found 20 feet south of the north end of the mound, three feet west of the long axis at a depth of eight inches and was in very fragmentary condition. Burial C°4-7 was that of an adult female flexed on the left side with the head to the north and was found 35 feet south of the north end of the mound and four feet east of the long axis at a depth of two feet. There was a previous pit adjacent to this burial and the skeletal parts were in poor condition.

Burial C°4-8 was an adolescent male extended on the back with the head to the west. C°4-8 was found 33 feet south of the north end of the mound and five feet east of the long axis at a depth of three feet eight inches. Over the knees and lower legs of the skeleton were found a fragmentary Baehr Zoned Punctate pottery vessel, a bone pin, a shell pendant, a shell spoon and two unworked mussel shells (Pl. 46,*b*; 47,*a*). The bone pin is made from a swan ulna (*Olor* sp.) and measures 19.6 cm. in length. It is well polished. The proximal articular surface is unmodified and the distal end of the shaft is cut diagonally to produce a blunt point. The shell pendant is a left valve of *Ligumia recta latissima* and is 14.7 cm. long and 3.9 cm. wide. All edges are ground, the hinge is partially ground away and there is a hole 2 mm. in diameter drilled at the wide end, presumably for suspension. The mussel shell spoon is a fragmentary handled right valve but the remaining portion is too small for accurate measurement or identification. One of the unworked mussel shells is a right valve of *Lampsilis anodontoides* measuring 8.3 cm. by 4.0 cm. and the other is a right valve of *Proptera capax* measuring 7.5 cm. by 6.0 cm.

The Baehr Zoned Punctate jar C°4-8 was apparently not complete when placed with the burial. The portion of the vessel in the illustration is 11.3 cm. high, and the body diameter is 10.5 cm. (Pl. 47,*b*). The tempering is crushed limestone particles less than 1 mm., to fragments 2.5 mm. long. A small number of them are leached. The upper accentuated rim is 1.4 cm. high and has an inner channel 7 mm. wide which begins 5 mm. below the slightly flattened 3 mm. wide lip. There is a series of small dentate stamp impressions placed right to left on the outer rim and spaced 4 mm. apart. Just below the rim there is a horizontal row of closely spaced ovoid punctates pushed into the clay from the right. Below the punctates is a smooth horizontal band 1.4 cm. wide which is bordered by a shallow horizontal incised line 1 mm. wide which was made by the same pointed tool which separates the punctate and plain zones on the lower rim and upper shoulder area. The decorated panel is 4.5 cm. wide and is delimited below by a slightly undulating line setting off a smooth band bordered below by a similar line which delimits the horizontal brushing which covered the body. The punctates on the body are ovoid to trianguloid and were pushed into the clay from the left. The vessel was slightly lobed. This jar is only 4 mm. thick in the lower rim and 3 to 4 mm. thick in the body. The lower rim or neck has a greater height area than most vessels of the Hopewell-Baehr types. The zoned punctate decoration is also unusual and has some similarity to the Churupa Punctated style in the related Middle Woodland sites in the Lower Mississippi Valley. It is one of the vessels that stimulated the formulation of the hypothesis of a gradual decline of the

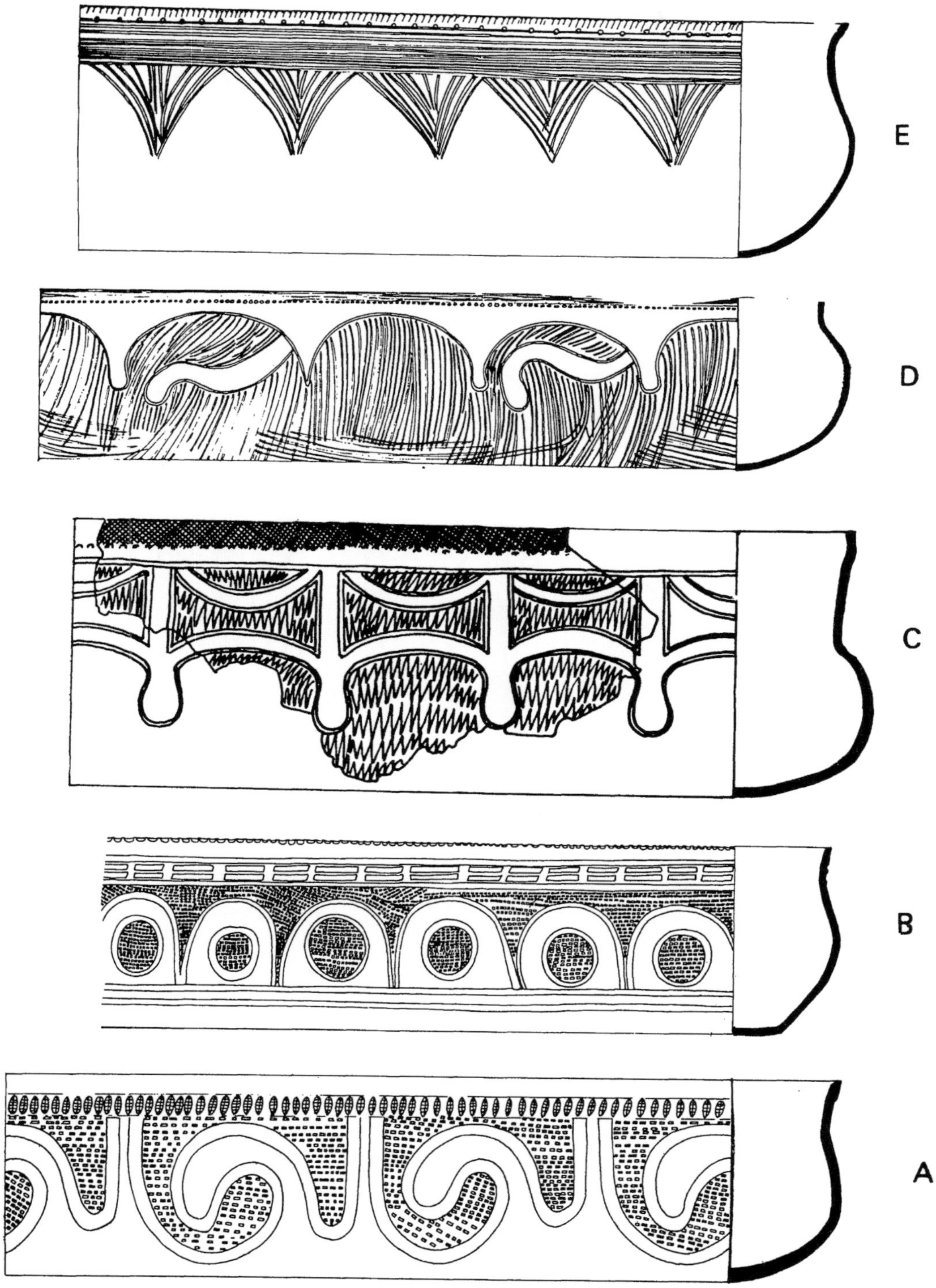

Fig. 6. Design patterns of some of the vessels from the Knight Mound Group. A. Havana Zoned Dentate Stamped jar C°16-5; B. Havana Zoned Dentate Stamped jar C°6; C. Small Hopewell Zoned Rocker Stamped jar C°8-4; D. Baehr Brushed jar C°8-3; E. Baehr Brushed jar C°5-4.

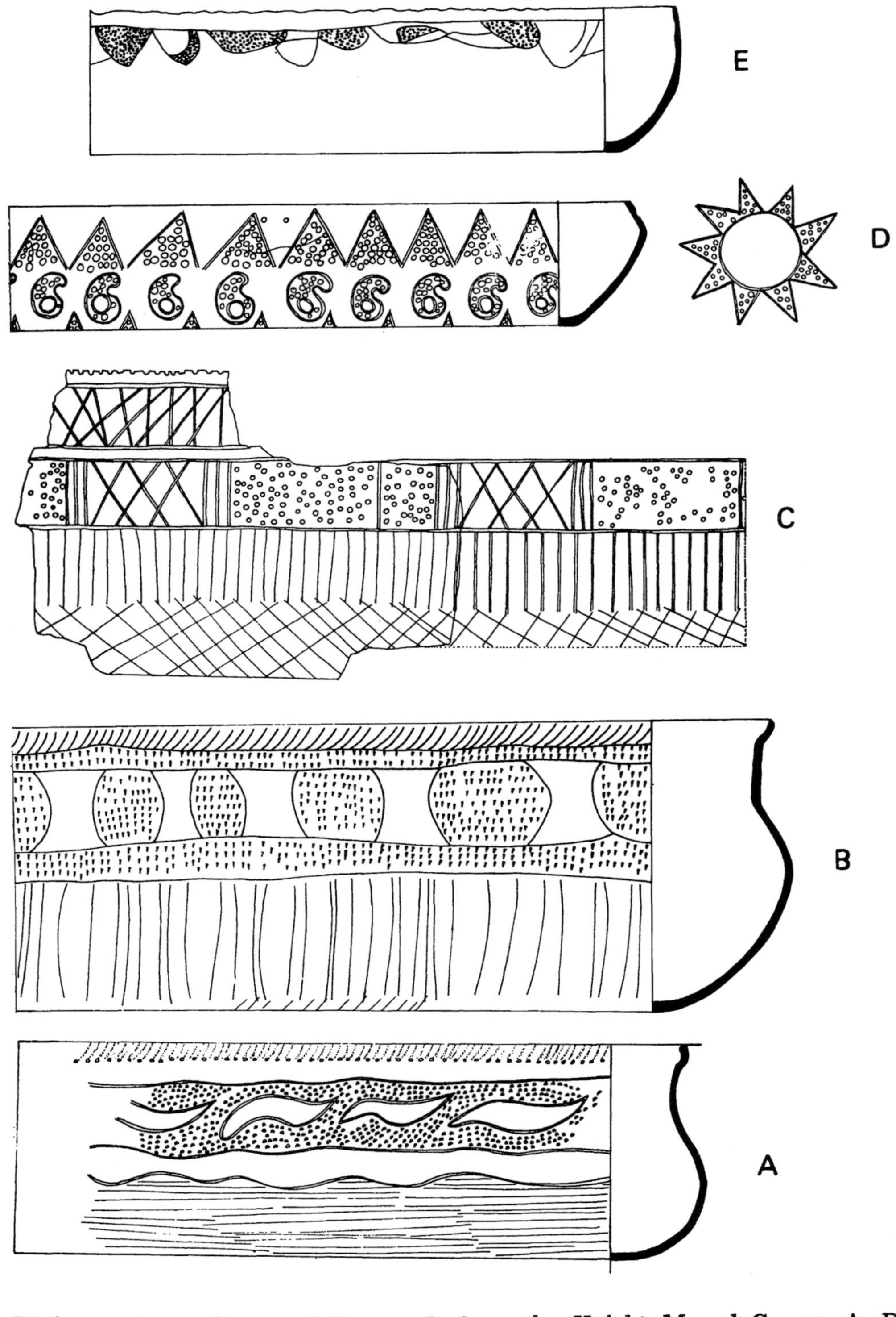

Fig. 7. Design patterns of some of the vessels from the Knight Mound Group: A. Baehr Zoned Punctate jar C°4-8; B. Baehr Zoned Punctate jar C°8-33; C. Canteen Zoned Incised jar C°2-74; D. Canteen Zoned Punctate jar C°2-85; E. Canteen Zoned Punctate bowl C°1-7.

quality of the Hopewell style in the Illinois area (Griffin, 1952*a*: 119-28). The design patterns of ten of the decorated vessels from the Knight Group are presented in Figures 6 and 7. The older designs are on Figure 6 from bottom to top and then on Figure 7 from bottom to top. These should be compared with the designs from Havana Mound 6 (McGregor, 1952: Pl. XXV); from the Norton Group in this volume; and from the Klunk Mound (Perino, 1968: Figs. 8, 9, 12, 41, 42).

The burials in the central portion of the mound were contained in a shallow pit which had been dug six inches to eight inches into the underlying red clay. The pit measured ten feet six inches long north to south, by eleven feet six inches wide east to west and, according to the photographs, was approximately nine feet six inches deep from the top of the mound. There were four rows of limestone slabs three layers deep laid immediately above the pit burials in an east-west direction and spaced approximately two feet apart, the northernmost row being six inches south of the north end of the pit (Pl. 48,*a*). The northernmost row was the only one left intact by the previous disturbance and it was ten feet six inches long from the east edge of the pit. There was another row of single slabs just to the north of the pit, measuring 13 feet long and not immediately over any burials, and a single row of slabs to the east of the pit lying in a north-south direction and measuring 17 feet in length. This north-south row extended two feet south of the pit and three feet north of the north row where it covered evidence of a small fire pit. This row was approximately one foot higher than the pit floor and was raised by four inches of "made dirt" containing a greenish-yellow clay. The north-south row underlay the east-west rows where they were seen to curve upward at the east edge of the pit. It was assumed that the same pattern held for the west edge of the pit but, as stated before, this side had been destroyed by previous excavation. The floor of the pit had been covered with ash and there was also a thin ash line one inch thick on the north and barely one-quarter inch thick elsewhere, over and around the rows of slabs. The ash line could be seen to curve upward with the rows of slabs at the edge of the pit and to continue upwards to a height of approximately two feet beyond the pit margin after which it curved downward slightly and disappeared (Pl. 48,*b*). The top of the mound was composed of light colored loess but the profile underneath and to the east of the ash line showed a dark loess over the red clay, suggesting either that a smaller mound had been covered over or that the original surface had been excavated for the pit burials and then filled in with the light loess (see C°3 for a comparable soil profile).

The burials remaining in the pit after the previous disturbance were in rather poor condition but 13 individuals could be identified (Pl. 49,*a* and Fig. 8). Through the center of the pit at least five individuals had been extended on the back with heads to the north. From east to west, C°4-25 was an adult female, C°4-24 was an adult male and C°4-23 was an adult female. C°4-21 was represented by the entire left leg and lower right leg and C°4-20 by both lower legs. The size of the bones suggests that these two were adult males. C°4-26 was an infant situated over the feet of the eastern-most female (C°4-25) and C°22 was an infant found over the thighs of the other female (C°4-23). C°4-28 was an adult female extended on the back with the head to the west and was found approximately on the centerline of the pit against the north wall. There was a small child (C°4-27) extended on the back with the head to the west situated over the lower legs of this burial. The northwest corner of the pit contained a compound

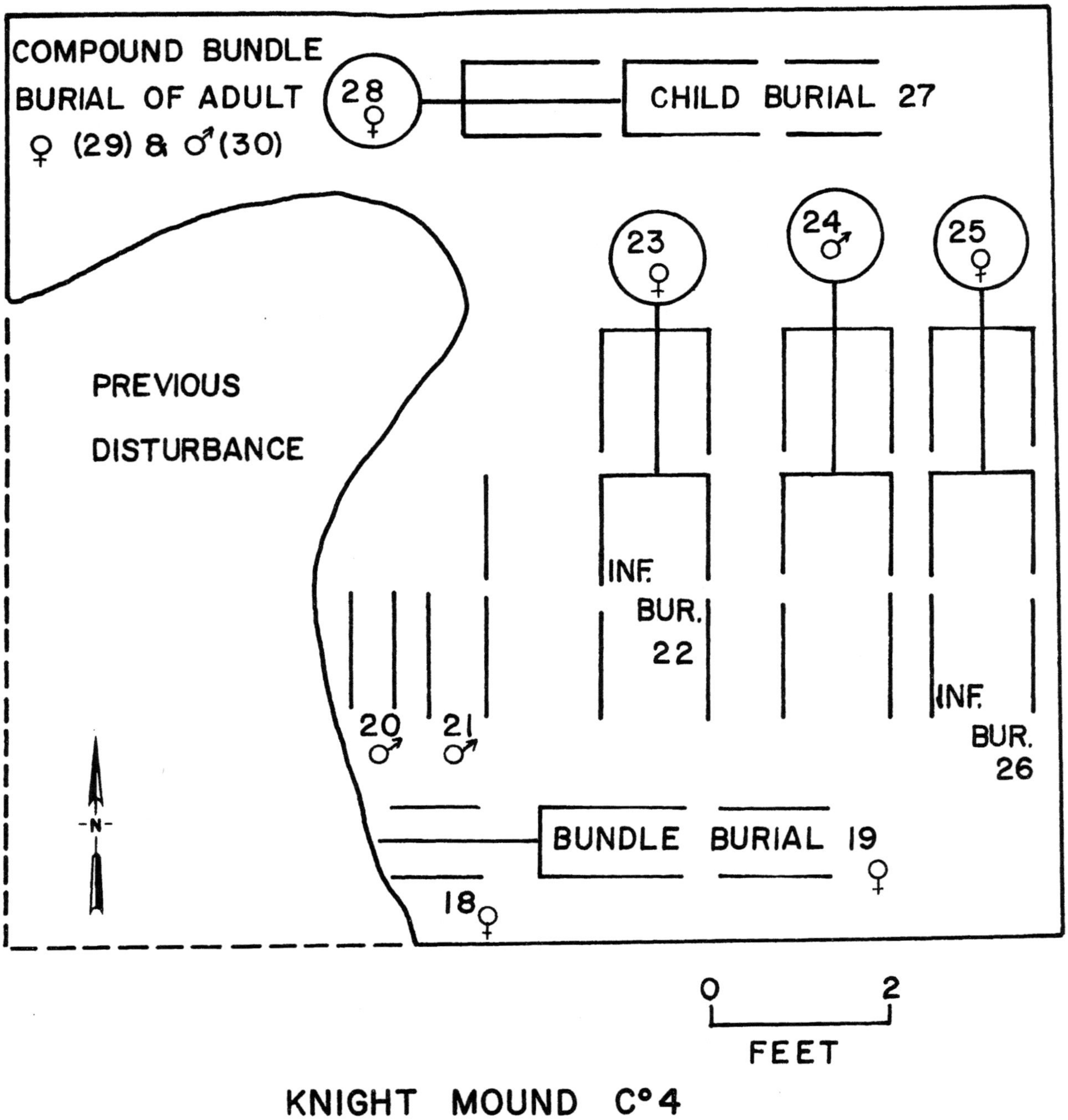

Fig. 8. Location of burials within central burial area of Knight Mound C°4.

bundle burial of an adult male (C°4-30) and an adult female (C°4-29). An adult female (C°4-18) had been placed extended on the back with the head to the west at the south wall of the pit but the portion from the thoracic area up had been removed with the previous excavation (Pl. 49,*b*). There was a bundle burial of an adult female (C°4-19) over the lower extremities of C°4-18.

Three artifacts were found in the area of the skull of an adult male C°4-24 (Pl. 50 and 51,*a*). At the right side of the skull was a flake knife, an unmodified incomplete blade 7.2 cm. long and 1.8 cm. wide of white flint with discontinuous flake scars. To the left of the skull was a fragmentary left half of a dog (*Canis* sp.) mandible 12.4 cm. long with no apparent modifications. An owl effigy pipe was located partially under the top of the skull. The pipe shows excellent workmanship and is carved from a mottled reddish-brown and bluish-grey Ohio pipestone. The owl effigy bowl is facing the smoking end and is 6.1 cm. long, 3.1 cm. wide at the wings and 2.3 cm. in diameter at the feet or bottom. The bowl is 1.5 cm. in inside diameter and 3.9 cm. deep. The platform is 9.8 cm. long, 3.8 cm. wide at the center, 2.0 cm. wide at the ends, 1.2 cm. thick at the center and 8 mm. thick at the ends and is markedly curved downward from the center at both ends. The top of the platform is flat and the bottom convex and there is a small nick worked into the right side of the end facing the front.

A number of artifacts were found in the mound fill that were not in direct association with burials. C°4-9 to -17 are seen in Plate 51,*b*. C°4-9 is a mottled tan flint projectile point found in the previous disturbance on the top of the mound. It has an ovoid blade, convex base and side notches, is 7.5 cm. long (approximately 3 mm. is missing from the tip), 3.3 cm. wide at the barbs and 8 mm. thick with a stem 2.2 cm. wide and 1.8 cm. long. It seems to be closest in type to Gibson Diagonal Notched. C°4-10 consists of 161 white flint percussion flakes which were found together in the south end of the mound at a depth of two feet. C°4-11 is a baroque pearl bead with a 1.5 cm. hole drilled through it for suspension which was found on top of the mound. C°4-12 is an antler drift found six inches over the center of the south side of the burial pit. It is 13.0 cm. long, cut and ground on both ends and ground over the entire surface. C°4-13, -14, and -15 are flint points found scattered immediately above the burial pit. All are ovate, straight-based blades with patterned, discontinuous, lamellar retouch and slightly constricted stems (Pl. 51,*b*). C°4-13 was found two feet east of the antler drift, C°4-12, and at the same level and is of white flint, 11.0 cm. long, 3.0 cm. wide at mid-blade, 2.2 cm. wide at the base and 1.5 cm. thick at the thickest point. C°4-14 was found one foot above the north edge of the pit and three feet east of the west wall and is of white flint mottled with tan and gray. It is 12.6 cm. in length, 2.9 cm. wide at the widest point (3.2 cm. from the basal edge), 1.7 cm. wide at the base and 1.2 cm. thick at the thickest point. C°4-15 was found immediately above the center of the pit and is of white flint, 12.4 cm. long, 3.1 cm. wide at midblade, 2.2 cm. wide at the base and 1.5 cm. thick at the thickest point. These points are similar to the Sedalia and Nebo Hill forms (Perino, 1968), and it may be doubted that they were made by the people who made the burials in the mound. C°4-16 consists of four flake knives, all incomplete, unmodified blades with discontinuous scars and ranging from 2.1 cm. to 4.8 cm. in length. C°4-17 is a flat, worn rose quartz pebble 2.4 cm. in diameter, found seven feet deep in the center of the mound. C°4-18 is a large red and white mottled flint core, 17.5 cm. long, 8.5 cm. wide and 11.0 cm. high from which a number of parallel-sided flakes have been removed (Pl. 52,*a*). It is from the northeast corner of the central pit. No number is assigned to an ovate, straight-based point of white flint found by Wadlow just above the burial pit and probably associated with the other blades C°4-13, -14 and -15 of the same type. It is 12.5 cm. long, 2.9 cm. wide at midblade, 2.0 cm. wide at the base and 1.1 cm. thick at the thickest point (not illustrated).

A ten foot trench was excavated between Mounds C°4 and C°5 six feet deep to a point just past the low point between the mounds and a six-foot square was continued downward in the southeast end of the trench. At a depth of seven feet six inches from the original ground surface a refuse pit five feet in diameter was encountered. It contained a large number of small rocks up to the size of a fist that had been subjected to fire, 28 pot sherds, a large number of animal bones, five flake knives and three projectile points (Pl. 52,*b*). The flake knives are unmodified blades of reddish to white flint, all approximately 1.6 cm. wide, two of them 4.4 cm. long and the other two 5.6 cm. and 3.1 cm. long. One projectile point is of gray flint and appears to be a Steuben Expanding Stem variant with a straight edged blade and convex base. About one-third of the blade is missing but the remaining portion is about 5.0 cm. long and 2.5 cm. wide at the barbs. The second projectile point is of black flint with excurvate sides, a concave base, wide, shallow side notches and a flaring stem. The point is 3.5 cm. long, 1.9 cm. wide at the shoulder and 2.1 cm. wide at the base with a stem 1.2 cm. wide and 9 mm. long. The third point is gray flint with straight edges, a straight base and a flaring stem. It is 3.7 cm. long, 1.2 cm. wide at the shoulder and 1.3 cm. at the base with a stem 8 mm. wide and 1.1 cm. long. The latter two points are probably also Steuben group variants.

In the pit excavated between Mound C°4 and C°5, 28 sherds were recovered. There were three Canteen Cordmarked body sherds, and one Canteen plate rim. There were 18 Baehr Brushed body sherds and one rim, one body and one rim of Pike Incised and one rim each of Montezuma Punctate, Pike Rocked Dentate and Baehr Zoned Brushed. Some of these are illustrated in Plates 53,*a* and 53,*b*. The large restored rim section of Baehr Brushed might have been zoned on the body. This rim is an excellent example of the quality of execution of much of the Baehr ceramic group. In the collection there is one fragment of a young deer mandible and two fragments of the proximal ends of deer ulnae, one 10.5 cm. long and the other 10.0 cm. long with no apparent modification (Pl. 52,*b*).

COMMENTS ON MOUND C°4

This mound was begun during the Hopewellian period by excavating a subfloor pit about eleven feet square some six to eight inches into the reddish soil zone of the loess on the ridge. From this pit thirteen burials or portions of thirteen were removed by Titterington. To some degree the orientation of the bodies was influenced by the size and shape of the pit. A compound burial of an adult male and female was in the northwest corner of the pit and another bundle burial C°4-19, an adult female, was placed over the lower legs of an extended adult female C°4-18 which had its head to the west along the south wall of the pit. Except for infant burials C°4-22 and C°4-26, the rest of the pit burials were extended. The main group C°4-20, -21, -23, -25 were extended north-south with heads to the north, but C°4-28 was extended along the north wall of the pit with head to the west and thus parallels the extended burial along the south wall.

In this pit there were three bundle burials of two adult females and one male. There were three infant burials, one placed between the legs of adult female C°4-23 and the second at the feet of adult female C°4-25 and the third over the legs of C°4-28. The seven extended burials included four females and three males, Five were extended north-south with heads to the north and two were east-west with heads to the west. Two later burials which are clearly Hopewellian, C°4-3, which was an adult male extended east-west with head to west and C°4-8, an extended young male east-west with head to the west. Two additional adult males without grave goods, C°4-5 and -6 were also extended east-west. The first with head to the east and the second with head to the west. One adult female C°4-7 was flexed in a north-south position with the head to the north. In addition three extended burials found by Wadlow were extended.

The most striking object recovered was the superb owl effigy pipe found under the right side of the skull of the adult male, C°4-24, in the main burial pit. This pipe of bluish-gray to reddish-brown Ohio pipestone is in the classic style of the Scioto Valley school of pipe manufacture and is one of the few items at the Knight Mound Group that can be confidently identified as originating in Ohio. The other items with this burial, a lamellar flake knife and the dog mandible, were the only additional grave goods with the thirteen recovered burials, except for the large flint nodule in the northeast corner of the pit.

The limestone slabs placed over the central pit were aligned east and west in five rows, with a north-south row just to the east of the pit. There may have been a similar row of slabs on the west side, but if so, the slabs had been removed before Titterington's observations. The limestone slab arrangement is similar to that of the central tomb of Mound 9 of the Kamp group (Streuver, 1960). The thin ash line of Titterington is almost certainly niter which results from the disintegration of vegetal materials incorporated in the grave construction. It is a fairly common feature of Hopewellian burial mounds. In this instance it would appear to have resulted from matting, bark, or other relatively thin covering. For some years it has been thought that the use of limestone slabs in the construction of Hopewellian burial areas was an indication of a late temporal position in that complex and that there was then continuity from late Hopewellian into early Late Woodland. While this continuity does exist, the association of limestone slabs with burials is also a feature of late Archiac to early Woodland in the Upper Mississippi Valley.

The burial of extended adult male, C°4-3, at a depth of five feet was apparently after the completion of the central pit and a few feet south of it. The mica plates with this burial are clearly Hopewellian in time. The burial of the extended adolescent male C°3-8 was about on the same level and about three feet east of C°4-3. The Baehr Zoned Punctate jar with this burial is a clear indicator of a late position within the Illinois Valley Hopewellian time scale and is comparable in time to the vessels placed in the main construction of Mound C°8. The long bone pin or awl of a swan is unusual. The shell pendant with this burial made from a long narrow mussel has been identified as *Ligumia recta latissima*, also known as the Black Sand shell. This form was common in the medium to large streams in Illinois in strong current at a depth of a few inches to four feet and on a coarse sand to gravel bottom. Another possible identification is *Elliptio shepardianus* (Lea) from the Altamaha River which flows through east Georgia into the Atlantic, about halfway between the northern and southern coastal border of Georgia. If the Georgia identification is the correct one, it would be one of the more unusual examples of long distance transport. Whichever species and source is involved, this pendant form is quite rare, but is exactly matched by one from the Snyders Mound group some fifteen miles to the south, found with an extended adult male burial C°114-1, one of the primary burials in that mound. One of the unworked shells, *Lampsilis anadontoidea*, the Yellow Sand shell, lives on sand, gravel or mud bottoms, in swift or slow current and at varying depths.

The four whitish flint knives found in various places over and near the central pit area are difficult to attribute to either the Hopewellian or Jersey Bluff complexes because such forms are not reported but it is also difficult to think that they could have been included in the mound fill. They are regarded at the moment as Archaic forms perhaps manufactured at the Archaic flint-working camp below the ridge on which the mounds were located.

The unusually incised Canteen ware jar with a shell spoon and Marshall Barbed point with adult burial C°4-1 was either an intrusive burial or one which was placed on the mound and then covered in early Jersey Bluff times. It is the only clearly Fox Creek phase burial in this mound.

It is difficult to provide an accurate estimate of the time at which the subfloor pit and limestone slab construction were made. There were so few preserved grave goods associated with the burials that placement in terms of what is primarily a ceramic chronology is hazardous. On the basis of the use of limestone slabs in the burial pit, that is similar to that of Kamp Mound 9 (Streuver, 1960) which clearly belongs to an early part of the Pike phase, it is reasonable to regard the mortuary activity which initiated the construction of this mound as taking place about the same time. It has been proposed in this monograph that Bedford Mounds 9 and 12 also belong in the Pike phase and it is in these two mounds that the five "imported" effigy platform pipes were found. The Knight owl pipe then would be in about the same time period as far as its placement in the burial pit is concerned. How long such a means of communicating with the "spirit" world have been kept in a society is unknown. If it was part of a medicine bundle, and as such intimately associated with a single individual, the time span is not likely to have been very long.

At some later period of time than the pit burial a number of Pike phase extended burials were made. The mica plates with burial C°4-3 are the only other objects in the mound which were clearly brought in from some distance. The plates, raccoon penis bones and beaver incisors may well have been enclosed in some sort of a container. The adult extended male near the top of the mound with late Baehr style vessel C°4-8 places a terminal period for the Hopewellian burials near the end of the Pike phase. Whether the first burial discovered in Mound C°4 by Wadlow and Gibson was a late inclusion or an intrusion is not known.

MOUND C°5

Mound C°5 is the fifth mound from the north on the low ridge in the middle of the valley. The mound measured 55 feet to 60 feet in length, 42 feet in width and 10 feet four inches in height at the center. The length could not be determined exactly because the area between C°4 and C°5 appeared to have been filled in. The long axis of the mound lay on an approximate azimuth of 300 degrees (Fig. 9). There was an old filled-in pit six feet in diameter and two feet six inches deep at the center of the top of the mound. C°5 was excavated during the summer of 1942 with work commencing on June 14, 1942. The mound was dug concurrently in two "levels," an upper level three feet six inches deep and a lower level. The upper level yielded several burials and unassociated pottery vessels and the lower level contained a central burial area at the bottom of the mound which had three levels of mass extended and bundle burials.

Three fragmentary pottery vessels were found in the upper level in the extreme west side of the mound at a depth of one foot (Pl. 54,*a*). The vessels were lying side by side and there was a child's radius

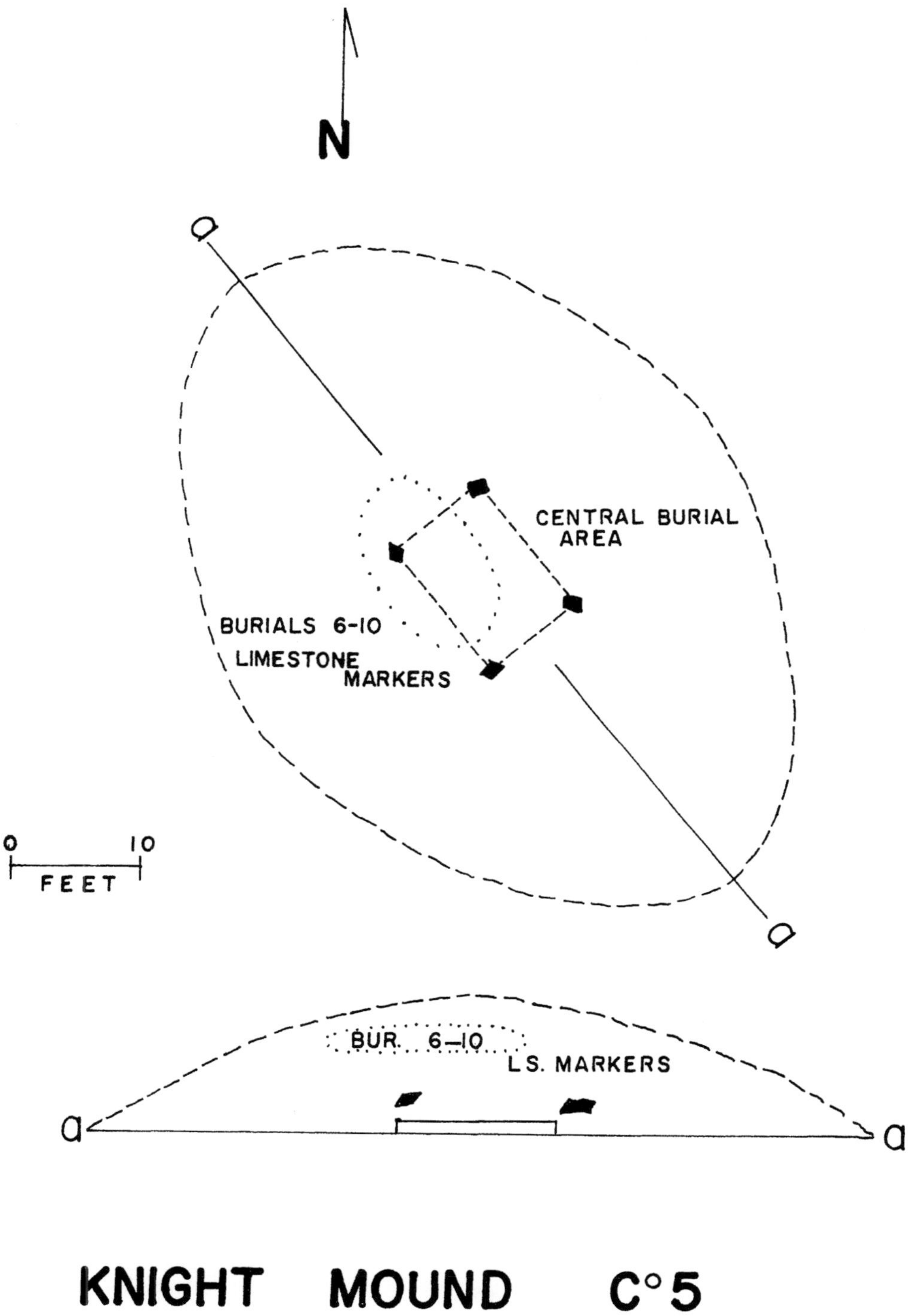

Fig. 9. Diagram of location of burials in Knight Mound C°5.

under the central vessel C°5-1A.

The small Canteen Plain jar C°5-1 (Pl. 54,*b*) has a height of 11.5 cm., a lip and rim diameter of 11.2 cm., and a body diameter of 11.4 cm. It has a very short vertical rim with a thickness of 5 mm. The body has the same thickness. The lip is uneven in height and is rounded to flattened and varied in width from 4 to 6 mm. The tempering material is granular which is well covered by the smoothing process. The interior is roughly smoothed and the exterior is also roughly smoothed with some faint vertical striations or brush marks. It has a smoke-darkened tan interior and blackened greyish exterior.

Vessel C°5-1A (Pl. 55,*a*) is an incomplete Canteen Incised jar of unusually good workmanship. The vessel is 13.8 cm. high. It has a body diameter of 13.5 cm., an estimated lip diameter of 11.5 cm., and 10.2 cm. for the lower rim. The rim is 2.8 cm. high and is vertical to outslanting. The lip is rounded 4 to 5 mm. wide. It has broad, 7 mm. wide transverse ovoid gashes spaced about 5 mm. apart. There is very little visible temper, but small holes in the paste suggest that fine limestone was used. The interior surface is smoothed and the exterior is smooth to burnished. The interior is smoke discolored over a light brown surface while the exterior is light tan to gray with some discoloration. The core is black. The rim is decorated with a band of line-filled triangles whose bases alternate at the lip and at the base of the rim. There are usually lines within each triangle. In the triangles with apex up, the lines slant from left to right, and from right to left in the triangles with apex down. There is a discontinuous horizontal incised line at the base of the rim which is narrow and shallow as are the lines of the triangles. This design resembles Yokena Incised of the Lower Mississippi Valley (Greengo, 1964: Fig. 23,*b*) but small line-filled triangles may be seen in any area of the world. There is a shallow horizontal line below the smooth band 1.6 cm. wide on the upper shoulder area. The width of the design area is 6 cm., and it is bordered on the base by a narrow shallow horizontal line. Within the design area are opposed pairs of L-shaped figures outlined by 2 mm. wide shallow incised lines. The horizontal arms of the figures are 5.5 cm. long and the vertical arms 4 cm. high. The vessel has a round base.

Only about one-third of the Canteen Plain jar C°5-2 was preserved (Pl. 55,*b*). It is 18 cm. high with an estimated lip diameter of 12.8 cm., and an estimated body diameter of 15 cm. The rim is vertical and rises from a constricted shoulder. The lip is rounded and 3 to 4 mm. wide. The side walls contract to a rounded conoidal base. The tempering is sparse amounts of small grit fragments. The interior and exterior surfaces are smoothed. There are faint vertical impressions of a pebble smoothing tool on the exterior body. The body thickness is 6 mm.

The surface of the west side of the mound was steep and the vessels were covered by only four to five inches of dirt on the outside. Three feet to the north of the first three vessels, two more fragmentary vessels were found at the same depth These are C°5-3, a Baehr Plain bowl and C°5-4 (Pl. 56,*a*), a Baehr Zoned Brushed Incised vessel with a row of exterior nodes.

There are fragments of about half of a small incurved rim Baehr Plain bowl C°5-3. It has a lip diameter estimated at 7.5 cm. and an estimated body diameter of 9 cm. and it is about 6 cm. high. The limestone particles with which the vessel was tempered are completely leached. The surfaces were well smoothed and there are faint horizontal brushing striations on the outer body. The outer surface is tan to light brown with some firing clouds and the inner surface is slightly smoke blackened. The lip is rounded, 4 mm. wide, and the body is 3 to 4 mm. thick.

The companion vessel to C°5-3 is a Baehr Zoned Brushed-Incised jar with badly leached limestone temper. C°5-4 has a rounded base, a vague low shoulder and a slightly flaring rim (Pl. 56,*a*). It is 13.5 cm. high, and has a diameter of 12 cm. at the lip, 11 cm. at the lower rim and 13 cm.

for the lower body. Both inner and outer surfaces were well smoothed, and are heavily smoke blackened with a few tan to brown areas. The core is black. The lip was flattened and is 4 mm. wide, while the body is 3 mm. thick. There is a row of short incised vertical gashes along the rim at the lip level 4 to 6 mm. long which cut deeply into the flattened lip surface. Just below the gashes there is a horizontal row of small bosses 4 mm. in diameter and spaced 8 mm. apart made by punching a narrow cylindrincal object from the inside. The nodes were made after a group of nine closely spaced horizontal lines were drawn around the rim in a zone 2.8 cm. high. Pendent from the lower narrow shallow horizontal line are five triangular areas with apex down. These areas are 6.5 cm. wide at the top and extend 5 cm. toward the base. They are filled with three to four incised lines parallel to the sides of the triangle. The rest of the body has brush marks.

A fifth fragmentary pot, C°5-5, was found five feet in towards the center of the mound from C°5-1. This is a Canteen Plain vessel with a well smoothed, almost polished surface (Pl. 56,*b*). It is one of the larger funerary jars with a height of 23 cm., a lip diameter of 16.2 cm., at the rim 16 cm., and of the body 18 cm. It has grit temper of small to medium size and a tan interior and upper exterior with a lower section which is smoke blackened. The lip is rounded to flattened and of uneven width from 3 to 5 mm. The rim is 6 mm. thick.

Burials C°5-6 to C°5-10 were encountered in the upper level at the center of the mound, east of the pottery vessels and from 2.5 feet to 3.5 feet deep (Pl. 57,*a*,*b*). C°5-6 was the burial of a female extended on the back with the head to the northeast. All the lower extremities with the exception of the upper half of the left femur were missing and the other parts of the postcranial skeleton are poorly preserved. The head is turned slightly to the left and has suffered some distortion from ground action. C°5-7 consists of the lower extremities and a portion of the left innominate bone of an adult male extended on the back with the head to the southwest near C°5-6. The remaining skeletal parts of these two burials are in articulatory positions, suggesting that the burials had been disturbed. C°5-8, located to the southeast of C°5-7, was a fragmentary Canteen Plain pottery vessel and a crushed child's skull, the top of the skull to the east. This jar has not been reconstructed although at least half of it is available. The rim diameter is estimated at 16.5 cm. and the height would have been somewhat greater. The rim is vertical, 4.5 cm. high and there is a very slight shoulder. The lip is rounded and 4 mm. wide. The tempering material is sand and angular grit. The particles are not well covered by the interior and exterior smoothing. There are some very faint possible cordmarkings. There are some horizontal brushing or scraping marks on the exterior rim. The exterior is brown to grey and the interior is dark grey. The core is black.

C°5-9, directly to the south of C°5-8, was an adult female extended on the back with the head to the northeast and appears in the photograph to have been a primary burial. The head is turned to the left and the upper trunk and rib cage were caved in by ground pressure. Plate 57,*b* shows the relative positions of burials C°5-6 to -9.

C°5-10 was the burial of an adult, reportedly male. The burial cannot be located from either the notes or the photographs but is presumably from the upper level of the mound. A Canteen Plain vessel was found immediately to the north of the fragmentary skull (Pl. 58,*a*). The left humerus was lying on the east side of the pot and a rib fragment was located on the upper portion of the pot. About one foot south of the skull was a portion of the left innominate bone and both femurs in approximate anatomical position. If the skeleton was articulated when interred, the skull would have been lying over the upper abdomen and the pot over the upper chest. This could have been the case as the cervical portion of the spine was found to the north of the pot. A shell spoon made from a left valve of *Lampsilis ventricosa*, 10.5 cm. long and 7.2 cm. wide with all surface ground, was also associated with the burial.

Vessel C°5-10 was badly warped from the weight of the mound earth above it (Pl. 58,*b*). It has granular tempering with some particles 3 to 4 mm. wide, and the tempering appears to be about 25 per cent on the basis of the paste. The interior is roughly smoothed with some horizontal striations on the inner rim. The outer surface is also smoothed and has parallel vertical brushing lines particularly on the shoulder and upper body. The vessel is about 23.5 cm. high. The rim and body are so laterally compressed that their diameters as well as the lip are difficult to estimate. The lip is of uneven height, most of it was flattened and is from 4 to 7 mm. wide. The rim is 5 to 6 mm. thick and is vertical with very little construction between it and the body of the jar. The base is conoidal.

At a distance of about four feet from the south end of the mound and at a depth of approximately three feet a lensing of black, grey and yellow dirt three to four feet thick underlain by compact red clay was encountered (Pl. 59,*a*). The red clay layer was found to be four to five feet thick when test trenches were excavated in the south end of the mound and under the central burial area. The burials in the central area occurred in this clay layer and Titterington remarks that there was no evidence of a pit having been cut into the clay. The clay layer was underlain by a slightly yellow loess and the upper portion of the mound was made up of a dark loess.

In the approximate center at the bottom of the mound was a burial area eight feet wide on the north, eight feet six inches wide on the south, twelve feet long on the west and eleven feet six inches long on the east. The pit was marked on each corner by piles of limestone slabs which were three to four feet above the burials. The southwest marker was a pile of four slabs measuring one foot by one foot three inches and was found six feet eight inches deep. The northeast marker consisted of six slabs in a one-foot-square pile and was found nine feet deep from the surface. The northwest marker was 13 limestone slabs in an area about two feet square and was found seven feet six inches deep. The slabs were evidently not intentionally shaped but were probably chosen for their regular dimensions. The smallest were six inches by four inches by two inches and the largest one was 14 inches by 20 inches by eight inches. As the southwest corner marker was uncovered during excavation, a white ash line one-eighth inch thick was noticed at the level of the lower portion of the top slabs. This ash line continued straight across the face of the trench wall and turned upwards abruptly at a 45 degree angle to meet the southeast corner marker. When the central burial area had been completely excavated, it was found that the ash line dipped down toward the center from all four margins and lay on top of the red clay over the burials (Pl. 59,*b*).

The first burials encountered in the central area were at a depth of ten feet six inches below the top of the mound and about two inches into the red clay below the lensed dirt (Fig. 10). They consisted of four adults, very badly disintegrated, which had evidently been extended on the back, side by side, with the heads to the north. Identifiable parts include the long leg bones, pelvic girdle and sacral and lumbar vertebrae of the west burial, both femurs and the right tibia of the next burial

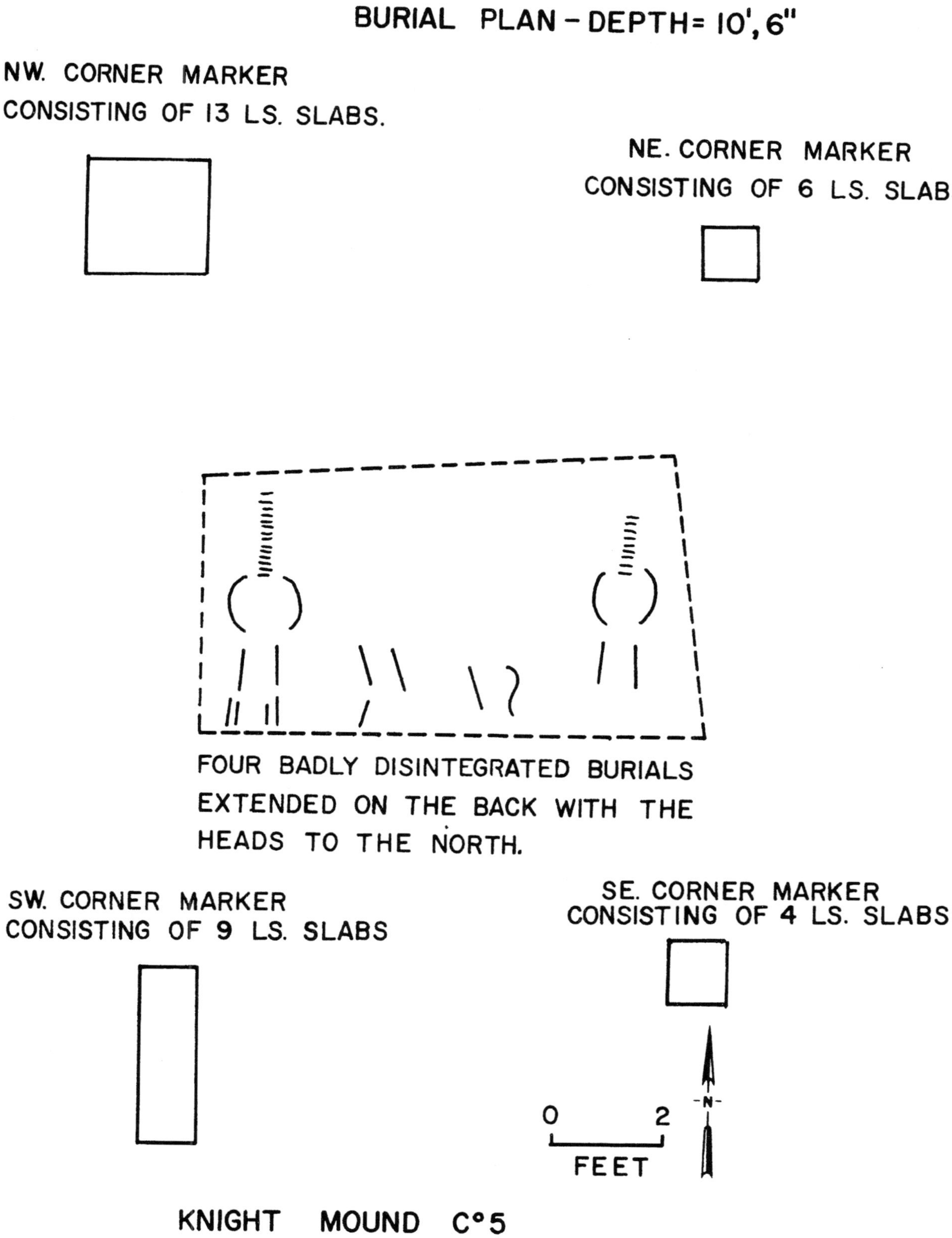

Fig. 10. Location of burials within central burial area of Knight mound C°5 at a depth of 10 feet 6 inches.

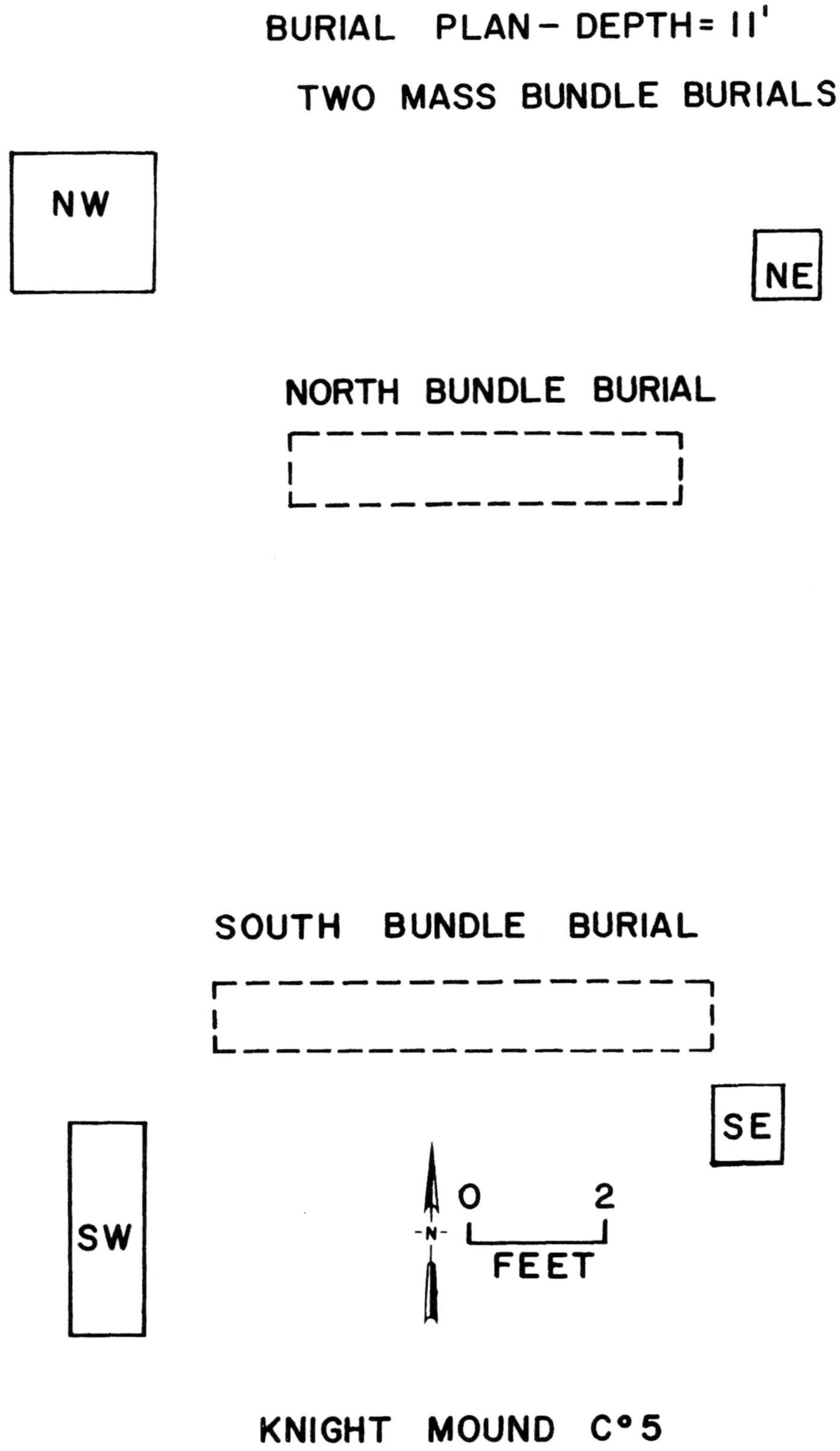

Fig. 11. Location of burials within central burial area of Knight Mound C°5 at a depth of 11 feet.

to the east, both tibiae of the next burial to the east, and the long leg bones, pelvic girdle and sacral and lumbar vertebrae of the east burial. These burials occurred in an area approximately eight feet by five feet in the center of the burial area (Pl. 60,*b*).

The next layer of burials was 11 feet from the top of the mound, bounded by the markers, six inches below the four extended burials, and consisted of two mass bundle burials, one on the north end of the central area and the other on the south end (Pl. 61,*a*). The bundle to the north measured five feet six inches east to west, one foot north to south, was six inches thick and located two feet south of the inner margin of the north markers (Fig. 11). Titterington states that the bundle consisted of the larger bones of possibly three or four skeletons, most of the bones lying in an east-west direction. The bones in the eastern one-third of the bundle were in a much poorer state of preservation than the rest. Small skull fragments in the western one-third of the bundle, the head of a femur, a right innominate bone, two clavicles, and portions of several ribs are identifiable in the photograph. A platform pipe, shell bead and bone effigy bear canine were located in the middle third of the north bundle (Pl. 61,*b*). The pipe (C°5-15) is of a hard, polished grey Ohio pipestone. The base is concave, 8.3 cm. long, 3.7 cm. wide, and 1.2 cm. thick at the center, 1.9 cm. wide and 5 mm. thick at the ends. The bowl is in the center of the platform and is 3.1 cm. high, 2.5 cm. in diameter at the base, and 2.1 cm. in diameter at the lip. The bowl is 3.8 cm. deep and the internal diameter is 1.6 cm. The bead C°5-17 is 2.2 cm. long and 1.3 cm. in diameter and has a cylindrical hole 4 mm. in diameter drilled through it. Eighteen hackberry seeds 5 mm. in diameter were found with the bead. The bone effigy bear canine C°5-16 is 7.9 cm. long, 2.1 cm. wide and 6 mm. thick and has a hole 4 mm. in diameter drilled in the basal end for suspension. There are two other holes 3 mm. in diameter and filled with a lime-like material in the center of the tooth and there is an incised line indicating the enamel border (Pl. 62,*b*). The south bundle burial was located between six inches to one foot north of the south corner markers. It measured seven feet long east and west and one foot wide north and south and contained the bones of possibly four or five individuals.

At a depth of eleven feet six inches from the top of the mound and immediately below the two bundles described above were found two mass burials composed of one group of three extended skeletons and the other of five extended skeletons and two individual bundle burials (Pl. 63,*a* and Fig. 12). The bundle burials were encountered in the area between the north corner marker. The center of the west burial was one foot three inches east of the northwest corner marker. No description is available for the contents of the bundles.

The north mass burial consisted of three individuals extended in the flesh, two with the heads to the west and one with the head to the east. The burial measured eight feet six inches east and west and one foot north and south according to the notes and no features are distinguishable from the photograph. The west end of the burial was one foot south of the northwest corner marker and the east end was one foot southwest of the northeast corner marker. The south mass burial contained five individuals extended in the flesh, three with the heads to the east and two with the heads to the west. This burial measured eight feet six inches east and west, and two feet north and south and both ends of the burial were located one foot north of the respective south corner markers. The photograph was taken after most of the bones had been removed and identification of po-

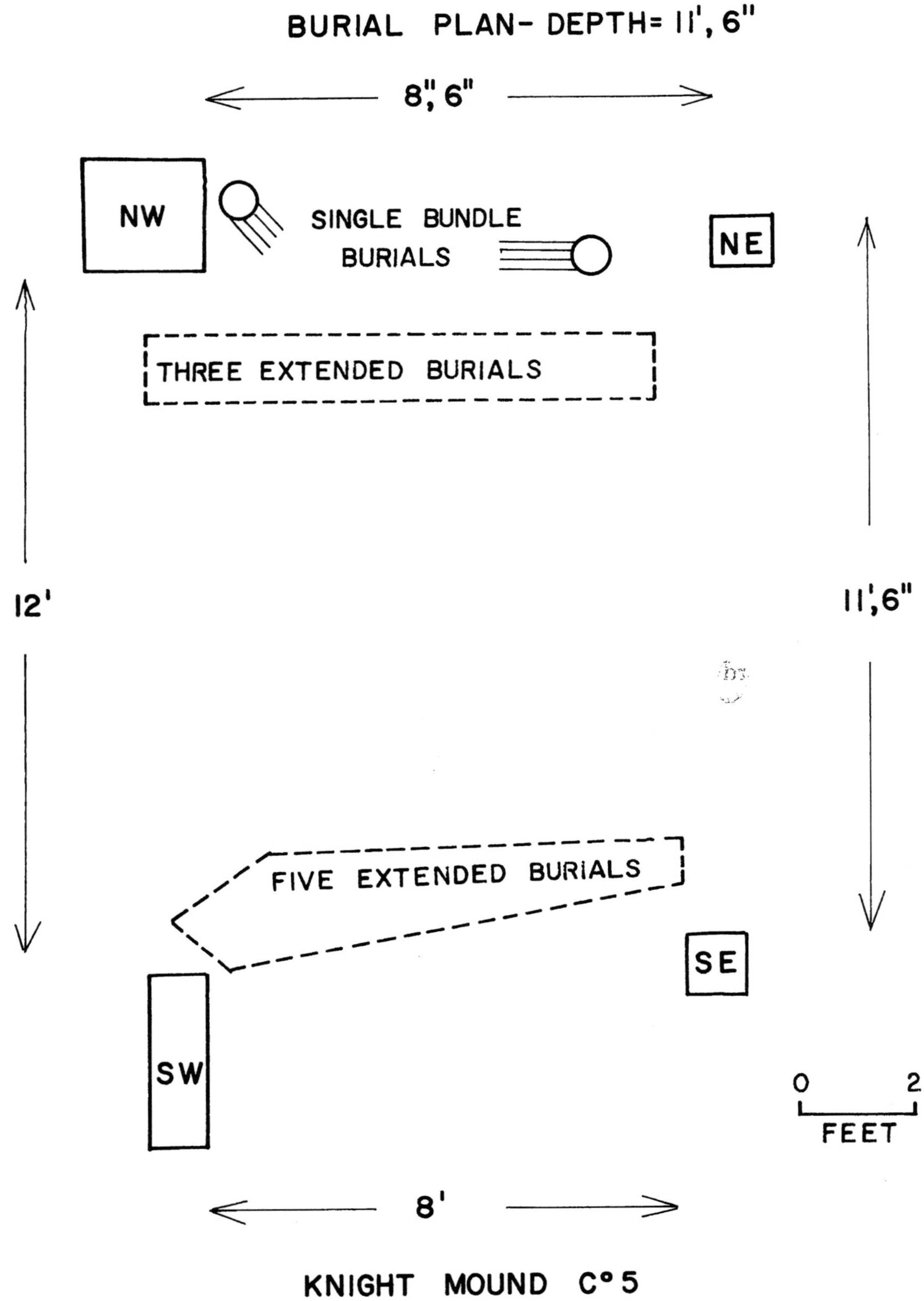

Fig. 12. Location of burials within central burial area of Knight Mound C°5 at a depth of 11 feet 6 inches.

sitions of the individuals was not possible. The two mass burials and the two individual bundle burials were left uncovered overnight June 20, 1942, and it was found next morning that four-legged intruders had disposed of most of the skeletal material (Pl. 63,*b*).

In summary, the central area bounded by the limestone markers contained three layers of burials, one immediately above the other and all within the red clay stratum. The bottom layer at eleven feet, six inches, consisted of two individual bundles and two "mass" burials, one containing three extended individuals and the other five extended individuals. The second layer contained two multiple bundles, one containing portions of at least three individuals and the other remnants of at least four individuals. The top layer consisted of the poorly preserved remains of four extended adults.

A number of artifacts were found in the general area of the central burials, some of which are illustrated in Plate 64,*a*. C°5-11 is an unnotched ovate point of pinkish flint found eight inches above the bones in the east end of the south mass bundle burial at a depth of eleven feet. The blade is 6.2 cm. long, 3.3 cm. wide at a point 2.0 cm. above the base, it is 2.5 cm. wide at the base and 1.6 cm. thick. C°5-12 is assigned to four small grit tempered Havana sherds, three of which are Havana Zoned Dentate Stamped. The sherds were found seven feet three inches north of the southwest corner marker in the lensed dirt ten inches above the red clay. C°5-13 is a projectile point or knife of yellowish-white flint and was found two feet north of the north mass bundle burial in the upper part of the red clay at a depth of eleven feet. The point has an ovate blade, a straight stem and a convex base and is 9.7 cm. long, 3.2 cm. wide at mid-blade, 3.0 cm. wide at the shoulder and 1.8 cm. wide at the base with a stem 1.8 cm. wide and 1.2 cm. long. C°5-14 is a Norton Notched projectile point of dark grey flint and was found in the top of the lensed dirt five feet four inches below the surface, 16 feet north of the south end of the mound and one foot west of the long axis. This point has side notches 7 mm. deep, a convex base and straight sides and is 7.0 cm. long, 4.2 cm. wide at the shoulder, 2.9 cm. wide at the base and 1.0 cm. thick with a stem 2.1 cm. wide. C°5-18 is assigned to an unworked left valve of *Ligumia recta latissima*, 10.5 cm. long and 5.7 cm. wide, found near the north mass burial of the bottom level after the hogs had disturbed the area. Number C°5-19 is a left femur and the left half of a mandible from the south mass bundle burial at a depth of eleven feet. C°5-20 to -23 were sherds found in the upper three feet of the mound. C°5-20 to -22 are all representative of Canteen Cordmarked and C°5-23 is an incised, grit-tempered Canteen Incised sherd (Pl. 64,*b*). C°5-24 is a blade 5.8 cm. long and 1.2 cm. wide with nibbling edges along one edge, location unknown.

Two trenches were excavated in the mound for the purpose of checking the soil profile. One trench, 20 inches wide and 52 inches deep, was cut through the center of the burial area from north to south for twelve feet and revealed red clay for a depth of 42 inches, underlain by yellow loess to the bottom of the trench. The dividing line between the clay and loess was straight. The second trench, 20 inches wide and 55 inches deep, was excavated from south to north in the south end of the mound for a distance of eight feet and showed the clay to be 45 inches deep in this area. There was a pile of eight limestone slabs just to the east of this trench, three feet north of the south end of the mound, under which there was an infant burial. A pile of limestone slabs with no associations occurred on and just below the sod about one-third of the way up the east side of the mound, but Titterington states that they may have had no connection with the construction of the mound.

COMMENTS ON MOUND C°5

The burial activities connected with this mound began with the delimitation of a rectangle eleven feet six inches north and south and eight feet east and west in yellow loess. Titterington remarked a number of times that he found no evidence of a pit. This burial area was eleven feet six inches deep and the first group of ten burials included two groups of extended individuals and two individuals who were bundle burials. Lack of further identification is because they were given preliminary clearing on a Saturday and the property owner requested they be left in place so that the neighbors could see them on Sunday. Not only were the neighbors notified, but there was also loose stock so that animals, quite properly identified as swine, prevented more accurate recording and interfered with the recognition of grave goods, for only a mussel shell was found along with the displaced skeletons. The two bundle burials were placed along the north edge of the burial rectangle at a depth of eleven feet six inches, one with the skull on the west side of the bundle and the other with the head on the east side. The three extended burials in the northern quarter were oriented east-west, and two of them had the head to the west and one to the east. The five extended burials in the south section were also aligned east-west and of these two had the head to the west and three to the east.

Some six inches above the first ten burials were two mass bundle burials, one in the north section and one in the south section both placed above the two groups of extended burials below. With the north bundle of the three or four individuals, whose skeletal remains were aligned east-west, was the slightly concave platform pipe apparently of Ohio pipestone, a shell bead, hackberry seeds, and the bone effigy bear canine. The south bundle of four to five individuals had no artifacts.

About six inches above the two mass bundle burials were four extended adult burials lying north and south with heads to the north. They also had no artifacts. The lower approximately twenty burials described as being in red clay, with the implication that the clay was carried in, are certainly Hopewellian. The absence of observed and recorded grave goods is an interesting feature. In the capping lensed earth over one of the corners were Havana Zoned Dentate Stamped sherds and one Havana Plain sherd.

In the upper central part of the mound were three adult extended burials without grave goods; these are presumably either very late Hopewell or early Jersey Bluff. The male, C°5-7, was oriented southwest-northeast with head to the southwest, while the two females were aligned in the same way but had their heads to the northeast. There is no orientation data for C°5-10 which was an adult male with a Canteen Plain jar and mussel shell spoon nor for the crushed child's skull, C°5-8, also with a Canteen Plain vessel.

All of the eight vessels in the mound were in the upper part. Of these the Baehr Plain bowl and Baehr Zoned Brushed Incised, C°5-3 and -4, found close together, were probably the first ones interred. The bowl is one of the relatively few Hopewellian bowls in the north. The decorated vessel is an excellent example of Baehr ware with the unusual feature of a small horizontal row of rim bosses with the interior perforation holes covered with clay. The rim bosses are first found on Early

Woodland Black Sand pottery, become a diagnostic feature of Havana pottery, and continue in use into Late Woodland complexes in the Illinois area. They are not a part of the Woodland tradition in the central Ohio Valley but are a part of the Alexander series pottery in northern Alabama and are regarded as an intrusive element in Tchefuncte pottery in the Lower Mississippi Valley.

The three vessels found close together at a depth of one foot or so form an interesting and probably later interment. The Canteen Incised vessel, C°5-1A, with a line-filled triangle rim and zone incised body is believed to be an example of the continuation of the Hopewellian decorative tradition on to Canteen ware vessels. The other two vessels are normal examples of what is believed to be early Canteen Plain in this area, and the same interpretation is made for C°5-5, -8 and -10.

The whitish flint point, C°5-13, from deep in the mound, is a stemmed form which resembles the Macon-Pontchartrain point of Late Archaic and Early Woodland time in the Lower Mississippi Valley. There are similarities to other Late Archaic stemmed forms and this specimen does not have a clear association with either burials or other materials in the mound. On the other hand the point C°5-14 is an example of the corner notched forms of the Norton-Manker melange and is clearly a Hopewellian form.

The body sherds found in the upper fill of the mound attest to the relatively late addition of this zone for they belong to the Canteen ceramic complex. The Canteen Incised sherd is believed to represent the continuity of Late Baehr-Pike decorative concepts into Jersey Bluff times.

Construction of this mound was begun during Middle Woodland times and the initial rectangular central burial area, but without a pit, is a common Hopewellian practice. As in Mound C°4, there were so few preserved mortuary materials that it is difficult to estimate when this took place within the proposed chronological framework of this paper. The assumption will be made that it was relatively early in the Pike phase because of the construction features, the lay out of the burials and because of the imported platform pipe which is the only non-locally made item recovered. The Havana Zoned Dentate Stamped sherds in the mound-fill are only indicators that the burial pit is not earlier than the production of the vessels of this "type" at the Knight village.

If the ceramic typology is correct the capping of the mound, or at least the upper burial and artifacts, were placed in the mound over some period of time and not as part of a single burial ceremony. The Baehr Zoned Incised vessel and its companion bowl are well made examples of the style of the Pike phase and should have been manufactured close to the time of the central burials in Knight Mound 8. For many years such vessels were spoken of as though they were only burial or ceremonial vessels and the decorative styles associated with them had a similar restricted use in the society which produced them. While there certainly was a tendency to include small vessels in burial association there are now enough known representative village site pottery collections to realize that similar vessels both in size and design had other functions. It is significant that these Pike phase vessels were not placed with burials as they might have been but were placed in the tumulus during the late construction activities connected with the concept of inclusion of ceramic containers with human burials.

The Canteen ware vessels in the top of the mound are a part of the continuation of this same concept. The three vessels found together are important in the recognition of a gradual shift from late Pike phase to the Fox Creek phase of Late

Woodland. A search has been made for similarities to the incised body decoration on vessel C°5-1A but it has not produced satisfactory results.

MOUND C°6

Mound C°6 was the sixth mound from the north on the low ridge in the center of the valley. The mound was excavated by Mr. L. M. Gibson in June, 1944, and is reported to be the second smallest mound in the group. The method of excavation and exact provenience of artifacts and features is not reported but several general features are included in the notes.

A Canteen Plain vessel and a small conch shell container were found in the top of the mound. The shell is described as approximately 17 cm. long, about the same size as C°2-78, but no other information is available. The vessel C°6-1 is a Canteen Plain jar badly broken up during the excavation. It has a lip diameter of 15 cm. and an estimated height of 17.5 cm. The rim is slightly flaring and there is a vague shoulder. The rim diameter is 13.8 cm., the lip is rounded and of uneven width from 5 to 7 mm. The rim and body thickness vary from 6 to 8 mm. The temper is grit but there is only a small amount of it. Some of the pieces are 4 by 4 mm. but most of them are much smaller. The interior and exterior surfaces are smoothed and some exterior areas are burnished. Smoothing striations on the outer rim are horizontal and on the body they are vertical. They could have been done by a pebble. The upper interior half is heavily smoke blackened and the exterior is greyish-brown to tan. The core is black except for the thin layer of oxidized clay on the outer surface. The base is rounded with only a slight conical appearance. This vessel should have been recovered.

A subfloor pit reportedly lined with bark was encountered in the central portion of the mound. The pit contained an undetermined number of burials, possibly as many as twelve or fourteen, about evenly divided between secondary bundle burials and burials extended in the flesh. Mr. Gibson reported that several types of shell beads (Pl. 65.*a*), a pair of imitation shell animal mandibles and two projectile points were found associated with the burials. The shell beads included fresh water pearls and the projectile points are variants of Norton points, according to Dr. Titterington, with convex base and sides and corner notches, made of hornstone. They are not with the Museum of Anthropology collections. Mr. Gibson observed that two of the extended burials had groups of pearl beads around each of the upper arm bones in a position suggesting arm bands. This was reported before the excavation of the human figurines in C°8 which are portrayed with such armlets. The central pit also yielded a complete pottery vessel and 22 sherds.

This vessel is Havana Zoned Dentate Stamped (Pl. 65,*b*) with both grit and limestone temper which is badly leached. This unusual feature for a Havana style vessel may mean it was made about the time of the postulated shift to the predominant use of limestone which characterizes the Baehr and Pike ceramic complexes of the lower Illinois Valley area. The vessel height is 14.9 cm. It has a lip diameter of 15.2 cm., of the rim 14.8 cm., and 16.3 cm. for the body. It has a flat circular base 7.2 cm. in diameter. The lip is flattened, slopes inward, and is 7 mm. wide. The rim and body are 9 mm. thick. Most of the interior and exterior surface has a slightly reddish-tan to reddish-brown color which is quite distinctive among the other vessels from the Knight Mound Group.

The interior and exterior surfaces were smoothed before the decoration was applied. The outer lip and upper rim had a very closely spaced horizontal row of ovoid impressions 4 mm. wide and high. The plain horizontal rim band, 1.5 cm. wide, is bounded below by a broad, 4 mm. shallow horizontal incised line. On the lower part of the rim there are two parallel broad horizontal deep grooves, 5 mm. wide, made with a flattened-ended tool, placed one above the other. They are from 4 cm. to less than 3.5 cm. long and each group of two is separated from those to the left and right by a narrow plain vertical panel about 1 cm. wide. There are ten to eleven of these around the rim. Below this zone is a horizontal line similar to the one at the top of the decorated rim zone.

On the body there are six circular areas 3 to 4 cm. in diameter filled with horizontal dentate stamp impressions which are closely spaced. The stamp made seven indentations in a row 2.2 cm. long so that it was necessary to fill in areas with only part of the tool applied to the surface. The stamped areas are encircled by a wide shallow incised or trailed line. This line is the inner member of an arch which outlines a wide plain band. In the area above and between the arches and up to the base of the rim the potter placed usually horizontal, closely spaced dentate stamp impressions made with the same or a similar tool to that used in the circular areas. At the lower border of this decorated band 8 cm. wide, there are two parallel broad shallow horizontal lines. There is a plain horizontal zone 2.3 cm. wide between them and the flat base.

The sherds include one from another Havana Zoned dentate pot, one unidentified grit-tempered sherd with a reddish exterior color and 20 body sherds with grit and limestone temper, two with a straight dentate stamp, six with zone-type broad incising and twelve with a smooth undecorated surface. These sherds with limestone temper are identical in paste characteristics, thickness and color to the Havana vessel from the pit and the Havana rim from the mound fill. Three sherds from the mound fill are: a Havana Plain body sherd, a Havana Cordmarked body sherd and a Havana rim with inbeveled lip, placed on a plain upper rim, exterior nodes placed on a plain upper rim and at least two horizontal rows of large ovoid punctate neck decoration. This Havana rim also has some small limestone granules mixed into the temper and there are hematite inclusions in the paste.

Miraculously from somewhere in the mound there was recovered a small white flint chisel (?) 6.9 cm. long, 2.5 by 2.9 cm. wide and 1.5 cm. thick at midsection. It is biconvex with battered thinned edges at each end.

COMMENTS ON MOUND C°6

This mound was clearly started by a Hopewellian group because of its bark-lined subfloor pit, combination of extended and bundle burials, the Havana Zoned Dentate Stamped vessel placed in the central tomb, the pearl and shell beads, Norton type points of blue-grey hornstone, according to Titterington, and the effigy animal mandibles cut from shell. All of these are Hopewellian in character. Unfortunately, only the beads and the vessels are now in the Museum of Anthropology collections. The fact that most of the sherds from the mound fill are of the Havana tradition is interpreted to indicate that only pottery of this type was present in the earth dumped on the mound. The small white flint chisel may have belonged to the earlier Archaic occupation. The small Canteen Plain jar C°1 and associated *Busycon* sp. shell are regarded as a late addition to the mound. The shell could be one of the last marine shells associated with burials in the Knight Mound Group.

This mound was begun somewhere near the shift from the Bedford phase to the Pike phase in the lower Illinois Valley area, if our ceramic sequence is reliable. While more material may have been placed with the dead in the central subfloor pit than was recovered or reported it is more likely that the majority of the Hopewellian burials were not only not accompanied by HIS[1] ceremonial articles, but that none of the burials were.

MOUND C°7

Mound C°7 was the seventh mound from the north on the low ridge in the center of the valley and was trenched with a slip scraper and team in the fall of 1943 by Mr.

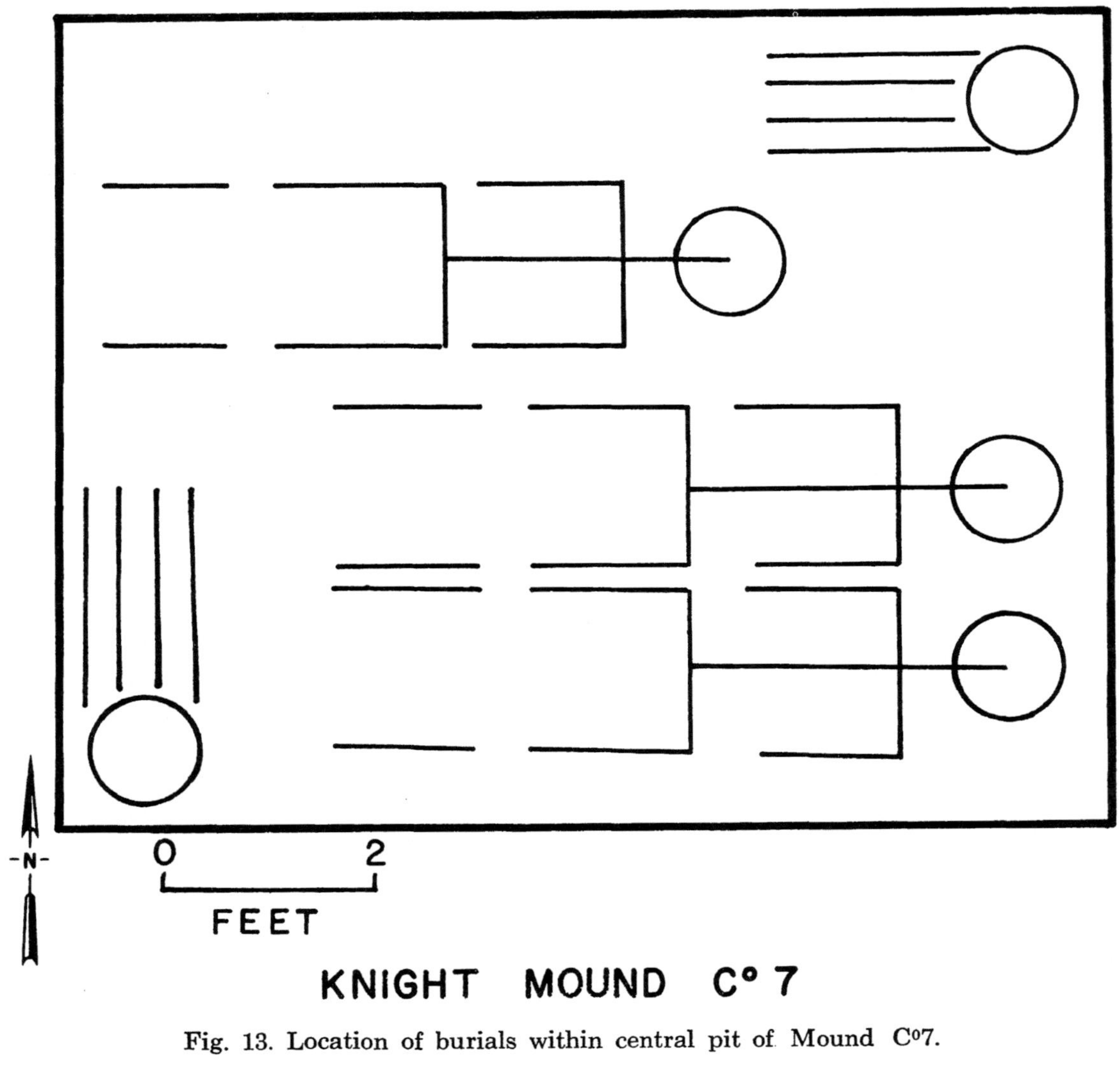

Fig. 13. Location of burials within central pit of Mound C°7.

[1]An abbreviation for Hopewell Interaction Sphere which is pronounced with a strong lingering unvoiced sibilant sound.

Walter Wadlow. The trench was put through the center of the mound in an east-west direction. In the spring of 1945 it was discovered that the trench had missed the south edge of the central burial pit by about five feet and subsequent excavation was carried out on the pit. The dimensions are given in the notes as roughly ten feet east and west, eight feet north and south and 12 to 14 inches deep. The pit contained three adult burials extended on the back with the heads to the east and two bundle burials, one in the northeast corner of the pit and the other in the southwest corner (Fig. 13). There were no artifacts in association with the burials but along the east half of the north wall of the pit there was a layer one-half to one inch thick of a tan to brown powdery material. Titterington suggests that this material represents disintegrated objects of wood since it did not seem to be earth or bark. Five pottery sherds picked up from the excavation dump include one large Cahokia Cord-marked rim, three body sherds from the same vessel and a badly eroded unidentified rim sherd with shell temper and a reddish paste.

This mound has the familiar bark lined or covered subfloor pit. The three adult extended burials with heads to the east lay parallel to the long axis of the pit. The bundle burial in the northeast corner had the skull on the east of the bundle which was oriented east-west. The bundle burial in the southwest corner was oriented north-south according to the drawing with the head to the south. None of the burials had recovered artifacts in association but this is not conclusive evidence that perishable grave goods were not included.

The central rectangular pit certainly fits the Hopewell burial pattern and it is assumed that the extended bundle burials on the floor belong to the Hopewell occupation even though no grave goods were found in the pit.

MOUND C°8

Mound C°8 was the eighth mound from the north on the low ridge. The mound measured 50 feet long, 40 feet wide and 6 feet high and the top was flattened as the result of the mound having been used by cattle for shade and a "fly stomp." The long axis was northwest by southeast (Fig. 14). Excavation was begun on October 8, 1942, by Mr. Walter Wadlow and his father by means of a 20-foot-wide trench in the southeast edge of the mound. The total excavated area was represented by a trench 35 feet long, 20 feet wide and 6 feet deep. None of the photographs of the excavation of this mound are suitable for reproduction.

A group of five burials (Fig. 15) consisting of three adults and two children, all extended on the back, was found about twelve feet northwest of the southeast end of the mound and about five feet northeast of the long axis at a depth of five feet, or about one foot above the base level of the mound. The skeletal material was in a poor state of preservation and none of it was saved. No assessment was made of the sex of the three adults. Two of the adults (C°8-1 and -3) with one of the children (C°8-2) between them were disposed with the heads to the northwest and the other child (C°8-4) and adult (C°8-5) were six inches higher with the heads to the southeast. Each of them had a pot to take with them. Burial C°8-1 had a Baehr Plain vessel (Pl. 66,*a*) in association near the head, C°8-2 had a Baehr Brushed vessel (Pl. 66,*b*) at the head, C°8-3 a Baehr Zoned Brushed vessel (Pl. 67) over the left shoulder. Burial C°8-4 had a Hopewell Zoned, Plain Rocker Stamped vessel (Pl. 68,*a*) in associ-

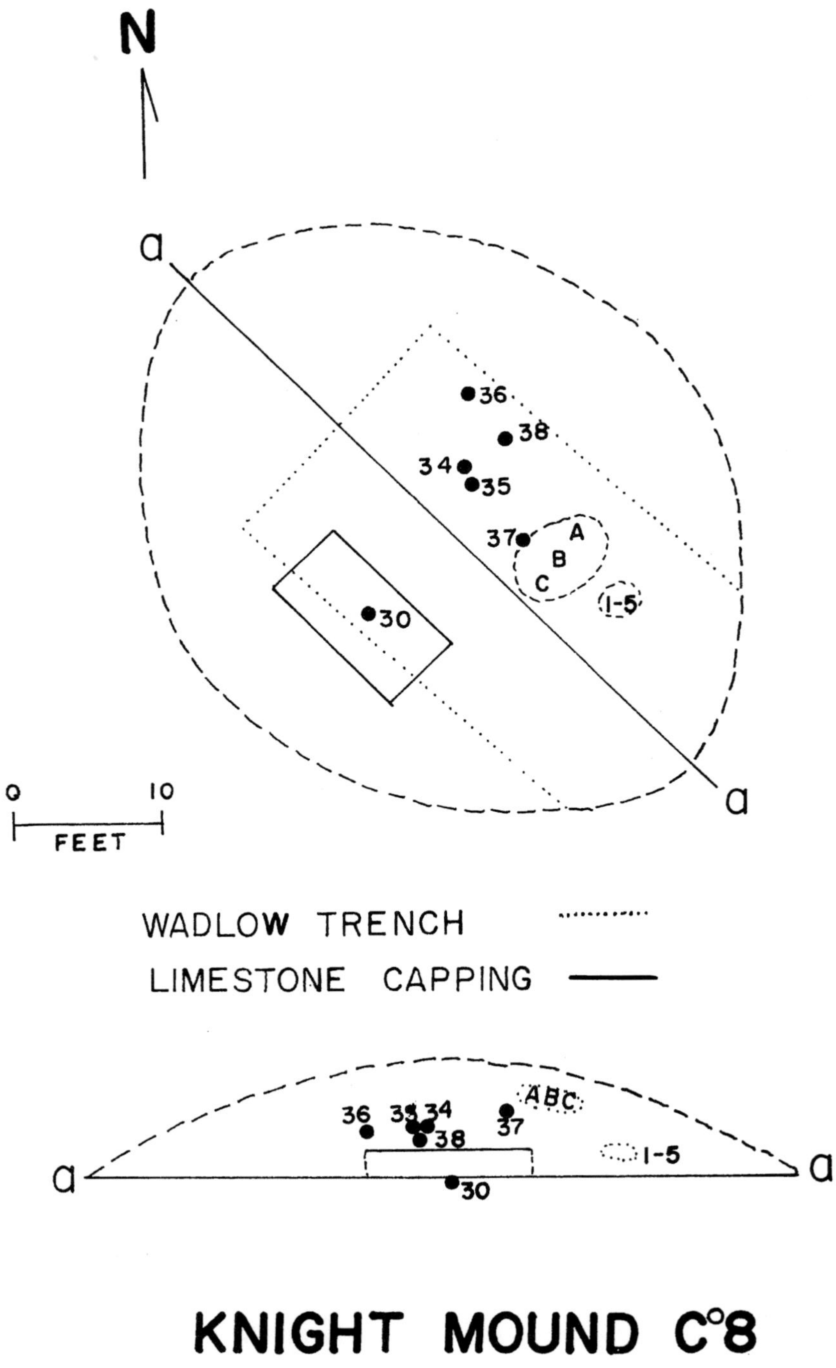

Fig. 14. Diagram of burial location in Knight Mound C°8.

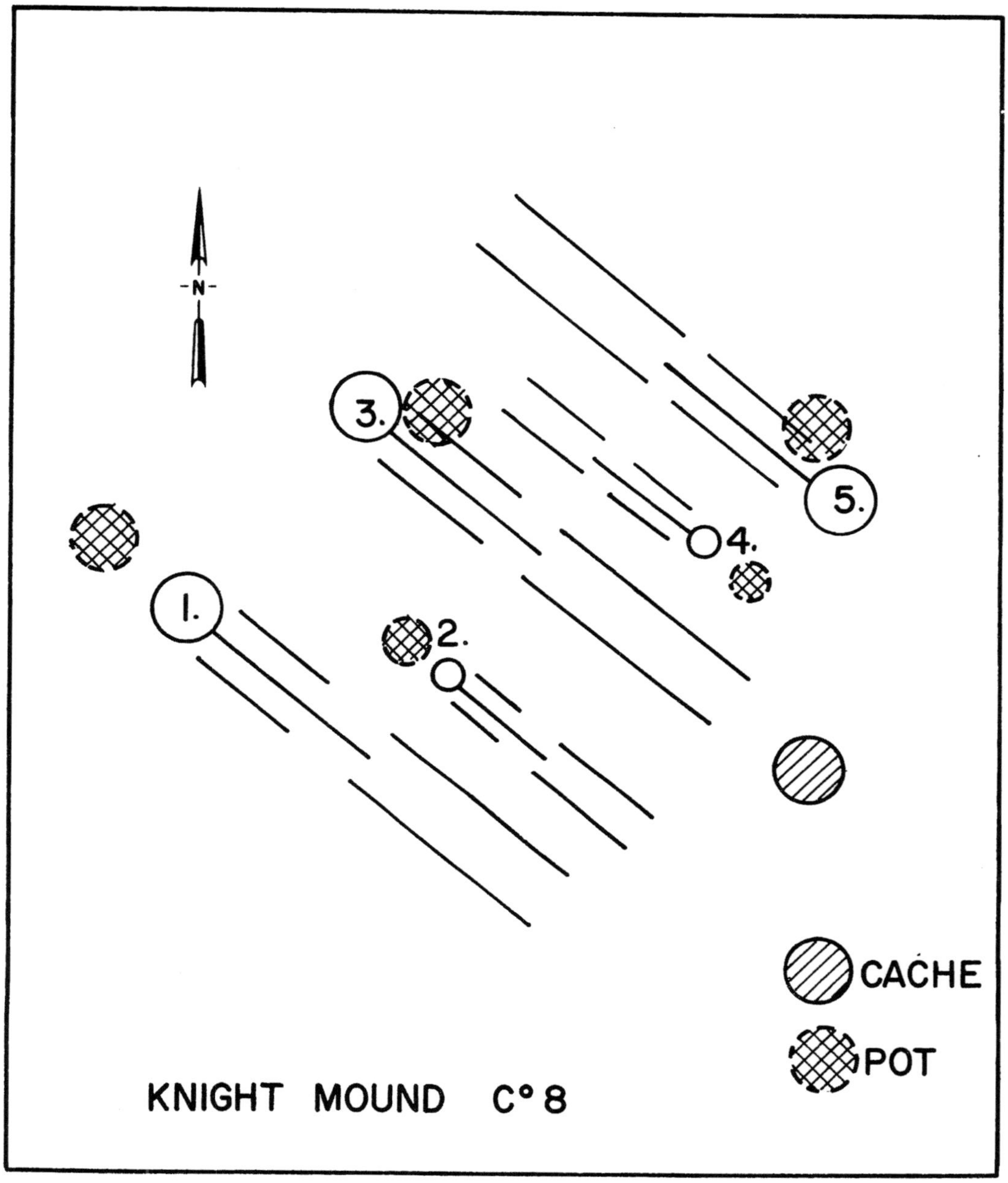

Fig. 15. Location of Burials within central burial area of Knight Mound C°8.

ation near the head and C°8-5 a Baehr Zoned, Plain Rocker Stamped vessel (Pl. 68,*c*) over the right shoulder.

The Baehr vessel with C°8-1 had a badly preserved mussel shell spoon inside it but the spoon is not available in the collection.

The Baehr Plain vessel C°8-1 is 10.3 cm. high (Pl. 66,*a*). It has a lip diameter of 8.7 cm. and a rim diameter across the slightly accentuated and channeled rim of 9 cm. The body diameter between the four lobes is 11.2 cm., and across the lobes it is 12.2 cm. The tempering material is badly leached limestone particles. Both interior and exterior surfaces are heavily smoke blackened. The interior surface is smoothed and the exterior is smooth to burnished. There is some evidence of brushing on the rounded vessel base. The lip is rounded and 2 to 3 mm. wide. The rim is 4 mm.

thick and the body is 3 mm. thick. The only decoration is a very narrow shallow incising forming a series of four low broad arches over the four lobes of the vessel.

Vessel C°8-2 appropriately is a child's pot found with the burial of a child (Pl. 66,*b*). This small Baehr Brushed jar should have limestone temper but it does not, even though the particles are small and white. It is 7.8 cm. high, has a lip diameter of 6.5 cm. and a body diameter of 8 cm. The shoulder, body and base are rounded. The lip is rounded and is 3.5 mm. wide. The rim is vertical, 5 mm. thick, as is the body. The interior surface is smoothed and the exterior is roughly smoothed on the body with horizontal brushing marks, except on the base where the brushing marks are not consistently applied in one plane. The exterior color is reddish-tan to smoke blackened and the interior is greyish-tan to slightly blackened. There is a smoothed 1 cm. wide upper rim which has very shallow and irregular brushed impressions. At the base of this upper rim there is a horizontal row of small irregular hemiconical punctates made from the right. Below the punctates is a burnished horizontal zone which is separated from the body by a 2 mm. wide horizontal incised line.

There was a cache of material in an area about one foot in diameter at the feet of the central burial, C°8-3, reportedly a male. It consisted of the fragments of five clay figurines, a small fragment of galena, a plano-convex rubbing stone of diorite and six complete and three fragmentary flake knives. The galena fragment, C°8-11, measures 2.5 cm. long, 2.0 cm. wide and 1.7 cm. high and only one side appears to have been faceted by rubbing. The rubbing stone, C°8-12, is 7.2 cm. in diameter and 3.4 cm. in diameter. The convex surface is pecked to shape and the plane surface is smooth as a result of use. The complete flake knives, C°8-13 to -18 (Pl. 78,*b*), are blades averaging 4.6 cm. in length and 1.2 cm. in width and all show secondary retouch on the proximal dorsal surface. The fragments, C°8-19 to -21, are distal tips of blades and average 1.9 cm. in length. All the blades are of a pinkish white flint, from the same core; all four fit together.

The figurines were described in an earlier publication by W. C. McKern and his description is reproduced below (McKern, Titterington and Griffin, 1945). The figurines from this mound are now in the Milwaukee Public Museum.

> Of the five painted figurines, one represents a seated man and four portray women, two standing and two seated. Two of the women, one standing and one seated, are carrying nude infants. All of the little effigies exhibit a rigid style in proportion, surface treatment, and in methods of modeling feet, hands, and the details of faces, suggestive of work done by a single artisan. The figures are ill-proportioned, with long bodies in contrast to short legs, and with large heads in contrast to minute feet; but the life-like postures effected and the professional sureness of the general treatment serve greatly to strengthen and preserve the impression of realism in spite of stylistic inaccuracies. The eyes are represented by pinched-up elongated ridges disposed obliquely. The upper lips are rather carefully modeled to show the philtrum and adjoining lip cleft.
>
> All heads are equipped with widely protruding, discshaped ear-plugs. That these are ear-plugs rather than stylized ears is clearly indicated by the fact that in one of the standing female figures the ears are realistically modeled above these elements.
>
> The only male of the series [Pl. 69] stands 3 1/16 inches high. He is represented as kneeling and sitting on the medial aspect of each foot, with his feet turned inward toe to toe. He is holding before him a staff-like object with the head or handled end, which is painted red, placed under his chin. This staff has at its lower end the suggestion of an atlatl hook. The man is wearing the simplest kind of breech-clout. The entire body above the breech-clout and the left arm above the wrist are painted a dull purplish red, suggesting a shirt. The right arm is missing from just below the armpit to the wrist. There is no artificial coloring on or below the breech-clout. Looping from the top of each shoulder to pass under the adjoining arm

is painted a broad band of white bordered with red and sectioned by transverse black lines at wide intervals. Lateral extensions of this garment or painted design extend outward from the neck well over each shoulder. The face is painted completely white. The headdress, whether representing hair or hair augmented by artificial accessories, suggests a low, long-haired pompadour anterior to an oval plat extending over the frontal region and separated at the crown from a similar plat covering the back of the head. Centered in the latter plat and protruding sharply from the back of the head, is a flatly disposed, thick disc. Both plats and the disc appear to have been painted black. The white color on the face extends up over the crown of the head between the two plats of "hair." The protruding ear-plugs are solidly red.

All of the female figures are nude above the waist and are similarly dressed in short, kilt-like loin-cloths extending from the small of the waist to barely below the knees. They all wear black or red foot coverings of uniform style, with tops extending well above the ankle and terminating in points above instep and heel with V-shaped depressions at the sides. Three of the women exhibit black and white arm bands. Three share the same basic style of hair arrangement: the back hair hangs down well below the waist. It is arranged in a flat plat which, at the neck, is the full width of the falling head of hair but which tapers down to a relatively narrow squared or rounded end toward the waist. This coiffure could be most easily effected through the use of some plastic element such as clay. The creator of the figurines provides no evidence of plaiting or artificial shaping accessories. To what extent realism in these representations is defeated by the artistic style of the modeler can only be conjectured.

One of the female figures [Pl. 70] which is 3 3/16 inches high, is represented as sitting with both knees disposed obliquely to the right and both feet, one above the other, resting with heels against the left hip. This sitting posture is practiced not uncommonly by Indian women of the historic period. A Dakota woman, now residing in northern Wisconsin, recently demonstrated the posture to me and volunteered the information that this position was known as the Sioux women's method of sitting. In our figure, the right hand claps the knees and the left hand rests on the abdomen. The kilt, which appears to be held in place without the aid of a belt, is solidly red. The "moccasins" are black with specks of white suggesting beads. Two broad black arm bands, similarly speckled with white, are placed just below the armpits, and an undecorated black band ocurs above the right wrist (the lower left arm is missing). The hair is parted in the middle and curves smoothly down on either side of the face to pass back over the shoulder. Faintly surviving elements of both red and black paint are variously present on the hair. Ear-spools appear to protrude through falling strands of hair.

The other seated female figure [Pl. 71], which is 3⅛ inches high, assumes the same sitting position described for the first, but she is holding a nursing infant to her breast. Her kilt, generally, has vaguely defined decorative elements in black and red, but as viewed from the rear the garment is red with a broad white stripe, disposed somewhat obliquely from the vertical, extending down to the right of the center. The "moccasions" are black. The hair, arranged as described for the other seated female, seems to have been painted a solid black. The original color of the ear-spools is not now apparent. The infant's hair is not parted down the middle as in the adults but does curve down each side of the face. There is no plat down the back. All of the hair area above the adult's hand, which covers the occiput of the infant, is painted a light red, suggesting a head covering. There are black "moccasions" with faint white speckles on the feet.

The shorter of the standing figures [Pl. 72], which is 3 11/16 inches high, holds an infant on her back; her right hand extends back to clasp the child's right knee and calf, her left hand passes over her left shoulder to grasp the child's left wrist. The "moccasions" are black with white speckling, apparent particularly above the left heel, The kilt retains some of the original red color, and there are irregularly disposed white spots along both thighs. Black arm bands with white speckles are placed just below the armpits, and two similar bands occur above the wrists. The hairdress as seen from the front is identical to that of the two seated female figurines, but as seen from the back, it differs from all the others. A heavy rope of hair is doubled back on itself in a diagonal direction and is fixed in place by means of cross-ties on the right side of the back of the head. The hair area at the back is painted red, with a mixture of black at the center of the occiput. The black extends up on the medial arm of the loop of roped hair. The mixture of black and white on the top and front area of the hair, as seen in the accompanying illustrations, is accounted for by a slight scuffing or abrasion of the original surface so that the fresh clay is exposed. This is more or less solid at the top front, while at the left front it has more of a scratched appearance, with some of the original surface remaining intact. There is no evidence of paint on the infant. The hair or head covering has the same outline as on the other infant. The ear-spools, protruding through the hair of the adult, show no positive artificial coloring.

The fifth of the series of painted figurines, representing a standing women [Pl. 73], is 4⅜ inches high. It represents a lady with a considerably more decorative costume than the others. The right "moccasin" is black and the left one is red, but each is decorated about the top with usual white speckles. The kilt is black with a decorative stripe at top and bottom consisting of two parallel rows of laterally disposed white bars. Unlike the kilts worn by the other female figures, this one appears to be supported at the top by means of a broad red belt with decorations consisting of variously directed lines in pale orange. At the back, there is a bustle-like apron, white except for a black band across the top, which falls to mid-buttocks. A bulge of somewhat irregular outline dominates the center of the white area. A small portion of this seems to be broken away. Although there is a definite incised division line between the bottom of the characteristic plat of hair hanging down the back and this "bustle," the outline of the latter is a continuation of the former. This would permit an interpretation of the "bustle" as the terminating end of the plat of hair. There are very wide arm bands, black with white speckles, at the usual places on both upper and lower arms, although an excavator's tool has nearly removed the evidence from the upper left arm. A necklace, consisting of several rope-like strands in white, conceals the throat. The face seems to be unpainted save for five white dots under the left eye. The headdress is basically like those of the two seated female figures, with certain curious additions. Two knobs protrude from the head, one diagonally forward from just within the hair line above the forehead, the other rearward from a point just back and to the left of the crown of the head. In shape, these are smooth domes set in broad basal rings. The dome parts are red and the encompassing rings are white. In addition, on the right side of the head there is a boldly protruding fillet, painted red, which curves high above the ear from the temple region to a corresponding point behind and above the ear. The right ear-spool is damaged and partly missing, but the left one, painted red, appears in correct position below the realistic representation of an ear done in bas-relief. Both ear and ear-spool appear to protrude through the hair. The two hands are placed above the upper legs and appear to be holding foot-like objects disposed heel to heel. One of these "feet" is crossed just above the toes by a broad band of white; the other is black, like the kilt on which it rests.

The vessel with Burial C°8-3 is the best quality production of the vessels in the mound. This Baehr Zoned Brushed jar (Pl. 67) is 10.5 cm. high. It has a lip and rim diameter of 11.2 cm. The body between the four lobes is 13.4 cm. wide and across the lobes the diameter is 14.6 cm. The tempering material is crushed limestone, badly leached, with most of the particles less than 1 mm. thick. The exterior color is greyish-tan to slightly blackened particularly on the burnished to polished areas. There is a uniformly grey interior. The interior is smooth as was the exterior before the polishing and brushing. The lip is rounded to flattened and is 4 mm. wide. The rim and body are 3 mm. thick.

The rim varies in height from .7 to 1 cm. and is slightly channeled on the interior. On the exterior there are uneven, parallel, closely spaced incised lines which are narrow and shallow. There is a horizontal row of small punctates poorly and irregularly made, spaced close together below these lines. They were made with a narrow hollow cylinder usually from the right. Below this is a well polished primarily horizontal neckband which projects downward between the lobes a distance of 6 cm. from the lip. The polished area is delimited from the brushed body by a single medium wide and medium deep U-shaped line. From each of the two opposite polished band's downward projections there is a horizontal polished band *ca.* 1.5 cm. wide which swings to the left and almost extends to the next vertical band before it curves downward. These horizontal bands have the same type of incised delimiting lines. The rest of the body has a "brushed" surface which was produced by closely spaced single strokes by a tool which left impressions 1.5 mm. wide and with a flattened appearance. These are usually vertical or from right to left on the body, but on the base this produced an overlapping pattern.

The second of the two children in the first group of burials also had a child's size pot with it (Pl. 68,*a*). This Hopewell Zoned Plain Rocked Stamped vessel has a lip diameter of 6.3 cm., a lower rim diameter of 4.8 cm. and an estimated height of 7.8 cm. It has a narrow and rounded lip 2 mm. wide, and the neck and body are 2 mm. thick. It has very fine granular limestone temper which is badly leached. The exterior surface is smoke blackened while the interior is greyish-tan. A portion of the exterior surface has eroded exposing a brownish-tan paste which is also the color of the core.

This small vessel was completely decorated with a fine degree of precision and excellent design planning. The upper rim band with slightly channeled interior is 8 mm. high and has a fine line crosshatched design. At the base of this is a horizontal row of small hemiconical punctates made from the left. Below the punctates is a narrow, 5 mm. wide polished horizontal band which is terminated by a horizontal narrow, 1 mm. incised line. The same tool was apparently used for the incised lines on the lower rim and body. Most of the rim, or neck, has four zones of identical design with a polished vertical panel 6 mm. wide on each of the rectangular zones which are 4 cm. wide and 2.2 cm. high. In the upper portion of each zone is a polished narrow, 3 mm. festoon band running from one upper corner of the rectangle to the other. The areas above and below the festoons are covered with fine line vertical plain rocker stamping. The lower section of each rectangle is delimited by an arched polished band which swings over each of the four lobes of the body and then joins the vertical panels which descend half-way between the lobes where they broaden to form a spoon-bill-like or key-hole shape. The lobes and presumably the rest of the body are covered with plain rocker stamping vertically placed in horizontal bands.

The Baehr Zoned Plain Rocker Stamped vessel C°8-5 (Pl. 68,*c*) is called Baehr and not Hopewell because it does not have a crosshatched rim, and the overall rocker stamping on the body has not quite the character of good Hopewell execution. There are other design deficiencies. The name shift may also be somewhat deliberate to help emphasize the thin and arbitrary dividing line between the Hopewell and Baehr groups in Griffin's typology (Griffin, 1952*a*: 119-20). The tempering material is badly leached limestone. The exterior and interior are greyish to smoke blackened. The interior and exterior surfaces are smooth. The height of the vessel is 16.5 cm. The lip diameter is 14 cm., the rim 12.8 cm. and the body 14.5 cm. The lip is flat at 4 mm. wide. The rim and body are 4 mm. thick. The rim is slightly flared and is thickened in the upper segment. The body is very slightly lobed. The upper thickened rim has a horizontal band of vertical V-shaped lines 8 to 9 mm. long and spaced 2 to 3 mm. apart. Below the thickened rim is an incised horizontal line with small shallow punctates in the horizontal line spaced 2 to 3 mm. apart and applied at a right angle to the surface. There is then a plain polished horizontal band 1.2 cm. wide terminated by a horizontal medium wide and medium deep U-shaped line. Above the lobes on the body there is a burnished to polished band *ca.* 1.5 cm. wide which arches over the lobes. These arches are outlined by the same kind of incised lines as on the rest of this vessel. Above these arched bands the area is filled with plain impressions, vertically placed and convex to the right. On the body below the polished arch bands are closely spaced, roughly horizontal, convex to the right plain rocker stamp impressions. This decorative pattern covers the lower body and base of the vessel with the same consistency. It must be recorded that the potter, in executing the design, did not get the arches truly centered over the lobes.

At about 15 to 20 feet northwest of the southeast end of the mound and ranging from the long axis to eight feet northeast were three scattered burials consisting of two children and one adult, each with a pot in association. The remains of the children were near the surface. The pots, C°8-32, a Baehr Brushed Incised vessel with a notched rim (Pl. 74,*a*) and C°8-33, a Baehr Zoned Punctate vessel with a flaring rim (Pl. 74,*b*), were quite fragmentary. The adult C°8-31 was at a depth of about one foot and had a Baehr Zoned Brushed vessel, C°8-31 (Pl. 75,*a*), in association. C°8-33 is reported to have contained a badly disintegrated mussel shell spoon.

Vessel C°8-31 is perhaps the best quality vessel of the three placed with the scattered burials. This Baehr Zoned Brushed jar is 12.4 cm. high. It has a lip diameter of 9.1 cm., of the rim 8.8 cm., and of the body 12.2 cm., estimated, between the four lobes. The tempering material was composed of a great deal of now badly leached limestone. The interior is greyish-tan and the exterior is the same color to slightly blackened. The core is dark grey. The interior is smooth and so was the exterior before the decoration was applied. The lip is narrowed, rounded to flattened and is 2 to 3 mm. wide. The rim is 4 mm. thick, but the body is 3 mm. thick. The base is rounded.

The upper rim is slightly accentuated and channeled on the interior. It is 1 cm. high and has widely spaced left to right slanting incised lines. Below this is an incised line with shallow punctates irregularly spaced but most often about 1 cm. apart placed over the incised line. There is then a burnished to polished horizontal band 1.3 cm. wide terminated by a horizontal incised line which, like the others on this vessel, is narrow, shallow and U-shaped. Then there is a narrow horizontal band 8 mm. wide also terminated by a horizontal line. Within this lower rim band there is a series of left to right oblique, irregularly spaced incised lines. Above the lobes is the normal incised line in a series of four arches and on the body the horizontal brushing of this Illinois style.

C°8-32 (Pl. 74,*a*) is an unreconstructed Baehr Brushed low rim jar with a shape and surface treatment almost identical to C°8-54 except that it is smaller. The tempering material is almost completely leached limestone. The surfaces were smoothed on the interior and exterior and are blackened on both surfaces. There is a short vertical rim with a flattened and slightly inverted lip. On the outer lip edge there are short, medium wide and medium deep vertical gashes spaced 4 to 7 mm. apart. On the shoulder area and down the body are the "brushed" or incised vertical lines arranged in pairs, then a space, another pair and so on. The lip is 3 to 6 mm. wide, the shoulder area is 5 mm. thick and the body is only 3 mm. thick. The base is rounded.

The Baehr Zoned Punctate vessel C°8-33 is 17 cm. high (Pl. 74,*b*). It has a lip diameter of 14.2 cm. while at the base of the flaring rim it is 12.8 cm. The lower rim has a diameter of 12 cm., and the body is 14.5 cm. The lip is narrowed to 2 mm. but the base of the upper rim is 5 mm. thick and so is the body. The vessel has a smoke blackened interior and a blackened upper exterior and a light brown lower body. The interior is smooth and so was the exterior before it was attacked by the person applying the design.

The upper unusually flared rim is 1.8 cm. high and has on the exterior; parallel, irregularly spaced, shallow, narrow U-shaped right to left slanting lines. This band is delimited by a medium wide, rather deep V-shaped line which is also the upper border for a band 1.2 cm. wide of two horizontal rows of triangular punctates with apex down. This band is bordered below by an incised line similar to that of the upper border. On the lower rim there is a 4 cm. wide band which alternates with a plain area and an oval area which has small triangular punctates with apex down, arranged in horizontal rows. The plain and punctate areas are separated by narrow incised lines. On the shoulder area there is another horizontal band of irregular width 1.7 to 2 cm. wide with three horizontal rows of the same vertically placed trianguloid punctates. This band is outlined above and below by narrow, medium deep horizontal lines. On the body there are vertical incised lines irregularly spaced which continue to the rounded conoidal base. A distinct series of such lines was applied across the base.

There was an area of limestone slabs in the west side of Mr. Wadlow's trench and over one-half of them had been removed when Dr. Titterington was invited to continue the excavation. The slabs were estimated to have covered an area about twelve feet from east to west by six feet from north to south and were piled about two feet high. The lowermost slabs were on a level with the mound base, a depth of six feet at this point. Some material was found in between the slabs but not in direct association with the burial (C°8-30, Pl. 76,*a*), located under the central area of the slabs. The burial was that of an adult female, according to Titterington, extended on the back with the head to the west. The material includes two conch shell containers, four drilled bear canines (Pl. 76,*b*), a copper adze and two pearl beads. One of the conch shells (C°8-28, Pl. 77,*a*) is a *Busycon* shell 18.1 cm. long found two feet south of the skull. This shell furnished the radiocarbon date of M-164, of 1700 ± 150 (Crane, 1956: 668). The second, C°8-29 (Pl. 77,*b*) is a *Cassis* shell 24.4 cm. long found one foot six inches south of the right hip. Both shells are cut approximately in half longitudinally, the columella and inner whorls are removed and the edges are smoothed. The four drilled bear canines, C°8-22 to -25 (Pl. 76,*b*), are all 8.3 cm. long and the perforations, on one side only, are placed at an angle so that they intersect at the pulp cavity. All show some cutting and grinding on the root end. The copper adze, C°8-26 (Pl. 78,*a*) is 11.3 cm. long, 6.2 cm. wide, and 8 mm. thick. The celt is widest at the slightly convex bit and the sides taper slightly toward the straight poll. The cross section shows one side flat and the other slightly convex and the flat side shows fabric impressions on the copper residue suggesting that the celt had been wrapped in fabric. The two pearl beads, C°8-27, both drilled and approximately 6 mm. in diameter, were found in association with the bear canines and may have belonged to an ornament.

A compound bundle burial, C°8-34 and -35, was found 26 feet northwest of the southeast end of the mound, and four feet northeast of the long axis, at a depth of four feet six inches. It consisted of the long leg bones, both skulls and one mandible of the two individuals, reportedly females. The skulls were lying side by side, the long bones resting on top of one, and the mandible was between two of the femurs. C°8-36 was the burial of an adult female extended on the back with the head to the northwest and turned to the right and was found 30 feet northwest of the southeast end of the mound, and eight feet northeast of the long axis, at a depth of five feet four inches.

C°8-37 consisted of the fragmentary tibiae and fibulae of a small child, evidently the only remains of an extended burial. The bones were found 20 feet northwest of the southeast end of the mound, and three feet northeast of the long axis, at a depth of three feet six inches. In the region where the lower left chest would have been there was an unpainted figurine of brown clay 6.9 cm. high. The body of the figurine is a simple flat oblong shape, the only feature being a roughly conical projection in the shoulder region suggesting arms. The lips, eyes and nose resemble those of the larger figurines but with less attention paid to detail. There is an incised line encircling the top of the head, possibly indicating hair or a head covering (Pl. 79). In May, 1943, Mrs. Victoria Harper of the Ceramic Repository of the Museum of Anthropology compared clay from the figurine with clay from miscellaneous Canteen, Baehr and Havana sherds from surface collections by means of thin sections and found no apparent significant difference in the mineral content of the clay. The figurine was found to be "practically untempered" and was examined by means of immersion in refractive liquids. Close to the figurine were two small unidentifiable masses of clay, thought by Titterington to be disintegrated parts of figurines.

On October 18, 1942, the excavation was continued to a point 15 feet southeast of the northwest end of the mound. One burial, C°8-38, was found 26 feet northwest of the southeast end and seven feet six inches northeast of the long axis at a depth of six feet. The burial was in a very poor state of preservation and was on the back with the head to the southwest and the legs flexed. No photographs were taken of this feature.

A number of artifacts occurred in the fill unassociated with burials. Twelve flake knives, C°8-39 to -50 (Pl. 78,*b*), were found scattered through an area three feet long at the center of the mound, just to the northeast of the central axis at a depth of two feet six inches. The knives are all blades of white flint with an average length of 4.4 cm. and an average width of 1.6 cm. Six of the blades show longitudinal retouch flakes on the dorsal side of the striking platform and the sides of two pairs fit together, suggesting that all are from the same core. Four artifacts, C°8-51 to -53, were encountered in a group 30 feet northwest of the southeast end of the mound and two feet eight inches northeast of the long axis at a depth of five inches. C°8-51 is an oval granite hammerstone or anvil 12.3 cm. long, 9.4 cm. wide and 4.1 cm. thick. The cortex of the stone has been removed by pecking around the periphery and the stone has been pitted approximately 1 mm. deep on both flat surfaces. C°8-52 is a round quartzite hammerstone 6.3 cm. in diameter and 3.8 cm. thick. This stone shows use marks around the periphery. C°8-53 consists of two fragmentary mussel shell hoes, both reportedly about 11.3 cm. long. One is located in the collection and has been identified as a right valve of *Megalonaias* sp., it is 11.3 cm. long with a hole 2.2 cm. in diameter through the center. C°8-54 (Pl. 75,*b*) is a fragmentary Baehr pottery vessel found 31 feet northwest of the southeast end of the mound, and four feet northwest of the long axis at a depth of six feet. This is another vessel which is difficult to type. It is clearly vertically incised on the exterior surface but was done in such a haphazard fashion that it closely resembles the brushing technique on the Baehr and Pike pottery group. In addition, it is not as large nor as thick as most Pike vessels but it is not as thin as most Baehr vessels. Also, it has the same very low rim and constricted shoulder area as C°8-32. These two vessels could be the product of the same potter.

The vessel shape resembles a low wall Mississippi jar more than it does the normal contemporary shapes of late Hopewellian times. The temper is crushed limestone with some particles 2 to 3 mm. in size but most of them are smaller. The interior was smoothed and the exterior smooth. The interior is smoke blackened and the exterior varies from brown to grey to blackened. There is a contracted shoulder area and a low slightly flaring rim. The lip is narrowed and rounded, it is 2.5 mm. wide, and the rim is 4 mm. thick. The shoulder area is 6 mm. thick and the base 8 mm. thick. The shoulder area and body to the base have narrow irregularly placed vertical incised lines. The estimated height is 10 cm.

COMMENTS ON MOUND C°8

This mound with the famous figurines and other grave goods has produced much interaction among archaeologists irrespective of what it has to do with the Hopewell Interaction Sphere of some contemporary archaeologists. The first five extended burials in the southern part of the mound are presumed not to have been in a pit. This may have been an oversight on the part of the prehistoric Indians, or of the excavators, although Titterington specifically said they were unable to find one, in a letter to Griffin dated October 29, 1942. The extended burials were oriented northwest-southeast and were aligned with the long axis of the mound. The two adults and the child between them in the western part of the group had their heads to the northwest, while the child and adult in the eastern part had their heads to the southeast.

The five vessels, one with each of the burials, is the best known group of late Hopewellian Baehr vessels that have been excavated. The small vessel, C°8-4 with a child, is called Hopewell Zoned Plain Rocker Stamped because it has the characteristics of this present day classification of Middle Woodland pottery. Its association with the four Baehr vessels in the same burial group is an excellent example of the continuity between Hopewell and Baehr style pottery. An almost identical small vessel was found at Spoonville, Ottawa County, Michigan (Pl. 68,*b*).

The best quality Baehr Zoned Brushed vessel, C°8-3, was placed with the central adult burial which had the figurines and other items placed at its feet. It is unfortunate that the sex of this burial and the other two adults is not known for certain, but none of the skeletal remains from this mound were preserved. The fine Baehr vessel C°8-5 has a design of a polished arched band above the slight lobes that is similar to the late Hopewell Zoned Incised vessel from near Nutwood, Jersey County, Illinois (Griffin, 1941: 218-19). The use of an incised arched line over the four lobes of two of the other vessels is also of importance in recognizing the concept of pottery decoration of the potters over a fairly large area in Illinois.

The import of the galena cube, outside of the probable use of galena to provide white paint, is not known. There were probably multiple sources but they have not been studied and the identification of the source is not now possible. Galena as an important item of burial goods first appears in Late Archaic over a wide area of the eastern United States but is most common in Hopewell association and in other Middle Woodland period sites such as Copena in northern Alabama. The flake knives, C°8-13 to 18 were specifically struck from a core to place them with the central group of burials, and a similar motivation is represented by the lamellar blades scattered in the mound (C°8-39 to

50), for their placement was also done for specific burial reasons.

The five figurines are remarkable not only for their information on female costume and other data but the fact that they were placed with a burial group is unusual. The two male effigy figures from the big Baehr Mound in Brown County, Illinois (Pls. 80 and 81), were associated in one instance with a burial, the figurine resting on a mica plate, with flint chips (lamellar blades?), and bone-perforated pulley type earspools. In the other instance the figurine had been wrapped in a woven bag of vegetable fiber also containing a copper celt and a very small four lobed vessel with a tall neck (Griffin, 1941). The figurines described by Dr. J. F. Snyder were not in the American Museum when Griffin studied the collection. They are now known to be in the collections of the St. Louis Academy of Science. Struever (1960), recovered figurine fragments from Kamp Mound 9 but they were in the mound fill along with other village debris. The best figurine fragment from the Kamp site was from a village area.

Figurine fragments were found in village sites in Pike County, Illinois by the University of Illinois. Epstein (1958: 60) reports on a head from the Pool site, and there is also one from the Irving site (Taylor, 1958: 75). Dr. Dan Morse of Peoria found a figurine torso on the Macoupin site in Macoupin County, and subsequent excavations on the site by Frank Rackerby have produced other figurines from the village. These will be described in Rackerby's Ph.D. thesis at Northwestern University. The University of Chicago recovered a crude figurine from the Whitnah village site, F^{v}49, probably in the stratigraphic pit excavated by Olive Eggan, although this location is not specifically identified in the publication (Cole and Deuel, 1937: 162). The most northern figurine of Hopewellian style (Pl. 82,*b*) is from the Steuben site, Marshall County, Illinois (Schoenbeck, 1947: 41). This is as far north as figurines are known for they have not been recorded in northern Illinois, northwestern Indiana, Michigan, Wisconsin or Iowa.

A few years ago a group of baked clay figurines was discovered on a Hopewellian village site in Schuyler County, Illinois (Pl. 83, 84, 85). The photographs of these specimens have been provided by Dr. Dan Morse of Peoria. They are not to the same scale and the measurements given were obtained from the metric scale included in the negatives. A large piece of ocean shell was noticed near human bones which had been plowed during the fall of 1963. Careful sifting of the earth in this area and patient reconstruction of the fragments resulted in the recovery of nine figurines and two additional heads (Clark, 1965). Where the legs are available they have the same bent knee posture as on the Adena effigy pipe and on most, if not all, of the Hopewellian figurines. The women have a colored wrap around skirt which ends just above the knees, and the men wore a breech clout. None of the Schuyler figurines have footgear. Three of the female figurines have the hair knot on the back of the head and also have a bun of hair portrayed on each side of it that extends beyond the sides of the head. In effect the hair was gathered into a central and two lateral head knots. It is somewhat reminiscent of the hair style of Hopi unmarried women, one hesitates to say "maidens," of the turn of the century. Earspools are shown on four of the female heads and on one of the male heads. One of the female figures is in an unusual posture which is that of a person lying prone with legs raised at the knees and the upper body also raised slightly. This position is very similar to a small figurine, "Naughty Marietta," from the Marietta group in Ohio (Pl. 86,*b*) that was in the collection of E. H. Davis in the mid-

1800's but is now in the Peabody Museum, Harvard University, with catalog number 58. This information and the photograph was provided by Olaf Prufer, who has also informed us of a fragment of a very crude figurine from the Hopeton Works, Ross County, Ohio, which is in the Ohio State Museum. The Schuyler County figurines, like the group at Knight, look as though they could be the product of an individual sculptor. They may have been with a burial, which may have been in a village area or possibly on the basal portion of a low mound now plowed down.

In western Jackson County, Illinois, the multiple occupation Twenhofel site has produced a complete figurine and portions of some 22 others which range in quality from the one illustrated (Pl. 86,*a*), to examples as crude or cruder than the sixth figurine from Knight. This site has produced more figurine fragments than any other in Illinois. The Sugar Camp Hill site on the border of Jackson and Williamson Counties, about six miles east of Carbondale had "a small crude clay female effigy 5.35 cm. long, 1.28 cm. wide. The figure is highly stylized with a pinched node for the nose, conical modelled and carved breasts and incised looping lines which apparently are intended to indicate legs. This effigy bears a general resemblance to one found in the Whitnah Village site in Fulton, County, although the Crab Orchard piece is cruder and more stylized than the Fulton County one" (Maxwell, 1951: 107).

In the Carlyle Basin of the Kaskaskia drainage, Clinton County, Illinois, 37 figurine fragments were found at the Texas site (Morrell, 1965: 37-38). One of the heads is said to be in "Havana" association but the range of time is not known for "Havana" at this site. This figurine head was in a pit intrusive into Feature 17, and miscellaneous charcoal from the intrusive pit produced a date of 1800 ± 90 B.P. (GX-0362). Rackerby reports six arm and leg clay fragments from human figurines in midden areas at the Boulder site (1966: 114-16) which probably belong to the Hopewellian occupation.

The Museum of Anthropology has a small crude clay figurine fragment in its collections from the Damiansville site in Clinton County, Illinois in the Kaskaskia drainage. Our collection from this site was given to us by Gregory Perino in 1953. The material in amateur hands as well as our collections indicate that this site was occupied from Late Archaic to early Late Woodland. The figurine has a short body with a length of 3.2 cm. from neck to crotch. The width of the shoulders is 2.7 cm. and the body thickness is 1.8 cm. The small head is missing and arms were not modelled. There are two short stubs 8 mm. long for legs. In crudeness it resembles some of the Poverty Point figures or the poorly formed effigies from northern sites.

The Crable site in Fulton County, Illinois produced a small excellent example of a female effigy head which is quite close in style to some of the heads from the unnamed site in Schuyler County. A cast of this head presented to the Museum of Anthropology by Dr. Dan Morse in 1964 has a height of 2.3 cm. from the crown of the head to the chin, and a head width of 2 cm. The eyes slant slightly, the nose is broken, and the hair is smooth and combed to the sides of the head from a saggital line. The ears are indicated but there are no earspools (Pl. 82,*a*). The appearance of the face resembles that from the Twenhofel complete figure. This is the only item of clear Hopewellian provenience from the Crable site which has a dominantly Mississippian occupation with some earlier Weaver to Tampico or Maples Mills remains. From the Clear Lake Village site of southwestern Tazewell County and northwestern Mason County, E. Schoenbeck (1941: 65), reported on a Y-shaped baked clay object that may be part of a figurine.

Across the Illinois at the Hopewell house on the Weaver site a crude figurine fragment was recovered (Wray and MacNeish, 1961: 43). A figurine torso is reported from the burial area of the Frederick site (Young, 1960) in Schuyler County, Illinois.

In Indiana, figurines are known from two sites. The first is the Worthington site in Green County, Indiana (Black, 1933: Pl. 31) and the second is the Mann site in Posey County (Adams, 1949: 56-58). Dr. James H. Kellar of Indiana University informs us that a great many figurine fragments have been found at the Mann site from excavations under his direction and from local amateurs. While the Mann site has a long period of occupation from Middle Woodland to Mississippi, the figurines illustrated by Adams are almost certainly Hopewellian. Narrow, primarily vertical striation represent the hair on two of the heads. The figurine fragment from near the Worthington mound had striation to represent the hair style.

The Turner figurines form the largest group that have been described (Pl. 87, 88). The description of these by C. C. Willoughby and E. A. Hooton (1922: 71-74) is pertinent to the presentation in this report and is quoted below to accompany the reproduction of the illustrations. Most of the figurines came from the so-called altar 1 of Mound 4.

> Perhaps the most interesting objects from this altar are the figurines illustrated on plates 20 and 21 [Pl. 87, 88]. There is every reason to believe that the artists who fashioned them belonged to the group of people who resided here, and that the effigies represent individuals or types of the same people. Dr. Hooton has called attention to the fact that the peculiar form of head shown in the figurines corresponds closely to the crania from the mounds and burial places of this group.
>
> Unfortunately, none of the effigies is perfect. They were either deliberately broken before being placed on the altar, or the heat from the fire caused them to splinter. Probably both agencies contributed to their destruction. Such fragments as could be fitted together have been carefully joined. In this way, the complete outlines of several were restored, as shown in plate 21 [88].
>
> The figures were modeled from clay without the addition of shell. They were apparently roughly formed with the fingers, and finished with modeling tools, some of which had sharp edges for trimming and paring the surface. The ears, ear-ornaments, garments, and some other portions were prepared separately and luted on. So far as can be judged by the fragments, both arms of each individual occupied the same relative position. This is another illustration of the symmetry so characteristic of the art of the Great Earthwork Builders and the Northwest Coast tribes.
>
> Two fragments of similar figures were obtained in the general digging of mound 4, and another fragment was found under the northern embankment of the great enclosure.
>
> These figures have little in common with the crude terracotta effigies from other sections of the United States. The modeling is much superior, and an unusual variety of postures is shown. As portraitures of the human form, these effigies compare favorably with many of the figurines from the Maya and Nahua regions.
>
> The largest of these effigies (plates 20 and 21,g [87, 88]), represents a man with hands crossed over his abdomen. The face is destroyed but the shape of the head is easily determined. He wears spool-shaped ear-ornaments of the same form as those of copper taken from the graves and altars of this group. The large knot of hair shown above the forehead in the drawing was among the fragments, and undoubtedly belonged to this figure. He wears a belt, and a broad breech-cloth, which has been painted red.
>
> The greater part of the surface of the effigy shown in a, of both plates, is badly mutilated. This man, also, wears a belt, breech-cloth, and large ear-ornaments. His fore-knot is bound with a fillet which is carried around the back of the head. His foot coverings consist of moccasins with short leggings attached. The upper edge of the legging is scalloped. The moccasin proper has the U-shaped inset characteristic of the northern Algonquian and neighboring tribes.
>
> The seated figure, f, in both of the above plates, represents a warrior with sides of the head shaved, leaving a ridge of short hair extending across the crown from front to back,

a method of arrangement characteristic of the warriors of the Pawnee, Sauc and Fox, and various other tribes of the northern half of the United States.

The kneeling effigy, illustrated in e, has the usual fore-knot, and wears a breech-cloth. The lower legs are flexed, and the toes turned inward, as shown somewhat imperfectly in the rear view. In the seated figure, c, no attempt has been made to restore the head, as the entire outer surface has scaled off.

In the upper row in plate 20 [87] is shown the lower part of a face, and one ear with a large perforation in the lobe. The head is restored in d, plate 21 [88]. Detached ornaments were probably inserted in the perforations. Portions of two other male figurines are illustrated in k, plate 20 [87]. Both of these wear the usual breech-cloth.

Aside from a few small fragments of one or two individuals, three women are represented in the figurines. The most perfect of these is shown in b, of both plates. This is 6½ inches in height, and represents a matron dressed in a short blanket-skirt, and low foot coverings of the general form of the woven shoes from the Kentucky caves. The hair is neatly parted, and gathered in a chignon at the back of the head. The ears are not pierced. The whole skirt is colored a dull red, and traces of paint may be seen on other portions of the figure. The eyeballs show traces of white, and the lips are colored red. It seems probable that the whole effigy was originally carefully painted. The skirt is short and reaches nearly to the knees. It is of the type worn by the Natchez and other tribes of the South, and is in the form of a long narrow blanket, wrapped around the hips, one corner being tucked in at the waistline at the back to hold it in place, as shown in the back view of the drawing.

The effigy of another woman is illustrated on plate 20, h [87]. This has been so badly injured that few details can be made out, a considerable portion of the exterior having flaked off. She wears the same type of skirt, but instead of the outer end being brought around under the right arm before tucking in at the back, it is carried in the opposite direction under the left arm.

The third woman is represented by a few fragments only. These have been joined together, and are shown in plate 20, i [87]. This apparently was one of the most carefully modeled in the group. It represents a young woman dressed in the characteristic red blanket skirt, and low shoes, sitting in the usual fashion of Indian squaws, with the lower limbs flexed and the feet carried backward to one side, the weight of the body resting principally upon the lower half of the left leg. The portions of the exterior of the figure which remain show unusual care in modeling and finish. It is possible that these figures when properly arranged may have formed one or more mortuary groups, and the large effigy with crossed hands may have represented a corpse, around which the other figures were placed.

In Missouri the first of the Hopewellian figurines to appear was from the Givens site in Saline County (McKinney, 1954). "An interesting specimen found here was a clay effigy (pottery) of a human head and shoulders. It is finished in rather light buff color and contains very little tempering material. The figure, including the head and shoulders is 3 cm. in height, width of the head at the ears is 2 cm., and width of the shoulder including arm projection is 3.5 cm. All of the features are quite clear cut and distinct. Considerable attention to detail has been given to ears, eyes, and nose. The head, entirely bald, is dome shaped and rests directly on the shoulders. There is no suggestion of a neck." Figurines have been recovered from a Hopewellian village site in Cooper County on the Lamine River. They are said to be crude. Three crude figurine fragments from the Trowbridge site in Wyandotte County, Kansas are illustrated by Shippee (1967: Fig. 51). These have the head and upper part of the body. A third clay figure may be a bird from the Renner site north of Kansas City.

One small figurine head from the Cooper Hopewellian site in Delaware County, Oklahoma has been described by Baerreis (1940:1): "It is a portion of a figurine which was modelled in clay and then baked. The ears are elongated and contain an ornament similar to an ear spool in the lobe of the ear. The elevated area on top of the skull resembles the copper head plates which are occasionally found in position on skulls of burials in the Ohio Hopewell mounds. The knob of the rear, right side of the skull may be some type of hair dress or ornament. A lower portion of this figurine, clothed only in breechcloth, was also found. Figurines, somewhat resembling this specimen, have been found in the Turner Mound in Ohio." This figurine is that of a male and if the normal sex ratio of figures at other sites is valid here, there should be others on the site.

The excavations by University of Georgia field parties at the Mandeville site in Clay County, on the Chattahoochie River, have recovered figurines in a Middle Woodland context in Mound A.

> In Layers IA and II, one human figurine head and two torso fragments were recovered. The head fragment is somewhat crudely executed, though some fine nose and mouth detail is present. One ear is broken away, while the other stands out from the head and may represent an earspool. The head is 1¾ inches high, from vertex to the break at the base of the neck. The two torso fragments are somewhat crude compared to another figure from the base of Mound B. One represents the complete upper portion of a female torso, broken at the waist, neck, and lacking arms; while the other is three-quarters of the upper torso, again possibly female, with the arms broken away. The former torso shows an area in the midriff where a strip of clay has broken away, and Bettye Broyles suggests this to be where arms originally were, folded over the abdomen. In general, there are striking similarities to human figurines in Illinois Hopewell. However, since the paste of these figurines is micaceous, and much like local pottery pastes, it is likely that these were made locally, in a style probably inspired from elsewhere (Kellar, Kelley and McMichael, 1962: 344).

From Mound B a complete figurine was found which is described as follows:

> Though figurine fragments were recovered from Mound A and the village, this figurine is the only complete example. It is 3½ inches high and was found in a pit (Feature 10). The upper part of this pit had been subjected to much heat and a large mass of charcoal was still present. The figurine was at the base of this depression lying face down and adjacent to a fragment of galena. It is a representation of a women bent slightly forward at the waist with hands at the side with fingers extended. Though the hands were detailed even to the knuckles, the left thumb had not been modeled. The skirt, portions of the feet, hairline, and armbands are painted red, while the hair and portions of the back are painted black. Her hair is parted to the left, tapers down the back, and is squared off just above the waist. Stylistically, it appears to have much in common with some of the Illinois examples and, possibly, the standing female from Turner, though the Mandeville example is unique in the extreme breadth of the mandible. The bigonial spread is remarkable and one commentator has suggested a goiter is indicated. Particular points of similarity are the hair down the back, the hair part, the short stubby legs, the relatively broad shoulders, the use of paint, as well as the techniques for differentiating physical features (Kellar, Kelly and McMichael, 1962: 351).

Along the west Florida coast, excavations by Florida State University in Swift Creek period middens has produced figurine fragments that are part of the general Hopewell styles. Further investigation of Florida sites of this period would probably produce more examples. In the Lower Mississippi Valley during W.P.A. excavations of the Crooks site in La Salle Parish, Louisiana, a clay figurine head was recovered with scratches indicating hair. The head is hollow and the facial portrayal is not suggestive of the Hopewell style. It was found in the secondary mantle and it is not possible to say that it is a Hopewell period figure (Ford and Willey, 1940: 119). The Greenhouse site, in Avoyelles Parish, also excavated by W.P.A.-sponsored crews, produced some ten figurine fragments but since the specimens, like most of the material from the mound, was deposited from village occupation areas, it is difficult to know their original context or period of manufacture (Ford, 1951: 112). Figure 44,*a*, a small head in the Greenhouse report, appears to be of the Hopewell style.

Some of the other fragments may also be of this period. The Manny site, in Issaquena County Mississippi, had one Hopewell period figurine head (Greengo, 1964: 78) which Greengo thought might have been attached to a vessel rim because no body fragments were found. If it was on a vessel rim it would be the only known instance at this time period, for effigy head bowls are a rather common feature of Mississippi period ceramics but not of Middle Woodland pottery.

One of the clan bundles among the Prairie Potawatomie when Skinner (1924: Pl. 5) studied them was that of the Man or Human Clan. In this bundle were two male and two female carved human figures from five to eight inches long regarded as clan ancestors. One of the male figures has a bun on the top of its head. Other items in the bundle were three medicine pouches of woven beadwork, a medicine plume of split and dyed owl feathers, a small wooden tablet covered with mnemonic song figures, and a magic arrow with a brass point. The bundle was to aid the clan in war, misfortune and disease. Skinner provides a lengthy description of magical properties and observances connected with the bundle. It is not implied here that the Hopewellian figurines were part of a clan bundle but it is one of the rare reports of human figures which were part of the cultural complex of an Indian group from the Upper Mississippi-Great Lakes area.

There are some stylistic similarities in the figurines from the various sites over the wide geographic area listed above which allow us to recognize them as Hopewellian. On the other hand, the five major Knight figurines represent a distinct group, so do those from Schuyler County, Illinois, and both are recognizably different from the Turner group. The interpretation favored here is that figurines were not an item of trade, barter or exchange. At least the variations of either style, dress, ornaments or materials do not suggest that such was the case. There are no figurine features which are held in common at all of the sites, perhaps because of the inadequate sample from most of the sites. Wherever the legs are shown the figures are almost always in a bent knee position similar to that of the Adena human effigy pipe and of the many Olmec figurines. Earspools are fairly common for they occur at Turner, Knight, Schuyler County, Illinois, and the Baehr site.

The time period of the Knight figurines is presumably about A.D. 200 to 300 but the temporal position of the other figurines is less well documented. The Turner site is said to be late Ohio Hopewell but it almost certainly had an occupation by shortly after the birth of Christ. A time period for Hopewellian figurines would probably be between A.D. 100 to 300. A connection to Middle America is possible but debatable and is not supported by distributional, stylistic or chronological data. One would hardly consider the crude blobs at Poverty Point to be directly stimulated from Mexico, or even to be a prototype for Hopewellian figurines. As sculptured representations they should be also considered along with other representations of humans and animals such as appear on platform pipes or produced from bone, copper and other materials, which had a strong development for the first time in the Eastern United States in Hopewellian art.

In this mound, which is certainly the most famous of the Knight group because of the quality of the five figurines, there is not a subfloor tomb or a log structure or very much in the way of burial goods or practices which suggest either a strong amount of long distance exchange or the necessity of interpreting the burials as evidence of a highly organized status-differentiated society. The pottery vessels with the five burials associated with the figurines are the best quality vessels recovered from the Knight mounds and serve to place the early levels of burials in this mound as early in the Pike phase.

The other deposits perhaps contemporary with the figurine group were the marine shell containers, the bear canines, pearl beads and copper axe which were under the limestone slabs but not directly associated with the adult female extended burial. Marine shells were brought into the Illinois area as early as Late Archaic times but many arrived during Middle Woodland and as the result of the quickening of the inter-area connections, the increased population and the interest in exotic materials for burial purposes. The copper adze may or may not represent a trade item, even though the copper itself is probably from the Lake Superior Basin. The copper adze, axe and celt forms were widely distributed during Late Archaic and Early Woodland and there is no need to regard them as being distributed from any single source. The adze certainly has no indications of use as a woodworking implement or any other mundane activity. The field notes do not indicate that the objects under the slabs were close together to suggest their inclusion in a single container.

Near the end of the burial activities resulting in Knight Mound C°8 was the placement of the three vessels with the scattered interments of two children and an adult. These vessels are clearly within the Pike phase but their construction and design suggest they were later than the group of five vessels with figurines. The position in the mound of Burial C°8-37 with the small poorly made figurine indicated that it was also made during the latter part of the mound construction.

MOUND C°10

C°10 is the tenth mound from the north on the low ridge and was test pitted by Mr. Wadlow. No details concerning location of the pit or provenience of artifacts are available. Two pottery sherds and a projectile point were found in the pit (Pl. 89). One sherd is part of the rim of a Pike Plain large jar with a pronounced inner channel 2 cm. high below the lip. Most of the tempering is leached out. The second sherd is a portion of a Havana Plain rim with flattened inward-slanting lip and impressions of a cordwrapped stick 6 mm. wide, 5 mm. apart on the exterior rim at the lip. The projectile point, C°10-3, is a Steuben Expanded Stemmed type of white flint with a flaring stem, straight base, straight sides and long, shallow notches. It is 8.7 cm. long, 2.6 cm. wide at the shoulder, 2.5 cm. wide at the base and 8 mm. thick with a stem 1.6 cm. long and 1.8 cm. wide at the shoulder.

MOUND C°14

C°14 was situated on the east end of the high ridge surrounding the valley. The mound measured 50 feet long, 38 feet wide and approximately nine feet six inches deep with the long axis running east and west. A trench 20 feet wide was excavated from the south edge of the mound to a point five feet north of the center and to the undisturbed original surface.

The only burial feature encountered was a bundle of a skull minus the mandible, the right femur and right innominate bone of one individual, reportedly a female (Pl. 90). The bundle was found at a depth of nine feet two inches at the approximate center of the mound. There was a large, roughly rectangular block of flint just to the south of the bones (Pl. 90,*b*). At a point 36 feet west of the east end on the long axis at a depth of nine feet eight inches were found three flint projectile points, C°14-2, -3, and -4 (Pl. 91), that had been placed on edge, side by side, on the original ground surface. Why they were so placed, and when, is unknown. C°14-2 is a point of blue-white flint with convex sides, a straight stem and slightly convex base and basal notches. It is 10.7 cm. long, 6.8 cm. wide and 1.2 cm. thick with a stem 1.9 cm. long and 1.9 wide. C°14-3 is of blue-white flint with ovoid sides, corner notches and a straight stem with a straight base. The point measures 10.2 cm. long, 5.1 cm. wide and 1.3 cm. thick and has a stem 1.4 cm. long and 1.7 cm. wide. A piece 2.7 cm. long and 3 mm. wide has been broken off one side of the tip. C°14-4 is a crudely made point of porous white flint and has convex sides, a straight stem and base and basal notching. One barb extends down even with the base, the other to within 1.1 cm. of the base. The point measures 13.1 cm. in length, 5.9 cm. wide and 1.4 cm. thick and has a stem 1.5 cm. long and 2.1 cm. wide. A fourth projectile point (C°14-1) was found seven feet eight inches east and four feet south of this group at approximately the same depth. It is of white flint with fairly straight sides, a straight stem and base and basal notching such that both barbs extend to the base line. The point measures 7.0 cm. in length, 5.0 cm. wide and 1.0 cm. thick with a stem 1.4 cm. long and 1.3 cm. wide. These implements have very little indication of use. The west side of the wall at the north end of the trench where most of the lensing of dirt occurred was undercut for a distance of three and one-half to four feet but no subfloor pit was encountered. Other instances are known of Archaic points being excavated in a later context such as those reported by Perino (1963: Fig. 2) from Koster Mound 5, in Greene County, Illinois.

Two of the points or knife fragments from the Black Sand village in Fulton County belongs to this style (Cole and Deuel, 1937: Fig. 28; White, 1968: Fig. 46A). The forms called Smith points by Baerreis and Freeman from northeastern Oklahoma (1960) and also some of the Eva forms from western Tennessee (Lewis and Kneberg, 1961) are probably related to those under Mound C°14. Illinois seems to be, like western Tennessee, on the eastern border of the distribution of these forms for their major concentration would appear to be from southern Missouri to eastern Oklahoma. The time range is not definitely known but somewhere around 3000 to 2000 B.C. is probably about right.

MOUND C°15

C°15 was an elevation measuring 33 feet east and west by 22 feet north and south and was situated just to the east of C°14 on the crest of the high ridge. A ten-foot-wide trench was started on the north side of the elevation and was excavated two-thirds of the way through. The deepest part of the trench was in undisturbed clay and a four foot six inch deep pit excavated at the center of the elevation showed several more inches of clay underlain by undisturbed loess. Two roughly rectangular white flint tools were found near the surface (Pl. 92). C°15-1 is 10.6 cm. long, 5.9 cm. wide and 2.0 cm. thick near the working edge. The tool is bifacially worked on both sides and one end although the worked end is plano-convex in cross section. C°15-2 is 7.9 cm. long, 4.2 cm. wide and 1.5 cm. thick and is bifacially worked on all edges. The two tools appear rather crude and might have functioned as choppers, adzes or even scrapers. Dr. Titterington thinks this was a natural elevation, not a mound.

MOUND C°16

Dr. Titterington reports that all of the 1946 season prior to and including his vacation was spent in the excavation of this mound. C°16 is situated on the west end of the high bluff surrounding the valley and was the largest of the 11 mounds on this bluff. The mound appears to have been about 60 feet in diameter and from 20 to 25 feet high (Fig. 16).

The first 15-foot-wide trench was started in the west side of the mound at a point approximately 25 feet below the top. After nothing was encountered in several feet, the level of the trench was raised five feet and continued. Burial C°16-1 was found two feet below the surface at this point, probably close to the east edge of the mound. C°16-1 consisted of the skull of a young adult male, a few fragmentary long bones and some small fragments of a child's skull. The bones were scattered over an area about three feet six inches in diameter and were underlain by a thin layer of charcoal. The trench was widened to 30 feet after finding C°16-1. Burials C°16-2 and C°16-3 were encountered 20 feet east and ten feet north of the center of the mound just below the sod line. This was a compound burial of two infants, both flexed on the left side with heads to the north.

Burials C°16-4 to C°16-7 (Fig. 17; Pl. 93,*a*) were found in a group about twelve feet east and three feet south of the center at a depth of about 15 feet. C°16-4 was an adult male extended on the back with the

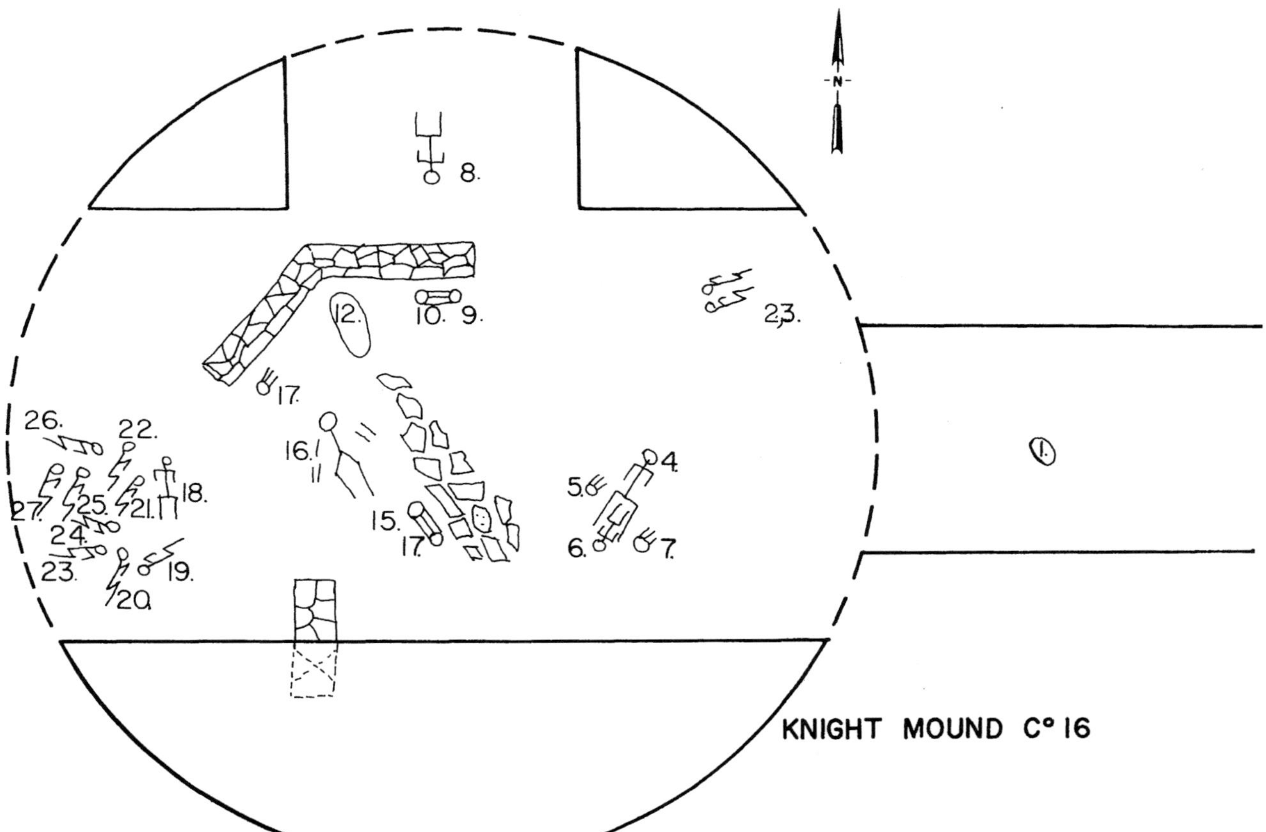

Fig. 16. Floor plan of Knight Mound C°16 according to Dr. P. F. Titterington. Diameter of mound about 60 feet.

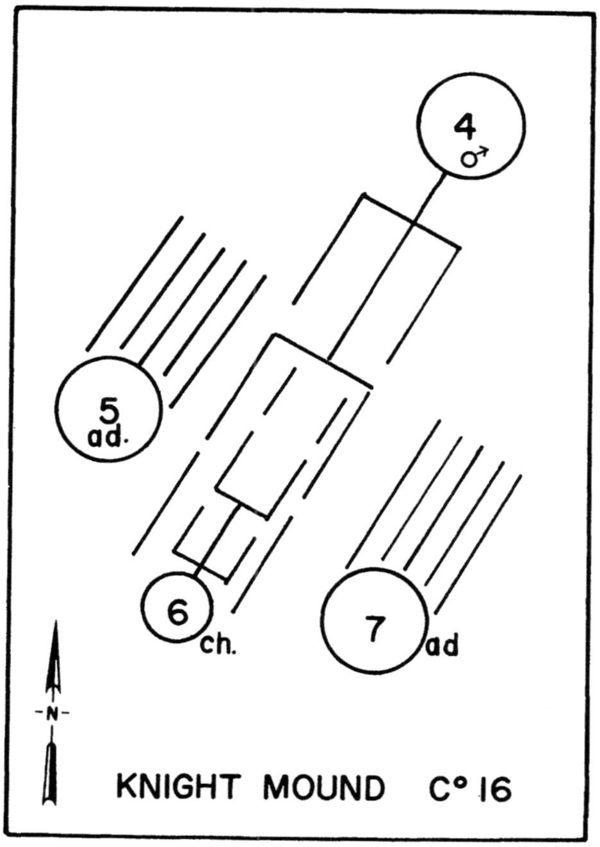

Fig. 17. Diagram of Burials C°16-4 to 7, one of the primary interments in the mound.

head to the east. Black clay had been forced into the orbits, nose aperture and mouth, suggesting at least partial decomposition before burial although the skeletal parts in the photographs seem to be in articulatory position (Pl. 93,*b*). C°16-6 was that of a child about six years old extended on the back with the head to the west between the lower extremities of C°16-4 (Pl. 94,*a*). A total of 343 shell disc beads were scattered under C°16-6 and around the legs of C°16-4, some of them appearing to have been strung. The beads are 1.0 cm. in diameter, vary from 3 to 6 mm. in thickness with a hole approximately 3 mm. in diameter, and were cut from the columella of a large marine univalve (Pl. 94,*b*). Over the lower rib cage of C°16-6 was an ovate knife of purplish flint with a length of 13.0 cm., a width of 6.6 cm. and a thickness of 9 mm. (Pl. 95,*a*). C°16-5 was a bundle burial consisting of a crushed skull and several fragments of long bones located just to the north of the lower extremities of C°16-4. There was a crushed, complete Havana Zoned Dentate Stamped vessel (Pl. 95,*b*), immediately above the skull. The vessel contained a badly disintegrated mussel shell spoon.

This small funerary example of Havana style has every attribute of its class, except perhaps for the rounded base. It is 13 cm. high. The lip diameter is 13 by 13.5 cm., 11.7 cm. at the base of the rim and the body diameter is 14 cm. The lip is flattened, 7 mm. wide and has a slight inward slant. The rim has a slight outward slant and is 7 mm. thick on the upper plain band and 5 mm. thick at the decorated lower band. The body is 7 mm. thick. The temper is medium to fine sand and sparse angular grit. Some of these grit particles protrude on both surfaces. The inner and outer surfaces are smoothed, and the surface colors are light brown to dark brown with some smoke blackening on the base.

The vessel was decorated by preparing a smooth upper rim band 1.2 cm. wide and on the lower rim a band of similar width containing vertical closely spaced impressions of a small ovoid cross-barred stamp 5 mm. wide. On the body the plain and stamped areas are separated by broad 9 mm. wide deeply impressed trailed lines which produced a slight bulge on the inner surface. The dentate stamp that was used had at least eight "teeth" and most of the stamp impressions are horizontal.

A 20-foot-wide trench was started in the north end of the mound and Burial C°16-8 was encountered about ten feet into the mound at a depth of three feet. The individual was an adult female extended on the back with the head to the south. One fragmentary and one complete pulley-type earspool or pendant of antler were situated over the upper chest region (Pl. 95,*a*).

The semi-circular fragment fits the dimensions of the complete article. The outside diameter is 4.0 cm., the diameter of the "groove" is 3.4 cm. and the central hole is 1.7 cm. in diameter. The objects are 1.6 cm. thick at the outside and 7 mm. thick next to the inside hole. There are eight irregularly spaced holes 3 mm. in diameter drilled through the groove into the central opening and the outer edge and the 4 mm. wide "flange" appear to have been polished.

Approximately 10 feet north of the center of the mound base a wall of limestone slabs was encountered. This wall consisted of two sections, each about ten feet long, which met at a 45-degree angle, one starting two feet east of the center line of the mound and running east and west, the other going from the west of the first and angling to the southwest. No dimensions are given in the notes but the wall would appear to be three to four feet high and two feet wide in the photographs and to be made of horizontally laid slabs approximately six inches thick and up to two feet square (Pl. 96,*a*, *b*). A compound bundle burial of an adult female, C°16-9, and an adult male, C°-16-10, was located at the base of the wall just south of the east end. There was a split, perforated, incised bear canine with the bundle, the medial half of the right lower incisor of *Ursus americanus* (black bear). The tooth is 5.4 cm. long, 1.7 cm. wide and 5 mm. thick (Pl. 95,*a*). Parallel lines 1 to 3 mm. long have been cut into both edges of the root and a 3 mm. hole is drilled through the end of the root. Burial C°16-11 was the fragmentary calvarium of a young adult, sex undetermined, found in a "pocket" on top of the wall four feet west of the east end.

C°16-12 was a bundle burial, minus the skull, of what was apparently an adult male. The bundle was found in a pit six feet four inches long, three feet wide and possibly one foot deep, the long axis running east-west and the west end of the pit two feet six inches southeast of the angle in the wall (Pl. 96,*a*). The burial was overlain by six small limestone slabs and there were four post molds, ranging in diameter from two and one-half to three and one-half inches, which formed a rough rectangle about six feet by three feet around the pit. There were no associated artifacts. Three feet to the southeast of this pit there was a row of flat limestone slabs which ran for 15 feet to the southeast through the center of the mound. Burial C°16-13 was a skull, presumably male and without the mandible, in a pocket in the southeast end of the row. C°16-14 and -15 represent a compound bundle burial found just to the south of the east end of the row of slabs.

C°16-16 was an adult male extended on the back with the head to the northwest (Pl. 96,*b*). The arms extended from the body and the right leg was partially flexed. The bones were very poorly preserved and a large portion of the skeleton was removed in excavation. However, the remaining skeletal parts, the right and left legs, right foot, right humerus, right and left radius and ulna and skull, indicate a flesh burial. The burial was located in a pit 15 inches deep in the mound floor and approximately eight feet wide across the north end where the outlines of the pit were clearly indicated (Pl. 97,*a*). The east edge of the pit was lost under the row of limestone slabs and the west and south edges were not clearly outlined, the soil in this area being soft, dark in color and containing numerous bone fragments to a depth of three feet above the pit floor. Several artifacts were found with this burial (Pl. 97,*b*). About one foot to the west of the skull there was a conch shell container 20.8 cm. long, 15.2 cm. wide and 10 cm. deep, made by cutting a shell of *Cassis madagascariensis* approximately in half (Pl. 100,*a*). The cut edges and the surface from which the columella had been removed show cut marks and are polished. A platform pipe of reddish Ohio pipe-stone was uncovered six inches to the south of the conch shell, along with a group of seven worked sections of bird bone. The pipe is 12.0 cm. long and 4.7 cm. high from the bottom of the platform to the top of the bowl (Pl. 98,*a*). The slightly concave platform is 3.6 cm. wide and .9 cm. thick at both ends and 4.5 cm. wide and 1.3 cm. thick at the center. The bowl measures 3.4 cm. high, 4.1 cm. in diameter at the base, 3.1 cm. in diameter at a constriction 1.3 cm. above the base and 4.5 cm. in diameter at the flanged lip which is flat on top. The interior diameter is 2.0 cm. and the depth of the bowl is 4.1 cm. Part of the platform had been broken off and was found a short distance away, leading Titterington to suggest a deliberate mutilation. The sections of bird long bone (Pl. 98,*b*) consist of sections of a right and left tibiotarsus of the turkey (*Meleagris gallovo*), 18.5 cm. long and 1.5 cm. wide at the proximal end from which the articulatory surfaces have been cut, and sections of a right and left ulna of the whistling swan (*Cygnus columbianus*), one 11.0 cm. long and splintered at both ends, the other 18.7 cm. long and 1.5 cm. wide at the proximal end, the distal end having been cut obliquely and polished to form a gougelike point 8 mm. wide. The other three bone artifacts are sections of swan radii (*Cygnus* sp.), two of them 19.0 cm. long, one 18.5 cm. long and all were 7 cm. wide through the shaft. All three have been modified, one having been broken so that only a small portion of the oblique cut is left, one is obliquely cut to form a rounded edge like that mentioned above, and the last cut to form a long and fairly sharp point, suggesting use as an awl. All three of the latter artifacts had been polished along the cut edges. There was a large mussel shell spoon about one foot to the east of the skull which was subsequently broken by a visitor stepping on it. It is described in the notes as a right valve 20 cm. long with a handle cut into the posterior end and appears in the photographs to be a species of *Proptera* or *Lampsilis*. Two flat bone imitation bear canines were also found with C°16-16, one in the loose soil six inches above the burial and the other in contact with the upper thoracic vertebrae (Pl. 98,*b*). The first is 6.9 cm. long, 1.5 cm. wide at the center and 4 mm. thick with a 2 mm. hole drilled through the top and two more holes drilled 6 mm. apart through the center. The imitation canine found near the spine is 7.2 cm. long, 1.8 cm. wide and .4 cm. thick, with the same arrangement of holes. Both of these objects show striations and polishing on all edges and surfaces and the one found near the spine is partially decomposed, possibly, as Titterington suggests, through contact with decaying body tissues. There were several copper articles with C°16-16 (Fig. 98,*b*). Three copper earspool discs and fragments of a fourth were found near the skull, one complete disc just over the left frontal bone and the other two discs and fragments in the area of the neck. The discs have a rolled rim and a circular depression in the center approximately 2 cm. in diameter and 4 mm. deep, and they vary in diameter from 4.8 cm. to 5.2 cm. and in thickness from 0.5 mm. to 1 mm. One of the discs has a short, cylindrical "shank" projecting from the center suggesting some method for connection of a pair of them. Of the 20 copper fragments, one is the circular depressed area of the disc and another is a semicircular fragment of a band 7 mm. wide and 1.6 cm. in diameter with rolled edges. According to Titterington there were two pairs of "sticks" covered with sheet copper, one pair over the abdomen and the other over the lower chest. The "sticks" are described as being about three inches long and about the size of a finger but only nine fragments of the copper were saved. The fragments are 0.5 mm. in thickness and a little of the organic material has adhered to the interior of some of the fragments. This is definitely not wood but some type of grasslike stalk. This sounds very much as if the objects were conjoined tubes or "panpipes." In the region of the upper thoracic spine, near one of the effigy bear canines described above, was a fragment of sheet copper 3.4 cm. long, 1.6 cm. wide at the bottom, 1.2 cm. wide at the top and 2 mm. thick. Halfway up one side is a thin silver inclusion .7 cm. long and 5 mm. wide and there is another fragment approximately .5 cm. square near the top of the object. A constriction .9 cm. below the top still has what is reported to be the original twisted string knotted around it. (Pl. 99,*a*). In the region of the neck there were 33 pearl slug beads, ranging in size from 3 mm. to 9 mm. in length with 2 to 3 mm. holes in diameter. Some of these are illustrated at the top and extreme right of Plate 99,*b*. Twenty cylindrical shell beads cut from the columella of a marine univalve and averaging 9 mm. long and 6 mm. wide were found in the region of both ankles, ten apiece, and there were two planoconvex shell beads 2.5 cm. long and 9 mm. wide, drilled obliquely through each end, with each of these groups of beads. These are illustrated on Plate 99,*b*; bottom center. Titterington states in the notes that the arrangement of these beads in the area of the right ankle suggests attachment in a row around a foot covering of some type.

Burial C°16-17 was a bundle burial under several limestone slabs and was found just to the east of the south end of the limestone wall. There was an eight-foot row of limestone slabs about ten feet to the south of C°16-16 which lay underneath a boundary marker post on top of the mound, so no more of the south end of the mound was removed. C°16-18 was a fragmentary burial consisting of the left leg and left arm. The burial was 20 feet west of the center of the mound at a depth of two feet. In the region of the abdomen was a small amount of hematite and two Ansell projectile points of white flint (Pl. 100,*b*). The points both show short, slightly flaring stems, convex sides, slightly convex bases and slight shoulders. The first, which has ochre-stained sand on one side, is 8.4 cm. long, 2.5 cm. wide at the shoulder, 2.4 cm. wide at the base and 9 mm. thick with a stem 2.2 cm. wide and 1.3 cm. long. The second point is 8.5 cm. long, 2.5 cm. wide at the shoulder, 2.1 cm. wide at the base and 8 mm. thick with a stem 2.0 cm. wide and 1.2 cm. long. Burials C°16-19 through -27 were all flexed burials interred with no special alignment at two-to three-foot intervals south of the midline in the western portion of the mound that was removed. The burials had been penetrated by the roots of a tall, wiry grass and no attempt was made to work them out sufficiently for photographing. C°16-19, a child burial, had a projectile point in association (Pl. 100,*b*). The point, of white flint, has a short, slightly flaring stem, pronounced barbs reaching almost to the base line, straight blade sides, a concave base and some basal thinning. Measurements are 5.3 cm. long, 3.1 cm. wide at the end of the barbs, 1.7 cm. wide at the base, and 4 mm. thick with a stem 1.3 cm. wide and 7 mm. long (White's Marshall Barbed). Three dental specimens were saved: C°16-19 is the right half of a mandible showing an impacted third molar, C°16-20 is a maxilla and mandible with the upper left second bicuspid displaced buccally by a supernumerary tooth consisting of one set of roots and a pair of fused crowns and C°16-21 is a maxilla and mandible.

Artifacts found in the mound fill unassociated with burials (Pl. 100,*b*) include a flint knife, two bifacial flint artifacts, 22 shell and two copper beads (Pl. 99,*b*, lower left). C°16-28 is a gray flint knife with convex sides, flat ends and fine retouch and measures 13.5 cm. in length, 4.3 cm. wide at the middle, 2.5 cm. wide at the ends and .8 cm. thick. This knife was found in the sod near the center of the mound. C°16-29 is the number given to two unnotched points or knives of white flint, found at a depth of 18 inches in the west end of the mound near the flexed burials (Pl. 100,*b*). Both show slightly convex sides and convex bases and both are somewhat curved in the side view as if the original form of the flake had been retained. The larger measures 8.5 cm. in length, 3.3 cm. wide, 2 mm. above the base, 2.8 cm. wide at the base, and 1.0 cm. thick. One side of the base shows a stepped series of hinge flakes. The smaller blade measures 5.4 cm. in length, 3.0 cm. wide and 7 mm. thick. The original surface of the flake (probably an old flake-scar) is unmodified for 1.0 cm. above the base except for a few small flakes removed from the periphery and the "point" is formed in part by another section of unmodified cortex. There were 22 shell beads ranging in size from 2.1 cm. long by 1.6 cm. wide to 3 mm. long by 5 mm. wide, all out from the columella of a marine univalve and other shell beads. The two copper beads measure 7 mm. long by 6 mm. wide and 4 mm. long by 7 mm. wide and were made from rolled copper strips. The beads were all found in the fill dirt but are not mentioned in the notes.

The copper pendant with a silver inclusion with Burial C°16-16 is a rare item for it has little or no indication of aboriginal workmanship but it was apparently of enough value to utilize as an ornament. Such a piece should probably not be recorded as one that had been formed somewhere in Ohio or the Upper Peninsula and traded as a manufactured item. The cord that was tied around the upper slightly constricted "neck" of the piece has been examined by Volney H. Jones of the Museum of Anthropology. His statements is given below:

> The cord averages about 1.5 mm. in diameter. It is composed of two strands, each twisted individually in a counter-clockwise or Z twist direction, and the two combined in the opposite clockwise or S twist direction. The cord is neatly made with smooth and uniform composition, but is not tightly twisted (about 3 spirals per centimeter).
>
> The cord is exceptionally well preserved, with little apparent deterioration, although it is not heavily impregnated with copper salts. It has a somewhat glossy, silky appearance.
>
> The fibers were examined under high-power magnification, and were found to fall into the category of "herbaceous bast," that is, fibers from the stems of herbaceous plants (as opposed to "woody bast" from schrubs and trees). The most common source in this area for such strong, silky fibers were the so-called "Indian hemp" (*Apocynum cannabium*) and various species of milkweed (*Asclepias* sp.) These are not readily distinguishable, and the precise source has not been determined.

The shell beads at the right ankle of C°16-16 recall the indications of such beads as part of the limb ornamentation which usually is on the arms.

The shallow Burial C°16-18 with hematite and two Ansell constricted stem points may be a Bluff burial or one of Late Hopewell. The points and the hematite found with this burial are not diagnostic enough to be certain. The same may be said for the Marshall Barbed form with child burial C°16-19. The other points in the mound fill and most of the shell and copper heads are not specific nor can they be associated with other features.

COMMENTS ON MOUND C°16

The occurence of limestone slabs around the central features at the base of the mound is similar to the use of limestone in Mounds C°4, C°5, and C°8. The purpose of the limestone wall is difficult to understand for it is not an enclosure, not a capping over a tomb or burial area, nor otherwise significant for the burial activities. There were relatively few burials and a small amount of grave goods for the size of the mound.

One of the major interments was Burials 4-7 made near the mound floor but southeast of the central area. The adult male was extended with head to the east while the extended child between his legs had its head to the west. The two bundle burials were also oriented east-west with the skulls on the west side of the bundle. The placement of black clay into the eyes, nose and mouth of the adult male may be connected with two concepts associated with Hopewellian burials. Two burials in Mound 10 of the Cyrus Thomas Mound Group in Barron County, Wisconsin, had baked clay masks resulting from the exposure to firing of the skull after clay had been modeled to the head of the deceased (Cooper, 1933). Another possible connection may be the blockage of the nasal aperture with copper plugs at the Hopewell site in Ohio (Shetrone, 1926: 141-44). Other than these probably not too pertinent practices there do not seem to be many reported similarities. It might be thought that the black clay was the result of the deposition of a layer of black clay over a burial group or area which was a fairly common Hopewellian maneuver in the Illinois area, but Titterington was an experienced excavator and would have observed such a deposit.

The Havana Zoned Stamped vessel associated with bundle burial C°16-15 is one of the best extant examples of this decorative style. While this style has been recognized for some time as part of an early Hopewellian ceramic complex in the Illinois area there is rather poor temporal or areal control over its variations through time. This vessel then cannot be used to claim an Early Illinois Hopewell placement because this style lasts well into the period when the Hopewell style was being produced and even into the beginning of the period of the Baehr-Pike development in the lower Illinois area. It should not then be asserted that this burial group and the vessel were placed in the mound before the Hopewell or Baehr style had developed. The other artifacts such as the beads or knife are not particularly helpful in assessing the age of the burials.

The extended adult female C°16-8 in the northern part of the mound with the perforated antler pulley-type earspools is certainly a Hopewellian burial. This type of earspool of bone, clay or other material is fairly common in the lower Illinois Valley area and is almost a locally specific artifact. They are identical in concept to those of cannel coal from the Rutherford Mound in southeastern Illinois (Fowler, 1957: 31-33), although there are marked differences in size and probably in the function of the objects. As Fowler emphasized, the Rutherford perforated rings are much larger than the ones of baked clay in the altar of Mound 3 at the Turner site (Willoughby, 1922: 60-61), and in an ash bed in the embankment around the Great Enclosure. Stone rings were found in altar 1 of Mound 25 of the Hopewell group made of slate and cannel coal. Some were pierced with four holes, and others with eight holes in pairs opposite each other (Moorehead, 1922: 139-41). There were fourteen rings, but at least one was not of the pulley type. One pulleywheel type earspool of sandstone was discovered at the Seip Mound 1 (Shetrone and Greenman, 1931: 457) but in the same mound there were 56 copper earspools of the more common forms. Probably the first recorded occurrence of this pulley type of earspool was from a burial near a large oval mound in the downtown Cincinnati area (Sargent, 1799; Drake, 1815; Starr, 1960: 23-24). One spool was a large one of cannel coal and a smaller one was of baked clay with four holes pierced from the outer to inner surface of the wheel. These were associated with stone plummets, a carved bird effigy head of stone, a panpipe form of copper, carved bone, galena, mica, marine shells, beads and copper spools. They are decribed below and illustrated in Plates 101, 102. Almost thirty burials were said to be in rude coffins of stone found in the mound nearby.

One of the rare identifications of earspools in the northern Mississippi Valley is from a mound at Moline along with other indications of a Hopewellian complex in the tri-cities area made famous in the late 1880's by the fake effigy pipes and an engraved tablet (Bennett, 1945: 116). A description of this earspool was not found in the publication cited by Bennett.

Burials 9 to 15, and 17 and 18 were either bundles, compound, or a skull with no body and vice versa so that little can be said of their orientation. They are important in emphasizing the great variability of Hopewellian burial procedures within a mound; between mounds in a single group and close together in time; and between mound groups on adjoining ridges, and so on.

The major burial from the standpoint of associated grave goods was the adult male C°16-16 which was extended northwest-southeast and with the head to the northwest in a subfloor pit. The *Cassis* shell with this burial was well preserved. While not limited to Hopewellian sites this shell is strongly associated with Hopewell, particularly in the Illinois Valley area. According to one authority (Abbott, 1954: 193-94), *C. madagascariensis* is very rare in Florida where it is replaced by the Clench's Helmet, the subspecies *spinella* Clench. This is very similar in shape to the typical *madagascariensis* but has a top row of small evenly spaced spines. It is fairly common in 20 feet of water off the Florida Keys. Most of the identifications of the Helmet shell from archaeological sites simply refer to *madagascariensis*. The important point is, of course, that this shell does not occur in the Gulf area as was pointed out some years ago (Griffin, 1946: 65) and requires some social mechanism for its transport into the Upper Mississippi Valley. If there was an exchange network, there must have been a long distance between knots, for the Helmet shell is not a common type in prehistoric sites in the Southeast or even Florida.

The flat shell beads perforated from each end and from the base near each end so that the two adjoining perforations meet, is a rare form. Other examples are from the big Baehr mound (Griffin, 1941: Pl. 2, No. 1), from Gibson Mound 4, Calhoun County, Illinois, and from the central altar of Mound 3 of the Turner site near Cincinnati (Willoughby, and Hooton 1922: 54).

The reddish Ohio pipestone plain platform pipe is, of course, from Ohio and was almost certainly made there, as were the bird effigy pipe from C°4 and the curved base pipe from C°5. These pipes would seem to indicate, on stylistic grounds, that they were made at about the same time as the ones of the large deposits in the Tremper Mound and in the Mound City Group in the Scioto Valley in Ohio.

The long bone awls of turkey and whistling swan are indications of the importance of the turkey which had a close association with the oak-hickory forests and the swan with the Mississippi Valley flight movement of migratory birds. The swans would have been available during the spring or fall but there is no control over the length of time between the death of the swan and the burial of the bone with the body with which it was associated.

The copper earspools are of the thin copper style with a concave outer central portion. They are almost identical to specimens from the Rutherford Mound (Fowler, 1957: 24, 25), where both of the connected copper discs are about the same size. The earspools in Mound C°104 and C°114 of the Snyders Group are much heavier, the inner disc is about two-thirds the size of the outer one and the connect-

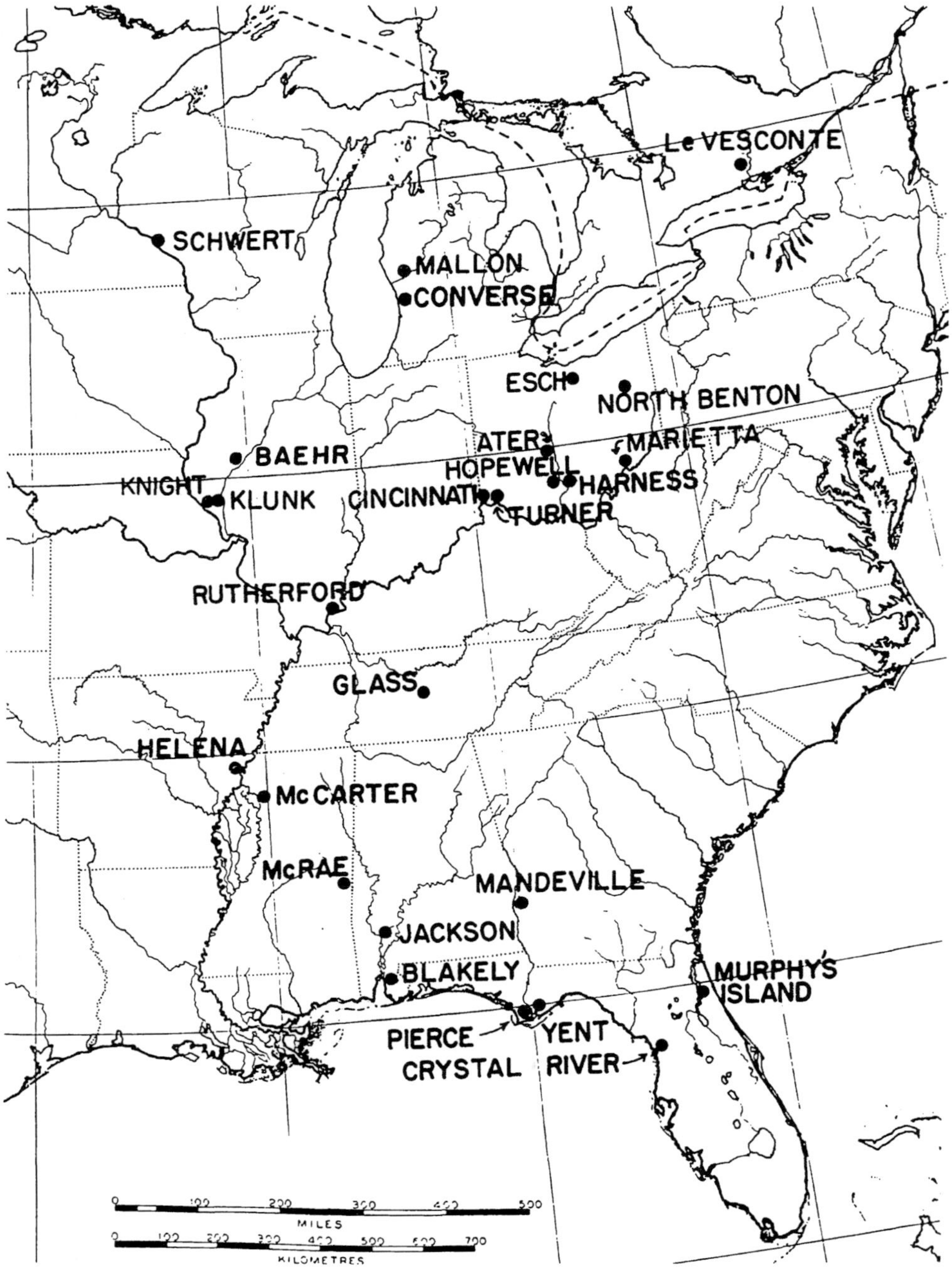

Map 2. Geographical distribution of sites where panpipes have been recovered. UMMA Neg. 152-1.

LIST OF 27 SITES WITH 55 HOPEWELLIAN PANPIPES

1. **Burial at Cincinnati, 3 tube copper**
2. **Burial in mound at Marietta, Ohio, 4 tube silver**
3. Hopewell site Mound 25, Ross County, Ohio
   a. 4 tube copper, clay tubes (?), FMNH* cat. 56708
   b. Altar 1, 4 tube copper and meteoric iron, FMNH cat. 56588
   c. Cut No. 2, burials 249-59 (?) 3 reeds 5 inches long, copper gone, FMNH cat. 56093
   d. Copper deposit, thin semi-tubular straight copper object with rivet (?) hole at top, FMNH cat. 56218
   e. f. Copper deposit, 6 pieces of cane 5¼ inches long (interpreted as remains of 2 pipes), FMNH cat. 56237
   g. Burial 12 of Shetrone, Ohio State Museums, 1 tube copper, reeds (?) Hopewell site Mound 17
   h. A few fragments of curved copper objects, FMNH cat. 56593
   i. Two pieces of copper tubing, FMNH cat. 56589 Hopewell site Mound 20
   j. Burial of Shetrone, 3 tube copper, Ohio State Museum
4. Esch Mound, Erie County, Ohio, 3 tube copper with silver overlay, Ohio State Museum collection
5. Ater Mound, Franklin County, 3 tube copper, Ohio State Museum collection
6. Harness Mound, Ross County, Ohio, 3 tube copper, Peabody Museum, Harvard University
7. North Benton, Mahoning County, Ohio, 2 tube cooper, leather plugs, location unknown
8. Turner site, Hamilton County, Ohio, 3 tube meteoric iron, Peabody Museum, Harvard University
9. Converse Mound 2, Kent County, Michigan, Peabody Museum, Harvard University
   a. 3 tube silver
   b. 3 tube, copper (?)
10. Mallon Mound B, Newaygo County, Michigan 3 tube copper, UMMA cat.
11. *a-i.* Levesconte Mound, Northumberland County, Ontario, 4 copper and 5 silver panpipes, Royal Ontario Museum
12. Glass Mound, Williamson County, 3 tube copper, Peabody Museum, Harvard University
13. Mandeville site, Mound B, Clay County, Georgia, University of Georgia
   a. 3 tube copper
   b. 4 tube copper and silver
   c. 3 tube copper
   d. ? tube copper
   e. ? tube copper
14. Crystal River, Mound F, Citrus County, Florida, Heye Museum ?
   a. 3 tube copper
   b. ? tube copper
15. Pierce Mound, Mound A ?, Franklin County, Florida, ? tube, copper, Heye Museum
16. Yent Mound, Northernmost Island, Franklin County, Florida, ? tube copper, R. S. Peabody Foundation 39524
17. Murphy Island, Putnam County, Florida, Heye Museum?
   a. 3 tube copper
   b. 3 tube copper
18. Blakely Shell Midden, Baldwin County, Alabama, ? tube copper, Heye Museum ?
19. Mounds near Jackson, Clarke County, Alabama, 3 tube copper, Heye Museum ?
20. McRae Mound, Lauderdale County, Mississippi, ? tube copper and silver, U.S. National Museum
21. McCarter Mound, Panola County, Mississippi, 3 tube copper, private collection
22. Helena Mound C., Phillips County, Arkansas, 3 tube copper and silver, American Museum of Natural History
23. Rutherford Mound, Hardin County, Illinois, Illinois State Museum
   a. 3 tube copper
   b. 3 tube copper
   c. 4 tube copper
24. Knight Mound C°16, Calhoun County, Illinois, ? tube, copper, University of Michigan Museum of Anthropology
25. Klunk Mound 13, Calhoun County, Illinois, ? tube copper, Gilcrease Foundation
26. Baehr Mound 1, Brown County, Illinois, 3 tube copper, location unknown.
27. Schwert Mound 12, Trempealeau County, Wisconsin, Milwaukee Public Museum
   a. 3 tube copper
   b. Mound 4, 3 tube copper, Wisconsin Historical Society
   c. Mound 25, 3 tube copper, Wisconsin Historical Society

* Field Museum of Natural History

ing copper shaft has an open passageway through the center of the earspool.

The presumed copper conjoined tube or tubes with Burial C°16-16 is one of the more interesting items, for their use is not definitely known even though they are called "panpipes." They are one of the specifically Hopewellian time markers and have been used for many years to show the wide spreàd interaction of prehistoric groups in the Eastern United States Map 2. The find of panpipes nearest to the Knight Group is some eight or ten miles to the east in Mound 13 of the Pete Klunk Mound Group. In a subfloor pit with a log roof the male and female extended burials had been placed west to east with heads to the west. The pottery in the fill of this mound is primarily of the Baehr Group of late Illinois Valley Hopewell.

> The skeletons lay side by side, the female wearing a pair of limestone-tempered clay earspools with eight tiny perforations radiating from the central perforation of each. The male wore a series of artifacts consisting of: Two pairs of large bear canines at each ear which had been drilled on one side . . . surrounded with conch-shell disc beads, five-sixteenths of an inch in diameter, a copper panpipe, surrounded with two hundred and three disc beads, which lay on the sternum, thirteen large pearl slug beads and six barrel-shaped beads about the ankles, and, in addition, a copper earspool tightly clenched in each hand (Perino, 1968: 109-14).

The first recorded panpipe in Illinois came from Baehr Mound 1, in Brown County. It was excavated in September, 1897 by Dr. J. F. Snyder.

> At G unconnected with any other object, the ornament of sheet copper . . . was turned up. It is very smoothed and as accurately corrugated as though pressed by machinery. It seems to have been with those old savages a favorite form of decoration, as several of the same type have been found in Ohio, Florida, Georgia and other sites (Snyder, 1898: 20).

If I understand the description of the excavation this conjoined copper tube panpipe was one of the shorter forms, about 6 cm. long, and was located in the upper layers, about 20 inches deep, of the west half of Mound 1. At about the same depth in the western trench made by Snyder were the two Baehr figurines, a perforated bone and a wooden (clay?) earspool, and pottery vessels of the small Baehr Brushed types.

The Rutherford Mound, in Hardin County, Illinois, had three panpipes or conjoined copper tubes. It should be noted that in this mound there is no consistent burial orientation although most of the Hopewellian burials were extended. Burials 30 and 31 and 27 and 28 were on or below the mound floor and so precede by some unknown length of time Burials 14 and 15.

> Burials 30 and 31 were on top of the red clay subsoil under the mound, but due to the soil condition, only the enamel caps of the teeth, a fragmentary femur, and portions of lower leg bones remained. The two individuals were apparently buried side by side with the head of one placed by the feet of the other. Both had an ear spool in each hand. The ear spools were 4.5-5.5 cm. (1¾ to 2⅛ inches) in diameter and were wound with string on the axle. Burial 31 had on its chest a panpipe, a prismoidal flake knife and a cuboid of galena. The panpipe, 3¾ inches (95 mm.) long and 1⅞ inches (48 mm.) wide, was made of a sheet of copper wrapped around three reeds, fragments of which were preserved. On the back side of the panpipe were what appear to be fabric remnants, possibly part of the garment of the individual (Fowler, 1957:17).
>
> Burials 27 and 28, extended side by side, were among the richest burials in the mound. Burial 28, although apparently complete, was in a poor state of preservation, and it was possible to determine no more than its position and relationship to the others. Burial 27 was also extended and although better preserved was not as complete as 28. The feet, the left hand, and many of the ribs were missing, and the skull was badly crushed. Again we have only a partial skeleton which appears to have been articulated at the time of burial. No evidence of fire was found that would indicate partial cre-

mation at the burial location. This phenomenon is present with several other burials in the mound and its possible explanation will be discussed in a latter section of this report.

Several outstanding artifacts were found with Burial 27 (Plate VI). In the right hand was a small copper celt (3 3/16 inches [81 mm.] long and 1 9/16 inches [40 mm.] wide at the bit). This celt was plano-convex in cross section with squared edges. A three-tubed copper panpipe, the best preserved one in the mound, was on the left chest area of this burial. Inside it were preserved several fragments of the reeds that had been encased in a sheet of copper. The front surface was indented between the tubes whereas the back was flat. In the back the two ends of the original sheet overlapped about ⅜ of an inch. Holes had been perforated in the two ends of the copper sheet just at the edge of the overlap. These holes were possibly used to tie the ends together and hold them in place. This panpipe was of exactly the same size as the one found with Burial 31. Since the only preserved portions of the tubes were those parts encased in copper, there is no way of determining how long the tubes were originally.

Under the left lower leg of this burial was a platform pipe made of soft stone. This pipe (4 23/32 inches or 120 mm. long, 1¼ inches or 31 mm. wide and 2⅛ inches or 54 mm. tall) had a flat platform and a bowl with an expanded base. It was very soft when found and warped out of shape due to the pressure of the earth.

Many beads were found with Burial 27—some (236) around the neck and some in the abdominal region (see Plate VII and Table II). Those around the neck appeared to be in three parallel lines and probably were a necklace or "choker". Those in the abdominal region indicated no particular pattern but may have been sewn to a garment. The beads were small globular and disc-shaped beads of cut shell (Plate VII, *b* and *c*). Other beads were found under the right wrist indicating that they may have been part of a bracelet (Fowler, 1957), pp. 19-21).

Burials 14 and 15 were found in Square 30 L 5. As in many other burials in this mound the foot bones were missing from these burials and the chest area was incomplete and deteriorated. On the chest of Burial 14 was a copper panpipe made up of four tubes. It was crushed by the weight of the soil upon it (see Plate IV, *c*). Fragments of reed and other materials from which the tubes had been made were found preserved in the copper tubes. Many beads were found in the neck area of Burial 14 and probably made up a necklace at one time. These beads were unusual for this mound; that is, they were disc-shaped with the hole drilled through the diameter of the disc. A mussel shell was found under the right lower arm bones of Burial 14, and in it were 10 globular beads of mussel shell (Fowler, 1957:28).

The placement of the panpipes on the chest area for the Klunk and Rutherford burials is regarded as supporting evidence that the copper-covered "sticks" on C°16-16 were panpipes. The difficulty of recognizing these panpipes is emphasized by the fact that when the first one was found at Cincinnati, a copper-covered three tube pipe, it was simply called a thin copper tube (Starr, 1960: 24), while the next one found at Marietta, Ohio, was thought to be part of a sword.

The Cincinnati panpipe was apparently not in a mound but in a grave near one as Sargent (1799: 177-78) wrote on Sept. 8, 1794:

> I have the pleasure, my dear Sir, to transmit you a drawing of some matters more extraordinary than have heretofore come under my observation, in all the researches into the antiquities of this country. The multiplicity of my avocations leaves not leisure for more than rough delineations; and you must be contented to receive them in this style. I possess all the originals, and intend by some safe conveyance presenting them to the Philosophical Society, should they believe them of importance enough for a deposit of my disposition to promote the purposes of their institution. The drawing, perhaps, is too imperfect to stand the test of criticism, and it might not be prudent to hazard it to their view. Your judgement, however, should govern. [The Philosophical Society received the articles.]
>
> It may be proper to add, that the body with which this collection was interred, was found lying in a nearly horizontal position, about five feet from the surface of the earth, with the head towards the setting sun, and at the S. W. side of, or about fifteen feet from an extensive artificial mound of earth, raised probably for

the purpose of a burial ground, upon the margin of the second bank of the Ohio River (suddenly rising fifty feet above the first) and now elevated, in the extreme, eight feet from the general level of the same, with a gradual slope in the various directions, and a base of about 120 feet by sixty. One of the main streets of the town passes through the Western part of this grave, and in the frequent repairs of the acclivity, human bones have often been found. You have, I think, been heretofore told by me, and perhaps received a sketch, of very extensive ancient fortifications at Cincinnati, not regular as those of Muskingum, but very worthy of notice. I should not omit to mention to you, that upon this mound are the stumps of oak-trees, seven feet diameter; and within seven feet, one of small size........ years of age. Many, in its vicinity, that might have been of more duration, are removed by the opening of this road, or street. In addition to the matters of which you have the drawing, were several utensils, or ornaments, lost or mislaid. If hereafter they come to my view, you shall receive information.

In the meantime, and always, believe me desirous of contributing to your amusement, and of promoting science all in my power.

Adieu,

W. Sargent

The finds with this burial include beside the panpipes, the artifacts illustrated in Plates 101 and 102. There were five plummets, a carved bird head, a large and a small pulley-type earspool, a small copper pendant and a carved bone. Identification of the material from which they were made was done by George Turner, who also made the mistake of saying they were from a mound (1802: 74-76). Plummet No. 1 was made of grey porphyry; No. 2 of jasper "marked with blood-coloured veins and spots on a green basis;" No. 3 of transparent rock crystal; No. 4 porphyry of mixed black and yellow; No. 5, a ferruginous stone and perhaps of volcanic origin. The fine bird head he identified as a rapacious bird and probably represented the beak of an eagle. The large earspool is cannel coal and the small one of clay.

The account of the Marietta find written by Dr. S. P. Hildreth and published by Atwater (1820: 168-78), describes copper and silver earspools, found on and near the skull, the three-tube panpipe was "near the side of the body" which could mean alongside the chest area (Pl. 103). These items have, of course, nothing to do with a sword or sword belt.

In removing the earth which composed an ancient mound in one of the streets of Marietta, on the margin of the plain, near the fortifications, several curious articles were discovered the latter part of June last. They appear to have been buried with the body of the person to whose memory this mound was erected.

Lying immediately over, or on the forehead of the body, were found three large circular bosses, or ornaments for a sword belt, or a buckler; they are composed of copper, overlaid with a thick plate of silver. The fronts of them are slightly convex, with a depression, like a cup, in the centre, and measure two inches and a quarter across the face of each. On the back side, opposite the depressed portion, is a copper rivet or nail, around which are two separate plates, by which they were fastened to the leather. Two small pieces of the leather were found lying between the plates of one of the bosses; they resemble the skin of an old mummy, and seem to have been preserved by the salts of the copper. The plates of copper are nearly reduced to an oxide, or rust. The silver looks quite black, but is not much corroded, and on rubbing, it becomes quite brilliant. Two of these are yet entire; the third one is so much wasted, that it dropped in pieces on removing it from the earth. Around the rivet of one of them is a small quantity of flax or hemp, in a tolerable state of preservation. Near the side of the body was found a plate of silver which appears to have been the upper part of a sword scabbard; it is six inches in length and two inches in breadth, and weighs one ounce; it has no ornaments or figures, but has three longitudinal ridges, which probably correspond with edges, or ridges, of the sword; it seems to have been fastened to the scabbard by three or four rivets, the holes of which yet remain in the silver.

Two or three broken pieces of a copper tube, were also found, filled with iron rust. These pieces, from their appearance, composed the lower end of the scabbard, near the point of the sword. No sign of the sword itself was discovered,

except the appearance of rust above mentioned.

Near the feet, was found a piece of copper, weighing three ounces. From its shape it appears to have been used as a plumb, or for an ornament, as near one of the ends is a circular crease, or groove, for tying a thread, it is round, two inches and a half in length one inch in diameter at the centre, and half an inch at each end. It is composed of small pieces of native copper, pounded together; and in the cracks between the pieces, are struck several pieces of silver; one nearly the size of a four penny piece, or half a dime. This copper ornament was covered with a coat of green rust, and is considerably corroded. A piece of red ochre, or paint, and a piece of iron ore, which has the appearance of having been partially vitrified or melted, were also found. The ore is about the specifick gravity of pure iron.

The body of the person here buried, was laid on the surface of the earth, with his face upwards, and his feet pointing to the northeast, and head to the southwest. From the appearance of several pieces of charcoal, and bits of partially burnt fossil coal, and the black colour of the earth, it would seem that the funeral obsequies had been celebrated by fire; and while the ashes were yet hot and smoking, a circle of thin flat stones had been laid around and over the body. The circular covering is about eight feet in diameter, and the stones yet look black, as if stained by fire and smoke. This circle of stones seems to have been the nucleus on which the mound was formed, as immediately over them is heaped the common earth of the adjacent plain, composed of a clayey sand and coarse gravel. This mound must originally have been about ten feet high, and thirty feet in diameter at its base. At the time of opening it, the height was six feet, and diameter between thirty and forty. It has every appearance of being as old as any in the neighbourhood, and was, at the first settlement of Marietta, covered with large trees, the remains of whose roots were yet apparent in digging away the earth. It also seems to have been made for this single personage, as the remains of one skeleton only were discovered. The bones were much decayed, and many of them crumbled to dust on exposure to the air. From the length of some of them, it is supposed the person was about six feet in height (Atwater, 1820: 168-78).

The Marietta and Cincinnati finds were forgotten for some time. Moorehead's final but incomplete statement on his 1891 excavations of the Hopewell group refers to a three-tube panpipe (Pl. 104,*c*; *d*).

There were several copper cylinders, one of which is shown in Fig. 22. These originally covered bone tubes. They were badly decayed, and all but the one shown were in fragments. Usually they appear to have been a union of three cylinders. Similar copper cylinders have been found by other explorers in the mounds (Moorehead, 1922: 128).

Shetrone reports a three-tube pan pipe four and three-eights inches long by one and five eights inches wide with Burial 1 in Mound 20, which was a cremated burial surrounded by rocks and which also had copper earspools. In Mound 25, Burial 12 as described by Shetrone was an adult burial within a log enclosure. "With this burial the skeleton of a medium sized adult in early middle life were found, at the neck, a large number of seed pearl beads; copper plates beneath the right shoulder and the knees; and a short copper tube, enclosing slender reeds, in the left hand" (Shetrone, 1926: 150). In discussing these objects, Shetrone wrote:

The present survey found, with Burial 12, of Mound 25, a copper specimen of this type consisting of a single tube. In the Hopewell material at the Field Museum there are fragmentary specimens having from two to four tubes. From the evidence it would appear that specimens of this type were not confined to the triple tube form but ranged from one to five or more tubes.

Specimens examined all appear to have contained tubes either of bone or reed, the interstices being filled with clay. The reverse sides are flat, over-lapped, and usually bear one or more holes for attachment or suspension. Their form suggests a flute-like musical instrument and the presence in some specimens of fibers, cane or reeds, is taken by some to indicate their use as torches; neither suggestion, however, appears to account satisfactorily for the purpose of the objects (Shetrone, 1926: 267).

There are no one-tube panpipes, for a one-tube wind instrument is not a panpipe. The Marietta specimen is not a five-tube but a three-tube instrument as the description, but not the illustration, demonstrates.

A check of the Field Museum collections did not provide specific evidence for the location at the Hopewell site of the specimen illustrated by Moorehead (1922) as Fig. 22. This is not the same specimen that was used for a reconstruction of panpipes for the Field Museum (Martin, Quimby and Collier, 1947: 277). It is the only specimen reported to have bone in the tubes and is probably from Mound 25. Moorehead illustrated a three-tube panpipe said to have had bone tubes, while the reproduction is based on specimen catalog no. 56708 which is a four-tube pipe. Some of the other specimens that Shetrone reported were in the Field Museum may be ones described below. From Mound 25, Field Museum catalog no. 56588, are two fragments of copper tubing almost certainly a panpipe. From altar 1 in section 3 in Moorehead's excavation came catalog no. 56588 which is described as "Four fragments of copper cylinder covered with meteoric iron." It is identified as a copper panpipe band and a later entry states that it was exchanged with Mexico. "Three 5 inch long reeds badly crushed, originally covered with copper" is the wording for catalog no. 56093. This number is tied into the following statement in the catalog. "Ten skeletons were found in cut no. 2, *without objects or ornaments*. They lay upon the base line in the same end of the trench with (Burial) no. 248 and are shown on diagram of Cresson's drawings. All were extremely decayed and none of them could be preserved." The person who underlined "*without object or ornaments*" had drawn a line to catalog no. 56087, and wrote "eight perforated bear claws; 56088, six stone copper covered buttons; 56089, two canine jaws cut; 56093; 56094, pieces of bark." This would suggest that this panpipe was associated with Burials 249-259 along the east side of the mound according to Moorehead.

For catalog no. 56218, from the Mound 25 copper deposit, the catalog says it is a "thin semi-tubular straight copper object with rivet hole at top" that is presumed in this paper to be a panpipe. Also from the copper deposit under entry no. 56237 there is listed "Six Pieces of cane about 5¼ inches long", which are presumed to be from panpipes. There would probably have been two of them. There are fragments of what are presumably panpipes with a catalog no. 56593 identified as "Md. 17, a few fragments of thin curved copper objects." A great many of the copper objects buried at the Hopewell site were in cremation ceremonies and suffered considerable damage. These objects also inevitably suffered from the excavation techniques and subsequent museum attrition. It is a reasonable assumption that the nine or so specimens identified at the Hopewell site are not the total number actually buried there.

Dr. Olaf Prufer recorded in his unpublished and non-microfilmed Harvard doctoral thesis that a four-tube panpipe of copper with silver overlay was found at the Esch Mound in Erie County, Ohio, but Greenman (personal communication) has called it a three-tube pipe; a copper three-tube panpipe was found at the Hopewell Ater Mound, Franklin County, Ohio, and a three-tube copper form at the Harness Site in Ross County, Ohio.

One of the most recent panpipes from Ohio was published by W. H. Magrath from the North Benton Mound near Akron in the Muskingum River Valley. Burial No. 11 was an elderly man extended east-west with head to the east within a stone enclosure some eleven feet long and six feet in width and 18 inches in thickness around the skeleton and with a stone capping.

> Among the remains of the fingers of the right hand, resting on the chest and surrounded by a mass of bright red paint, was a conjoined tube, consisting of three parallel cane tubes encased in a copper jacket. The whole is 6 inches long

and two inches wide, the individual canes having an interior diameter of 5/8 inch. One side of the copper jacket is corrugated, conforming to the shape of the canes, the other is flat, with the copper overlapping in the middle. Inspection of the interior of the tubes revealed that plugs, probably of leather, had been placed inside at varying distances from the ends to produce three closed columns of air of graduated lengths. Probably this instrument was a panpipe (Magrath, 1945: 43-44).

A conjoined tube of meteoric iron came from the Turner site near Cincinnati where it was in the altar of Mound 3 which also produced the clay perforated pulley-type earspools. Willoughby says of the find and others he had available for comparative purposes:

> The best preserved object of this metal is made of a thin sheet about 3½ inches square, bent into the shape shown in figure 21. One side is corrugated, and the other flat. A number of similar specimens have been taken from the mounds of this culture group, made of silver, copper, and meteoric iron. The one of silver, found by Dr. Hildreth in a mound at Marietta and mistaken for a part of an European sword scabbard, is the most noted of these. There is a well-preserved example in the Museum from central Tennessee, from a mound belonging to this culture. It was accompanied by a copper adze blade, spool-shaped ear-ornaments, and mica plates, This Tennessee specimen had originally surrounded what appears to have been three tubes of cane or reed, fragments of which have been preserved by copper salts. It is probable that each of the specimens above mentioned served to bind together three similar tubes. These tubes must have been usually about ½ inch in diameter; but in one example in the Museum, a silver band from a mound at Grand Rapids, a northern outpost of this culture, the tubes were probably about the size of an ordinary lead pencil. Perhaps the tubes may have been whistles of different notes joined together into a single instrument (Willoughby and Hooton, 1922: 50-51).

Willoughby's reference to the Grand Rapids specimen is from Converse Mound 2 excavated by W. L. Coffinberry. There is no evidence available of the placement of this Michigan specimen with a burial or its relationship to other items in the mound which only included Goodall Hopewell material. Another panpipe of silver, apparently a three-tube specimen, came from this mound, according to James E. Fitting who examined the collection in 1969. The pottery vessel from this mound is a western Michigan example of Baehr Zoned Plain Rocker Stamp (Quimby, 1941: 145). Recently a three-tube copper panpipe was found in Mallon Mound F in the Muskegon River Valley by Earl Prahl who will furnish a detailed description in his forthcoming thesis (Pl. 105). This panpipe had reeds on the interior but they definitely did not have anything except sand in them for they were first X-rayed and then the sand was removed with great care. A "probable" panpipe was found in the Franz-Green Mound in Porter County, Indiana according to the information provided McAllister (1932) by Amos Green. This panpipe is not identified on the map showing the distribution.

The first record of panpipes in the Trempealeau variant of Hopewellian was obtained by W. C. McKern in Schwert Mound 12 in Trempealeau County, Wisconsin. In contrast to some other panpipe associations this one was one of the few recovered specimens placed with the burials. Other mounds in the Trempealeau Lakes area had a considerable amount of the classic grave goods of the Hopewellian climax period. The tubes were 10.5 cm., or four and one-quarter inches long with three reeds.

> The single inclusive feature of importance in the mound was a compound burial placed in the center of the mound floor, covering a rectilinear area 17 feet in length and 13.5 feet in width, with the major axis extending west 26° north. At least thirty-one individuals had been interred here, of which eighteen were represented by reburials of bundled disarticulated bones. The remaining thirteen individuals were extended in the flesh in a prone position. Of these, the heads of six were directed to the northwest, five to the southwest,

and two to the southeast. With the exception of one half-grown child, all were adults. Two male skulls supplied the only positive data on sex.

A relatively large bundle reburial was so situated, with the bones cascading down to the burial floor from an originally higher placement, as to suggest interment after the mound was partly erected and a subsequent displacement due to settling. The result was to confuse some of these bones with those of the floor burial.

All skeletal parts were in a highly advanced state of decomposition, and it is quite possible that more than thirty-one individuals had originally been placed in the grave.

A roughly shaped disc, or scraper-knife, chipped from chalcedony, was found near the southwestern corner of the burial floor, not directly associated with any surviving skeletal parts. This specimen is 19 cms. in length and 10.2 cm. in maximum width.

At a point on the burial floor three feet northeast of the stone implement, one foot removed from the head of an extended individual, was the remains of either one sheet-copper sleeve made to represent three conjoined copper tubes, enveloping sections of reeds which were partly preserved through contact with the copper, or of two sleeves, one made to represent two conjointed tubes, and the other, a single tube. The question involved originates in the poor state of preservation of the thin, highly disintegrated copper (McKern, 1931: 260-61).

During the 1966 excavating season Dr. Joan E. Freeman of the State Historical Society of Wisconsin recovered two copper panpipes from the same mound group. In a letter of September 30, 1966, she said,

We got two panpipes from the 1966 Trempealeau or Schwert mound excavations. Both are of copper, three tubes with something inside of them which I have not yet taken to the Forest Products lab for identification. There are no stops in the tubes.

One pipe came from Mound 25 (we used McKern's numbering system for the mounds so you can locate them on his maps), from the subfloor burial pit but not in association with any of the bundle reburials. None of the artifacts in this mound were with burials, instead they apparently were just placed in the pit. The second pipe was from the subfloor pit in Mound 4. This pipe lay next to an extended burial along with three large bifacially flaked blades and a grit tempered bowl.

The most northern and also one of the most startling panpipe finds was at the LeVesconte mound excavated by Walter Kenyon for the Royal Ontario Museum. Within a small mound there was a considerable number of burials of various positions in subfloor pits and at various levels within the mound. In the mound were four copper and five silver panpipe covers (Ritchie, 1965: 217-18). An article in the New York Times, sent from Toronto and prepared by Canadian Press, said that "Museum minerologists have identified the unsmelted silver, along with a small piece of cobalt mineral, as coming from the northern Ontario mining area of Cobalt, about 250 miles distant. Mr. Kenyon says, "This find on the Trent River south of Campbellford is a Point Peninsula site with some items indicating its temporal association with Hopewells to the south." One of the copper pipes is five and one-quarter inches long by one and one-half wide. The three reeds were tied with cord to keep them in place. There is no indication of plugs (Pls. 106, 107).

The copper panpipe from Tennessee is from the Glass farm at Franklin, Tennessee. According to Putnam:

In 1879, Mr. Curtis opened a mound on the farm of Mr. F. S. Glass, in Franklin, Tennessee, which was twenty-one feet high and of a similar character to the one just referred to in Ohio, inasmuch as the deposit of human bones found in it were the remains of a body which had been cremated, and this mound was also remarkable for the several copper objects which it contained. Eight feet from the top of the mound were the burnt human bones, principally fragments of the cranium, with which were found the spool-shaped objects described farther on, and two small shell beads. Near the bottom of the mound, in the center, was a large piece of mica, and six inches under the mica, in a bed of ashes, were the copper axe described under No. 18314, and the copper band represented of full size by the two views in fig. 16. Just under the ashes, at the very bottom

> of the mound, was a small cavity covered by a stone, in which was a small amount of red oxide of iron and a large piece of mica. At various depths in the mound, there were found a bone implement, a large crystal of galena, a piece of burnt limestone, a small mass of burnt clay, and a number of animal bones which were not burnt.
>
> The copper band is four and one-half inches long and a little over one and a half inches wide. It is very brittle and at both ends on the grooved side the copper has turned to a green carbonate and is considerably decomposed. This band was probably made from thin sheets of native copper which were pounded together, and in some places two layers of copper can be traced by the laminations, although its thickness is not more than double that of good letter paper. The sheet of copper thus prepared was a square of four and one-half inches. Two deep grooves were then made parallel to each other, and extending the whole length of the piece, leaving a central raised portion about a quarter of an inch wide, between them as seen in Fig. 16, b.
>
> The band seems then to have been folded over a piece of wood half an inch in thickness, to which it was secured, as indicated by four holes at the corners where the band overlaps, on the surface opposite the grooves, as shown in figure 16, a. Portions of the wood are still preserved within the band.
>
> Of course it is impossible to determine the exact use of which such an object as this was put, but it seems probable that it was an ornament of some kind, and it is not unlikely that it was attached to a belt of some other part of the dress of the owner (Putnam, 1882: 106-07).

The copper earspools with the cremated remains had a vegetable fiber cord wrapped around the copper cylinder connecting inner and outer symbols and this in turn was covered by a buckskin thong. On one of the spools the thong ended in a loop as if for suspension. The earspools were probably not worn by the individual when the cremation took place. The copper axe was one-quarter inch thick in the center and one-eight inch thick at the belt. It was 23 inches long and had a bit two and one-quarter inches wide. The description certifies that it was a celt and not an adze.

An earlier excavation by Dr. W. M. Clark of Franklin, Tennessee had been made in this mound group and the published report may well have stimulated F. W. Putnam to send Curtis to dig there. There were three small mounds and the large mound in this group in which both Clark and Curtis found most of the materials they recovered. Clark found a copper earspool in the lower part of the mound. The other copper object was a most unusual find.

> No. 1 is a face or mask, and is composed of four pieces. The main pieces are beaten together in the center by some instrument of stone, the mark of the blows being distinctly visible. One piece is riveted on each side to represent ears, and the rivets are exceedingly well put in and firmly united. It is oval in shape, 6 inches long and 4 inches wide, being about as large as the average face of a man. By aid of a sharp tool small dots were made to trace the location of the eyes, eyebrows, nose, and mouth, and a horizontal line beneath the nose shows the place of the nosestick, which has a pendant on either end, with a bead or other ornament resting on the cheek. At its lower edge, below the chin, are three rivet-holes, by which it was possibly fastened to a wooden or stone body, and then raised upon the altar, with its burnished surface glittering in the sun, an object of pride and admiration to the assembled nation. One side of this mask is eroded, and the whole is heavily coated with the oxide of copper (Clark, 1878: 272).

In a recent publication Griffin (1965: 139) discussed the find of obsidian and mica by Joseph Jones and expressed the hope that it had been found by him on the Glass farm. Clark mentions in his report that on two small mounds he examined he found a three-pound piece of galena and a copper earspool with 18 inches of flax thread around the central cylinder, associated with an elderly adult male whose teeth had all been lost. In the other mound he found nothing "it having been previously opened and examined by Dr. Joseph Jones of New Orleans." The Glass farm is one of the very few sites in Tennessee that have an association with the Hopewellian artifacts. It would seem to be important to try and locate the village area and identify the industrial complex and other features of the society who buried their dead in the Glass Mounds. Where is the remarkable mask?

The excavations at the Mandeville Site in Clay County, Georgia, on the lower Chattahootchie provides an example of a society participating in the Hopewellian cultural developments while retaining a strong local flavor of the late Deptford to Early Swift Creek complexes. Besides the female figurine discussed in the section on Knight Mound 8 there are lamellar flake blades of Flint Ridge origin, thin bi-cymbal earspools with one having an overlay of meteoric iron, copper beads, a steatite and a clay plain platform pipe and five copper panpipes that were, perhaps, hijacked on their way to Florida.

Artifacts from the gravel layer at the base of the intrusions into the primary mound included sherds, a bi-cymbal spool and three conjoined tubes. The latter, like others from Mound B, were constructed by enclosing either three or four cane tubes in a copper sheet. Heavy cordage was used in at least one instance to pack the cane more securely in its metal enclosure. One of the above was covered with silver foil in addition to the copper. An interesting observation for our examples is that the four tube variety seems to be smaller than those with three tubes.

Contained in the previously mentioned large rectangular pit on the south side of the mound [B] was another copper-covered pan pipe, tube number indeterminable, a broken pottery vessel, and a clay platform pipe. The pot was crushed and friable, but it seems to be nearly complete. It has a slight flared orifice, small tetrapodal supports, and although generally plain, exhibits some irregularly spaced simple stamping. The pipe is short and stubby and not one of the better examples of its type. . . .

On the east side with the three burials was a fifth pan pipe and a possible conch shell container. Only a fragment of the shell remained, but the cleavage plane resulting from the deterioration of the material suggested the artifact. The midfacial area of one of the isolated skulls had been stained with copper, but the artifact was completely oxidized (Kellar, Kelly and McMichael, 1962: 351-52).

The authors of the Mandeville report felt that the origin of the copper earspools, panpipes, the use of meteoric iron and silver, and platform pipes "though of infrequent occurrence are so widespread as to mask the immediate points and direction of contact" (*op. cit.*: 353). This is a good conservative position to adopt but in their case was strongly influenced by the misconception that the origin for eastern United States panpipes was Mexico.

A series of radiocarbon dates from the Mandeville site was processed at the University of Michigan Radiocarbon Laboratory (Crane and Griffin, 1962: 190; 1964: 9). These are pertinent to the time period of the panpipes which are assigned by Kellar, Kelley and McMichael to Phase III of the Mandeville site in their report to the National Park Service. Phase III materials apparently are in both their Mandeville I and II occupations. They believe that several centuries of Woodland development are present in Mounds A and B. M-1042 has a radiocarbon date of 1960 ± 75 B.P. and is from the premound village Late Deptford assemblage under Mound A. M-1044 has a date of 1420 ± 75 B.P, and is from Layer 3 of Mound A which is called Swift Creek or Mandeville II. M-1045 is 1460 ± 75 B.P, from layer 4 of Mound A and is also called Swift Creek or Mandeville II. Another date from the peripheral lenses of Mound A, M-1043 at 1030±75, probably pertains to Mississippian occupation. The only date from Mound B, which contained the panpipes, is from a redeposited cremated burial of an adolescent in Feature 5. This feature in their Park Service report is regarded as Phase IV at a somewhat later time than Phase III. The date of M-1215A is 1530 ± 120.

There is then no definite association of radiocarbon charcoal with the panpipes.

The Mandeville I and II dates range from roughly A.D. 1, plus or minus 75 radiocarbon years, to just over A.D. 400 plus or minus 120 years so that we are left with the unfortunately imprecise statement that panpipes at Mandeville were deposited sometime during the first half of the first millennium of what is called in some circles "our era."

One of the most commonly referred to traits which connected the Florida Middle Woodland sites to northern Hopewell are the panpipes found by Moore at the Crystal River site on the central Florida west coast along with other items which indicated strong ties to the Ohio center. Unfortunately Moore's excavation technique and reporting leave something to be desired and there is no data as to the connection of the two panpipes at Crystal River with a burial or other items. "An ornament of fluted sheet-copper, badly broken, came from this mound (Fig. 61). This pattern was a popular one among the aborigines. We have met with it at least twice before, once at Apalachicola and once in the fine mound on Murphy Island, Fla." (Moore, 1903: 412). Part of a second panpipe was also found at Crystal River. The Apalachicola site is at Pierce Mound A, where "also in caved sand, a fragment of sheet copper with fluted decorations, badly carbonated was found" Moore, 1902: 225).

This mound and village is regarded as having a definite Hopewellian level. There is difficulty in the assignment of a relatively short time period to the panpipe in Florida or for that matter of being able to clearly segregate the Hopewellian material in Florida into temporal divisions by sites as Sears has done (Sears, 1962). From the vessels illustrated by Moore, Griffin has had the opinion that most of the illustrated or described materials from Pierce Mound A would be transitional between Santa Rosa-Swift Creek and Weeden Island and this would mean that the panpipe was probably deposited about A.D. 300 to 400. Sears, in commenting on copper panpipes, says that C. B. Moore's notes referred to a "badly carbonated fragment of copper from Yent in his field notes. If this is the specimen catalogued only as Franklin County in the R. S. Peabody Foundation for American Archaeology (No. 39524), it is another panpipe" (Sears, 1962: 6). Moore referred to the specimen from Pierce Mound A as "badly carbonated" and it is also in Franklin County, Florida. It was found loose in the sand by Moore's excavators. Moore could certainly have used the same terminology for a specimen at Yent. Where is the one from Pierce Mound A?

On the St. Johns River, ten miles south of Palatka in Putnam County, Moore's men demolished a twelve-foot-high mound on Murphy's Island in four and one-half days. On the floor of the mound,

> . . . each with a separate interment were: (1) fragmentary remains of an ornament of wood overlain with very thin sheet copper. One side is flat, the other respousse. The breadth is 2.2 inches, its original length is undetermineable. With it was a large sheet of mica. (2) An ornament of sheet copper, bent over and repousse as shown in Fig. 59 [the panpipe]. A part of one side is missing through corrosion. At one end of the broken side are two perforations. Length, about 7 inches; width about 2 inches. (3) An ornament of thin sheet copper apparently at one time coating a tube of some long-fibered substance like cane. It was recovered in several fragments, but probably when entire had a length of about 8 inches, with a slightly irregular diameter averaging 1.5 inches. (4) A fine specimen of sheet copper, entirely unbroken, and not materially affected by corrosion, representing the crescent moon. Distance between horns, 10.3 inches; maximum width, 1.7 inches; thickness, .04 of one inch. About one-half inch from the central part of the convex margin of the body, 1.7 inches apart, are two perforations by the aid of which this ornament, in early times doubtless highly polished, could be fastened to the chest or suspended from the neck, the horns pointing down (Fig. 60).

> Toward the center, in the eastern portion of the mound, 12 feet from the surface, with human remains, together, associated with a pendant of shell, were: (1) apparently a number of separate discs, each about 1.8 inches in diameter, of sheet copper firmly cemented together through corrosion and too greatly carbonated to permit any successful attempt at separation. (2) A disc of sheet copper, centrally concavo-convex, about 2 inches in diameter. (3) A much corroded object of sheet copper apparently of the sort known as spool-shaped, supposed by some to have served as an ear-plug, by others, as a button or stud for garments. Similar objects have frequently been figured as coming from Ohio mounds and elsewhere. Diameter of upper and lower portions, about 1.8 inches. (4) An ornament of sheet copper consisting of a disc centrally perforated and symmetrically bent and repousse, as shown in Fig. 61, with section [the second panpipe]. Maximum diameter, about 2.1 inches.
>
> Loose in caved sand was a small disc 1 inch in diameter. Within its slight concavity lay remains of wood (Moore, 1896: 507-09).
>
> Twelve feet from the surface, toward the central portion of the mound, in association with human remains was taken out, in our immediate presence, an object resembling the lower portion of a small nail (Fig. 70). Its length is .8 of one inch. It is affected by the magnet, and is therefore iron or steel or iron ore.
>
> It may be well to explain to the general reader that the aborigines were unable to reduce iron from its ores, and that this metal, in a native state, if it exists at all on this earth, is of extreme rarity, and that the only iron in aboriginal use in pre-Columbian times was that obtained from meteorites, as is shown by the high percentage of nickel present when analytically tested. There is no reason why the aborigines of Florida should not have been possessed of some small piercing implements of meteoric iron. Unfortunately, the original material of this specimen cannot be determined by analysis, as it weighs but 215 milligrams and is corroded through and through (Moore, 1896: 514).

The panpipes, copper crescent, copper covered reed tube, copper earspools, and a meteoric iron awl are indicative of the intrusion of this metal complex into a society with very little other indication of Hopewellian characteristics. It was the presence of these highly specific Hopewellian forms that led J. B. Griffin in the late 1930's and early 1940's (Griffin, 1946), to separate a Racy Point period, now called St. Johns *Ia* Early, and a Murphy Island period, now called St. Johns *Ia* Late (Goggin, 1952: 40; 49-50). Sound dating for this complex or complexes in Florida is still somewhat conjectural. The panpipe from Murphys Island is the largest one known.

In the Blakeley shell midden in Baldwin County, Alabama, of northeastern Mobile Bay, Moore's men obtained a copper panpipe.

> In one hole, not far from the surface were parts of four skulls, and other scattered bones. At a depth of 16 inches was a circular deposit of fragments of cremated, human bones, 10 inches in diameter, 4 inches deep. No sign of fire marked the immediate vicinity of this deposit. Just above the bones lay a tool with blunt point, made from an antler of a deer, showing no mark of fire. Thirty-two inches from the cremated remains, in the same hole, at about the same level, was a mass of fragments of calcined shell, including, however, a number of shells showing no trace of fire. No charcoal was present with this deposit. About 1 foot below a skeleton which lay near the cremated remains, was another skeleton, flexed on the left side. One hand resting on the neck was in contact with an ornament of sheet-copper that had imparted a green color to some of the bones of the hand and to at least one of the cervical vertebrae. This ornament, 3 inches long by 1.5 inches wide, is corrugated on one side and belongs to a type common to the mound at Crystal river, northwest Florida; the larger mound at Murphy Island, St. Johns river, Florida, and other localities. With the copper lay two mussel shells. One (*Lampsilis anodontoides*) shows a perforation at one end; the other was broken to fragments in digging. Near the skull of the skeleton on which was the copper ornament lay an isolated calvarium (Moore, 1905: 284-85).

The other recorded copper panpipe in Alabama is from one of the mounds in the "Mounds near Jackson," Clarke County, in the Lower Tombigbee drainage. In the central area of a mound only two feet high was a number of burials. "Presumably having been with a skeleton which had decayed away was an ornament of sheet copper (Fig. 10)," (Moore, 1905: 259). Moore then says that it was similar to the one from Blakeley and the other places he mentioned above. This mound group is a part of what could be called the Porter Hopewellian complex located midway between the Santa Rosa-Swift Creek sites to the east and the Marksville-Troyville sites in the Lower Mississippi Valley.

There are two records of panpipes in Mississippi. The first is from the McRae Mound in Lauderdale County, Mississippi which was excavated by Henry B. Collins. "Within this small inner mound or clay dome was found a rectangular ornament of sheet copper and silver enclosing a core of wood, shown *in situ* in figure 93. Both copper and silver are shown by analysis to be native American, probably from the Lake Superior region. Silver and copper ornaments practically identical to this have been found in small numbers in Florida, Tennessee, Ohio and Michigan" (Collins, 1926: 92). The illustration looks like the panpipe was five to six inches in length. J. B. Griffin examined the pottery from this mound and concluded that it belonged to an Early Baytown or Middle Woodland level (Phillips, Ford and Griffin, 1951: 438-39). Subsequent examination of the lamellar blades in 1966 in the National Museum suggests that the bluish gray, white and mottled white specimens look like the Illinois Valley and southwestern Illinois material and that they are not from Ohio.

The second find of panpipes in Mississippi is from Panola County on the south side of the Little Tallahatchie River near Batesville. A brief report on the excavation of the McCarter Mound appeared (Johnson, 1969) and subsequent correspondence from Glen Johnson has also been helpful. This is one of the shorter forms of about three inches in length.

Burial #3 consisted of three adults. This burial was located in the north-west corner of the mound and represents an earlier (or first) stage of the mound construction. These burials were in such poor condition that in two cases all that remained was the enamel caps of the teeth. An outline of the skull and jaw could be traced in the remaining one. From dark casts, or "shadows" in the soil, we could determine that the burials were oriented south to north and were extended.

Of particular interest with this burial group was the sheet copper covering of a three tube pan pipe which was found in the chest region of burial #3-C. There is no evidence at the moment to indicate the type of material the copper had originally covered; however, it is clear that the tubes were small. The copper was indented between the tubes on the top side and appears to be flat on the bottom side.

The pottery which was recovered includes a small plain cup, a medium size bowl, and fragments of several other vessels. All seem to fall in the Tunica phase and the bowl and part of another vessel have been classed as Twin Lakes Punctate and Crowder Punctate (Johnson, 1969).

The ceramic complex is similar to that from the Tallahatchie-Coldwater area of the eastern Delta for the Tchula to Early Baytown period. This distinctive ceramic and cultural assemblage is both more complex and has a different time span than was conceived by its publishers (Phillips, Ford and Griffin, 1951: 432-37). In the photographs sent by Johnson to Griffin in March, 1969, there are five rim sherds of what might have been one vessel with a decoration of at least five horizontal rows of what appear to be punctates. They are very similar to ones from the Crooks site (Ford and Willey, 1940: Fig. 20, *j*, *k*.) identified as "unusual sherds of the Marksville occupation." The Crooks site example "is covered with impressions made with a small stick wrapped with cords. A close examination reveals the twist of the cords. The stick was applied horizontally and the impressions are very close together" (*ibid*: 88). A temporal placement for this specimen should be close to that of the Helena site to be discussed below which would probably be about A.D. 100 with an unknown plus or minus factor. The radiocarbon dates obtained from the Helena site certainly do not have the consistency or short time span that the archaeological complex indicates.

An important panpipe was found in the southern extension of some of the Illinois Hopewell burial practices at Helena, Arkansas. In tomb A, Mound C there was a small rectangular subfloor pit containing an extended individual of about 13 to 15 years old identified as probably female. It was oriented southwest to northeast with the head to the southeast. A *Busycon* shell dipper was placed in the southwest corner of the pit. Around the neck were 45 or more fresh-water pearl beads. Around both upper arms were shell bead armlets 7 cm. wide and similar sets were around each wrist. Each band had enough beads to make a strand 30 inches long. A few of the upper beads were pearls and about seven inches of each wrist strand were pearls. Around the lower waist was a belt composed of doughnut shaped shell beads and the lower jaw canine teeth of eight red wolves. Held in each hand of this burial was a bi-cymbal copper earspool. This individual burial has a remarkable similarity to finds in the Illinois Valley area from the standpoint of specific items, and their placement is strikingly like that of the decoration shown on the female figurines from Mound C°8. In addition the panpipes follow a pattern of chest placement known from Illinois and other areas where the burial or excavation procedure would allow it.

A set of copper-jacketed panpipes (Find 108: Fig. 10) lay on the sternum of Burial 61. The copper jacket was badly corroded and quite fragile. It is 20.7 cm. long and 5.5 cm. wide and was made to hold three cane tubes approximately 1.3 cm. in diameter, side by side. On the side that may be referred to as the front of the instrument, the copper was bent into flutings to conform to the curves of the three cane tubes. The jacket is flat on the reverse where the edges of the copper sheet were brought together and held by two cord ties that passed through holes in the sheet.

At the mouthpiece end only, on the front side of the instrument, the copper has been coated with a thin sheet of silver for a distance of 3.2 cm. from the end. The method of attachment of the silver to the copper is not clear. David M. Seaman of the Department of Mineralogy of the American Museum suggests that the Indians may have taken advantage of what are termed "half-breed crystals". These curious crystal growths are composed for a foot or more of copper crystals, then abruptly the crystals are silver for additional inches of the formation. Examples of these formations are found in the Lake Superior area. The cane tubes have been preserved by copper oxide. They run the full length of the copper jacket and apparently did not extend beyond. When the instrument is viewed as shown in Fig. 10b, the three tubes can be described as left, center, and right, The left-hand cane tube was wrapped for part of its length near the center with twisted bast fiber string. Two layers of vegetable material, possibly the inner bark of a tree, has been wound over this in strips 3 mm. wide. This wrapping perhaps helped to secure the cane tube in the copper covering.

Usually in the making of panpipes of cane or bamboo, the septum that closes the tube at each joint is utilized to control the length of the tube, but such is not the case with this instrument. The three cane tubes run the full length of the copper jacket, and no joints are visible. The right-hand tube has been plugged with a small stick for 11.5 cm. of its length, leaving an open tube 9.2 cm. long. The plug is a small twig of a variety of wood that has a pith center. It is about 3 mm. in diameter, wrapped with a two-ply yarn which, in turn, is covered with a wrapping of ribbon-like strips about 3 mm. wide, probably the inner bark of some tree. (The string wrappings used in these panpipes are described by Junius Bird as "Two-ply yarn with Z spinning twist and S doubling twist." The string is made of a bast fiber that cannot be identified with certainty.)

No plug is visible in the central tube. A wooden plug in the left-hand tube extends to within 4.5 cm. of the end of the tube. Evidently this was the high-note side of the panpipe.

Adhering to the upper side of the instrument, as it lay on the chest of Burial 61, are fragments of bast—fiber—twined cloth preserved by the copper salts (Ford, 1963: 16-17).

Ford's identification of the panpipes as

having two stops in the outside cane tubes is paralleled by that of Magrath from the North Benton, Ohio mound. Either because of the preservation problem, or because the plugs were not there, no other examples have been reported. The actual length of the reported cane, bone or wood tubes when placed with burials is not known, so that they may have projected evenly or were graduated in length above and below the copper sheathing. The most popular term for them is certainly panpipes but this identification is not a certainty. It is difficult to understand if they were musical instruments, that they did not continue in use up to the European colonization in the southeast and Mississippi Valley. A search of the literature has not produced a record of panpipes in North American (Roberts, 1936) or in Middle American ethnographic accounts but there are a few reported from prehistoric Mexican sources. Panpipes are known from the Peruvian area to tropical eastern South America and spread from there into the Caribbean. The prehistoric specimen from Mexico which intrigued McMichael, 1964: 129) is from Tres Zapotes in southern Vera Cruz. It is of baked clay and the item as shown (Weiant, 1943: Pl. 53, 13) had a four-tube appearance but the piece is not complete. It was identified as a panpipe by Dr. George Herzog who identified the various musical instruments at the site for Weiant. The panpipe is said to be of the yellow and pink wares associated with the upper Tres Zapotes surface burials. This is an interesting category but is not too helpful in placing the unique panpipe, if it is, with relation to anything else. Illustrations of pottery with "surface burials" cover some range of time with most of them in post-Classic times.

The companion volume on Tres Zapotes by Drucker says that figurines were attached to panpipes and that "Several fragments of panpipes—small clay tubes of various lengths joined side by side—have been found. Their upper ends are open, and meant to be blown across. Clay panpipes have not been reported elsewhere in Mexico, although Beyer (1920: 182ff.) has pointed out their probable occurance, as indicated by a figurine (from southwest Mexico?; Drucker, 1943: 88). Drucker associated the panpipes with his Upper phase which represented a strong intrusion of new elements. A recent summary of Vera Cruz and Tabasco archaeology associates the panpipes with strong Mayoid influences of the Late Classic period (Coe, 1965: 705). If this temporal placement is correct, then the hypothesis of a known Mexican source for Hopewellian panpipes is an impossibility.

The clay panpipe fragment illustrated by Weiant is very similar to one of pottery from Nasca, Peru (Isikowitz, 1935: 380). The only comprehensive review of panpipes is by Isikowitz who describes the considerable variety of forms and other features. He regards them as being limited to South America in this hemisphere and favors the idea that they developed there and were not introduced by Australoids from Melanesia, or from the Mediterranean. He found no record of them in the West Indies.

The best way to have provided a different pitch for the tubes would have been to have reeds of different length from the upper opening to the septum rather than having plugs in the tube to vary the sound produced by blowing across the open ends.

Whatever function the conjoined tubes had, it is clear that they were of some importance in Middle Woodland societies over a large area (Map 2). They are not found at the great majority of Hopewellian sites but when found they are normally with individuals of obvious importance and often placed in the chest area or in the hand so that they were in a handy location if they were to be blown by the person buried.

Perhaps the instrument most similar to the panpipe would be the flute or flageolet which was broadly distributed in the United States. From the Plains to the East coast area this multiple-hole wind instrument was commonly made of cedar. Over most of the eastern part of the United States the flute was not normally used for ceremonies or dances but was used for courting. The most extensive description of the use of the flageolet is by Speck in his study of the Yuchi.

> This type of flute is one that is found widely distributed over the continent. Here as elsewhere it is employed by men as an important aid in influencing the emotions of the opposite sex. Very plaintive and touching strains are produced on the flute. They seem to have a deep effect upon the Indians, often moving the hearers to tears. Young men intentionally play these tunes to arouse the emotions of young girls, and the players themselves appear to be as much affected as anyone. The owner of a flute keeps his instrument wrapped up in a package and treats it with extreme care. It was formerly put to another use sometimes. When the people were traveling from a distance towards the town square to attend ceremonies there, the flute was often made to give forth a few measures of music as a sort of traveling song. When passing isolated farms or settlements on the route the flute was also played to signal the presence of the travellers and to call the hearers to join them on their journey to the town square.
>
> One of the tunes played on the flute as a love song was recorded on the phonograph and a transcription of it is offered below. The man who gave this tune exclaimed something like the following when he had finished: "Oh, if some girls were only here! When they hear that they cry and then you can fondle them. It makes them feel lonesome. I wish some were here now. I feel badly myself (Speck, 1909: 62).

One of the early burials in Knight Mound C°16 was probably the extended adult male number 16 placed in the subfloor pit. This individual had more grave goods with him than any of the other Knight Mound burials. The distribution studies of the flat shell beads, the panpipes and of the thin copper earspools suggest that this burial was probably interred during the Pike phase. Because of the large number of copper earspools in Ohio Hopewell, particularly at the Hopewell site itself it is probable, but by no means certain, that the earspools were obtained by some mechanism similar to the gift exchange known from the early historic period. The small copper pendant on the other hand probably did not come out of Ohio. The panpipe is somewhat more difficult although the easiest interpretation would be to suggest that it was made by the copper craftsmen in Ohio who produced such a wide variety of copper forms. The LeVesconte site in Ontario, with its nine panpipes briefly discussed above, does not support such a conclusion. The Ohio made pipe was perhaps enclosed in a "medicine" bundle at the right elbow.

The burial group C°16-4-7, had a number of grave associations of which the Havana Zoned Dentate jar C°16-5 is, perhaps, the most interesting. According to the ceramic typology which is followed in this paper, this vessel would be regarded as a perfect example of the early Havana ceramic tradition and would on that basis be regarded as probably belonging to no later than the Bedford phase proposed in the Introduction and perhaps even to the Calhoun phase. Irrespective of when the vessel was made it would not seem to be earlier than burial number 16 and it is associated in this mound with the ovoid knife and shell beads with child burial number 6. Unfortunately they are not particularly helpful chronologically. Burial number 8 with the perforated bone pulley type earspools was interred subsequent to number 16 and probably somewhat later than numbers 4 to 7. Such earspools seem to be associated with the Pike phase rather than with the Bedford phase.

Most of the burials in this mound seem to belong to the Pike phase and to a relatively restricted time period. This is somewhat unusual at the Knight Group. The excavations of Perino at the Klunk Group and his earlier excavations at the Bedford Group have helped to emphasize that archaeologists can no longer regard the material from such groups as representing the short time burial procedures and concepts of a single society, but must instead attempt the recognition of the varied burial practices and associated offerings as these change through time.

MOUNDS C°17 and C°21

The ridge to the north of the valley has three large conical mounds (C°16, C°22, and C°26) and at least eight low oval mounds, five between C°16 and C°22 and three between C°22 and C°26. Titterington reports that the dense scrub oak and wild grapevine cover on the ridge made an accurate count or detailed photographic record of the mounds impossible. C°17 and C°21, three to five feet high, were situated between C°16 and C°22 and were opened after the completion of the work on C°16 in 1946. The mounds were opened in order to substantiate Dr. Titterington's idea that they were identical with the Bluff Focus burials found in Jersey County, Illinois and the two partial excavations proved the point to his satisfaction. No specific dimensions are reported for these mounds although it would appear from photographs and drawings that the length is close to the minimum of 35 feet reported by Titterington in his Jersey Bluff trait list (Titterington, 1942: 240). Complete excavation of all the burials was not attempted because some were close to the surface and badly disturbed by the roots of the brush covering the mound. Titterington reports that all the burials were flexed and presents photographs of some of the features in both mounds and a list of materials saved from the excavation.

Mound C°17 contained at least six burials, two of which are represented by photographs (Pl. 108,*a*). A compound burial of two adult males (C°17-4 and -5) was encountered at a depth of at least three feet according to the photographs. C°17-4 was on the back with legs flexed to the left, arms resting across the chest and head to the south, the skull being in direct contact with the skull of C°17-5 which was placed face down in the same direction and was missing the lower extremities. Burial C°17-6 was an adult male flexed on the right side with head to the north.

The north end of C°21 was opened and six burials were found in an area which appears from the photograph to be about 20 feet square (Pl. 108,*b*). The deepest point in the photograph, from a burial to the surface, appears to be about five feet. Burials C°21-1,-2 and -3 are all adult females, fully flexed, with heads to the west and found within three or four feet of each other at the west edge of the excavated area. C°21-4 was an adult male, head to the south, lying on the back with legs fully flexed to the left. C°21-5 was an adult male, head south, lying on the back with legs fully flexed over the abdomen. C°21-6 was a young adult male with head to the west lying face down with the legs flexed back so that the feet were directly over the pelvis. The skull had been displaced in position so that the face was pointed straight up, but aside from this it appears that these latter three burials had been interred at least partially in the flesh.

The skeletal material saved is listed but not identified as to location. The list includes two complete male skeletons, one male skull and upper extremities, two pairs of male mandible and maxilla, one complete female skeleton and one female mandible and maxilla. In addition, the mandible and maxilla of two young adults were saved, one showing impaction of the lower third molars. There were 33 river snail (*Anculosa praerosa Say*) shell beads in association with the former individuals (Pl. 109). There were 730 of these Anculosa beads scattered over and under the chest region of an infant burial, leading Titterington to suggest that they may have been attached to a robe or garment. There was also a cylindrical bead 9.1 cm. long made from the columella of a large marine univalve, found on the chest of a small child burial. A single Canteen Cordmarked body sherd was found in the mound fill.

MOUND C°19

This mound was one of the low oval mounds between C°16 and C°22 on the high ridge and was dug by Mr. Walter Wadlow in October, 1941. Titterington reports that Wadlow found a crushed skull, a few cervical vertebrae and a section of sternum with an associated pottery vessel containing a mussel shell spoon (correspondence, P. F. Titterington to J. B. Griffin, Nov. 28, 1941). The spoon is a left valve of *Proptera capax*, 10.6 cm. long and 6.3 cm. wide and is thinned and ground around the edge (Pl. 110,*b*).

This Canteen Cordmarked jar is 23.5 cm. high (Pl. 110,*a*). The lip diameter is 16 by 17 cm., the rim is 16.2 by 17 cm., and the body diameter is 23.5 cm. It has a short slightly flared rim which is 7 mm. thick. The lip is deeply and closely notched with wide U-shaped notches transversely across it. The vessel has a sloping shoulder area and a rounded base. The temper is grit and the surfaces have a sandy feel. The interior is heavily smoke blackened and the exterior is tan to brown with some blackened areas. The interior is roughly smoothed with horizontal rows of finger impressions where the vessel was held as it was being constructed and paddled. The exterior surface has fine closely spaced cordwrapped paddle impressions over the body except for some smoothing on the rim.

MOUND C°22

This mound is the central one of the three larger conical mounds on the high ridge to the north of the valley. The mound was 52 feet long, 38 feet wide and 9 feet high, the long axis being northwest by southeast (Fig. 18). It was excavated in October, 1942, by Dr. Titterington and his crew.

Nine flexed burials were found within two feet six inches of the top of the mound, all rather poorly preserved due either to scrub oak or grapevine roots or to large limestone slabs which had been placed over some of them. A compound burial of an adult male and a small child (C°22-1 and -2) was found ten feet northwest of the southeast end of the mound on the long axis at a depth of one foot three inches. The adult was fully flexed on the right side with the head to the south. The child was flexed on the left side with head to the west and was situated between the femurs and rib cage of the adult male. There was a double-pointed bone object, the point of an awl and an unworked mussel shell by the upper end of the adult's left tibia. The double-pointed object is 8.5 cm. long, 0.6 cm. wide and 0.3 cm. thick, made from the cortex of animal rib and showing marks and polishing on all surfaces. This object may have been used as a fish gorge, although the polish is finer

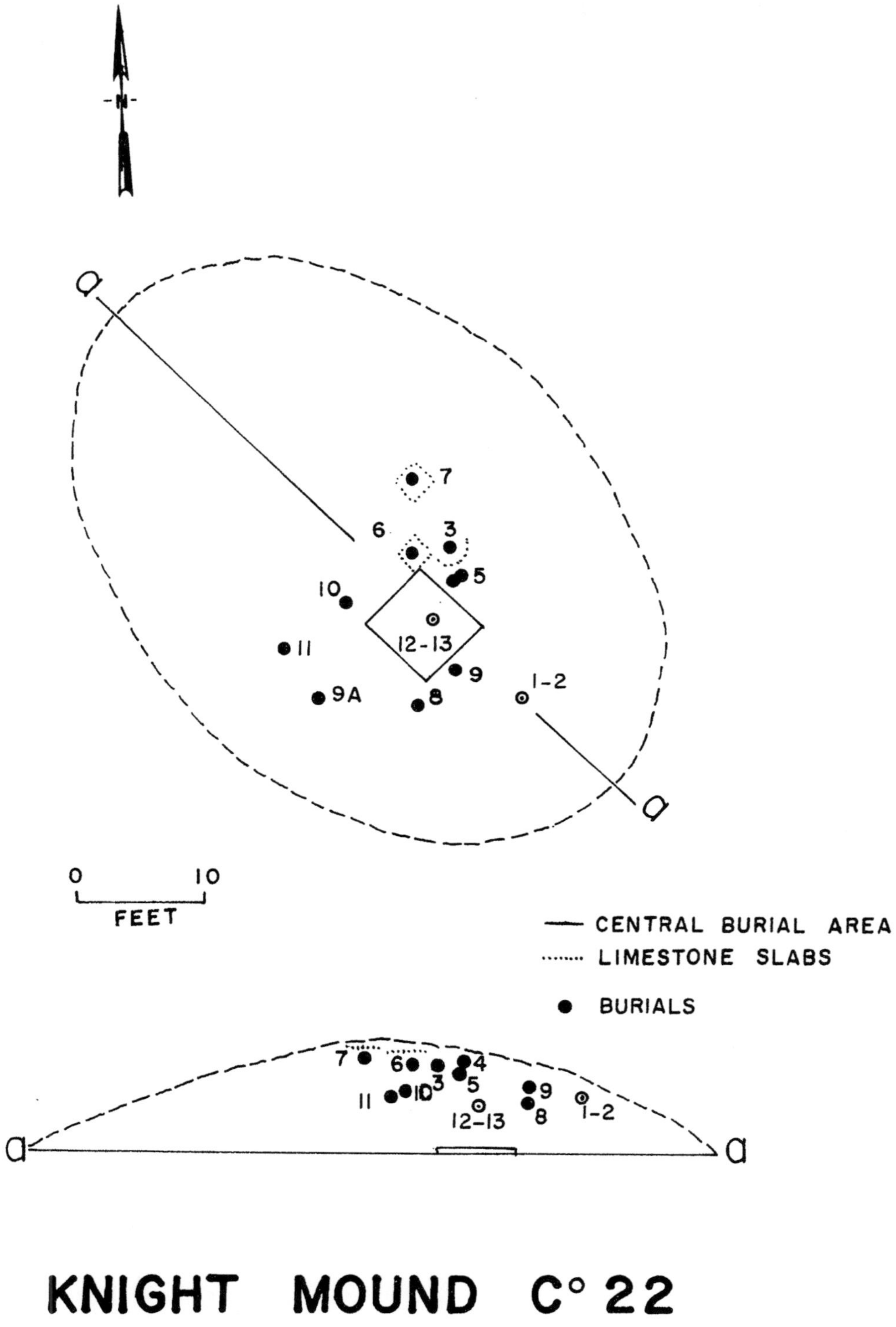

Fig. 18. Reconstruction of burial locations in Knight Mound C°22.

at the pointed ends suggesting use as an awl. Three of the nine burials were encountered 22 feet northwest of the southeast end of the mound, five feet northeast of the long axis at depths from 10 to 16 inches (Pl. 111,*a*). C°22-3 consisted of a semicircular row of limestone slabs two deep, with a child's skull under the center slab, the child having been flexed on the left side with the head to the north, according to the notes. C°22-4 was an adult female flexed on the left side with the head to the northeast and was found just to the south of the limestone slabs of C°22-3 and partially under the leg bones of that burial. C°22-5 was a flexed burial on the left side with the head to the northwest, found under a layer of limestone slabs just to the east of C°22-4.

Burial C°22-4, an adult male flexed on the left side with head to the northwest, was found underneath four large limestone slabs situated about two feet west of the above-mentioned group of three burials at a depth of 18 inches. C°22-7 was an adult female flexed on the right side with head to the west and was underneath one large and two small limestone slabs just beneath the surface of the mound. This burial was located 28 feet northwest of the southeast end of the mound and seven feet northeast of the long axis at a depth of 15 inches. C°22-8 was an adult male flexed on the left side with head to the south and was found 15 feet northwest of the south end of the mound and six feet southwest of the long axis at a depth of two feet six inches. C°22-9 was found in line with C°22-6 at a point two feet southwest of the long axis and 20 inches deep. This was an adult female flexed on the left side with the head to the southwest.

Five extended burials were found at depths ranging from three feet six inches to four feet six inches. C°22-9A was an adult female extended on the back with the head to the west and was found 21 feet northwest of the southeast of the mound, eleven feet southwest of the long axis at a depth of three feet six inches. Roots of a small elm tree had grown through the skull and there were fragments of a pot and a mussel shell spoon which had been placed at the top of the skull. The one sherd in the collection is a rimsherd from a Baehr Brushed vessel. (Pl. 115,*b*). C°22-10 was the burial of an adult, presumably female, on the back with head to the west. The skull, left humerus and left ribs were all that remained, the rest apparently having been removed through a previously dug pit. This burial was located 25 feet northwest of the southeast end of the mound, four feet southwest of the long axis at a depth of four feet. A large part of a Baehr Brushed vessel (Pl. 111,*b*) was located at the top of the skull.

This funerary jar is an excellent example of the Baehr Brushed type (Pl. 112,*a*). It is 15.3 cm. high and has a lip diameter of 12.5 cm., 11.8 cm. at the base of the rim, and the body diameter is 14.5 cm. Most of the limestone tempering material is still in the vessel. It has a greyish-tan exterior and a blackened interior. The interior surface was smoothed and the exterior surface was smoothed before the decoration was applied. The lip is rounded to flattened and is 4 mm. wide. The rim is 4 mm. thick but the body is slightly thinner being 3 mm. thick. The rim height is irregular from .9 to 1.3 cm. On the outer rim surface there are the irregular medium-wide-to-narrow flat bottom shallow, closely spaced horizontal lines so common in this group. At the base of this decorated slightly thickened and channeled rim is a horizontal row of roughly made hemiconical punctates punched from the left. The smooth to burnished lower rim is delimited by the single medium wide and medium deep incised line which runs in four arches over the slightly accentuated four lobes on the upper body. An unusual variant is found on this vessel for the "brush" markings on the lobes are horizontal, with the more normal vertical impressions covering the rest of the body. The rounded conoidal base has a badly eroded surface. The brush or simulated brush marks are 2.5 mm. wide, shallow and flat bottomed.

C°22-11 was an adult male extended on the back with the head to the northwest and was found 26 feet northwest of the southeast end of the mound, ten feet southwest of the long axis at a depth of four feet six inches. The skull, the lower legs, the right forearm and both hands were missing, the other bones occurring in articulated position although somewhat displaced from ground pressure. A perforated bear canine (Pl. 112,*b*) was found above the left clavicle. This artifact is 8.1 cm. long, 2.5 cm. wide and 1.6 cm. thick at the middle and has two holes 5 mm. in diameter and 1.0 cm. apart drilled obliquely toward each other on one side, presumably for suspension. There is a conical hole 1.2 cm. in diameter on the opposite side which intersects these two holes and which may have contained some kind of inlay. C°22-12 and -13 occurred in a compound burial 19 feet northwest of the southeast end of the mound on the long axis at a depth of four feet four inches. Both were adult males extended on the back with heads to the west. C°22-12 was represented only by the fourth and fifth lumbar vertebrae, pelvis and legs which were slightly flexed and C°22-13 was complete, although disarranged by ground pressure. There were no associations.

There was a central feature in C°22 at a depth of nine feet consisting of the remains of at least six individuals C°22-14 to -19 (Pl. 113,*a*), in an area six feet eight inches square paralleling the long axis of the mound, the center of the feature being 20 feet northwest of the southeast end of the mound and one foot southwest of the long axis. Four of the individuals were secondary burials and the other two were evidently interred at least partially in the flesh. There were no skulls or skull fragments in this immediate area. The feature was covered by a layer of white ash directly in contact with the bones (Pl. 113,*b*), the ash being thickest in the northwest corner of the area and extending past the burial area for an undetermined distance. Burial C°22-14 was a partial secondary burial which lay along the northeast margin of the burial area. It consisted of a pile containing, from south to north, a dorsal spine, several ribs, an ulna and a fibula, two innominate bones, two femurs, a sacrum, a tibia and the disarranged bones of the wrist and hand associated with a flake knife. The innominate bones had been placed with posterior surfaces upward and the head of each femur was in contact with the respective acetabulum although the anterior surfaces were rotated upward (Pl. 114,*a*). The flake knife, a blade of white flint 6.3 cm. long and 1.3 cm. wide, shows retouch on the dorsal side of the bulb end and has use marks along both edges. C°22-15, another secondary burial found along the southeast margin of the area, consisted from west to east of two femurs with a right innominate bone lying partly on top of one, two metacarpals with a flake knife were under the innominate bone, then a right tibia and fibula and a left innominate bone, a fifth lumbar vertebra containing the tip of a broken projectile point, a sacrum and the left tibia and fibula beside which lay two calcaneus and two talus bones. The flake knife is a blade of pink flint 5.2 cm. long and 2.0 cm. wide showing nibbling along one edge and retouch on the dorsal surface of the proximal end. C°22-16 was a secondary burial found on the southwest margin of the area and included from north to south a group of bones consisting of a tibia, fibula, a humerus, a radius and an ulna followed in line by a sacrum, a femur with superimposed left innominate bone, two ribs and finally the right innominate bone. C°22-17 was extended on the back with head to the southeast immediately beside C°22-16 and lacked the head, shoulder girdle, arms and the feet. The remaining bones of this burial seem to be in their normal articulatory positions except that the legs appear to be rotated laterally so that the femur heads are pointing upward. C°22-18 lying next to C°22-17 approximately in the center of the burial area was extended on the back with head to the southeast. This burial also lacked the shoulder girdle except for the left clavicle, the head, the arms and the feet. The lower legs were rotated similar to C°22-17. There were two femurs superimposed over the lower legs of this burial, two tibiae and part of a vertebral column between the upper legs, one innominate bone in the pelvic region and another under the right rib cage and fragmentary remains of what appear to be two more tibiae and a fibula at the center and left side of the rib cage.

A number of artifacts were located in the region of the right shoulder of C°22-18 (Pl. 114,*b*). These include two sandstone abraders, three fragments of antler, a flake knife, a projectile point, a cube of galena, two pieces of hematite and a modified flake (Pl. 115,*a*). One of the abraders, of tan sandstone, is 9.8 cm. long, 7.7 cm. wide and 2.8 cm. thick, roughly rectangular with evidence of use on at least one flat surface and all edges. The other, of ferruginous sandstone, is 5.6 cm. long, 4.5 cm. wide and 7 mm. thick This object shows indistinct striations on one flat side and very marked, highly polished vertical striations along one edge, possibly a result of grinding the stone for red pigment. The antler fragments consist of a poorly preserved section of base, 11.0 cm. long including a portion of the brow tine, and two smaller pieces of tine each 5.0 cm. long. The flake knife is a blade of tan flint 4.3 cm. long, 1.8 cm. wide and 3 mm. thick and shows retouch on the dorsal side of the proximal end and use marks on both edges. The small dark grey flint projectile point is 5.3 cm. long, 2.8 cm. wide at the shoulder, 2.3 cm. wide at the base and 0.5 cm. thick with a stem 1.6 cm. wide and 1.3 cm. long. It is a straight-sided, corner-notched concave base form identified as a late variant of the Snyder-Norton-Gibson-Manker continuum. The galena cube varies from 1.8 cm. to 2.2 cm. on a side and shows smoothing on at least three sides. One of the pieces of hematite is 5.5 cm. long and approximately 3.0 cm. wide, has a hardness of 2.0 and shows striations on one edge. The other is 4.2 cm. long, 3.0 cm. wide and 2.0 cm. thick, has a hardness of 3.0 and shows deep crisscrossed cut marks over one complete side. The modified flake grades from limestone to jasper and has been crudely retouched as a steep-sided scraper on the edge of the jasper portion.

Further excavation on the northern half of the mound was carried out in August, 1944, in an attempt to find the skulls of the burials in the central pit. A few scattered long bones and vertebrae and one skull fragment consisting of part of a right parietal and mastoid were found. In association with this skull fragment were five small mollusk shells of *Obovaria subrotunda* averaging 1.5 cm. in diameter and drilled through opposite edges and a clay pulley-type earspool or pendant (Pl. 115,*b*). This object is 4.4 cm. in circumference diameter, 3.4 cm. in inner grove diameter, 1.8 cm. thick at the outer edge and 1.0 cm. thick in the center. It has a central hole 1.5 cm. in diameter and nine small radiating holes through the body from the outer circumference to the central hole. The clay is tempered with a mixture of grit and limestone and the object shows a high polish on the outer rim and both faces.

Three artifacts from this mound are not

mentioned in the notes and presumably came from the fill. There is a white flint projectile point of the Mason-Dickson group (C°22-19) with a triangular blade and contracting stem which measures 8.3 cm. in length, 3.7 cm. wide at the shoulder and 1.0 cm. thick with a stem 2.0 cm. long and 2.2 cm. wide at the shoulder (Pl. 116,*a*). C°22-20 is a cube of galena measuring from 1.1 cm. to 1.3 cm. on a side (Pl. 116,*b*). C°22-21 is a blade of pink and white fossiliferous flint measuring 7.3 cm. long, 1.7 cm. wide and 3 mm. thick and showing "nibbling" on both edges (Pl. 116,*b*).

COMMENTS ON MOUND C°22

This mound was begun by Hopewellian people who placed the fragmentary and reassembled skeletal material of at least six individuals within a six foot, eight inch square. There were no skull fragments and very little burial furniture. They were covered by what Titterington called a "white ash" layer which was probably a bark layer turned to niter. The most noteworthy artifact group was a male tool kit at the right shoulder of Burial 18.

The group of five extended adults are presumably Pike phase burials because of the association of a Baehr Brushed vessel with Burial 10. Of the three adult males two were oriented east-west with heads to the west and one was northwest southeast with head to the northwest. The two females were also oriented east to west. One of the skulls was on the east end of the body and one was on the west end. The Baehr Brushed vessel is one of the best of its type and should date about the time of the Mound 8 vessels. The shell bracelets or anklets of *Obovaria subrotunda* are identical to ones found in two of the mounds at the Snyders site. This species occurs on a sand or gravel bottom, in current and at a depth of several inches to four to five feet. It apparently is not present now in the Illinois or nearby Mississippi rivers. It is uncommon in the lower Wabash and Ohio rivers and their tributaries. The anklets, or spangles, as Dr. Titterington used to call them, are not common in Hopewell or any other group.

The latest part of the mound construction covered nine flexed Jersey Bluff burials. One adult male flexed on the right side had his head to the south. Two adult males flexed on the left side had their heads to the northwest and the south. Of the three adult females, one was flexed on the right with head to the west. Two were flexed on the left, with one head to the northwest and the other to the southwest. Both children were flexed on the left side, one with head to the west and the other with its head to the north. Age and sex are not known for the burial flexed on the left with its head to the northwest. There was then some preference in the Jersey Bluff interments for placing the flexed burials on the left side with head from northwest to southwest.

Summary

The Knight Mound Group represents the burial customs of prehistoric Indian societies living on the east side of the Mississippi River in northwestern Calhoun County, Illinois from about A.D. 150 to about A.D. 400. This represents a time span of approximately 250 years during which the burial practices and the associated items underwent such marked changes that archaeologists can recognize them as belonging to different complexes. The first burial activities were those of people identified as participating in the Pike phase of Middle Woodland Hopewellian societies in the lower Illinois Valley area.

They placed some proportion of their

dead in burial mounds on the bluffs and ridges east of their village. In this they were following a precedent known for a thousand years in their area and in other areas of the Mississippi Valley. Initial activities included removal of the humus zone, excavation of subfloor pits with the long axis usually paralleling that of the ridge, or preparation of a central burial area; the use of limestone slabs for a pavement, a covering, marking corners of burial pits, or for delineating burial areas. The pit burials are often extended and tend to be multiple representing both sexes and both adults and children. There are however, other burial forms and consistency in these practices is not demonstrated at the Knight Group. Many of the burials have a north-south orientation or deviate slightly from these directions but others are also positioned east-west and no compulsive orientation is represented. For pit or central chamber areas the orientation of the prepared structure was important in determining the relationship of the burial to the cardinal directions. The orientation of the central pit or tomb could be affected by the shape and alignment of the ridge or bluff top.

The excavations by Gregory Perino at a number of mound groups in the lower Illinois Valley have produced a large number of burials outside the mounds, many of which were apparently of the same society as those in the mounds. This parallels the results obtained by Neumann and Fowler in White County, Illinois along the Wabash. The Knight Mound should be revisited to determine if the same situation is true there. The Pike phase burials in the mounds of which we have a record would not seem to represent the expected number of deaths in the community that occupied the Knight village for about 150 years.

Of the preserved grave goods placed with burials the copper artifacts, marine shell containers and beads, the mica plates, galena cubes, the Blandings turtle carapace, and perhaps Dongola flint, are items which were obtained from distant sources with the copper, mica and *Cassis* shell sources being the farthest removed. How these reached the Illinois area is still a matter of conjecture but it is likely that no single explanation will suffice for the inter-societal relationships. The geographic distribution of panpipes as presented in this paper (Map 2) is quite different from that of obsidian (Griffin, 1965: Fig. 1). It may be reasonable to believe that the earspools and perhaps the panpipes were made in Ohio but this is not certain. The three platform pipes of Ohio pipestone were obtained from that center. This is not a very impressive list of specific contacts with Ohio Hopewell given the presumed period of the Pike phase burials.

The rest of the items found with the Middle Woodland burials which have been described and illustrated in the report are assumed to have been produced by people of the Knight Village or to have been obtained from nearby groups following closely similar cultural patterns. Most of the items are also recovered from village site excavations and along with the rest of the evidence from the villages are a far better reflection of the total cultural pattern of the society than are burial customs alone. Certainly the most important program for Middle Woodland studies in the Eastern United States is a series of comprehensive excavations and analyses of villages by current techniques of recovery and interpretation.

The Fox Creek phase that has been proposed in this report is interpreted as having developed from the preceeding Pike phase by a gradual shift of interests, activities and implement styles. The causes of this shift are not understood but it can be predicted that they are not single but multiple, are not local, but widespread over the area occupied by Middle Woodland Hopewellian societies.

Fox Creek burials are usually flexed, but extended, bundle burials and single and multiple interments are a part of the pattern. They did not continue the emphasis on subfloor burial pits or log tombs of their predecessors. They did not place as many grave goods with the dead, nor did they acquire as many items of exotic materials. Their ceramic complex is markedly simple both in form and decoration, although the vessels in village use were as well made in terms of serviceability as those of the Havana ceramic tradition. They continued to make burial vessels specifically for burial purposes if this interpretation of the Knight Mound Canteen vessels is correct, and duplicated at other sites. Most of the Jersey Bluff collection of Dr. Paul F. Titterington is in the Illinois State Museum. This collection was studied about twenty years ago but it needs to be reanalyzed and integrated with the results of later excavations and new analytical techniques—a fine job for somebody.

THE NORTON MOUND GROUP

KENT COUNTY, MICHIGAN

BY

RICHARD E. FLANDERS

JAMES B. GRIFFIN

GENERAL DESCRIPTION AND HISTORY

The Norton Mound Group is situated in Sections 3 and 4 of Wyoming Township, Kent County, Michigan, in a city park between the cities of Grand Rapids and Grandville. The mound group is arranged roughly in two parallel lines with the three largest mounds in a line approximately parallel to and 700 feet south of the Grand River and the other 14 mounds in a curved line immediately behind the largest mounds (Fig. 19). The group is situated on a slight natural "dome"' which rises from two to five feet above the surrounding area and is approximately six feet above the present river level (Pl. 117). The area between the mounds and the river has undergone rather extensive modification in the form of a built-up road bed and some black-dirt stripping so that the original contours are obliterated. There has also been an indeterminate amount of soil stripping in the area between the mounds. The dark brown sandy loam topsoil varies from 0.3 to about 1.0 feet in depth in the immediate vicinity of the mounds and deepens to four feet within 100 yards to the northeast of the center of the group. The transition to the basal gravel under the sandy loam is very sharp. To the south of the mounds, the right of way for a freeway, Michigan I-96, comes to the middle of the road behind Mounds F to J and extends along the east side of the park where it crosses the river. The west side of the park is bounded by a gravel pit excavation which may have removed rather extensive village deposits and at least one mound. The park area is now covered by oak, hickory, hackberry, hawthorne, elm and poison ivy.

The data concerning the early history of the site are drawn largely from a copy of a W. L. Coffinberry manuscript "Mounds and Mound Builders of Michigan." Part of the manuscript describes a meeting of the Archaeological Committee of the Kent Scientific Institute (now the Grand Rapids Public Museum) of October 22, 1874 during which Coffinberry, Professor E. A. Strong and Dr. J. C. Parker were apointed as a committee to explore the mounds on the property of Captain A. N. Norton. The exploration was permitted on the condition that the mounds be left in their original shape and that all materials found in the mounds go to the Kent Scientific Institute. The committee explored seven mounds and a brief final report of the excavations was included in the manuscript. Coffinberry's original map unfortunately has been lost.

Coffinberry's notes contained enough data to convey a general idea of the appearance of the mounds. He describes them as being conical and regular in outline although somewhat flattened on top. The height of the tallest mound, identified by Coffinberry as Mound M in the notes, was essentially the same in 1874 as in 1963. The mounds are described as being composed of "surface" or "alluvial" soil and are "nearly homogeneous," an observation that led Coffinberry to suggest that no great length of time elapsed during the building of the mounds. Human remains were ". . . almost invariably found in an elongated, concave, irregularly oval pit a foot or two deep, surrounded by whatever objects of interests the mound contained. . . ." (Coffinberry, 1875: Article 9).

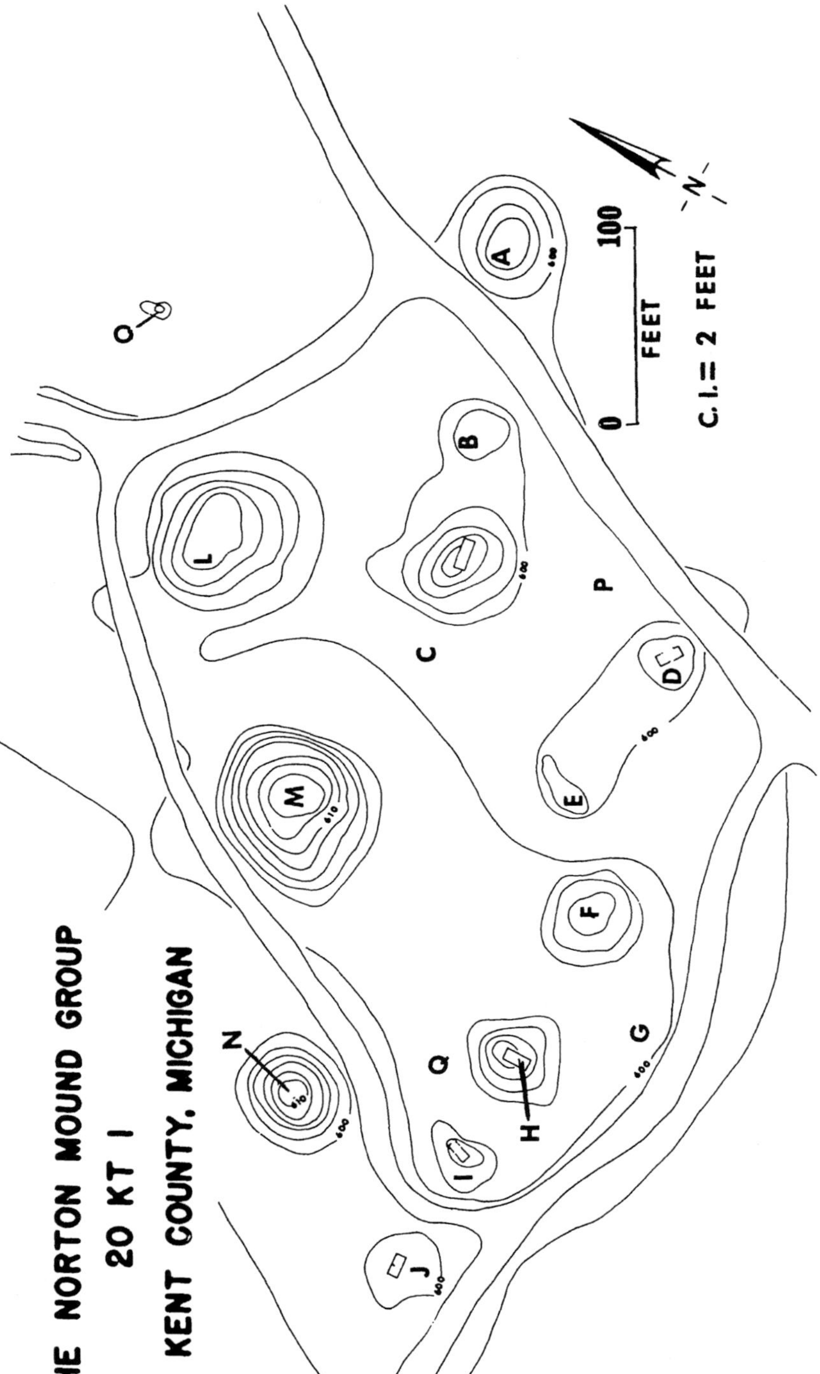

Fig. 19. Contour map of Norton Mound Group prepared by Richard Flanders. UMMA Neg. 15282.

Coffinberry's method of investigation consisted of sinking a pit into the top center of the mound in search of the central burial pit, then expanding the excavation when the burials were encountered to include the entire grave. A graphic illustration of this method can be seen in the description and profile of Mound D in this report. It is interesting to note that in his account of excavations, Coffinberry found nothing in four of the seven mounds tested. This is probably a result of digging only when the burial pit is actually at a greater depth. The only mound which can be identified from Coffinberry's notes is Mound M on Gibson's map, the largest of the group, which after 14 days of digging yielded "only one copper awl and a layer of ash."

Two more of the Norton mounds were opened in 1915 by H. E. Sargent, Director of the Grand Rapids Museum. Sargent filed a report with the Grand Rapids Museum and an article appeared in the Grand Rapids Herald, May 2, 1915, by T. O. Manchas, entitled "Breaking the Seals of the Mystery of the First Citizens of Grand Rapids of 1000 Years Ago." This article furnishes a few more details on Sargent's work. His first mound contained a subfloor clay-lined pit seven feet in diameter and 1.5 feet deep which contained three adults and two infants and a fair selection of grave goods. These included pottery vessels, shell spoons, bear canines and mandibles, turtle shells, turkey bone awls, beaver incisors, hammerstones and sandstone "abraders" and a large (9.75 in. long) well made shouldered point or knife of banded purple-white flint. Most of these articles are at the Grand Rapids Public Museum and are described in Quimby's Goodall focus report (Quimby, 1941*a*). The second mound yielded only some flint scraps, a bear canine and several beaver incisors. A clay-lined subfloor pit is described which is similar to the one in Sargent's first mound, suggesting that the second mound has not been completely dug, at least, by previous excavators. Thus there are records of nine mounds having been completely dug or tested prior to the present field session. However, the map done for the Kent Scientific Museum in 1936 by the late Edmond P. Gibson presents a little different situation than that found by the 1963 field crew.

Gibson furnished basal and top elevations for all 17 mounds originally reported for the group, and his outlines would seem to indicate that all the mounds retained at least their conical form, although Gibson's is not a contour map. The 1963 survey found 11 of the 17 original mounds still in a seemingly undisturbed, roughly conical outline (Fig. 19). Mound K on the west edge of the group is either completely leveled or is a part of the gravel pit excavation next to the site. There is no trace of Mound Q. A small portion of the north edge of Mound G remains but the access road seems to have taken the rest of the mound. Mound E appears to have been cut into so that only about one-third of the original surface structure remains. In the original location of Mound P there is only a slight depression about five feet in diameter down to the subsoil gravel. Mound O, the northernmost in the group, appears to have been cut off like Mound E with perhaps one-half of the original above-surface structure remaining.

The whole mound group has been included in a city park since 1936 when Mrs. W. B. Stiles deeded a portion of land containing five of the mounds to the city. The right-of-way for a section of the new freeway, Interstate 96, was originally mapped to run directly through the park but was diverted through the intercession of Mr. Fred See, Grand Rapids City Park Superintendent. There has been considerable black-dirt stripping in the vicinity of the mounds for a period of years which has destroyed or altered most of the original surface, including some of the mound profiles.

Late in 1962 a private individual indicated to Mr. W. D. Frankforter, Director of the Grand Rapids Public Museum, that funds might be available for excavation at the mound group. Mr. Homer Burch, then President of the Coffinberry Chapter of the Michigan Archaeological Society, appointed Mr. Frankforter a committee of one to check on the possibility of excavation. Mr. Frankforter then contacted Dr. James B. Griffin, Director of the Museum of Anthropology, University of Michigan, who indicated that a crew from the Museum would be available if funds were forthcoming and if permission from the proper municipal authorities could be obtained. Mr. James R. Sanderson, President of the Grand Rapids Museum Association, appointed a Committee for Indian Mounds Development consisting of Mr. Frankforter (Chairman), George W. Davis, Dr. Clarence J. DeBoer, H. Holmes Ellis, Edward V. Gillis, Dr. Austin Lamberts, A. Hugh Lilly, Dr. Martinus and Mrs. William VanDeventer. The Committee made numerous contacts during the remaining time before the field season both to secure funds and to make arrangements about the excavation. Dr. Griffin made several trips to Grand Rapids to aid in the arrangements and handled the details of the contract and University arrangements in Ann Arbor. The Committee contacted the Grand Rapids Foundation, a local philanthropic organization, which granted the full amount of $11,700 proposed by Dr. Griffin for the excavation, and private individuals donated $1000. The final agreements were reached in the afternoon of the day that the crew moved on to the site with poised shovels.

The archaeological field crew working under Richard E. Flanders in the first season's excavations were David M. Griffin, Elaine Grossbart, Sidney A. Harrison, John R. Halsey, Berry C. Kent, Suzanne Kish, Lewis Millenbach, Robert Modica, and Dwight Spenser. The drawings of the vessels from these excavations are by Dianne Foster Fisher. Most of the work on the preparation of the photographs is by George Stuber and the technical editing by Joanne Bailis.

The materials recovered in the excavations are the property of the City of Grand Rapids, Michigan and are housed in the Grand Rapids Public Museum. The negatives and original drawings are in the Museum of Anthropology of the University of Michigan.

In the summer of 1964 the University of Michigan Television Center sent crews to the site who filmed the excavations in progress. That fall a script was prepared and a half-hour program was recorded entitled "The Hopewell Heritage" which has now been shown 33 times on commercial television around the country, and before more restricted audio-visual groups in Michigan, and as far as Maryland.

Following the 1964 season an attempt was made to produce a program for the development of the Norton Mound Group and the surrounding area along the Grand River, which would stimulate the proper preservation of the mounds and establish a local nature center. Two class groups of the School of Architecture and Design at the University of Michigan worked on this project. One of these under the direction of Professor Charles W. Cares of the Department of Landscape Architecture prepared plans for the development of the area on both sides of the river including the mounds, and another group under Prof. E. V. Olencki, Robert M. Beckley, and Barry Yopp prepared a scale model and plans for a museum building. These were submitted to the Grand Rapids Museum. Unfortunately support has not been obtained for what could be an important educational and recreation area for west central Michigan.

The Norton Mound Group is one of the best preserved Hopewellian burial centers in the country and is one of the most important sites in Michigan. As the result of stimulation from the Museum of Anthropology and the Grand Rapids Public Museum the site has been named a National Historic Site by the National Park Service. Local, state and national support should be enlisted and combined to preserve this group and its natural environment as an example of man's utilization of the Grand Rapids area shortly after the time of Christ.

The initial description of the results of the 1963 season was prepared by Dr. Flanders as part of his Ph.D. thesis at the University of Michigan. Subsequently he prepared the description of the results of the 1964 season excavation of Mound M. There has been substantial exchange of ideas between Griffin and Flanders during this period between 1963 and 1969. The conclusions and interpretations of the relationships of the Norton site have undergone some modification from the statements in the Ph.D. thesis.

EXCAVATIONS

Mound H

The first mound to be tested was initially chosen for its rounded top contour (as opposed to the flattened appearance of some of the other mounds, suggesting disturbance) and for its intermediate size. Mound H was six feet high from the present ground level and 50 feet in diameter when excavation commenced (Pl. 118). It was decided to start through the mound with two ten-foot wide north-south trenches for the length of the mound, meanwhile leaving a five-foot wide balk through the center for the retention of profiles. The mound fill was to be run through a one-quarter-inch screen to check for village debris which might have been scraped up in the process of building the mound, although our preliminary testing seemed to indicate a very light occupation of the immediate vicinity of the mound group. The screening proved essentially unproductive and was discontinued at a depth of approximately three feet below the surface of the mound, although selected levels were screened from time to time as a check.

The stratigraphy of the mound established a model which was adhered to closely by the other mounds tested with two exceptions (Mounds J and M—Mound J was disturbed to the extent of obscuring stratigraphy and Mound M lacked only the subfloor pit). The top layer of H consisted of a thin sod and dark gray humus formation from the surface to a depth of about one foot in the center of the mound (Fig. 20). The bulk of the mound fill consisted of a layer of dark brown sandy loam varying from 0.3 feet to 2.0 feet thick which graded into a layer of lighter brown sandy loam, the latter soil being very similar to that directly under the sod around the periphery of the mound group. The stratum of light soil showed lenses of darker loam, presumably fill brought from a different location.

At a depth of approximately 4.0 feet from the top in the center of the mound a distinct break was encountered between the light sandy loam and a layer of dark gray organic soil which was recognized as a "cap" mentioned by the early excavators which seems to be a feature of the majority of Michigan Hopewell mounds. This dark cap was observed to dip toward the center of the mound from both ends as it was revealed in the profile and this slope of the cap was subsequently found to be

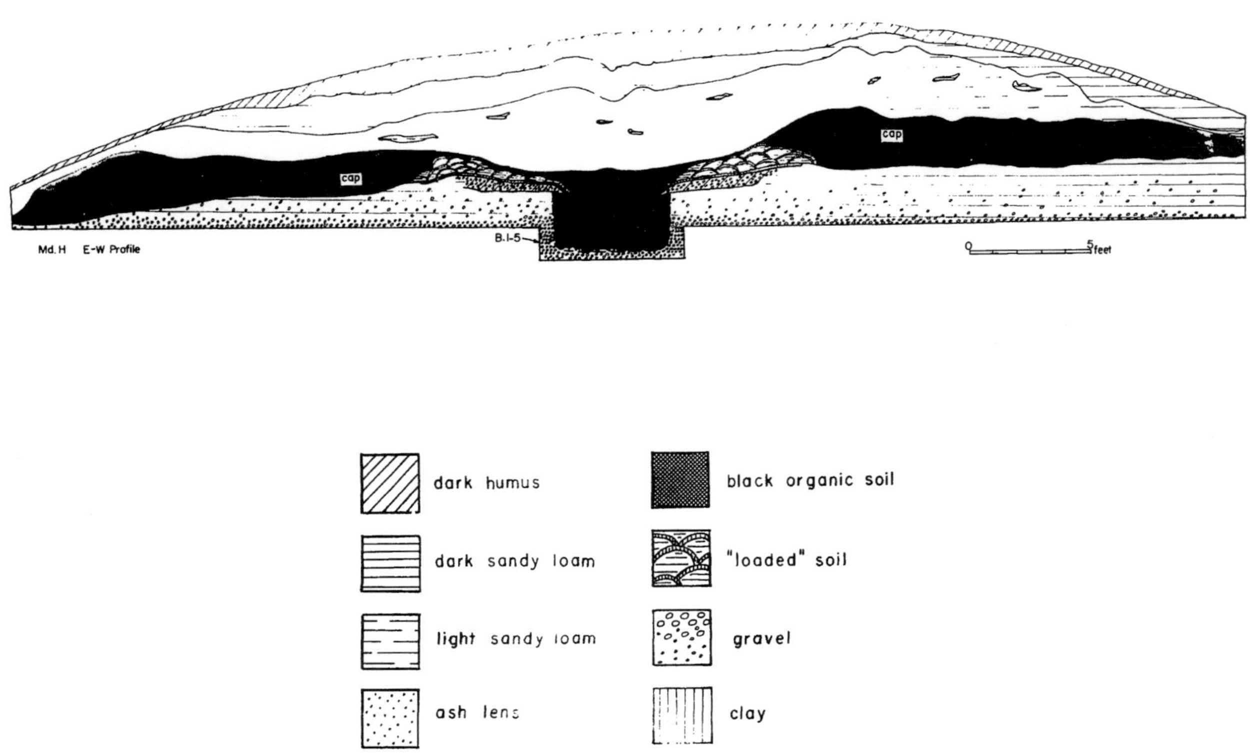

Fig. 20. East-west profile of Mound H. UMMA Neg. 15651.

directly over the central subfloor burial pit. The original appearance of this burial cap, as reconstructed, would have been a low ramplike structure surrounding the central pit. This cap varied in thickness from 0.5 feet at the extreme outer edges of the mound to a maximum of 2.5 feet at a point approximately one-third of the way through the mound. Within a diameter of 6.0 feet out from the edges of the subfloor pit, the cap was composed of "loaded" dark brown to black sandy loam (Pl. 118). The loads averaged 1.1 feet in length and 0.3 feet in depth and these dimensions compare favorably with the averages from Mound I (1.2 ft. by 0.3 ft.), Mound D (1.5 ft. by 0.3 ft.) and Mound C (1.2 ft. by 0.3 ft.), indicating that the same size container was probably used in all cases. Immediately underlying the loaded soil was a layer of material that was initially designated as an "ash lens" but was subsequently identified as bark partially replaced by calcium carbonate (see Mound M below). The bark layer was as thick as 0.3 feet and extended to the circumference of the loaded soil in some cases. Some of this material was used in an attempt to date the construction of this mound (see Radiocarbon Dates). The backdirt from the burial pit was represented by a lens of dark sandy loam with a heavy concentration of cobble-sized gravel. This backdirt did not extend quite as far as the "ash lens" and loaded soil and reached a maximum thickness of 0.5 feet. The dark sandy loam immediately below the mound base was 1.0 feet thick at the maximum and upon further excavation showed a mixture of pea- to cobble-sized gravel. The west half of the mound showed almost none of this gravel-free loam except for the area directly under the loaded soil, suggesting that the mound had been erected on a slight natural rise. Stratigraphic tests to the north of the mound in the center of the group and the profile of Mound I directly to the west supported this observation. There was no trace of a sod or humus formation under the mound, suggesting some preparation of the submound area prior to construction.

The Burial Pit

As soon as the profile of the cap was established with the dip in the approximate center of the mound, it was decided to remove the portion of the balk overlying the central half of the mound and continue down in search of the postulated subfloor pit. The outline of the pit appeared directly below the stratum of bark and backdirt in the form of a roughly rectangular area 9.0 feet north-south and 5.0 feet east-west which consisted of the dark organic soil of the cap in distinction to the surrounding light sandy loam and gravel (Pl. 119,*a*). It was found necessary to excavate a trench around the pit into the loose gravel to prevent loose gravel from sliding into the burial pit. The "pedestal" was then taken down with trowel, brush and dental probe. (Fig. 21).

The first artifacts to appear occurred in a group in the northwest edge of the pit at a point approximately 1.5 feet above the level of the burials. They were three fragments of worked copper and a burned human phalanx (Pl. 119,*b*). The copper fragments all showed some evidence of hammering and folding but were not recognizable artifacts. The phalanx shows a whitening of the cortex on the shaft due to heat and the condylar portions are encrusted with burned earth. In the south end of the pit at a depth of 0.3 feet to 0.7 feet above the burials were six projectile points (Pl. 123,*a*). Dimensions on these points are in Table 2. Points H1 to H5 show a steep marginal retouch on at least the lower one-quarter of the blade edge. This practice may be associated with hafting procedures. H1 to H5 are of a dark to light gray mottled chert, the type now being called Dongola chert, and H6 is of a smoky white coarse chert with crystalline inclusions. H2 and H5 were lying together in the southeast corner of the pit

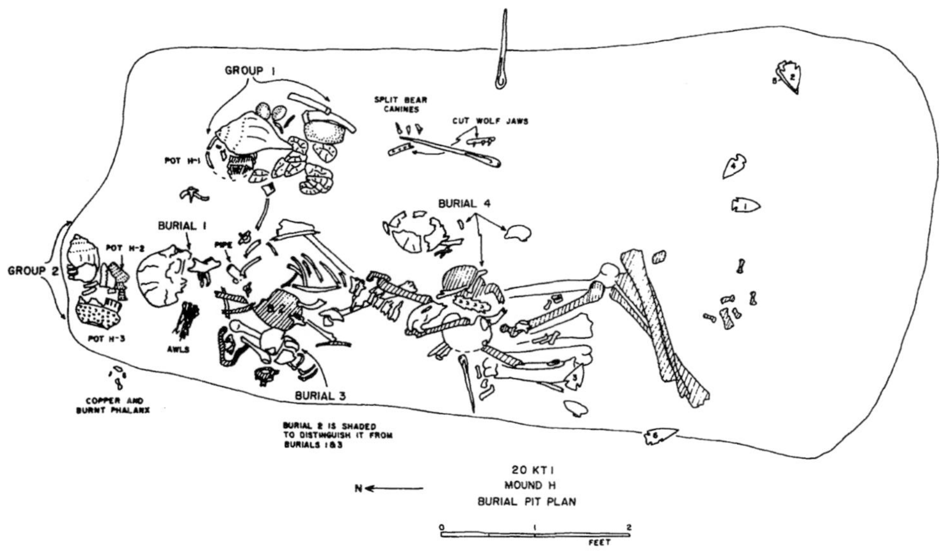

Fig. 21. Floor of burial pit in Norton Mound H. UMMA Neg. 15648.

0.7 feet above the layer of bones, H1 and H4 were together in the middle about 0.3 feet above the bones and H3 and H6 were placed in the southwest edge of the pit 0.5 feet above the lower leg of Burial No. 2. At about the middle of the burial pit there were three bone pins of split and ground elk metapodial (*Cervus canadensis*) ranging from 28.0 cm. to 30.0 cm. in length (Pl. 119,*b*). These metapodials are split so that one-half of the original distal condyle forms the head of the pin. The pin on the east side of the pit was evidently forced into the gravel forming the wall of the pit. The pin is broken and the point end in the gravel shows discoloration from the limestone which the head end does not. The other two pins were lying on the pit floor at the level of the burials, the one in the west edge *under* part of the burial. From the position of similar artifacts in the other burial pits, it is suggested that these pins were used to hold down some sort of cover for the burial pit. There were two cut and ground sections of wolf mandible (*Canis lupus*) and three fragments of a split bear canine (*Ursus americanus*) scattered around the pin in the center of the pit (Pl. 119,*b*). The wolf jaw fragments measure 6.2 and 6.5 cm. long and are of the right and left sides of the same individual. The fragments are cut and ground so that a portion of the interior of the tooth roots was exposed. The bear canine fragments average 2.8 cm. long.

Some other artifacts in the burial pit were found in two groups near the north end of the pit. The group in the northeast corner of the pit (Group No. 1, Pl. 120,*a*) consisted of a fragmentary Norton Zoned Incised vessel, a worked conch shell containing a lump of red ochre, 13 gray chert "blanks," or discoidal artifacts, a piece of iron pyrite, two granite grinding stones, a piece of sandstone, fragments of four worked beaver incisors, a lamellar flake, two worked pieces of deer antler and a mussel shell spoon. The pottery vessel (H1, Pl. 122,*a*) is represented by most of the rim and approximately one-half of the body, the rim being broken but essentially in place. The vessel is described below. Immediately above the vessel rim was a conch shell (*Busycon contrarium*) 25.4 cm. long and 13.0 cm. wide from which the columella, carinate ridges and mantle are removed by cutting and grinding. All cut and exposed edges are ground smooth. This shell contained a piece of red ochre 6.5 cm. long and 2.5 cm. wide with rubbed surfaces. The 13 blanks or discoidal artifacts were found in a group just to the south of the pot. They are all of the same mottled dark gray to light gray chert (Dongola chert) as the projectile points H1 to H5 and average 7.8 cm. in length, 5.1 cm. wide and 1.5 cm. thick. These discoidal artifacts are large flakes shaped by rough primary flaking, and some of the flake scars reaching more than half-way across the width of the piece. Five of the 13 show some remnants of the cortex of the original nodule. All show varying amounts of secondary flaking along the edges and most approach a "cordiform" outline (Pl. 120,*b*). The pyrite measures 5.4 cm. long, 4.2 cm. wide and 2.0 cm. thick and shows evidence of battering along one edge, possibly through use as a strike-a-light or as a percussion instrument (Pl. 121,*a*). The two oval grinding stones measure 8.0 by 7.0 by 5.0 cm. and 8.0 by 7.0 by 6.0 cm. respectively and both show a circular area 5.5 cm. in diameter on one face that has been modified by grinding or rubbing. This surface is not flat but is a little deeper in the center. The thinner of the two stones shows evidence around the periphery of use as a hammerstone. The sandstone piece has the form of a truncated cone and measures 10.0 cm. long with a diameter varying from 7.5 cm. to 6.5 cm. At least the truncated end appears to have been used for grinding. The beaver incisors (*Castor can-*

adensis) average 6.0 cm. in length and the inside of the cutting end is ground down to provide a square cutting edge, although none of the specimens shows evidence of use (Pl. 121,*a*). The lamellar flake of dark gray Dongola chert lay near the beaver teeth on the pit floor. It shows the characteristic three parallel flake scars on the dorsal side and measures 5.1 cm. long and 1.5 cm. wide (Pl. 121,*a*). The two worked pieces of deer antler were at the east edge of the group. These are both portions of the proximal end of antlers, 15.0 cm. and 13.6 cm. long respectively, and both are cut and ground on both ends. The longer specimen retains the burr. There is no clear evidence of use on either artifact (Pl. 121,*a*). The mussel shell spoon is a left valve of *Lampsilis ventricosa* 10.8 cm. long and 6.2 cm. wide. The shell is ground on all edges and a handle has been shaped into the anterior end by the removal of the hinge elements (Pl. 121,*a*).

The other group of artifacts (Group No. 2, Pl. 122,*d*) lay just north of the skull of Burial No. 1 next to the northern edge of the burial pit. It consists of one complete and one fragmentary Havana vessel, a worked conch shell, a fragmentary modified turtle carapace and two fragments of mussel shell spoons. The pottery vessels (H2 and H3) are described below (Pl. 122,*d*; Fig. 22). The conch shell (*Busycon contrarium*) measures 19.5 cm. long and 10.5 cm. wide and is modified like the shell in Group No. 1. The turtle carapace (*Emys blandingi*) is modified in the form of a scoop by the removal of all the marginal scutes except the three anterior ones which were left as a handle. The inner surface of the carapace is cut and ground smooth. The fragments of carapace underlay both the pottery vessels. The two mussel shell fragments (*Lampsilis* sp., both left valves) lay on top of the turtle shell fragments. They both show modification

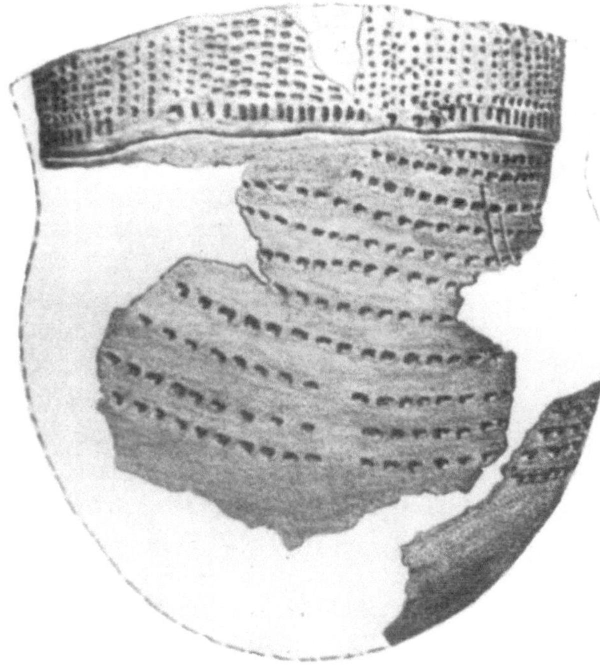

Fig. 22, Drawing of Norton Dentate Stamp vessel H-2, from Group 2 of central pit in Mound H. Height 14.0 cm. UMMA Neg.

in the form of removal of the hinge and grinding of the edges present.

A platform effigy pipe (Pl. 123,*b*) was found south of the mandible of Skull No. 1. The pipe is of a very soft limestone and was in contact with a piece of limonite which unfortunately had decomposed part of the upper portion of the pipe bowl. Enough of the effigy remained to establish an identification as the head of an elk. The treatment of the nose, especially, resembled closely the representation of the elk on the turtle carapace from Mound 1. The platform of the pipe measures 7.9 cm. long, 2.9 cm. wide and 1.3 cm. thick. The bowl is 3.5 cm. high and the estimated diameter is 2.5 cm. Some red ochre stain is left on the platform and bowl, suggesting that the pipe was originally painted or colored with this material. There was a group of 16 turkey metatarsal awls and a lamellar flake directly behind Skull No. 1 (Pl. 123,*a*). The use of the term *awl* here does not imply function but is used to differentiate these objects from the large split deer or elk metapodial pins whose function is more obvious. These awls were made by splitting the proximal end of the tibio-metatarsus of *Meleagris gallopavo* so that each awl included one of the articular surfaces of the original condyle and part of the posterior surface of the shaft. The awl was then pointed and the shaft and edges of the condyle ground smooth. These awls range in length from 10.4 cm. to 14.2 cm. with an average length of 12.5 cm. Dr. Charles Cleland has determined that the 16 awls represent at least eight individual birds. The lamellar flake of dark gray Dongola chert which lay under the group of awls is 3.6 cm. long and shows use retouch along one side of the distal edge.

The floor of the burial pit had been covered with a thin layer of mixed ash, charcoal and calcined bone fragments prior to the placement of the skeletal material and artifacts. This layer had become consolidated with the underlying gravel and the burial pit soil above it, but there is no evidence of its having been burned in place. The only recognizable bone was a burned section of deer cranium (*Odocoileus virginianus*) including a portion of one occipital condyle and the surrounding occipital bone.

Skeletal Remains

The burial pit contained the remains of five individuals. Burial No. 1 is the skeleton of a male close to 20 years old. The skull was in fairly good shape and a few of the cervical and thoracic vertebrae were in approximate anatomical position but the rest of the postcranial skeleton was disarticulated and out of order. Burial No. 2 is a male of late-middle or early old age afflicted with arthritis, rheumatoid arthritis with dental involvement, curvature of the spine and restricted use of the left shoulder and forearm. The bones of Burial No. 2 were for the most part disarticulated and out of order. The fragmentary right scapula shows postmortem cut marks on the acromial process indicating that the ligaments were cut in the process of dismemberment. The bones of Burial No. 1 and Burial No. 2 were so mixed that a "double bundle" type of interment is suggested. Burial No. 3 is the bundle burial of a child, estimated at 6 to 10 years old, which was placed next to the skull of Burial No. 2. Burial No. 4, to the east of the other three, is a bundled child perhaps three years old. Postmortem tooth loss is extensive, hindering an accurate age estimate. Burial No. 5 is represented only by a part of the palate and left malar of an adult that was found near the skull of Burial No. 2. All the skulls, both child and adult, show medium occipital flattening in the lambdoid region. Burial No. 1 has had postmortem removal of an ovoid section of bone from the region of the left parietal above and behind the left mastoid and Burial No. 2 has had a plaque of bone approximately 5 by 10 cm. in size removed from the left side of the occipital, behind and slightly above the left mastoid in the masto-occipital suture region. Burial No. 2 shows marked ear exostoses.

Burial Vessels

H-1 (Pl. 122,*a*) Norton Zoned Incised

Paste: Temper is angular crushed granite, some mica. Tends to foliate. Color buff to brown, some gray firing clouds.

Surface: Smooth, partially eroded on exterior. Interior smoothed.

Decoration: Vertical curved dentate stamp from lip down 2.5 cm., then a band of concentric incised triangles 6.5 cm. wide. Transverse dentate stamp on lip 3 mm. apart.

Form: Rim is slightly flaring, lip beveled inward. Neck is slightly constricted and body is sub-conoidal with rounded base.

Dimensions: Height 15.1 cm.
Rim height 3 cm.
Shoulder diameter 13.5 cm.
Rim diameter 12.9 cm.
Thickness 7 mm.

Similarities: The rim treatment is most similar to Griffin's type Naples Stamped with the addition of the dentate stamping on the lip. The body decoration is unusual, although one Hopewell Ware vessel from the Utica Mound Group described in Griffin and Morgan, 1941 (p. 46; Pl. 57, Fig. 2, p. 189) has a somewhat similar geometric design. Two grit-tempered vessels from the Brangenburg Mound Group in Calhoun County, Illinois have triangle designs as dominant decorative motifs but only the Hopewell Zoned Incised is directly analogous (ibid.: Pl. 50, p. 181). Concentric triangles or diamonds are a feature of some of the late Adena pottery (e.g. Griffin, 1947: Pl. III, p. 198) and go back as far as Stallings Island and Late Orange Period ceramics in the Southeast.

H-2 (Pl. 122,*c*) Norton Zoned Dentate

Paste: Temper is angular decomposed granite particles and sand, particle size up to 5 mm. Paste tends to crumble easily. Color is light brown with light gray firing clouds.

Surface: Smoothed, some temper particles protrude. Interior smoothed.

Decoration: Dentate stamp applied horizontally along outer lip, then band of light vertical dentate stamp 2 cm. wide bounded by a heavy horizontal dentate stamp and an incised line. The body shows diagonal single lines of dentate stamp about three-quarters of the way to the undecorated base and there is a faint attempt at zoning in the form of a "V" bounded by double incised lines.

Form: Rim is slightly flaring, lip is rounded to flattened and slightly insloping, neck is slightly constricted and body is subconoidal with rounded base.

Dimensions: Height 14 cm. (est.)
Rim height 3 cm.
Shoulder diameter 12.5 cm. (est.)
Rim diameter 12.7 cm. (est.)
Thickness 7 mm.

Similarities: Rim treatment is similar to Naples Stamped type.
This vessel, found with H-3, was evidently quickly made and inadequately fired for use as a burial vessel in Mound H.

H-3 (Pl. 122,*b*) Norton Zoned Punctate

Paste: Temper is angular decomposed granite, particles up to 4 mm. Paste tends to crumble easily. Color is light buff on top to gray on base, buff interior, dark gray core.

Surface: Smoothed, temper particles showing. Interior smoothed.

Decoration: Rim has lightly applied vertical dentate stamp for 1.6 cm. below the lip. The rim is bounded by a light incised line, then a plain zone 2 cm. wide, another vertical incised line and the remainder of the body is covered with punctate impressions which resemble vertically applied dentate stamping. The impressions of the tool are large (3 to 4 mm. in diameter) and appear rounded or, in some cases, semicircular as opposed to the usual rectangular form of a dentate stamp.

Form: Rim is vertical and slightly cambered with marked interior channel. Lip is flat, slopes inward. Neck is slightly constricted below the cambered area. Body globular with flat indented base.

Dimensions: Height 7.5 cm.
Rim height 1.4 cm.
Shoulder diameter 11.3 cm.
Rim diameter 10.2 cm.
Thickness 7 mm. on rim, 1.3 cm. on base.

Similarities: This vessel was found with H-2 and shows the same crude manufacturing techniques. The flat-based body and insloped lip are characteristic of some forms of Havana and the rim decoration is closest to Griffin's Naples Stamped type. The cambering and inner channel on the rim are usually considered characteristic of Classic Hopewell ware, however.

MOUND I

Mound I measured 35.0 feet in diameter and about 4.0 feet in height above the surrounding ground when surveyed. There was a pit 5.0 feet in diameter and approximately 1.5 feet deep directly in the center of the top which was evidently fairly recent judging from the consistency of soil within the pit. It was decided to test the mound with a ten-foot-wide trench through the center in spite of the obvious disturbance. The first 2.0 feet of depth in the test trench indicated that the disturbance was limited to a shallow pit which had been used as a fireplace and dump for refuse from a picnic.

There was a 1.0-foot to 1.5-foot thick

formation of humus over the south half of the top of the mound which disappeared on the center of the north half, evidently a result of erosion caused by a vehicle and foot path up to the top of the mound. Under the humus was a layer of dark brown sandy loam which graded quickly into a light brown sandy loam except in the region directly over the subfloor pit, where the dark soil directly overlay the cap. The dark gray organic soil of the cap reached a maximum depth of 1.5 feet at about one-third of the way through the mound from the periphery, from which point it thinned out over the central subfloor pit. Individual basket loads were discernible in the cap for a distance of from 3.5 to 4.0 feet out from the limits of the burial pit. The loads averaged 1.2 feet long by 0.3 feet high. There was a decomposed bark layer 0.1 to 0.3 feet thick underlying some of the cap but this was not a continuous layer like that in Mound H. A discontinuous lens of mixed gravel and light sandy loam appeared under the cap and ash layer, representing the material thrown out from the excavation of the subfloor pit. The original submound surface was represented by a layer of dark brown sandy loam which graded into light brown sandy loam for a total depth of two feet, underlain by the basal gravel. The burial pit had been dug down to this gravel level. There was no indication of a humus formation on the original surface, suggesting preparation of the surface prior to mound construction (Fig. 23 shows the profile).

The Burial Pit

The outline of the burial pit became apparent due to the dark organic soil inside the pit as soon as the submound level was reached (Pl. 124,*a*) and the original trench was expanded to include the central two-thirds of the mound. The pit was oriented northeast-southwest, and the dimensions of the pit at this point were 8.0 feet long and 4.3 feet wide (Fig. 24). At 0.5 feet below the original surface a split elk metapodial pin 26.9 cm. long was found in about the center of the east edge of the pit, lying horizontally with the tip of the point next to the pit wall. At a depth of 1.0 foot below the original surface there were the skull and articulated forelegs of a striped skunk (*Mephitis mephitis*) approximately in the center of the pit and other bones from this animal scattered through the pit at this level. There was a juvenile human rib next to the center of the east side of the pit and a juvenile tibia in the center of the south pit edge, evidently from Burial No. 10. The bottom level of the burial pit measured 6.5 feet in length and 3.5 feet in width. A thin layer of the dark burial pit fill and some patches of greasy hematite had been placed on the pit floor and the burials and grave goods laid in on top of it (Pl. 124,*b*).

In the southeast corner of the pit there were three split elk metapodial pins 21.1 cm., 26.2 cm. and 21.5 cm. long, respectively. One had been broken and the point end which was left in the gravel showed

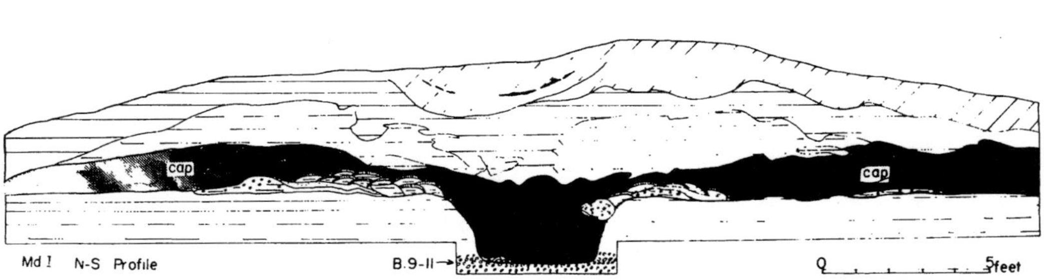

Fig. 23. North-south profile of Norton Mound I. UMMA Neg. 15651.

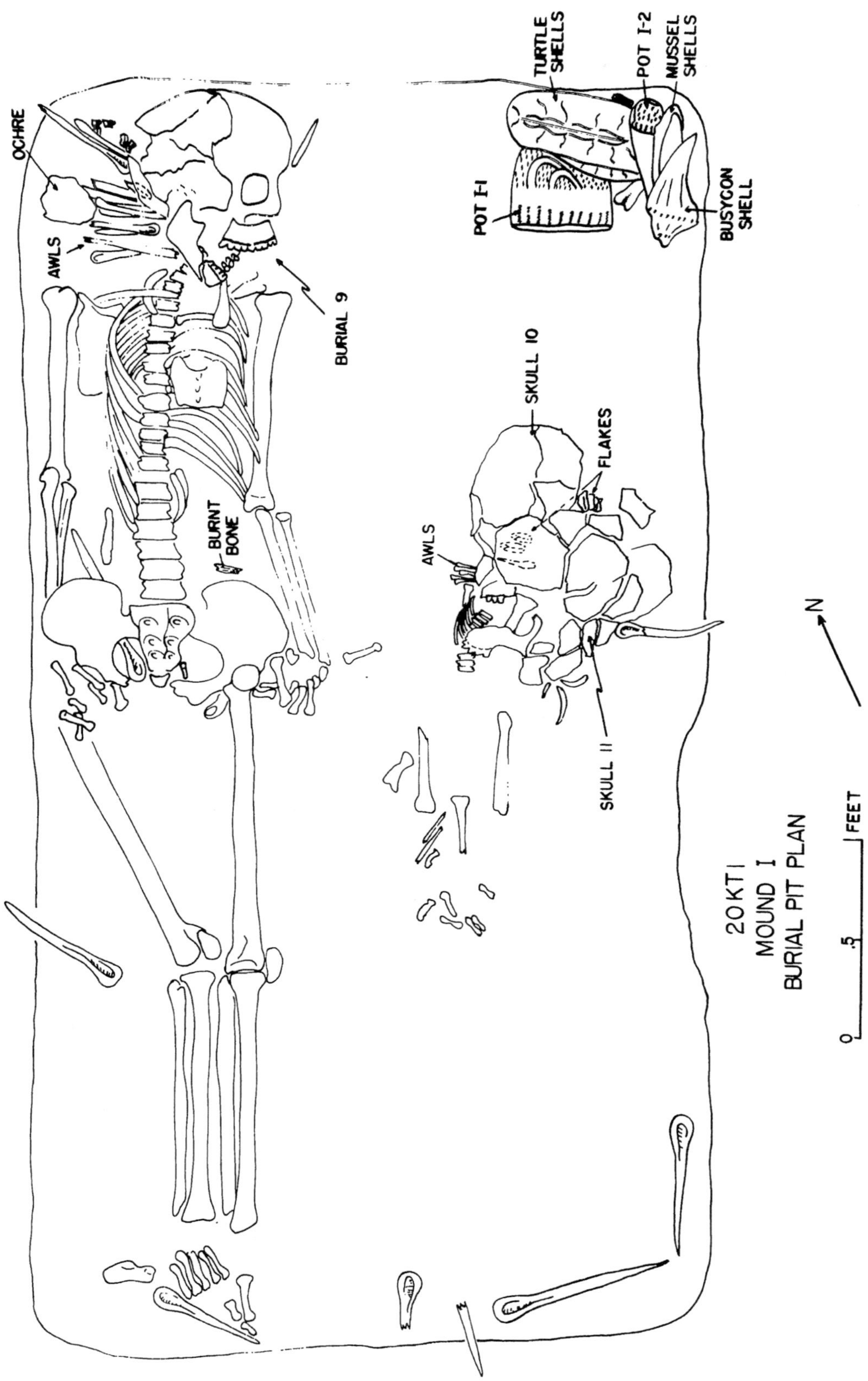

Fig. 24. Burial plan of the central pit of Norton Mound I. UMMA Neg. 15649.

staining from limestone. There was an elk bone pin 25.4 cm. long at the feet of Burial No. 9, another 22.3 cm. long to the west of the knees of No. 9, one 28.6 cm. in length under the right innominate of this burial and another 19.1 cm. long directly behind the skull. Another pin 23.4 cm. long was found immediately east of Skull No. 11 and one 30.3 cm. long was underneath the group of artifacts in the northeast corner of the pit. All these pins with the exception of the one under the pelvis of Burial No. 9 were pointing out toward the edge of the pit and were either partway into the gravel or touching it (Pl. 125,*a*).

There were groups of bone awls and chips beneath the skulls of Burials No. 9 and 10. The group of objects found under Skull No. 9 included seven cut turkey tibio-metatarsal sections, two worked sections of mammal bone, one fragmentary turkey awl and ten chert chips (Pl. 125,*b*). The turkey tibio-metatarsals averaged 13.5 cm. long after the distal end had been removed. These bones showed different stages in the removal of "extraneous" bone preparatory to splitting and finishing like the awls with Burial No. 1 in Mound H. The mammal bones include a section of long bone cortex 20.5 cm. long cut and ground to a blunt point and the proximal end of a split deer metapodial 19 cm. long which was cut and ground to a point. These two objects were located beside the cervical vertebrae of Burial No. 9. The chert chips average 3.5 cm. by 1.8 cm. and are the result of primary flaking of a gray chert identical to that from which the discoidals and points from Mound H were made (Dongola chert). Seven of the ten chips show use marks on at least one edge. The group of artifacts behind Skull No. 10 included six complete and four fragmentary split turkey bone awls (Pl. 126), the complete awls averaging 11.1 cm. long, and five Dongola chert chips. One of the broken awls shows notching along the anterior edge for a distance of 3.5 cm. from the head. The chips are of the same gray chert as the group under Skull No. 9. Three of the largest chips show use marks along one edge. A group of 10 complete and several fragmentary tubular shell beads were found under the mandible of Skull No. 10. These beads were formed by grinding cut sections of conch shell columella and the complete beads averaged 0.8 cm. long by 0.6 cm. in diameter. There was a lump of granular hematite 6 cm. in diameter between this group of awls and the edge of the pit.

The group of artifacts in the northeast corner of the pit included two pottery vessels, one a Norton Zoned Dentate vessel (Pot I-1, Pl. 127) and the other a miniature vessel and a notched rim and overall punctations on the body (Pot I-2, Pl. 127), a worked *Busycon* shell, three mussel shell spoons, three engraved turtle carapaces, one plain turtle carapace and three chert chips. The pots are described below. The conch shell is a *Busycon contrarium* 13.7 cm. long and 7.3 cm. wide which shows modification identical to that on the shells from Mound H (Pl. 127). One mussel shell spoon is a left valve of *Lampsilis ventricosa* 11.0 cm. long by 6.5 cm. wide which has a handle cut into the anterior end. Another is a right valve of *Lampsilis siliquoidea* 12.5 cm. long and 6.0 cm. wide with a handle at the anterior end. The third is a fragmentary *Anodonta* sp. right valve. All three shells show grinding on all surfaces. The turtle carapace dishes are all made from *Emys blandingi* and measure 22.5 by 12.0 cm., 19.7 cm. by 13.4 cm., 19.5 by 12.2 cm. and 14.8 by 9.0 cm. respectively. The lateral marginal scutes have been removed from the largest and the smallest shells and all show removal of the protruding interior bony attachments and grinding on all edges. The largest carapace has an engraved design consisting of

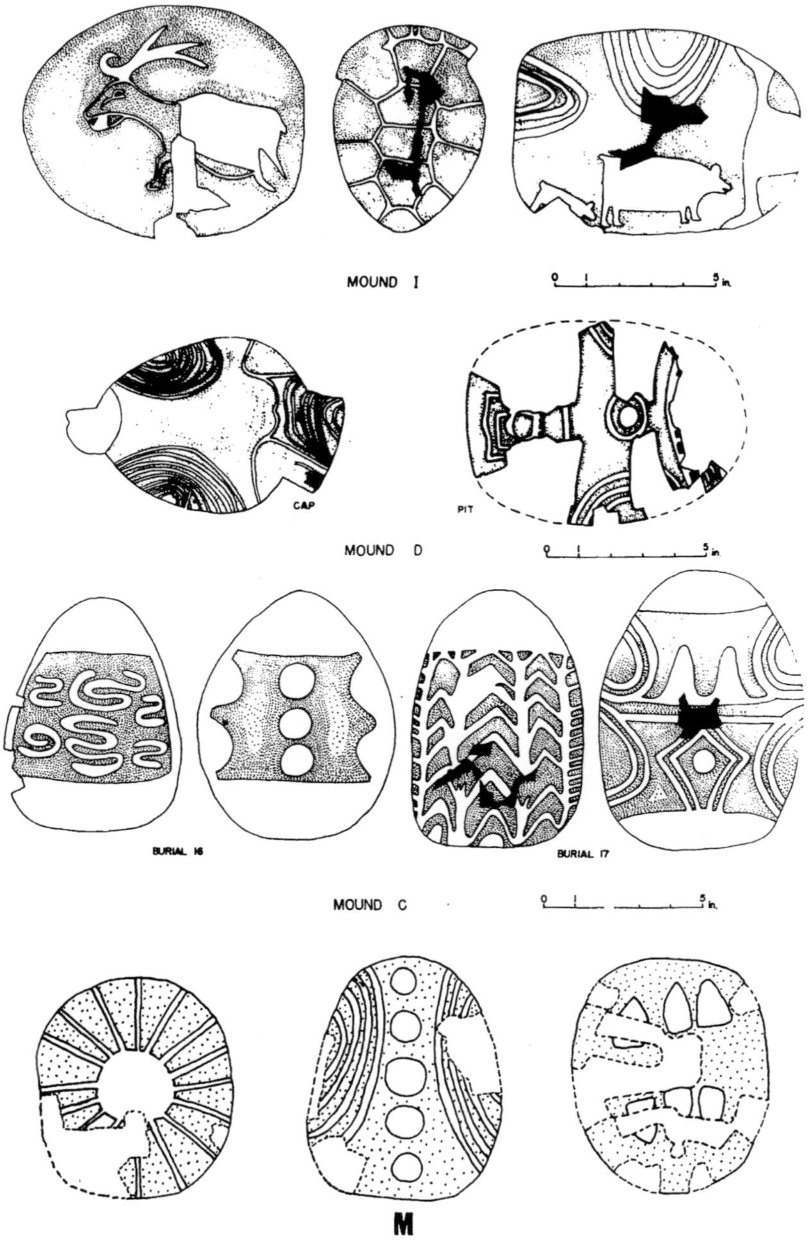

Fig. 25. Designs on turtle carapace containers from excavations in Mounds M, C, D and I. UMMA Neg. 15650.

two bears and two "rainbow" motifs, the next largest has an engraved elk design and the smallest shows a simple widening of the original seam pattern on the exterior of the shell (Fig. 25). The engraving on the shells was effected by removing small spalls of bone from the surface of the shell within the limits of the design. A similar effect was achieved in the laboratory by using the corner of one of the chert blades on dried turtle shell. The original skin probably afforded a nice contrast for the design, although the engraving is now so faint that it was necessary to trace the designs out in the laboratory with the aid of a binocular microscope. Mr. John Halsey of UMMA has duplicated the effect of engraving on an *Emys blandingi* carapace, producing an engraved dish which no doubt closely resembles the originals (Halsey, 1966: Fig. 3). Engraved turtle carapace containers would seem to be a trait specific to Michigan Hopewell, with the possible exception of brief references from Iowa and Ohio (Flanders, 1965: 362-3). Three dark gray Dongola chert chips average 3.4 cm. long by 1.5 cm. wide and one shows use marks on one edge.

Four sherds were also found in the pit fill. Two are 1.3 cm. thick sherds exhibiting heavy grit tempering, an oxidized interior layer and what appears to be rubbed-over cordmarking on the exterior surface. A third shows these same characteristics but is 6 mm. thick. The fourth sherd is 5 mm. thick with angular grit tempering and a uniform buff color throughout. This sherd is decorated on the exterior with four parallel incised lines 5 mm. apart which are intersected and halted by another line diagonal to them, identical to the decorative pattern of "nested triangles" on pot H-1 from Mound H. A few flecks of mica which might have come from the crushed granite temper show on the surface of this sherd.

Skeletal Remains

At least four individuals were represented in this pit, an extended adult and three bundled children. Burial No. 9 is identified as an adult female by morphological characteristics. The skull is badly warped but shows medium lambdoid deformation and a small plaque removal from the left side of the occipital behind and slightly above the left mastoid. The skeleton is complete and in anatomical position except for the left arm which had been rotated 180 degrees as evidenced by the humeral head displacement. There was a fragment of burned long bone, possibly human, just next to the left innominate of this burial—a possible parallel to the burned phalanx in Mound H. Burial No. 10 includes very fragmentary remains of two children, one about a year old and the other slightly older and Burial No. 11 is a child close to adolescence, also fragmentary.

Burial Vessels

I-1 (Fig. 26, A) Norton Zoned Dentate

Paste: Temper is mixed crushed granite and sand. Paste is compact, well-mixed. Color

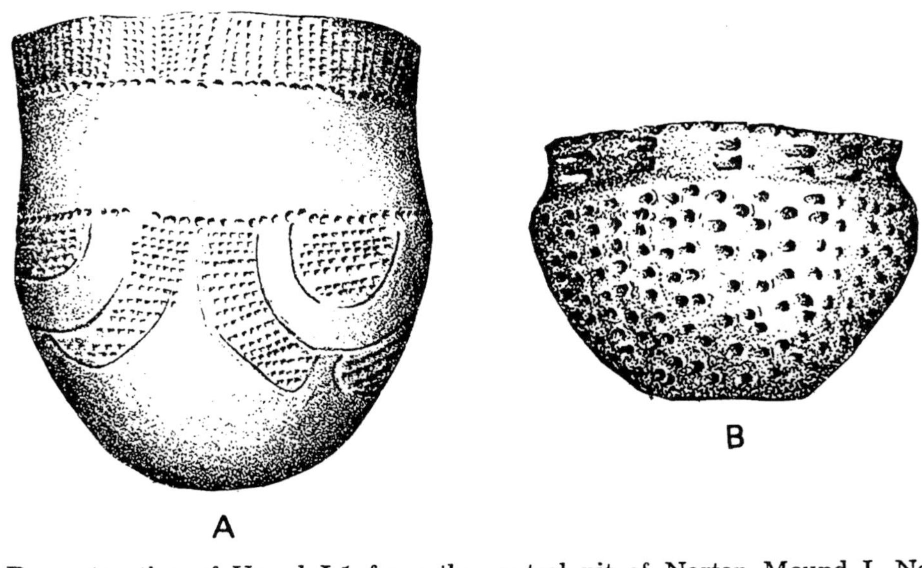

Fig. 26. *A*. Reconstruction of Vessel I-1 from the central pit of Norton Mound I. Norton Dentate Stamp, height 12.1 cm. UMMA Neg. 95-10. *B*. Reconstruction of Vessel I-2 from the central pit of Norton Mound I. Norton Punctate, height 4.0 cm. UMMA Neg. 95-10.

light to dark brown, some dark gray firing clouds vertically on three portions of circumference and around base. Core is dark gray.

Surface: Hard, well-smoothed approaching polish in plain zone. Interior smoothed.

Decoration: Lip shows longitudinal dentate stamp. Rim is marked by band of vertically to slightly diagonally applied dentate stamp 2 cm. wide, bounded by line of closely spaced punctates formed with hollow cylindrical tool applied from the right. Then a plain zone 3.0 to 3.4 cm. wide showing rubbed-out remnants of the lower design elements. Plain zone bounded by another row of punctates, then four semicircular design elements filled with dentate stamping. These design elements originally extended up to rim, but were obliterated probably before pot was dried.

Form: Sub-conoidal jar with off-center, slightly flattened base. Rim is slightly cambered, lip is flattened and rounded and slopes inward, neck is slightly constricted.

Dimensions: Height 12.5 cm.
Rim height 2 cm.
Shoulder diameter 11.2 cm.
Rim diameter 11.0 cm.
Thickness 7 mm.

Similarities: Semicircular design elements similar to these are found on Havana vessels from the Adler Mound Group (Winters, 1962: Fig. 38, p, 67) and the Utica Mounds (Griffin and Morgan, 1941: Pl. 54, p. 184, Pl. 55, p. 187) and are common in Goodall focus ceramics. The rim shows the Naples Stamped type dentate stamping and plain zone of the vessels from Mound H and Mound C and the slight cambering noted for vessel H-3, but the plain zone is bordered in this case by rows of punctates like one of the Utica vessels.

I-2 (Fig. 26,B) Norton Punctate

Paste: Temper is finely crushed granite and sparse sand. Paste is compact and well-mixed like vessel I-1, shows no tendency to foliate or crumble. Color is tan, with dark gray firing clouds. Core color is dark gray.

Surface: Smooth, hard, some temper protrudes. Interior smoothed.

Decoration: Exterior of lip is notched, rim shows one row of equally spaced, paired punctates applied from the left and body is covered with closely spaced punctates formed by blunt cylindrical tool applied from left. Base is undecorated.

Form: Flat-bottomed sub-conoidal jar with constricted neck, slightly flaring rim. Lip is thickened, round to flat on top and slopes inward. Base is indented like vessel H-3.

Dimensions: Height 4 cm.
Rim height 7 mm.
Shoulder diameter 5.8 cm.
Rim diameter 5.4 cm.
Thickness 3 mm.

Similarities: This miniature vessel has some similarity in both form and decorative technique to Griffin's type Montezuma Punctate as illustrated from the Brangenburg Group in southern Illinois (ibid., Pls. 46, 47, p. 175) and the Utica Group (ibid., Pl. 54, p. 185). Vessel I-2 is grit-tempered, unlike most of the Montezuma type, and lacks the cross-hatched Classic Hopewell rim sometimes found on this Middle Woodland form.

Mound J

This mound is indicated on Gibson's map as being only 1.5 feet high and this was the case when the overgrowth was removed. A north-south test trench ten feet wide was started through what was determined as the approximate center. The diameter of the mound was approximately 40 feet and the outline somewhat irregular, evidently due to recent excavations along the outer edges. There was a very thin dark humus layer encountered in the surface layer of the trench and the remainder of the profile consisted of dark brown sandy loam. At a depth of 1.7 feet from the surface in the center of the mound a slight color change was noted which troweling revealed as the rather indistinct outline of a burial pit. There was no indication of a cap in the upper layer of this mound and it appeared that this part of the usual mound structure was either not included or was obscured by the disturbance. The very irregular surface of the mound suggests that an undetermined amount of the upper portion of the mound was removed by stripping for black dirt.

The test pit was extended to the north by the excavation of a ten-foot wide section of the trench in an effort to determine the limits of the central pit. The pit, indicated by a darker and more organic soil, measured 7.75 feet long and 4.65 feet wide when first encountered (Fig. 27). It was found to be somewhat basin-shaped in profile so that Skull No. 6 and the turtle shell actually rested at a slightly higher elevation than the rest of the bones (Pl. 128). The depth of the pit actually ranged from 0.5 to 0.7 feet, very shallow for this pattern of mound construction, which again would seem to indicate recent removal of a good portion of the mound. It was immediately apparent from a slight mottling in the dark burial pit fill that some disturbance had taken place previously. The disturbance was localized to an oblong area in the thoracic region of Burial No. 6 and had resulted in the removal or scattering of most of the ribs, vertebrae, parts of the pelvis and the left humerus, scapula and clavicle.

The Burial Pit

The first artifact encountered in this pit was a straight-sided copper celt located about 0.3 feet above the pelvic area of Burial No. 6 (Pl. 129). The celt measures 10.0 cm. in length and is 5.3 cm. wide at the excurvate bit and 2.3 cm. wide at the poll with a plano-convex cross section and flattened edges. The bit shows some grinding 2.0 cm. wide on the convex edge, evidently in the process of forming the edge, and both hammer marks and unclosed fissures from the constituent fragments are evident on the sides of the celt. A turtle carapace dish (*Emys blandingi*) 16.5 cm. long and 10.0 cm. wide was found in the northeast corner of the pit (Pl. 129). The lateral marginal scutes were almost completely removed and the anterior and posterior edges were cut and ground smooth. The interior of the carapace was ground smooth except for a medial ridge of bone 3.0 cm. wide, the remains of the vertebral attachment, and no decoration was evi-

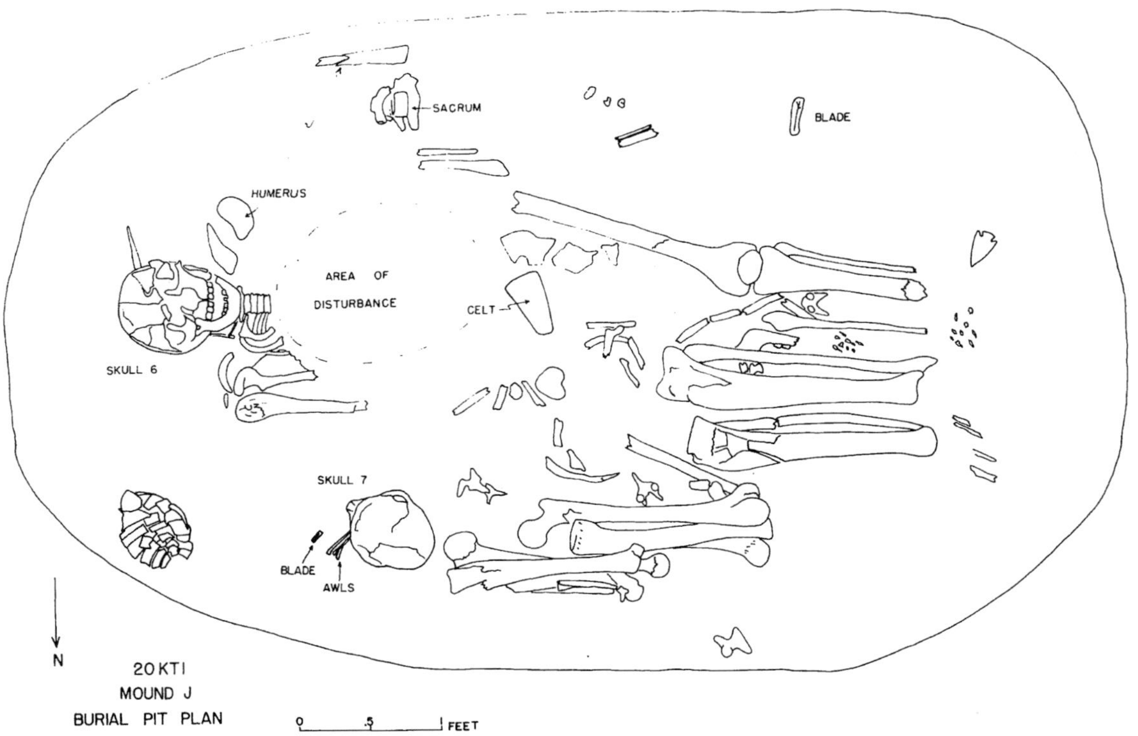

Fig. 27. Floor plan of central burial pit of Norton Mound J. UMMA Neg. 15646.

dent on the exterior. With this shell was an articulated portion of another carapace consisting of one costal and three vertebral scutes. The interior of the bones are smoothed like the dish and the last vertebral scute has been cut to a point, perhaps to serve as a tool of some sort. A corner-notched projectile point (Pl. 129) in the west end of the pit near the foot region of Burial No. 6 is of a tan and blue-gray mottled flint with quartz inclusions and is described in Table 2 (J-1). The material appears very close in color and constituency to some examples of "Flint Ridge" flint. A Dongola chert lamellar flake lay on the floor of the pit in the southwest corner. It measures 6.2 cm. long by 2.8 cm. wide at the widest point and has a limonite encrustation at the distal end (Pl. 129).

Skull No. 7, presumably associated with the bundle of long bones in the north part of the pit, was sitting on its base with the face to the east. Under the facial area were ten fragments of bone awls ranging from 2.0 cm. to 6.5 cm. in length, too small to be identified but presumably of turkey leg bones. With the fragments were two unretouched rectangular lamellar flakes of dark gray flint, one 3.5 cm. by 2.0 cm. and the other 2.2 cm. by 1.0 cm., both showing evidence of a prepared striking platform.

In the process of the removal of Skull No. 6, an oval plate of mica 14.8 cm. long, 8.0 cm. wide and 5 mm. thick was found directly under the back of the skull (Pl. 130,*a*). This plate had been stained by a thin deposit of hematite which underlay most of the skull. Directly on top of the mica plate were two lamellar flakes of yellow-white flint, one 5.9 cm. by 1.8 cm. and the other 6.2 cm. by 2.2 cm., both showing some modification of the striking platform. There was a fragment of a turkey tibio metatarsus, 18.0 cm. long with both ends broken off, extending past the left side of the skull and the pointed tip of an awl 5.5 cm. long and two small fragments 2.5 cm. long directly under the skull on top of the plate. These fragments are too small for identification but resemble the turkey bone forms from the other mounds. The fragments of Skull No. 6 were fairly well cemented together by the organic soil so it was decided to take the skull back to the lab as a unit. Upon removing the mixed dirt and ochre from the rear of the skull preparatory to reconstruction, it was found that a number of artifacts adhered to the skull, having been separated from the mica sheet by the dirt and ochre. These included one complete and two fragmentary lamellar flakes, one ovoid flint blank, one trianguloid flint blank, one corner notched projectile point, a portion of a bone awl and one fragment of worked bone (Pl. 130,*c*). The flakes are of yellow-white flint, all 2 mm. thick, and measure 4.7 cm. by 1.4 cm. for the complete specimen, 3.5 cm. by 1.6 cm. for the proximal fragment and 2.0 cm. by 1.0 cm. for the distal fragment. The other three chipped stone artifacts were stained by ochre in the dirt on and in the rear portion of the skull. The ovoid blank is of a tan and gray banded flint and measures 5.6 cm. long, 4.0 cm. wide and 1.4 cm. thick at the center. The parallel-sided trianguloid blank is of the same stone and measures 7.8 cm. long, 4.1 cm. wide at the base and 1.2 cm. thick at the center. Both of these artifacts show very little peripheral retouch but might have been used as knives. The projectile point, J-2, is decribed in Table 2. The awl is the proximal end, 4.3 cm. long, of one of the split turkey tibio-metatarsus bones and the worked bone object, also ochre-stained, appears to be a thinned-down section of an unidentified split long bone approximately 2.0 cm. wide with a 3 mm. hole drilled in one side.

The disturbed area of the burial pit also yielded several small fragments of mica, the proximal end 8.7 cm. long of a split deer metapodial which had been cut and ground to form one of the large bone pins, and three sherds. Two of the sherds are body sherds roughly 4.0 cm. square and 7 mm. thick with angular grit and sand temper and partially eroded surfaces. One sherd is smoothed on both surfaces and the other shows brush marks on both surfaces and three partially obliterated incised lines 2 mm. wide on the exterior, possibly part of a zoned decoration. The third sherd is a rim fragment 7 mm. thick with angular grit temper, an insloping lip, a band of crosshatched incised lines 2.2 cm. wide from the lip down to a single horizontal incised line and a row of hemiconical punctates 3 mm. wide and 8 mm. apart below this line. The rim is slightly thickened and channeled on the inside. This rim is identified as Norton Cross-hatched (Quimby, 1941,*b*), a local expression of the Hopewell Ware style.

Skeletal Remains

The remains of at least three adults and fragments of one child were found in the central pit. Burial No. 6 represents a fragmentary adult male extended on the back which had been disturbed by an intrusive pit in the thoracic and lumbar area. The cervical vertebrae were in anatomical position, the right humeral head was articulated and the left leg was in anatomical position. The left arm and scapula were scattered, a portion of the sacrum was found in the south edge of the pit, the upper right leg was missing and the pelvis was represented by scattered fragments. The skull shows medium-to-marked lambdoid flattening, ear exostoses and a plaque removal high on the left parietal. There was an extra fragmentary right tibia and two fibulae placed over the lower leg area of this burial. These bones are designated as both Burial No. 8 and Burial J, in Table 4, as the field analysis did not indicate two individuals. Burial No. 7 is a partial bundle burial of an adult male with the skull resting on its base at the east end of the bundle. The skull shows medium lambdoid flattening and ear exostoses. The child is represented only by carpal and finger bones and long bone fragments.

Mound D

Mound D is indicated on Gibson's map as being 6.2 feet high. The survey showed a present elevation of closer to 5.0 feet above present ground level, or approximately 5.3 feet above the original ground level, and a diameter of 50 feet. The exploratory ten foot trench uncovered a large intrusive pit beginning at the top center of the mound and gradually becoming smaller with depth, so it was decided to excavate a 15-foot wide trench begining ten feet in from the west edge of the mound to determine the limits of the intrusion.

The familiar dark organic soil of the cap, contrasting with the lighter sandy loam of the upper mound fill, was encountered about 3.3 feet below the top center of the mound. The cap reached a thickness of 2.3 feet at the edges of the intrusive pit but the "dip" of the cap over the central pit, so clear on the other mounds, was eradicated by the intrusion. The basket-load effect in this cap was not as clear as that in Mound H, for instance, but could be discerned for purposes of measurement. The loads averaged 1.5 feet long and 0.3 feet high. A bark lens underlying the cap extended 4 to 5 feet past the limits of the burial pit. The west edge of the burial pit was encountered at a depth of 7.5 feet from the top center of the mound and the trench was then leveled off at this depth in an attempt to trace out the pit. The original disturbance could be traced out to cover an area from the center about one-third of the length of the pit which measured 6.5 feet wide by 11 feet long, the long dimension being oriented northwest. However, upon "pedestaling" the burial pit and beginning the slow scraping of the pit fill, it was found that the original excavator had widened his excavation to encompass the whole burial pit except a narrow margin around the periphery (Fig. 28). The depth of the subfloor pit was 7.5 feet from the top of the mound, or 2.2 feet from original ground level (Fig. 28).

A small cache of burial goods was encountered under the cap in the bark lens in the north wall of the trench, approximately two feet above the level of the burial pit and even with the center of the pit (Pl. 131,*a*). The cache consisted from bottom to top of a thin layer of wood charcoal, a badly fragmented segment of a pottery vessel and a turtle carapace dish containing a mussel shell spoon and two cut and drilled bear canines (Pl. 131,*b*). The sherds average about 5 mm. in thickness and the color ranges from light brown to dark gray. The temper is mixed angular grit and limestone with the limestone predominating. The rim is slightly thickened and channeled with an insloping lip and the rim decoration consists of a band of

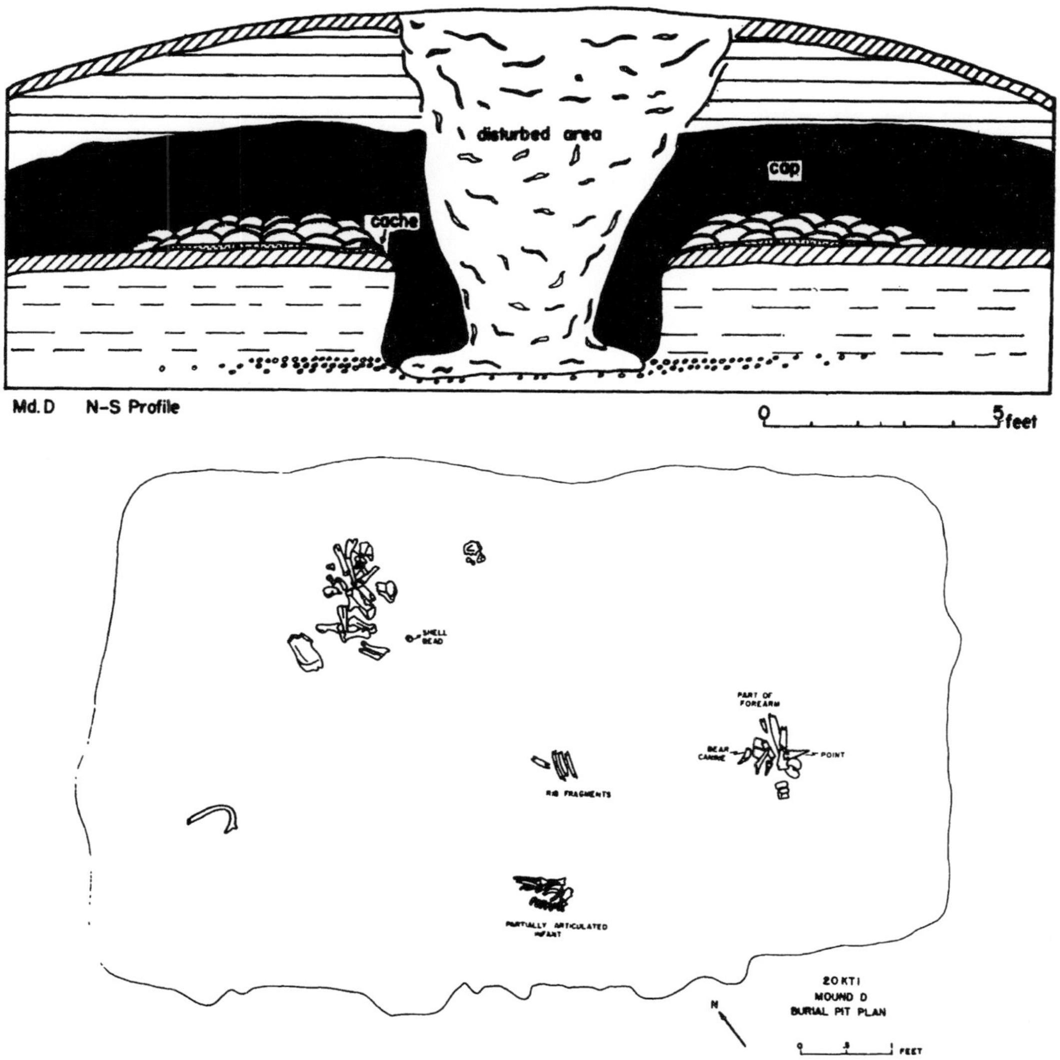

Fig. 28. *A*. North-south profile of Norton Mound D. UMMA Neg. 15652. *B*. Burial pit plan of Norton Mound D. UMMA Neg. 15655.

crosshatched incised lines 8 mm. wide on the thickened part on the rim, bordered by a row of hemiconical punctates. Although the body sherds are too small and scattered to permit reconstruction, there are indications of a lobate body form and a zoned decoration, the zones being filled with series of horizontal incised lines 1 to 2 mm. wide and up to 8 mm. long. The horizontal incised line design element is one that one would ordinarily expect with the Norton variant of the classic Hopewell style, although the limestone temper does not seem to be duplicated in Michigan Hopewell. The turtle dish is a carapace of *Emys blandingi* 19.2 cm. long and 11.0 cm. wide. Most of the marginal scutes have been removed and all protruding surfaces have been cut off the interior leaving a smooth surface. At the midpoint of the right edge two holes 2 mm. in diameter have been drilled 1.4 cm. apart, presumably to repair a split in the shell. A curvilinear design has been engraved on the outer surface of the shell (see Fig. 25). The shell spoon is a left valve of *Lampsilis ventricosa* 10.4 cm. long and 6.4 cm. wide with all edges and the outer surface ground smooth. A handle 5 cm. long and about 1 cm. wide has been cut into the anterior end of the shell directly opposite the umbone including some of the ventral margin and this handle has been decorated by notches cut into the edge from 3 to 5 mm. apart. The impression of this edge on plasticine closely resembles the dentate stamping on some of the burial pottery from this site. The bear canines (*Ursus americanus*) are both 8.0 cm. long, 1.5 cm. wide and 1.1 cm. thick at the widest point and appear to be the right and left mandibular canines of one small adult individual. A biconical hole 4 mm. in diameter is drilled through each tooth for suspension, the anterior edge of each root is ground flat and each tooth has a horizontal groove 3 mm. wide and 1 mm. deep in the center of one side (Pl. 131,*b*).

Contents of The Burial Pit

There were fragments of human bone scattered through the bottom layer of the burial pit where they had been left by the original excavators. The "tunneling" at the bottom of the original excavation had reached to the edges of the burial pit and nothing remained in its original position although a few articles were found in the backfill (Pl. 132,*a*). A black bear (*Ursus americanus*) canine is 5.5 cm. long and 1.5 cm. wide and is missing part of the root. A conch columella bead is 1.0 cm. long and 8 mm. wide and was found near some scattered foot and ankle bones in the northwest corner of the pit. A corner-notched point of dark gray flint has a base similar to the other Norton variant Snyders points but the blade is straight-sided and serrated. Dimensions are given in Table 2 (point D-1). Fragments of a turtle carapace (*Emys blandingi*) were reconstructed into a portion of an engraved dish (Pl. 132,*a*).

Mound F

Mound F was approximately 55 feet in diameter and 6.0 feet above present ground level when surveyed prior to excavation (Pl. 132,*b*). The mound presented a somewhat flat-topped appearance and the 20-foot wide preliminary trench indicated within the first few feet in depth that the mound was rather extensively disturbed. At a depth of two feet in the approximate center of the mound four large logs were encountered which were evidently placed in the pit in the process of refilling it. The trench was continued down approximately 7.0 feet to the basal gravel level. Several sheets of iron plating and some unburned and partially burned chunks of anthracite coal were found in the central area of the mound, evidently the remains of a makeshift fireplace used by the original excavators. The remainder of the mound, with the exception of the easternmost quarter, was excavated with the aid of an endloader from Rocks' Sand and Gravel Company which is located near the site. No clear evidence of the original structure of the mound was encountered and if a cap or subfloor was part of the original it was obliterated by the previous excavation. Traces of pre-mound occupation were found in the west half of the floor and these are described in the section Sub-Mound Materials, below.

Two artifacts came from the backfill of the original excavation where they were missed or thrown back in by the excavators. One is a worked conch shell and the other a bone effigy bear canine. The shell is a *Busycon contrarium* 24.3 cm. long and 14.8 cm. wide (Pl. 133). The columella and mantle have been removed and all cut and exposed edges have been ground smooth including the edge where the mantle was removed which presents a rather jagged appearance. The edge of the carinate has been ground so that only a slight ridge remains. The effigy bear canine is made of a section of mammal long bone shaft and is 9.1 cm. long, 2.5 cm. wide at the widest point and 0.8 cm. thick. The surface shows cutting and grinding marks on all surfaces and traces of the original cancellous tissue on one side. There is a 0.6 cm. diameter biconical hole drilled in the root end and another 0.7 cm. diameter hole in the area of what would be the enamel border, this last hole probably for an insert of some kind.

Mound C

The largest mound excavated during the season measured approximately 60 feet in diameter and 9.5 feet high from existing ground level, or 10.5 feet high from the original ground level. Excavation was initiated with a 20-foot wide trench into the west edge of the mound, using an end-loader for the upper mound fill which proved to be almost sterile in this case as it was for the other mounds. The first stratum under the light sandy loam top fill was a very hard layer of river clay and gravel varying from 0.5 to 1.0 feet in thickness and ranging in color from light gray near the central burial pit to a dark gray-brown near the edge of the mound (Fig. 29). The surface of this clay layer was very compact and what appeared to be individual loads of clay could be discerned. The dimensions of these clay "loads" averaged about 1.3 feet in diameter by about 0.3 feet thick, almost identical to the loading measurements in the dark soil caps. This clay overlay and graded into the familiar

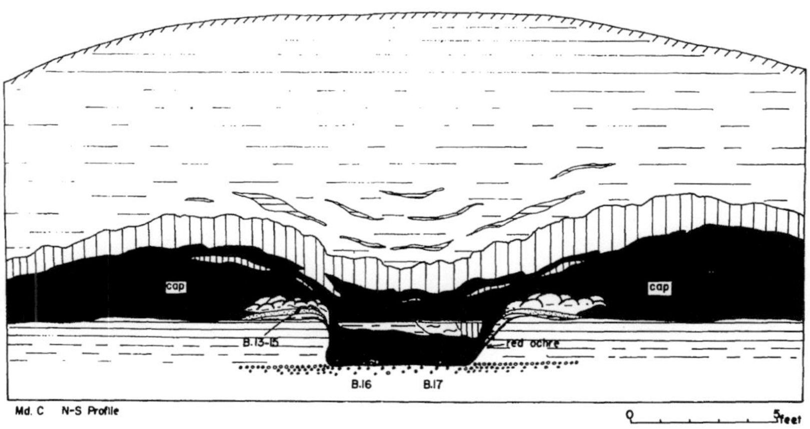

Fig. 29. North-south profile of Norton Mound C. UMMA Neg. 15652.

cap showing some loading near the center of the mound. This cap consisted of a dark gray to black organic soil with more clay content than the soils used in the other mounds, making careful excavation very difficult in most areas of this mound. The individual loads of soil which were discernible near the center of the mound averaged 1.2 feet long by 0.3 feet high. There was a two- to four-foot thick layer of decomposed wood and bark underlying this cap. The layer extended to a distance of approximately three feet past the margins of the central burial pit, covering a lense of light sandy loam which was later identified as having been thrown out in the process of digging the central pit. This backdirt rested in turn on the undisturbed original sandy loam which graded from a medium brown to a light brown color within 1.0 foot and which was approximately 2.0 feet deep above the gravel. At a point 20 feet in from the west edge of the mound the surface of the clay cap was seen to dip rather sharply toward the center and the work of clearing the cap down to undisturbed soil continued. North of the centerline 4.0 feet and resting on the bark layer immediately under the cap were the first long bones of the supplementary burials (Fig. 30).

The Supplementary Burials

Three burials designated Nos. 13, 14 and 15 in the field were found in a line running east and west above the north edge of the burial pit (Pl. 135). Burial No. 13 represents the bundled appendicular skeleton of an adult male, probably middle-aged, with some evidence of arthritis in the wrist region. There were several artifacts at the west end of Burial No. 13 (Pl. 136,*a*). The condylar end of a split elk metapodial pin was found under the middle of Burial No. 13 and a split deer metapodial pin 20.6 cm. long was at the west end of the bundle. Also at the west end of the burial were a pitted stone and four chert chips. The stone is an oval granite cobble measuring 8.0 cm. in diameter and 5.0 cm. thick. There is a small amount of grinding on an area 3.5 cm. by 5.0 cm. on one face and a pitted area 2.0 cm. in diameter in the center of this face. The chips are all of the dark gray Dongola chert and two of them appear to be the distal ends of small lamellar flakes. None show use marks.

Burial No. 14 represents the complete skeleton of a child approximately six to ten years old. The child was extended on the back with the head to the east. The skull shows lambdoidal deformation and a metopic suture, suggesting female sex. The appendicular skeletal parts were evidently disarticulated before burial but were placed in anatomical order. The bundle, Burial No. 13, was placed over the legs of Burial No. 14. Immediately under the mandible of Burial No. 14 there were 260 rolled sheet copper beads. (Pl. 136,*b*). The beads are of two types, a long tubular bead represented by eleven specimens ranging from 1.2 cm. to 2.3 cm. in length and 0.3 cm. thick and a short bead represented by 249 specimens ranging from 0.7 cm. long by 0.5 cm. wide to 0.3 cm. square. There was some attempt to obliterate the juncture of the copper sheet on all specimens and all show some beveling toward the ends, evidently from grinding. The beads were bound together in at least a double string with the long beads in the middle. A split deer metapodial pin 25.5 cm. long was found under the right humerus of Burial No. 14 and a piece of soft limonite and a chert lamellar flake were encountered just to the left of the skull. The flake is of dark Dongola gray chert and measures 4.5 cm. long by 1.5 cm. wide.

The right radius from Burial No. 15, an adult male, was found in the burial pit in the group of grave goods at the head of Burial No. 16, indicating that the burials

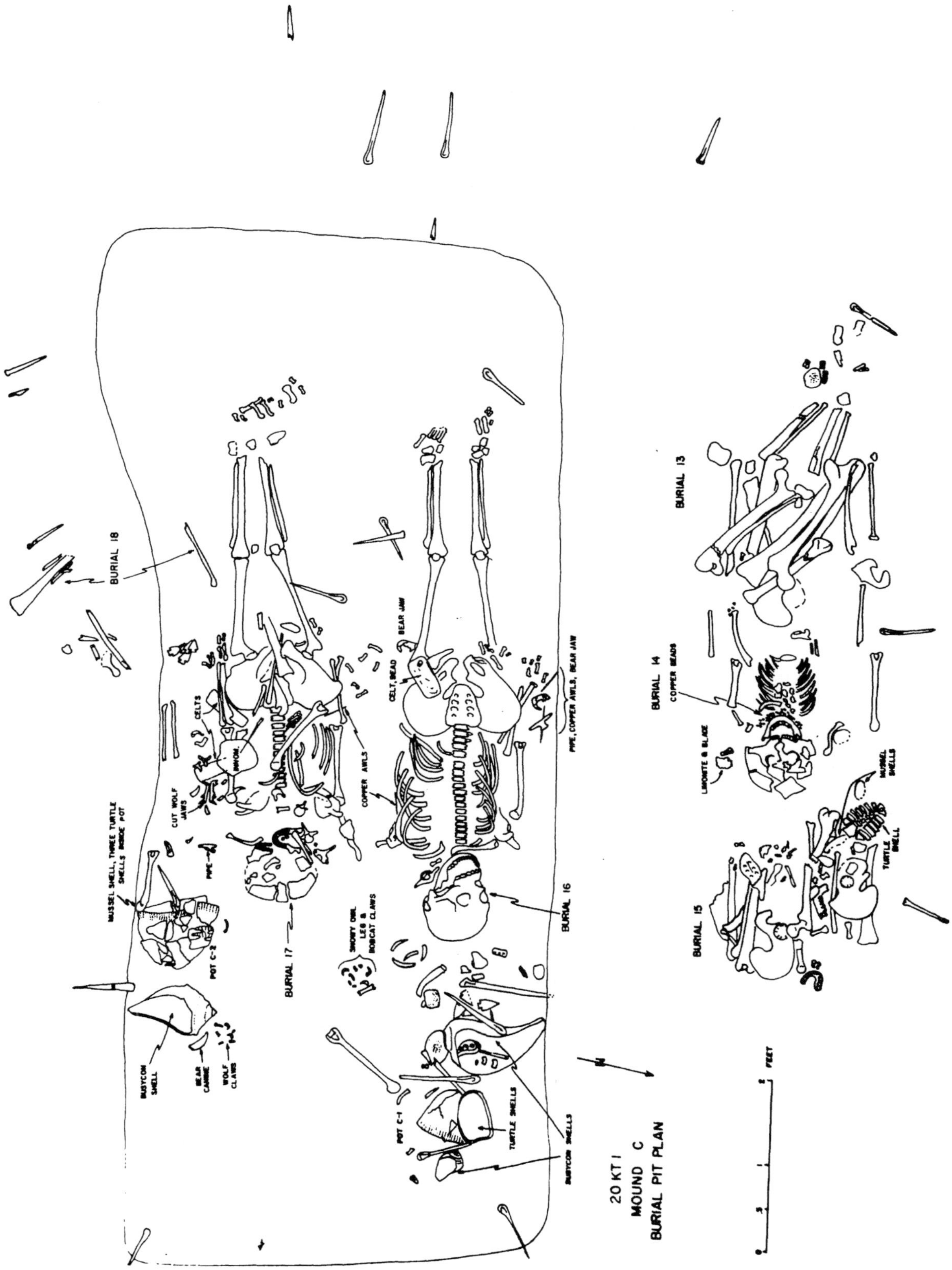

Fig. 30. Floor plan of burial pit of Norton Mound C. UMMA Neg. 15644.

in the pit and the cap were probably interred at the same time. There was a split elk metapodial pin sticking into the original surface north of the bundle. A turtle carapace dish and two fragmentary mussel shells were found at the north edge of the bundle. The dish is a carapace of *Emys blandingi* 13.4 cm. long by 9.0 cm. wide. The marginal scutes have been removed and the interior smoothed except for a slight ridge of bone along the vertebral scutes. One of the mussel shells is too fragmentary for identification and the other is a fragment of *Ligumia recta latissima* which shows grinding along the dorsal edge (Pl. 137,*a*). This *Ligumia* shell appears to have been modified the same as the *Ligumia* drilled pendant from the Illinois Knight Mound C°4-8 (elsewhere in this volume) although the decomposition has obliterated the hinge area.

Along the south edge of the burial pit and just outside the wall of the pit there were some fragmentary long bones including an adult right femur, some tibial and fibular fragments and a right patella. These bones were labeled in the field as "South End Fragments" and are now called Burial No. 18. Laboratory analysis revealed that there is a strong possibility that the extra fibula next to the left knee of Burial No. 17, a fragmentary tibia in the pubic area and a fragmentary female innominate over the left humerus of Burial No. 17 also belong to this fragmentary individual. There is also a possibility that the disarticulated arms included in the grave goods at the east end of the burial pit belong to Burial No. 18. It is probable that more skeletal material is present in the area to the east of Burial No. 18 and Burial No. 15, but permission could not be obtained to cut down a large live hackberry tree on top of the mound so further excavation in these areas was impossible.

Three bone pins were located in the east end of the burial pit at approximately original ground level. One pin made from the proximal end of a split elk metapodial was found along the southeast edge of the pit near the grave goods above the head of Burial No. 17. It is 20.9 cm. long and has a groove cut across the exterior surface. The pin in the southeast corner of the pit is 24.3 cm. long and is made from the distal end of a deer metapodial. The pin found in the northeast corner is of a split elk metapodial and is 23.3 cm. long.

There were several bone pins found at the original ground level around the west end of the burial pit, but outside the actual limits of the pit (Fig. 30). A pin 20.5 cm. long made from the distal end of a split deer metapodial was located just west of the fragments of Burial No. 18. There was a pointed end of a split elk metapodial at the southwest corner of the pit. All three of these pins were pointed toward the burial pit (Pl. 137,*b*). Along the west end of the pit there were two pointed ends of elk bone pins and two complete pins, 21.5 cm. and 25.7 cm. long, made from the distal end of split elk metapodials. One complete pin 22.0 cm. long made from the distal end of a split deer metapodial was located about 3.0 feet from the northwest corner of the pit.

The Burial Pit

When first defined at the approximate level of the original sandy loam, the burial pit was outlined with a thin layer of red ochre and then filled with a mixture of the dark organic cap soil, dark brown sandy loam and gray river clay. This mixture gave way to undifferentiated cap soil 0.5 foot below the level at which the central pit first showed up (see profile, Fig. 29). Two complete individuals and fragments of at least one other were found on the floor of the burial pit. Burial No. 16 was that of an adult male extended on the back on the north side of the pit. Burial No. 17 was an adult male extended on the back on the other side of the pit (Pl. 138,*a*; 141,*a*). The complete individuals were placed in the pit at the same time, evidently in an advanced state of decomposition (see the section on Skeletal Remains below).

The group of burial goods to the east of the skull of Burial No. 16 in the northeast corner of the pit includes three conch shell vessels, two turtle carapace dishes, a mussel shell spoon, a pottery vessel, six worked beaver incisors, a sandstone cobble and a hammerstone, two bone pins, one bone awl, two modified sections of deer antler, seven projectile points, a columella bead, a lamellar flake and some owl leg bones and bobcat claws (Pl. 138,*b*). The artifact closest to the northeast corner is a modified *Busycon contrarium* shell 12.8 cm. long and 8.6 cm. wide. The small dark gray chert flake 2.4 cm. long was found just to the south of the shell and a split elk metapodial pin 21.8 cm. long lay next to the conch shell. A Norton Dentate Stamped vessel, C-1, (Pl. 140) described in the following section lay next to the pin and two turtle carapace dishes and a fragmentary mussel shell spoon had been placed partly on top of the pot. The spoon is an unidentified left valve and has a notched handle cut into the anterior end. The dishes are *Emys blandingi* carapaces modified similar to those from the other mounds and both show an engraved curvilinear design (Pl. 140). They measure 17.1 cm. by 10.0 cm. and 17.5 cm. by 11.5 cm. respectively. Two of the six beaver (*Castor canadensis*) incisors lay next to the pot and the other four were directly beside the skull of Burial No. 16. These teeth average 6.0 cm. in length and all are modified by grinding on the cutting edge like those in Mound H. Next to the extra humerus in this group was a large *Busycon* shell vessel containing a bone awl, a series of adult carpal bones and a small *Busycon* vessel (Pl. 139,*a,b*). The larger shell measures 31.2 cm. long and 18.0 cm. wide and is modified like the other conch shells with the exception that the spire has been cut away. The estimated total length with the spire is 36.0 cm. The bone awl is a split and ground turkey leg bone 12.1 cm. long. The small *Busycon* vessel measures 11.1 cm. long and 6.1 cm. wide. Under the open end of the large shell there was a quartzite cobble hammerstone 7.0 to 9.0 cm. in diameter and 4.4 cm. thick which shows use on one end and one side. To the west of this stone was a rectangular piece of sandstone 6.0 cm. square and 3.0 cm. thick (Pl. 139,*a*). A conch columella bead 2.0 cm. long and 1.0 cm. in diameter lay next to the sandstone. One of the deer antler sections lay next to the sandstone piece and the other was under the large conch shell. These antler sections are cut diagonally to a length of 13.9 cm. and 13.1 cm. respectively. Both have been ground on all surfaces and both retain part of the burr. Neither shows use. Another split elk metapodial pin, this one 25.4 cm. long, rested on top of the largest conch vessel. There was another group of seven Norton variant points of light gray banded chert (C1-7), showing a remarkable internal similarity in dimensions (Table 2) beneath this pin and the conch and in no particular arrangement (Pl. 141,*b*). Next to the four beaver incisors were the right tarsometatarsus and phalanges of an adult male snowy owl (*Nyctea scandiaca*). The leg bone shows cut marks both on and around the proximal condylar surfaces, presumably a result of severing the lower leg while it was still attached with muscle and ligament. The snowy owl is ordinarily a tundra dweller, but is seen occasionally this far south (Flanders and Cleland, 1964). The owl bones were accompanied by four terminal phalanges of the bobcat, *Lynx rufus* (Pl. 142,*a*).

Several articles were placed directly on or next to Burial No. 16. A copper awl 8.9

cm. long and 4.0 mm. thick was found next to the left rib cage. The awl is square in cross section and a 2.0 cm. section of the wooden handle had been preserved by the copper. On top of the left innominate bone there was a straight-sided copper celt 19.2 cm. long, 6.8 cm. wide and 1.0 cm. thick with an unused convex bit (Pl. 142,*b*). Parts of a double fabric wrapping preserved by the copper showed a simple twined weave of twisted bast fiber with about 22 threads to the inch in the woof and eight to the inch in the warp (Pl. 143,*a*; 147). Fragments of an organic maeterial resembling bark were also preserved on one side over the fabric wrapping. A conch columella bead 2.4 cm. long and 1.1 cm. thick was resting directly on top of the celt (Pl. 143,*b*). Partially under the left femur of Burial No. 16 in the region of the scattered carpal bones there was a copper stained section of a cut bear mandible (*Ursus americanus*) (Pl. 143,*b*). This section of the right side had been cut off to a length of 6.5 cm. to include the second premolar. A biconical hole 4.0 mm. in diameter had been drilled in the rounded cut end. Three grooves had been cut across this end on the labial surface, one running across the hole. The section had been cut from the mandible so that part of the canine root was removed and two small notches had been cut into the bottom of the root. Two split elk metapodial pins, one from the distal end 23.5 cm. long and one from the proximal end 20.8 cm. long, were lying next to the left knee of Burial No. 16 and another elk bone pin 20.3 cm. long was next to the right foot.

A group of artifacts was encountered next to the pit wall in the region of the right wrist and hand of Burial No. 16. Two copper awls, one 11.5 cm. long and 3.0 mm. thick and the other 12.5 cm. by 4.0 mm., both showed square cross sections. The left side of the cut bear mandible mentioned above showed the same modifications with the addition of two grooves immediately behind the first premolar. There was a platform pipe with a "spool"-shaped bowl made of very fine-grained limestone. The platform of the pipe is 7.9 cm. long, 3.3 cm. wide and 1.3 cm. thick and the bowl is 2.8 cm. high with a diameter of 2.3 cm. (Pl. 144).

The group of artifacts at the head of Burial No. 17 includes a conch shell vessel, wolf claws, a bear canine, a pottery vessel, a mussel shell spoon, three turtle carapace dishes, a lamellar flake and a bone pin (Pl. 139,*b*; 144,*a*). Figure 30 shows the relative positioning of this group. The conch shell is a *Busycon contrarium* 25.8 cm. long and 13.7 cm wide, modified by cutting and grinding like the shells from the other mounds. The bear canine consists of the enamel and part of the root. The wolf bones include four claw cores and four second phalanges of *Canis lupus*, evidently the remains of four toes (Pl. 144). The pot, C-2 (Pl. 134,*b*), is a Norton Zoned Dentate Stamped vessel and is described below. The mussel shell spoon and three nested turtle carapace dishes were inside the pot. The spoon is made from a right valve of *Elliptio dilatatus* and is 14.0 cm. long by 8.3 cm. wide with grinding on all surfaces and with a notched handle cut into the anterior end. The three turtle shell dishes were made of the carapace of *Emys blandingi* and were 19.3 by 11.7 cm., 18.1 by 10.0 cm. and 16.0 by 9.8 cm. respectively. All three showed cutting and grinding on edges and interior and all had at least part of the marginal scutes cut off. The two larger dishes have engraved designs on the exterior which are reproduced in Figure 25. The bone pin is the distal end of a split elk metapodial 24.3 cm. long. The gray chert lamellar flake at the west end of the group is 3.8 cm. long and 1.3 cm. wide.

There were several articles directly associated with Burial No. 17. Three river pearl beads 6 mm. in diameter were found under the jaw (Pl. 134,*a*). Just to the south of the skull there was a small effigy platform pipe made of a very fine gray siltstone (Pl. 144,*b*). The slightly curved platform is 6.9 cm. long, 2.2 cm. wide and 1.3 cm. thick and the bowl is 1.9 cm. in diameter and 1.5 cm. high. On the bowl facing the smoker is the effigy head of an animal with bulging eyes, a small mouth and a crosshatched design on top of the head which resembles a turtle. Just to the south of the left humerus head was a pair of cut wolf jaws and two conch columella beads (Pl. 134,*a*). The cut jaws are both halves of a mandible of *Canis lupus* cut down to the roots of the teeth and to a length of 9.1 cm., bisecting the large molar. All the cut edges are ground and there is a hole 3 mm. in diameter drilled through the posterior cut edge on both pieces. The conch columella beads are 1.5 cm. long and 0.7 cm. in diameter. Next to the cut jaws and under the left humerus of Burial No. 17 was a straight-sided copper celt 18.5 cm. long, 6.7 cm. wide at the widest part and 1.0 cm. thick (Pl. 146,*b*). The bit edge was rounded but showed no signs of use. The copper had preserved fragments of a simple twined fabric with approximately 16 threads to the inch in the woof. The yarn is of a twisted bast fiber. There were also fragments of bark on top of the textile comparable to the material on the celt with Burial No. 16. A split elk metapodial pin 25.6 cm. long lay on top of the extra innominate bone. There was another copper celt under the left forearm of this burial, this one being 17.7 cm. long, 6.0 wide at the bit and 1.2 cm. thick. This celt was also unused and showed textile impressions on one side (Pl. 145). Seven Norton projectile points of dark gray Dongola chert were lying in a group with the points toward the foot of the grave, next to the left hand of Burial No. 17 (Pl. 146,*a*). Dimensions of these points (C8-14) are given in Table 2. These points show the steep marginal retouch mentioned for the points in Mound H. A split elk metapodial pin 27.6 cm. long was placed next to the right femur. There was a copper awl 11.1 cm. long and 4 mm. thick under the right radius and another awl 8.7 cm. long and 3 mm. thick in the area of the upper right rib cage of Burial No. 17. Both are round in cross section and show juncture marks and both show a relatively uncorroded end 1.3 cm. long where the awl was hafted. Two unmodified lamellar flakes of pink and white mottled chert were lying next to the thoracic vertebrae of this burial. They measure 4.4 cm. by 2.6 cm. and 3.8 cm. by 3.0 cm. respectively (Pl. 145).

Skeletal Remains From the Burial Pit

Burial No. 16 is that of a young-middle-aged adult male. The bones indicate a fairly robust individual with medium occipital deformation in the lambdoid region, slight ear exostoses and with a plate of bone 5 cm. long and 2 cm. wide removed postmortem along the posterior squamosal and masto-occipital sutures in the left mastoid region. The skull had been resting on the right parietal and a large piece of red ochre had caused bone mineral destruction, leaving a circular hole 6 cm. long and 5 cm. wide in the parietal. The left arm and clavicle of Burial No. 16 had been removed and placed over Burial No. 17 so that the clavicle was *under* the right scapula of No. 17, the humerus was over the right rib cage, the radius and ulna were over the pelvic region and parts of the hand were scattered around Burial No. 17's upper right femur. An extra tibia which was possibly from the fragmentary Burial No. 18 was placed over this radius and ulna.

Burial No. 17 evidently represents an old adult male. The cervical vertebrae and some of the ribs were missing and the upper postcranial skeleton was disarticulated but in approximate anatomical position.

Burial No. 17 shows marked lambdoid flattening and medium ear exostoses and there is some evidence of a plaque removal on the left parietal near the occipital suture, just above and behind the mastoid region. Although the mastoid and part of the parietal is missing in this area, the dimensions of the plaque are estimated at 2.5 cm. superior-inferior and 4.0 cm. anterior-posterior.

There were some human remains associated with the grave goods over the heads of Burials No. 16 and No. 17 which were mentioned in the preceding section. With the group of artifacts above Burial No. 16 in the northeast corner of the pit were a right radius belonging to Burial No. 15, a left humerus, radius and ulna perhaps belonging to Burial No. 18, an adult left patella and adult ankle bones, and a series of adult carpal bones inside the large conch shell. With the group of artifacts above the head of Burial No. 17 was a right humerus possibly belonging to Burial No. 18. The radius and ulna of this humerus were found against the burial pit wall next to the left forearm of Burial No. 17.

Burial Vessels

C-1 (Pl. 140) Norton Dentate Stamped

Paste: Temper is angular grit, probably crushed granite. Paste is poorly mixed, tends to foliate. Exterior color is light brown with extensive gray firing clouds. Core is dark gray.

Surface: Smoothed but rough-textured. Temper protrudes extensively. Interior smoothed.

Decoration: Outer rim has contiguous vertical rows of closely spaced dentate stamping 2.5 cm. long. Lower tooth of the dentate stamp is more strongly applied, giving appearance of a boundary to the rim decoration.

Form: Conoidal jar, slightly constricted neck, vertical rim, lip flattened and insloping.

Dimensions: Height 16.8 cm.
Rim height 3 cm.
Shoulder diameter 14.4 cm.
Rim diameter 13.8 cm.
Thickness 6 mm. at rim, 1.4 cm. at base.

Similarities: Within the site, the temper and paste characteristics of vessel C-1 are closest to those of the vessels in Mound I. This vessel appears to be a rather crude example of Norton Stamped.

C-2 (Pl.134,*b*) Norton Zoned Dentate Stamped

Paste: Temper is angular grit, about the same consistency as C-1 but paste appears better mixed and more compact with no tendency to foliate. Exterior and interior color is orange to brown, core is occasionally light gray.

Surface: Exterior is well smoothed, no temper showing. Interior shows horizontal to slightly diagonal smoothing marks.

Decoration: Row of vertically applied fine-toothed dentate stamp 3.5 cm. long on rim, plain zone 4 cm. wide, row of diagonally applied fine dentate stamping 1 cm. long bordered by horizontal incised line. Body decoration consists of five units of four-lobed curvilinear design elements, portions of which are filled with the same fine-toothed dentate stamping.

Form: Conoidal jar, slight neck constriction, slightly cambered rim with slight inner channel, flattened and insloping lip.

Dimensions: Height 25.7 cm.
Rim height 3.4 cm.
Shoulder diameter 19.5 cm.
Rim diameter 18.3 cm.
Thickness at rim 1.0 cm., at shoulder 7 mm.

Similarities: This vessel is almost identical to one of the three vessels in one of the Utica Mounds (Griffin and Morgan, 1941: Pl. 54, p. 185), the only difference being that the Utica vessel has a two-lobed instead of a four-lobed body design. The other two vessels in Utica Mound 1 are a grit tempered, flat-bottomed pot with a crosshatched rim and a zoned "bird" motif and a small limestone tempered Montezuma Punctate vessel with crosshatched rim. Vessel No. 1 from Utica Mound 8 (ibid.: Pl. 57, p. 189) is also very similar.

Sub-Mound Materials

Although all the mounds, with the possible exception of Mound J, showed indications in the profiles that some sort of clearing or preparation of the original surface had taken place before construction of the cap, there was some evidence of occupation of the area prior to mound construction. In both Mound F and Mound C there were small areas on the original ground level which had evidently escaped the "clearing." Both areas contained cultural material, ash, burned soil and some burned bone and may have been the remains of fire pits which extended deeper into the ground than the bulk of village material.

Mound F

In an area about five feet square in the center of the west half of Mound F, there were the remains of a hearth containing some cultural material. The remaining 0.2 feet of original sandy loam above the gravel had been burned a dull orange-red by repeated fires. A number of fragments of burned bone and shell in this deposit includes a fragment of a beaver mandible, a turkey carpal-metacarpus condyle and one fragment of the distal end and one of the proximal end of deer antler tines. The antler fragments appear to have been worked before being burned and may be the remnants of flaking tools. Also in this deposit were approximately 50 chips of light to dark gray chert, all showing signs of having been subjected to intense heat. One of these chips shows use as an end scraper and one is a fragment of a tool base showing some edge grinding. An unfinished celt made of compact brown quartzite lay next to, but not in, the burned area. The celt is 8.5 cm. long, 4.3 cm. wide and 1.3 cm. thick. The form is roughly flaked out but there is grinding on both dorsal and ventral edges and the broken bit shows grinding for 2 cm. from the edge. There was a rimsherd 8 mm. thick with angular grit tempering in the burned area. The sherd indicates a straight rim at least 3.2 cm. high with a somewhat flattened lip, small tool impressions on the outer lip and some horizontal brushing on the interior surface. The paste, temper and form agree with the Norton Dentate Stamped sherds from the base of Mound C (see below).

Mound C

There was a small area three feet to the west of the west end of the burial pit in Mound C which contained ash, mammal, bird and fish bones, mussel shell fragments and some cultural material. The original sandy loam did not have the burned appearance like the area in Mound F and the bone was not burned, suggesting that this deposit was part of a refuse pit. Identifiable bone includes two fragments of deer long bone and a fragment of woodchuck pelvis. Stone objects include a flake of light gray chert modified on all edges, the proximal end of a blade of white chert and an unmodified chip of dark gray chert. There was a portion of a dentate stamped rim 1.2 cm. thick with a flat lip, interior-lip notching and closely spaced rows of dentate stamp on the exterior running vertically from the lip. This sherd shows a thin light brown oxidized layer on both surfaces and angular grit temper. Other sherds in this deposit include one with rubbed-over cordmarking on the exterior and another with partially obliterated cordmarking on both surfaces. These two sherds are tan to orange in color with angular grit temper and appear to have been subjected to some heat. Charcoal in association with the sherds was used for a radiocarbon date (see below).

Radiocarbon Dates

Four radiocarbon determinations have been made on material recovered during the 1963 excavations (Crane and Griffin, 1966: 261). Three of these dates are from Mound H while the fourth is from Mound C. Two of the dates from Mound H are regarded as acceptable radiocarbon assessments. Sample M-1488 was composed of charcoal from a hearth at the base of the cap, in an ash lens, and above the black dirt from the burial pit and some five feet south of the pit. This radiocarbon date is 1790 ± 120 years ago or A.D. 160. Ash from the base of the cap and some five feet north of the burial pit, M-1490, has a radiocarbon date of 1850 ± 100 or A.D. 100 The questionable date is M-1489 which was composed of ash and charcoal from an ash lens below the cap and some five feet east of the pit. The radiocarbon result was 950 ± 100 B.P. An examination of similar material with Frederick Bevis, plant ecologist at Grand Valley State College, Allendale, Michigan resulted in the suggestion that contamination from ground water might have produced this result.

Another radiocarbon determination was carried out on charcoal obtained from the remains of the fire pit located on the original ground level just west of the burial pit in Mound C. This charcoal was directly associated with rim sherds of dentate stamped pottery described below. The date (M-1493) is B.P. 1960 ± 120 which fits well with the proposed ceramic sequence.

Mound M

General

Mound M is the largest mound of the Norton group and occupies the central position of the three large mounds nearest the mound (Pl. 148). The mound was designated as "M" on Paul Gibson's 1936 map and was described as being approximately 100 feet in diameter and 16 feet high at the time. The dimensions were the same in 1964 with a somewhat flattened top and several deep wheel tracks up the sides which disrupted the regular contours. This mound is the only one of the group definitely identified from Coffinberry's notes, both because of its size and because the quarter section line runs directly through the mound. According to the Coffinberry manuscript on file at the Grand Rapids Public Museum, his original excavation was an 8 by 15 foot hole into the top of the mound which passed through a layer of "ash conmingled with bones" to the basal gravels 17 feet deep. The "ash and bones" led Coffinberry to surmise that only cremated remains had been placed in this mound, and since only a copper awl was obtained from the trench, it was abandoned and refilled. Of course Coffinberry missed the central burial area and evidently identified the decomposed bark slabs as ash and cremated bone.

Dr. James B. Griffin of the Museum of Anthropology obtained a grant from the National Science Foundation for the purpose of excavating Mound M during the summer of 1964. The field crew was under the immediate direction of Richard Flanders assisted by Charles Cleland and consisted of John Halsey, Earl Prahl, David M. Griffin, Sarunas Milisauskas, Richard Wilkinson, Dan Higgins and Robert Modica. Work started on June 10, 1964 after permission to excavate was obtained from the Grand Rapids City Commission, and ended on August 15, 1964. The Kelsey Museum of Archaeology of the University of Michigan kindly loaned the aluminum photo tower seen in Plate 148,*a* from which most of the wide angle photographs were taken. The Central Fibre Products Company of Chelsea, Michigan contributed a Paradome seen in Plate 148,*a* for crew accommodations. The Consumers Power Company of Grand Rapids went to considerable trouble to furnish electric power to the site. The Michigan Bell Telephone Company of Grand Rapids kindly ran a telephone line into the crew's quarters. As in the 1963 season, members of the W. L. Coffinberry Chapter of the Michigan Archaeological Society made the summer very pleasant with their many kindnesses.

Excavation Procedures

Two large dead oak trees were removed

from the top of the mound and three other large trees were retained on "tree islands," adhering to a request by the Grand Rapids Park Department. The first step in excavation was to truncate the mound to a point past a large recent disturbance, a matter of about 1.5 feet, where it was possible to identify Coffinberry's trench as an area of mixed gravel and dark organic silt (Pl. 148,*b*). Datum was set at the top elevation of the mound, 615.5 feet above sea level according to a bench run from a U.S.G.S. bench mark in use by the freeway construction crew near the site. A north-south grid was set up to maintain provenience control for mound fill material. The mound was initially divided into quadrants and due to the relatively sparse cultural material from the fill, control was maintained this way to the point where the burial area was encountered. Although the cultural material from the fill was not plentiful, an interesting stratigraphic sorting can be observed in the occurrence of a thin, deeply cordmarked pottery in the upper two feet of fill, a predominance of either plain zoned or zoned dentate stamp ceramics in the area between the former and the primary construction features of the mound (the burial area and the "cap") and a definite majority of a thick, finely cordmarked ware on the floor of the mound (Pl. 149). A few sherds of what would seem to resemble Marion Thick were found immediately above the primary structure and these were probably included in the fill as a result of having been picked up in the preparation of the mound area. Plate 149 shows selected sherds from the floor of the mound with associated material including two antler tines, three flakes of dark grey chert and an ovoid chert knife. Plate 150 shows selected sherds from immediately above the cap and from the upper two feet of fill, respectively. The sequence and provenience of these types suggests a Marion Thick-like occupation before, possibly shortly before, the construction of the mound (see above, The Submound Floor), an occupation characterized by ceramics closely resembling Illinois Havana which funished the bulk of fill material for the upper mound, and some scattering of a type of ceramics usually identified in this area as Late Woodland after construction of the mound.

At the same time that the light sandy loam was removed from the top of the mound, tests were made with a soil auger from selected points in the outer half of each quadrant, and an eight-foot-wide trench was opened into the south edge of the mound in order to identify the burial cap characteristic of the other Norton mounds. The auger tests indicated a soil change from light sandy loam to darker, heavier soil at about nine feet below datum in the outer half of each quadrant, and at about 15 feet below datum in the middle quarter of the mound, suggesting a doughnut or ring-shaped cap demonstrated by the other mounds. The south profile trench (Pl. 151,*b*) revealed that the dark loam layer extended to the edge of the mound and that it showed the "loaded" pattern found elsewhere in this group. Due to the fact that the distinction between the dark cap soil and light sandy loam was so marked, it was possible to "sculpture" the surface of the dark cap. This resulted in this stage of the excavation being exposed approximately as we assume it appeared during construction of the mound (Pl. 151). The surface of the cap was not entirely regular. There was a depression in the cap, almost to the original ground level, on the north-south line, another approximately on the east line and a third depression on a line between the northwest and southwest quadrants. It was not possible to determine whether there was a similar depression on the south side of the cap due to the large tree island maintained there. During the excavation of the east half of the mound, it was noted that the cap showed two layers of the dark soil separated by a thin layer of light sandy loam in the area of the depression. This may have been the result of an attempt to fill in the depression after its function was fulfilled, perhaps as an entrance way to the burial area. When the cap was constructed, it likely resembled the quadrant construction noted for Illinois White County Mound 6 (Neumann and Fowler, 1952: 198).

The loads of earth isolated as a result of the "sculpting" adhered to the pattern found in the other mounds of this group. Approximately 20 loads were measured and an average size of 0.5 cubic feet and a weight of 25 pounds was obtained (Pl. 152). The present dimensions of the mound would require about 500,000 individual loads or 12,500,000 pounds of earth, assuming that the same hauling method was used throughout the process of construction. We might make a guess about the amount of work required to construct these mounds on this basis. If we assume at least seven months during the year of "good" working conditions (for example, the soil not frozen) we have a figure of about 2,400 loads per day. If we further posit the transporting of soil from a distance of not more than 300 yards, we might expect an individual accomplishment of a minimum of about 20 loads a day. The task of construction of Mound M, then, could be accomplished with a "work force" of about 120 people who of course would not be performing other tasks, such as those concerning subsistence. Assuming an efficient economic base for these activities, it would be entirely possible to complete the mound in one season.

At the time the light upper fill was being removed, it was noted that a line of white gritty material occurred near the central balk at about the level of the top of the cap. It was decided to remove the central portion of the balk in anticipation of some kind of central feaure which coincided with the "dip" in the burial cap. When the central balk was removed, the white gritty material was seen to extend in a roughly rectangular area surrounding a deposit of the light sandy loam mixed with a darker silty soil (Fig. 31). The dark disturbance was noted at the northeastern end of this deposit and this disturbance was again identified as the Coffinberry excavation. The white material was tentatively identified as ash in the field, although no charcoal or evidence of burning was found. Later analysis by Professor Fred Bevis of the Botany Department and Mr. James Funk, a student in the Chemistry Department of Grand Valley State College, Allendale, Michigan, made it clear that this material was wood and bark which had been partially replaced with calcium carbonate from ground water. A five-foot-square pit was opened in the center of this lighter rectangle with the purpose of testing the depth and structure of the expected burial complex before complete excavation was attempted. Basal gravel was reached in the bottom of the test pit directly underlying a stratum of hard yellow silt. No evidence of burial activity was encountered until the extreme southeast corner of the pit was cleared, yielding several fragments of modified turtle carapace (*Emys blandingi*). The work of clearing the mixed fill from the rectangular area within the decomposed bark line was started. The mixed fill was removed from the rectangular central area by following the bark layer down as closely as possible, except in the northeast end of the trench where it had been removed by Coffinberry's trench. As fill was removed from the burials and burial associations, it became clear that the burial structure in Mound M differed significantly from the subfloor pit pattern of the other mounds of

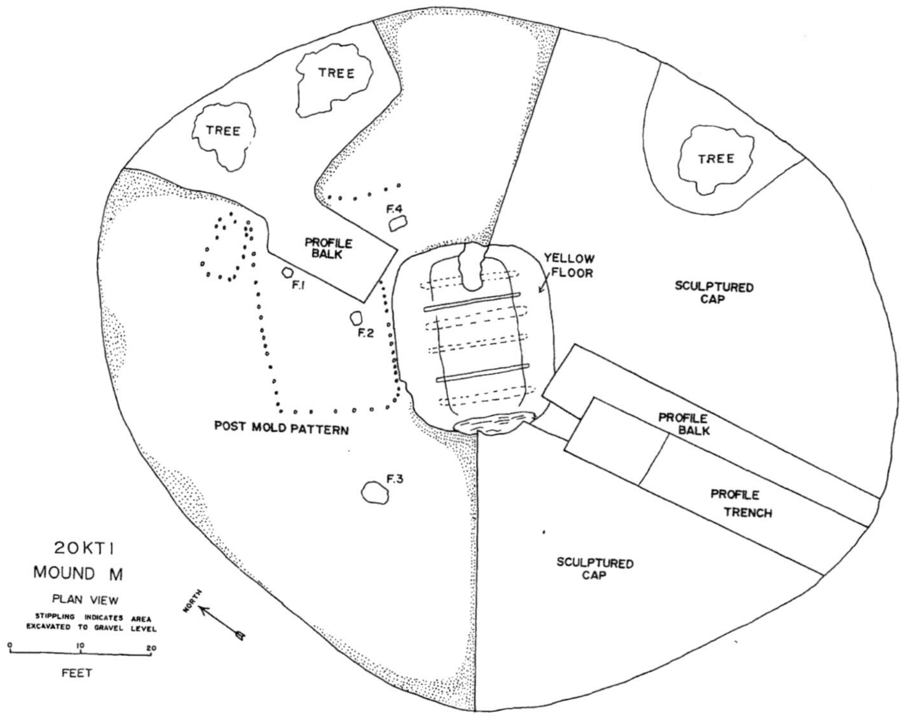

Fig. 31. Floor plan of Norton Mound, UMMA Neg.

this group. Figure 31 shows the floor plan of the mound and Figures 32 and 33 in major features of the east and west sides of the profile balk.

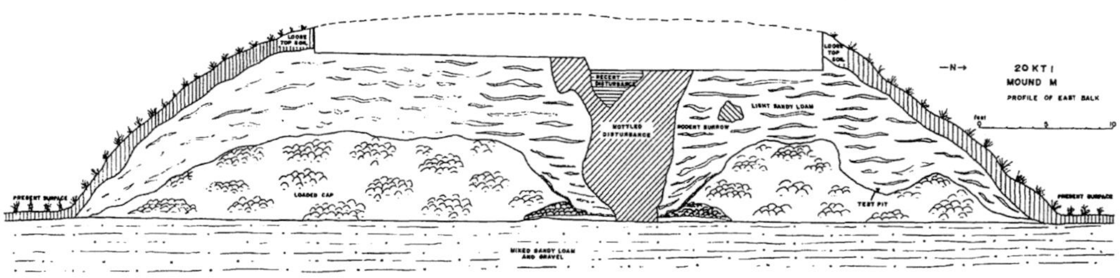

Fig. 32. East profile of central balk of Norton Mound M. UMMA Neg.

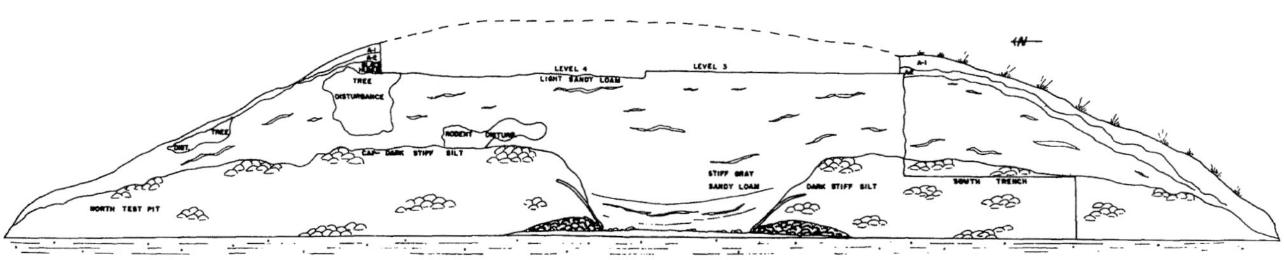

Fig. 33. West profile of north-south balk of mound M. UMMA Neg. 15274.

Burial Structure

Perhaps the best way to describe the results of the excavation in the central structure is to attempt a reconstruction in the order in which the evidence indicates the various features were built. The first stage of construction was the removal of the loam or humus from the entire original surface of the mound to within 0.3 to 0.5 feet from the basal gravel. The remaining original surface was very hard, dark gray silty loam mixed with pea gravel and sand and contained evidence of occupation subsequent to the mound-building activities (see below). At this level in the excavation, small fragments of mica were found *underneath* the cap structure in the profile trench at the north edge of the mound, on the surface northeast of the central burial area and in spots over most of the west half of the mound. This suggests a ceremonial practice of scattering mica flakes over the prepared mound area before the central structure and cap were built. In the center of the mound, an oblong floor of fine yellow silt was constructed on this scraped surface. The floor was 28 feet long and 21 feet wide with a somewhat irregular outline and varied from 0.5 feet thick in the center to a sharp edge on the periphery (Fig. 34). The long axis of the floor was northeast by southwest which at this point is approximately parallel with the river. There was some evidence of the use of water in the building of the floor in the form of laminar structure in parts of the floor, lines of washed reddish stain from minerals in the silt and the exceptionally hard, compact consistency. The hard consistency and reddish stain was uniform from top to bottom of the floor, suggesting one-stage construction rather than the repeated effect of rain on the unprotected structure. Several surface features were constructed at the time the floor was laid (Fig. 35). From southwest to northeast, these included a slab of wood and bark 1.5 feet wide laid across the southwest end of the area, a round trench approximately one foot wide and 0.5 feet deep, a smaller trench filled with the calcareous mold of a pole or log 0.4 feet in diameter, part of which was removed by the square test pit, and another trench 0.5 feet wide and about 0.5 feet deep. This sequence of trench-log-trench is repeated in the northeast part of the floor with a trench 1.0 foot wide and 0.5 feet deep with irregular outline, a cal-

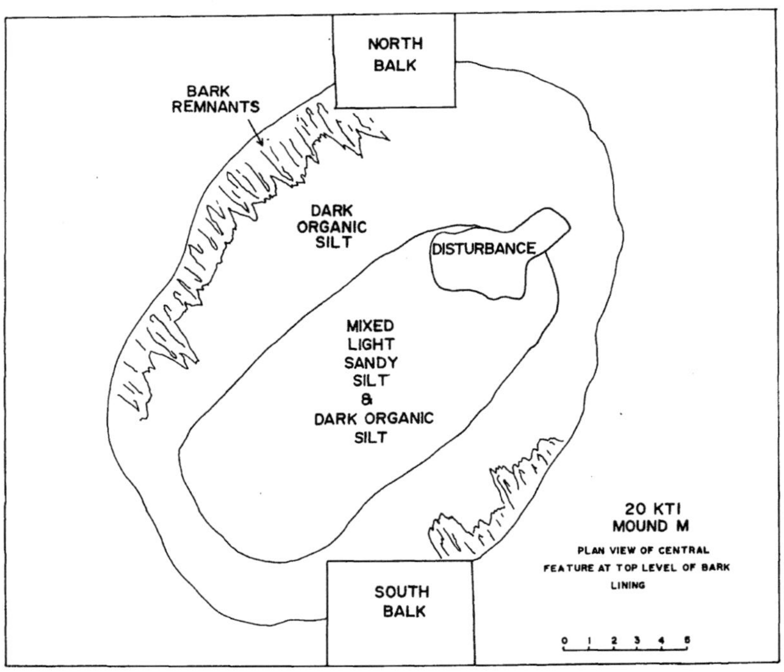

Fig. 34. Floor plan of the central feature at top level of bark lining, Mound M.

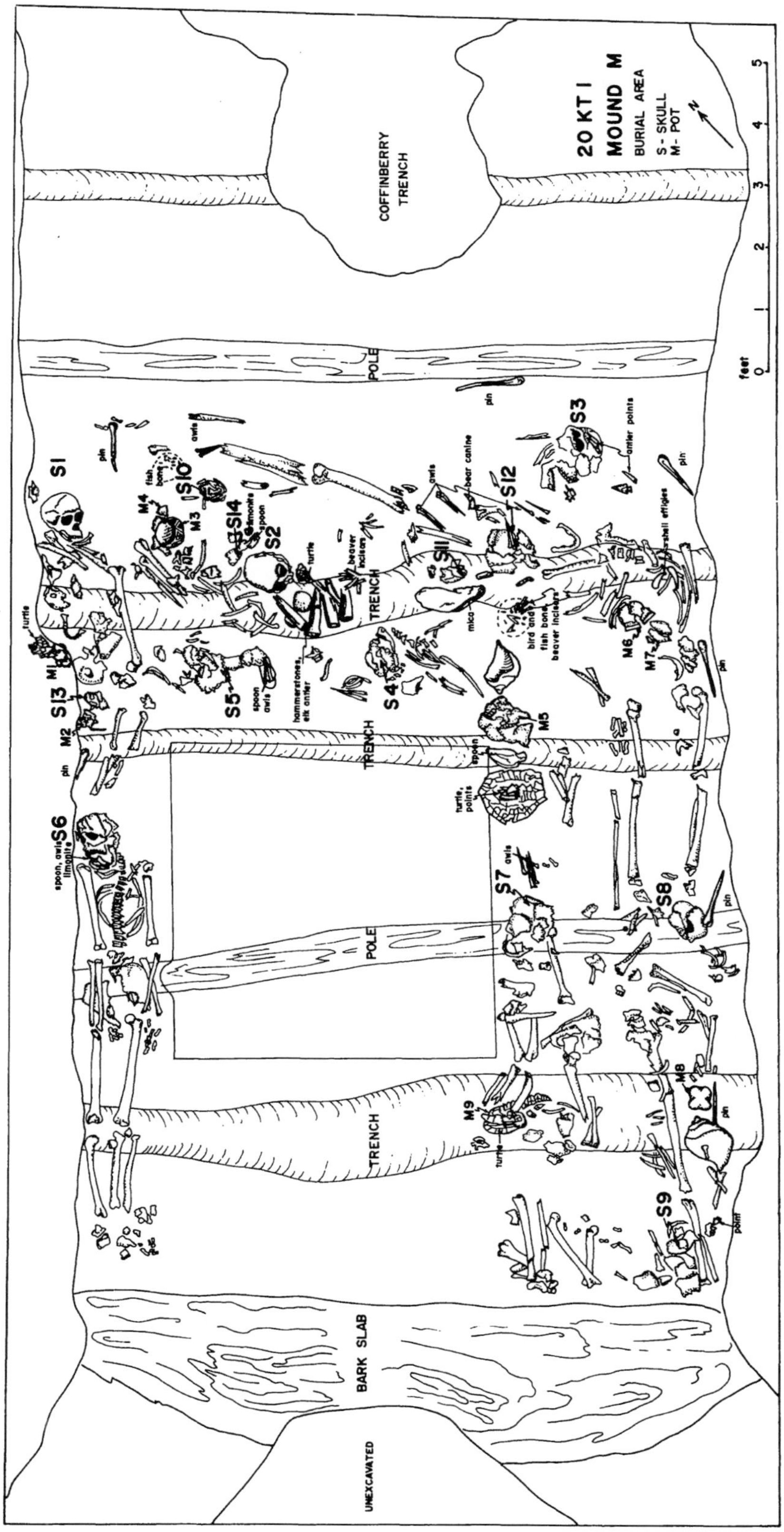

Fig. 35. Plan of central burial area of Norton Mound M. UMMA Neg.

careous log mold approximately 0.4 feet wide and a trench 0.8 feet wide and 0.3 feet deep. The end of Coffinberry's original trench destroyed part of this trench and most of the northeast end of the floor structure. If the large bark slab was repeated at the northeast end of the floor, the evidence was removed by this trench.

The next stage was the construction of a ramplike structure of dark organic silt around the edges of the floor. This structure covered the outer six feet of the floor on the long dimension and the outer three feet on the southwest end but was obliterated on the northeast end by the Coffinberry disturbance. It was 1.5 feet thick near the burial area and tapered down to match the floor edge on the long side. The material of this small ramp showed loading very clearly and was easy to distinguish from the larger burial cap by the darker color of the soil, almost black on some loads as compared to the gray to light gray soil in the larger cap. Next to the area where the burials were to be placed, there was a ledge one foot wide and about 0.5 feet high of this same soil. In the southwest end of this ramp, there was some evidence of washing on the upper and outer edges of this ramp in the form of several thin strata of light-colored sandy silt, contrasting with the dark organic silt of the ramp. This would suggest that this stage of the mound was left open for some time before the larger cap was added, perhaps for ceremonial activities. This washing was not noted in other portions of the small ramp, however. On this ledge and along the inside face of the small ramp, slabs of wood with bark were placed as a sort of lining. This organic material has largely deteriorated and been replaced by calcium carbonate, although a tentative identification of spruce was made by Professor Fred Bevis of Grand Valley State College. From evidence of soil impressions and calcareous remains, the slabs are estimated at from 0.1 to 0.3 feet thick. Evidently at this time the burials and associated goods were laid in place. Also at this time a portion of the larger cap was constructed to the extent that from one to two feet lay above the small ramp, and additional bark was placed upon this layer forming a double line of calcareous material. The rest of the large cap in this central area was constructed before the burial area was filled in, as the material above the burials was the light sandy loam of the upper layer of the mound. This indication of at least two stages of manufacture of the large cap may relate to the evidence of two layers of cap found along the east edge and possibly to the cap irregularities found in three of the quadrants. There is no other evidence of stratigraphic separation in any of the cap profiles, however. The final stages of construction were the filling in of the central depression over the burial area with mixed dark silt and sandy loam and finally with sandy loam, and the erection of the top level of the mound with the light sandy loam from the immediate vicinity.

Contents of the Burial Area

Several general characteristics of the burial area might be mentioned before a treatment of individual features. In comparison with the other mounds of this group, the fragmentary nature of the 14 burials is unusual and in some cases makes difficult the association of burial goods with particular burials (Fig. 35). The arrangement of the burials is also unusual for this group in that there is a fair amount of "wasted" space in the burial area as compared to the subfloor pits in the other mounds. Although there was some replacement of the bark lining over the caps in the other mounds by calcium carbonate from ground water action, there was very little calcareous deposit in the burial pits themselves. In Mound M, almost all the artifacts and bones were covered by a layer of calcareous material and there was a thin layer of calcium carbonate immediately on top of part of the yellow silt floor (Pl. 153,*b*). The soil in the upper level of Mound M is the same as that used for the top layers of the other mounds, a light sandy loam, but the different method of burial in both cases may account for the greater penetration of ground water to the burial area in Mound M. Subfloor pits in the other mounds were filled with the dark, compact cap soil after the interments which might have afforded more protection from ground water. As in the other mounds of this group, all but two of the turtle carapace dishes were made from *Emys blandingi*, the other two being *Terrapene carolina.*

All conch shell vessels were *Busycon contrarium* and all identifiable mussel shell spoons were some species of *Lampsilis*, probably *Lampsilis ventricosa.*

The contents of the burial area were catalogued by dividing the area into eight sections and by assigning numbers to skulls in order of discovery (Pl. 154,*a*). Burial 6, the only burial in close to complete anatomical order, was contained in Sections I and II. This was a male approximately 20 years old with medium lambdoid flattening and a plaque removal from the left parietal. Directly behind the mandible there was a group of artifacts including a lump of decomposed pyrites, one dark gray and one light gray flint chip, three fragments of a mussel shell spoon (Pl. 155,*b*) and two turkey bone awls, one 6.9 cm. long and the other 9.1 cm. long. Section III contained seven fragmentary burials. Burials 10, 13 and 14 were represented by fragments of infant skulls and sparse remains of postcranial skeletons. Burial 1 was an adult male in his forties with marked lambdoid flattening and with a green (copper?) stain along the left sagittal suture. Most of the postcranial skeleton was present. In direct association with the burial were two turtle carapace dishes (Pl. 156) covering a Norton Punctated variant pot (Pot M-1) and a lump of decomposed iron pyrites in front of the mandible. Skull 13, a fragmentary infant skull, was associated with a small flat-bottomed Norton Plain vessel (Pot M-2) Fig. 36,B and fragments of at least 65 columella beads (Pl. 157). Immediately below these two burials, Burial 5 was represented by fragments of a young subadult skull with slight occipipital deformation and a possible left parietal plaque removal. This skull was associated with a turtle carapace dish, fragments of six mussel shell spoons, seven turkey bone awls, one dark gray and one light gray flint chip and a worked fragment of animal bone (Pl. 158). Burial 2, a male in his forties with marked occipital deformation, was associated with about half of the postcranial skeleton. In front of the skull there was a group of artifacts including seven modified sections of elk antler, twelve modified beaver incisors, fragments of a turtle carapace dish, one hammerstone and a grinding stone (Pl. 160). The complete sections of antler were 17.5 cm. 14.3 cm. and 14.0 cm. long. The hammerstone is a granite cobble 7.3 cm. in diameter and 4.6 cm. thick with use marks around the periphery, one side smooth and slightly concave from grinding and the other side pitted from use as an anvil. The grinding stone is of ferruginous sandstone and measures 8.5 cm. long, 7.1 cm. wide and 3.2 cm. thick with clear evidence of grinding on one side. Directly behind Skull 2 were the remains of at least two mussel shell spoons, three dark gray Dongola chert chips, a small deposit of limonite and the fragments of infant Skull 14. The Norton Incised vessel with the nested triangle design, M-3, and the Norton Plain vessel M-4 (Fig. 36) were located between Skulls 1 and 2. Articles from this section not closely associated with burials include two deer metapodial pins, one 20.5 cm. long and one 23.5 cm. long, a group of fragmentary fish bones, three turkey bone awls and a dark gray chert chip near the fragments of infant Skull 10 and a dark gray chert lamellar flake 4.1 cm. long. The only article in Section V was a deer metapodial pin 25.1 long.

The three burials in Section VI were Burial 12, a subadult with medium lambdoidal deformation and a left parietal plaque removal, Burial 3, an old adult male with slight occipital deformation and a posterior left parietal plaque removal and Skull 11, a fragmentary infant cranium. Burial 12 was missing the hands, patellas, sternum, sacrum and lumbar vertebrae (Pl. 162,*a*). Immediately surrounding Skull 12 were five turkey bone awls and eight bone awl tips, a bear canine, a bear claw core and a fragment of a modified mussel shell (Pl. 161). The trench near Skulls 11 and 12 contained a sheet of mica 23.1 cm. long, 19.8 cm. wide and 0.4 cm. thick (Pl. 163), an *Oliva* shell 5.2 cm. long, six modified beaver incisors, a small group of fragmentary fish remains and a broken Dongola chert artifact 5.5 cm. long and 1.1 cm. wide which presumably had an original shape like a fish hook (Pl. 164). Also in this group of burial goods were two lower jaws of the golden eagle (*Aquila chrysaetos*) and one lower jaw of a female falcon (*Falco peregrinus* or *mexicanus*) (Pl. 164). Between the trenches but part of this group were a *Busycon* shell vessel (Pl. 165), a Norton Zoned Dentate Stamped vessel (Pot M-5) and fragments of two large mussel shell spoons (*Lampsilis* sp.).

In the northeast corner of Section VI, Burial 3 consisted of an old adult male with slight occipital deformation and a left posterior parietal plaque removal, very badly decomposed but complete except for the innominate bones. The burial was extended on the back with head to the northeast but only a few bones were in anatomical order (Fig. 35). There were four slightly tanged deer antler tine points in a group under the skull and one immediately to the left of the skull accompanied by a Norton variant point (Pl. 166). The antler tine points averaged 8.9 cm. in length. The Norton variant point is made from a very porous, granular dark gray stone. Dimensions are given in Table 1. Over the thoracic region of this burial were two fragmentary pottery vessels, two mussel shell spoons, two mussel shell effigies, five turkey bone awls and five awl tips, three flint flakes of dark gray chert (Pl. 167), ten bird claws and fragments of assorted bird bones. The pots are M-6, a Norton Zoned Dentate vessel with a cross-hatched rim and "rabbit track" punctates and M-7, another Norton Zoned Dentate vessel with an irregular lobed zone design (Fig. 37, *B*, *D*.). The mussel shell effigies are 8.2 cm. long, 2.3 cm. wide through the wide end and come to a rounded point on the other end. They are evidently effigies of bear canines. Next to the knee region of Burial 3 and partially in the trench were six turtle carapace dishes (all *Emys blandingi*) (Pl. 168,*a*, 169) covering a group of six Norton points of a banded light gray chert with fossiliferous inclusions (Pl. 170). These points are a better "matched" set in terms of similar dimensions than any of the three sets in the other mounds (Table 2). Just over the foot region of Burial 3 was the fragmentary skull of Burial 8, a bundled subadult female with slight occipital deformation and a possible left occipital plaque removal. Burial 8 was missing most of the postcranial skeleton except the long bones and pelvis (Table 4). In the region of the articulated right leg of this burial was a *Busycon* shell vessel with two holes drilled along the edge (Pl. 171) lying over a deer metapodial pin 27 cm. long. Next to the shell was a small quadrilobate vessel (M-8, Pl. 162,*b*) which was set directly over the trench on its mouth and

TABLE 2

PROJECTILE POINT DIMENSIONS 20KT1

(In millimeters)

Number	Max. Length	Max. Width	Basal Width	Index Length-Width	Stem Width	Notch Length	Notch Width	Thickness
Mound C-1	81.0	45.0	1.8	25.0	18.0	12.0	8.5	8.0
C-2	76.5	41.5	1.9	24.0	17.0	7.0	6.5	9.0
-3	77.0	41.0	1.9	27.0	18.0	10.0	8.0	8.0
-4	82.0	44.0	1.9	25.0	17.5	11.0	8.0	8.0
-5	77.0	43.0	1.8	26.5	19.0	9.0	7.0	8.0
-6	73.5	42.0	1.7	26.0	17.5	11.0	7.0	7.0
-7	74.0	41.0	1.8	26.0	18.5	8.5	6.0	8.0
-8	60.0	41.5	1.5	22.0	(18.0)	9.0	6.0	9.0
-9	66.0	40.5	1.7	26.0	17.0	9.0	6.0	8.0
-10	62.5	36.0	1.7	25.0	16.0	7.5	5.5	8.0
-11	65.0	40.0	1.6	24.0	17.0	8.0	4.5	9.0
-12	69.0	38.0	1.8	26.0	18.0	7.5	3.5	8.0
-13	63.5	45.0	1.4	24.0	19.0	9.0	7.0	7.0
-14	58.5	38.0	1.5	18.0	15.0	5.0	6.0	8.0
D-1	66.0	31.5	2.1	17.0	12.0	8.5	8.5	5.0
H-1	65.5	41.0	1.5	26.0	21.0	7.5	5.0	9.0
-2	61.0	32.0	1.9	(21.0)	15.0	8.5	9.0	9.0
-3	73.0	42.0	1.7	28.0	20.0	8.5	9.0	8.0
-4	82.5	39.5	2.1	27.5	(20.0)	(8.0)	(9.0)	7.0
-5	65.0	35.0	1.9	(24.5)	17.5	8.0	8.0	8.0
-6	81.0	39.0	2.1	(25.0)	20.0	7.0	8.0	10.0
J-1	82.0	39.5	2.1	(25.0)	19.0	7.0	7.0	7.0
-2	63.5	48.5	1.3	27.0	22.0	8.0	5.5	14.0
M-1	78.0	41.5	1.9	28.0	13.5	8.0	6.0	10.0
-2	79.0	48.0	1.7	23.5	18.0	9.0	7.0	9.0
-3	87.5	50.0	1.7	29.5	20.0	8.0	6.0	9.0
-4	81.0	48.5	1.7	27.5	17.5	9.0	6.5	9.0
-5	79.5	46.5	1.7	26.5	18.5	8.0	6.0	10.0
-6	81.0	46.5	1.7	27.5	18.0	8.0	6.0	9.0

Note:—Parentheses indicate estimates.

which contained three small engraved turtle carapaces (all young *Emys blandingi*), one plain *Terrapene carolina* carapace, and a fragment of decomposed and iron stained organic material which has been tentatively identified as a pine cone. The design on one of the carapace dishes is somewhat similar to that on a shell from Mound C of this group (Fig. 25). Burial 7, a subadult bundle with medium occipital deformation, lacked the hands, feet, spine and ribs like several of the other burials in this mound. Near the lower end of this bundle was a turtle carapace with eight lacing holes drilled from the exterior (Pl. 173) and the fragmentary remains of Pot M-9, a Norton Zoned Dentate vessel with long ovoid zones. Burial 9 was a bundled child with occipital deformation and left occipital plaque removal. Near the skull there was a projectile point of dark gray flint 3.4 cm. long and 3.0 cm. wide at the shoulder with a broken base (Pl. 172).

The Submound Floor

As much of the mound as time and trees permitted was removed to the gravel level, most of this area being in the northwest and southwest quadrants (Pl. 174,*b*). Directly beneath the cap and sharply demarked from it was an average of 0.3 feet of dark gray-brown sandy silt, only slightly lighter in color than the cap above and very hard-packed. This silt then graded directly into pea to cobble-sized gravel mixed with the sandy silt for approximately 0.2 to 0.3 feet above pure gravel. We might mention again the contrast between the profile in the center of the mound group and that on the periphery where the gravel is overlain by several feet of light silt.

There were several concentrations of cultural material in the dark sandy silt layer. Feature 1 covered an area approximately 4.0 feet in diameter in the northwest quarter next to the profile wall. Feature 1 consisted of 32 fragments of animal bone, one of them burned, a large fragment of mussel shell, a chip of dark grey banded chert and a stemmed point. The point is of very porous dark grey banded chert and is 4.0 cm. long and 2.2. cm. wide with a slightly contracting stem 2.0 cm. long. Although very crudely made, this point with its broad blade, slight shoulder and contracting stem resembles a familiar Early to Early Middle Wodland type. Feature 2 was found in the northwest quarter near the edge of the burial area floor in an area approximately three feet square. The feature consisted of one angular fragment of granite, two fragments of deer long bone, one agate core remnant, four light grey chert chips, one dark grey chip and 61 pottery sherds probably representing one vessel (Pl. 175). The body sherds vary from 1.0 cm. to 1.3 cm. thick and have a tan to orange exterior and a tan interior. The temper is coarse angular grit and those sherds with both surfaces intact show fine, closely spaced cordmarking, vertical on the exterior and horizontal on the interior. The straight rim tapers to a slightly rounded lip 8 mm. thick. There is a lug on one body sherd 3.5 cm. in diameter which also shows the fine cordmarking. These sherds are closely similar to the pottery in the lower levels of the Schultz site, Saginaw, Michigan and are identified as Marion Thick. Feature 3 was located near the edge of the southwest quadrant and consisted of 55 small bone fragments, an angular fragment of granite, two dark grey flint flakes, one slightly modified, and four sherds. The sherds are badly eroded and no decoration is visible on those surfaces that remain. The complete sherds are 1.2 cm. thick with a tan exterior, a reddish core and coarse angular grit temper. Several small fragments of mica were found in the area of Feature 3 and these are considered to be a part of the mica flakes scattered before the cap construction (see

Burial Structure). At the time these concentrations were being removed, a line of postmolds was picked up in the northwest quadrant. These molds showed up slightly darker than the dark silt in which they occurred and extended from the top of the dark silt into the gravel level where they became indistinct, precluding an outline of the lower end. The post molds averaged 0.25 feet in diameter and were on the average two feet apart although along the side nearest the burial area the average was closer to one foot. Forty of the molds outlined three sides of a roughly rectangular area 18 feet wide and 28 feet long, which incidentally is very close to the dimensions of the prepared burial floor (Pl. 174,*b*). Another group of 17 molds formed an oval pattern ten feet long by five feet wide immediately to the north of the large pattern. In the northeast quadrant, a slightly curving line of seven postmolds extended for twelve feet perpendicular to the long axis of the burial structure (Fig. 31). Because part of the prepared floor was removed to find some of the molds, it is clear that the structure was present before the mound area was stripped. The depth of the molds, not exceeding 0.5 feet, in relation to the size of the structure also suggests that an indeterminate amount of soil had been removed from the surface on which the structure stood. Within the rectangular area, some cultural material was encountered just above the mixed silt-gravel level. This included 60 sherds, one "thumbnail" scraper of light grey fossiliferous chert, nine light grey chert chips, two grey porous chert chips, one banded gray chert blank and a crude stemmed point (Pl. 175). The blank is 3.3 cm. long, 2.0 cm. wide and 1.1 cm. thick and is bifacially worked. The point has a square stem 1.3 cm. in both dimensions and is 2.6 cm. long and 1.4 cm. wide at the shoulder. The sherds are badly eroded and only five retained both surfaces which showed traces of fine, close-spaced cordmarking. The color is orange to brown on both surfaces with a grey core and the temper is coarse angular grit. These sherds match the Marion Thick described above in all observable characteristics. All the cultural material from inside the structure came from the same silt layer immediately above the gravel as that outside the structure. This seems to indicate that the structure was placed over an earlier occupation which was not disturbed by the building activities. There were no traces of features within the structure such as storage or fire pits and as far as could be determined, the rectangle was not closed off on the northeast end and was not directly connected with the line of posts in the northeast quadrant. It is tempting to interpret this structure as a part of the ceremonial activities connected with the mound, perhaps as a sort of charnel "storage" house which was removed just subsequent to the mound construction activities.

Another feature was located close to the line of molds in the northeast quadrant. Feature 4 was a pit approximately two feet in diameter containing ash, fragments of charcoal, several fragments of angular granite and 15 fragments of animal bone. The pit first showed up immediately below the cap and extended with an irregular outline to the mixed silt-gravel layer. On the top of the ash there were two fragments of mica, one about 5.0 cm. and the other 2.0 cm. in diameter, which were evidently part of the mica flakes scattered after the stripping. In the general area of the ash pit and just below the cap there was a fire-broken piece of dark grey chert with some calcareous deposit, a dark grey chert blade 5.4 cm. long and 1.4 cm. wide with retouch along the edges (Pl. 176) and a Havana body sherd 9 mm. thick with a section of dentate-filled curvilinear zone.

An elk scapula hoe or shovel was found immediately below the cap between the west edge of the burial area and Feature 3.

The article is from an immature *Cervus canadensis* with a maximum length of 22.8 cm. and maximum width on the blade of 13.5 cm. The spine has been removed and lateral cut marks from this operation are visible. The working end of the artifact is thinned and chipped from considerable use (Pl. 177).

Skeletal Material

Burial 1 is a male, 40 to 45 years of age at death. The right scapula, both clavicles, the ribs, right innominate, the patellae and most of the vertebrae are missing. The skull exhibits marked vertical lambdoid flattening, but there is no evidence of bifronto-occipital deformation (Neumann, 1942). There is some evidence of arthritis in the form of condylar lipping of the ulnae and lipping of the lower thoracic and lumbar vertebral centra; the skeleton is otherwise non-pathological. The dentition bears no caries, abscesses or ante-mortem loss; shovelling of the upper incisors is marked, and the maxillary left lateral incisor bears a well-developed lingual ridge.

Burial 2 is also a male of 40 to 45 years of age, with several of the long bones and other post-cranial bones being absent. The cranium exhibits slight bifronto-occipital deformation, with vertically directed lambdoid flattening. Ear exostoses are medium, the second lumbar vertebrae has lipping of the border of the centrum, and the fifth lumbar vertebra has an unfused neural arch. The dentition shows a marked degree of wear, but is otherwise without pathologies.

Burial 3 is an old adult male, with an estimated age at death of over 60 years. The post-cranial remains are very fragmentary and incomplete. The skull exhibits slight oblique lambdoid flattening, with no involvement of the frontal bone, as in bifronto-occipital deformation. An elliptical plate of bone has been removed from the posterior portion of the left parietal, immediately superior to asterion. The skeleton is quite pathological, with considerable evidence for arthritis. All vertebrae except cervicals one and two have lipping of the centra, and the long bones have condylar lipping and exostoses. The dentition shows extreme wear, the mandibular right first and second molars and the mandibular incisors having been lost ante-mortem. There are no observable caries, but abscesses occur in both the maxillary and mandibular dentition, as well as in the alveoli.

Burial 4 is a female, 15 years old at death. There is a slight amount of vertically directed lambdoid flattening, and a plaque removal from the posterior aspect of the left parietal, as described for Burial 3. No additional anomalies were observed on the skull. The post-cranial remains are complete except for the hands, the left patella and the sacrum. Other than a differential muscle response involving greater robusticity of the right clavicle, scapula, ulna and radius, the post-cranial skeleton is normal.

Burial 5, three years of age at death, has a slight amount of vertical lambdoid flattening; the presence of plaque removal is uncertain. Ear exostoses are absent, and the skeleton is without observable pathologies or anomalies.

Burial 6, a male of 18 to 20 years of age, is complete, and would therefore represent an in-the-flesh burial, unlike all other burials in Mound M. The skull has slight bifronto-occipital deformation, and plaque removal from the posterior left parietal. Ear exostoses are absent, and the skull is non-pathological. The maxillary incisors are strongly shovelled, and the dentition is without caries or abscesses. Post-cranial anomalies are confined to the vertebrae, as there is sacral lumbarization of the first sacral segment, and the neural arch of the fifth lumbar vertebra is unfused.

Burial 7 is a child of approximately ten years of age, the skull showing a slight amount of natural oblique lambdoid flattening. There is no plaque removal. The skeleton as a whole is strongly pathological, with several indications of congenital syphilis. The tibiae are strongly bowed anteriorly, with swelling of the anterior aspects. Both ulnae and the right radius have extensive decomposition of the periosteum of the shafts, the ulnae being identical to that illustrated by Moodie (1923: 468) which is from a pre-Columbian Indian from New Mexico, "showing a congestive osteitis which recalls the results of syphilis." The periosteal destruction and tibial alteration are restricted to the shafts, there being no joint involvement. The frontal bone, a classic site for treponemal lesions, exhibits no gross pathologies, although there is some resorption above the orbits; both the lack of gross destruction and the presence of resorption could well be a function of the young age of the individual. The palate shows strong involvement, with the posterior three-fourths having been destroyed. While claims of pre-Columbian syphilis are often subject to dismissal because of lack of concrete evidence or because other diseases cannot be ruled out, there are examples which exhibit all indications of treponemal infection (Morse, 1967).

Burial 8 is a 16 year old female. The skull is slightly deformed, but it is in the form of "natural deformation" (Neumann, 1942) as observed on Burials 3 to 7 discussed above. Viewed from the side, these skulls closely resemble undeformed Late Woodland crania from the lower Great Lakes area. The presence of plaque removal cannot be established with this skull, for the area of normal occurrence—the posterior left parietal and the left margin of the occipital—is missing, with no evidence of cutting as in the other crania. The absence of bone in this particular area of the skull most likely indicates that plaque removal has taken place, but in the absence of concrete evidence the skull will be regarded as questionable. From other skulls bearing the plaque removal, it would appear that the plate of bone was removed by a combination of cutting and smashing.

The skull of Burial 8 also has a bi-partite "Inca bone," and the left tympanic plate is absent. The dentition and post-cranial remains are normal.

Burial 9 is a child, 4 to 5 years of age. There is no cranial deformation, and the left posterior parietal bears a plaque removal. The remainder of the skeletal remains are without pathologies or anomalies.

Burials 10 and 11 are infants of less than one year, with no observable pathologies or anomalies.

Burial 12, a nine year old, exhibits both vertical lambdoid flattening and plaque removal. The post-cranial skeleton, complete except for the clavicles, patellae and sternum, is normal.

Burials 13 and 14 are both infants of less than one year of age. Burial 13 consists of fragments of the cranium and mandible, and a fragmentary post-cranial skeleton. Burial 14 is represented by cranial fragments.

Burial Vessels

M-1 (Fig. 36,*A*) NORTON PUNCTATE

Paste: Temper is angular crushed granite, core tends to crumble easily. Color is a uniform light brown to orange on both surfaces.

Surface: Smoothed, brush marks visible on both surfaces, particles well covered.

Decoration: Random pattern of angular punctates 7 mm. in diameter around the rim (6.3 cm. high).

Form: Flat bottomed jar with high vertical rim, flat insloped lip.

Dimensions: Height 12.1 cm., rim height 6.3 cm., shoulder diameter 9.9 cm., base diameter 4.5 cm., basal thickness 1.0 cm., rim thickness 7 mm., body thickness 5 mm.

Similarities: Annular punctates are similar to the decoration technique using a hollow cylinder of one variant of Sister Creeks Punctated (Griffin, 1952,*a* 100). The flat insloped lip indicates affinities with Havana Ware.

M-2 Fig. 36,*B*) NORTON ZONED CORDED

Paste: Temper is angular crushed granite and

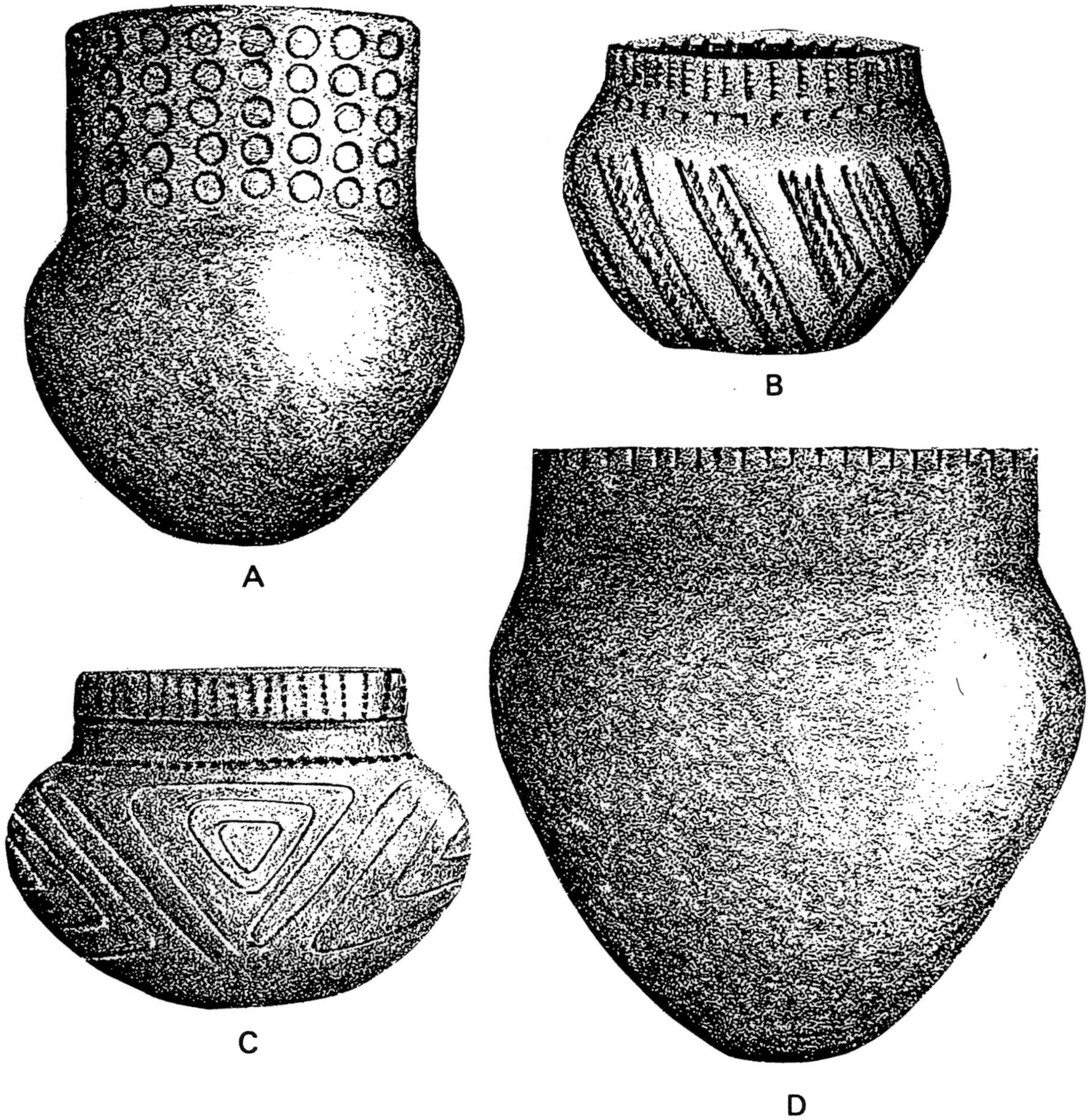

Fig. 36. *A*. Vessel M-1; Norton Punctate, height 12.1 cm. *B*. Vessel M-2; Norton Zoned Corded, height 4.9 cm. *C*. Vessel M-3; Norton Incised, height 8.2 cm. *D*. Vessel M-4, Norton Plain, height 14 cm.

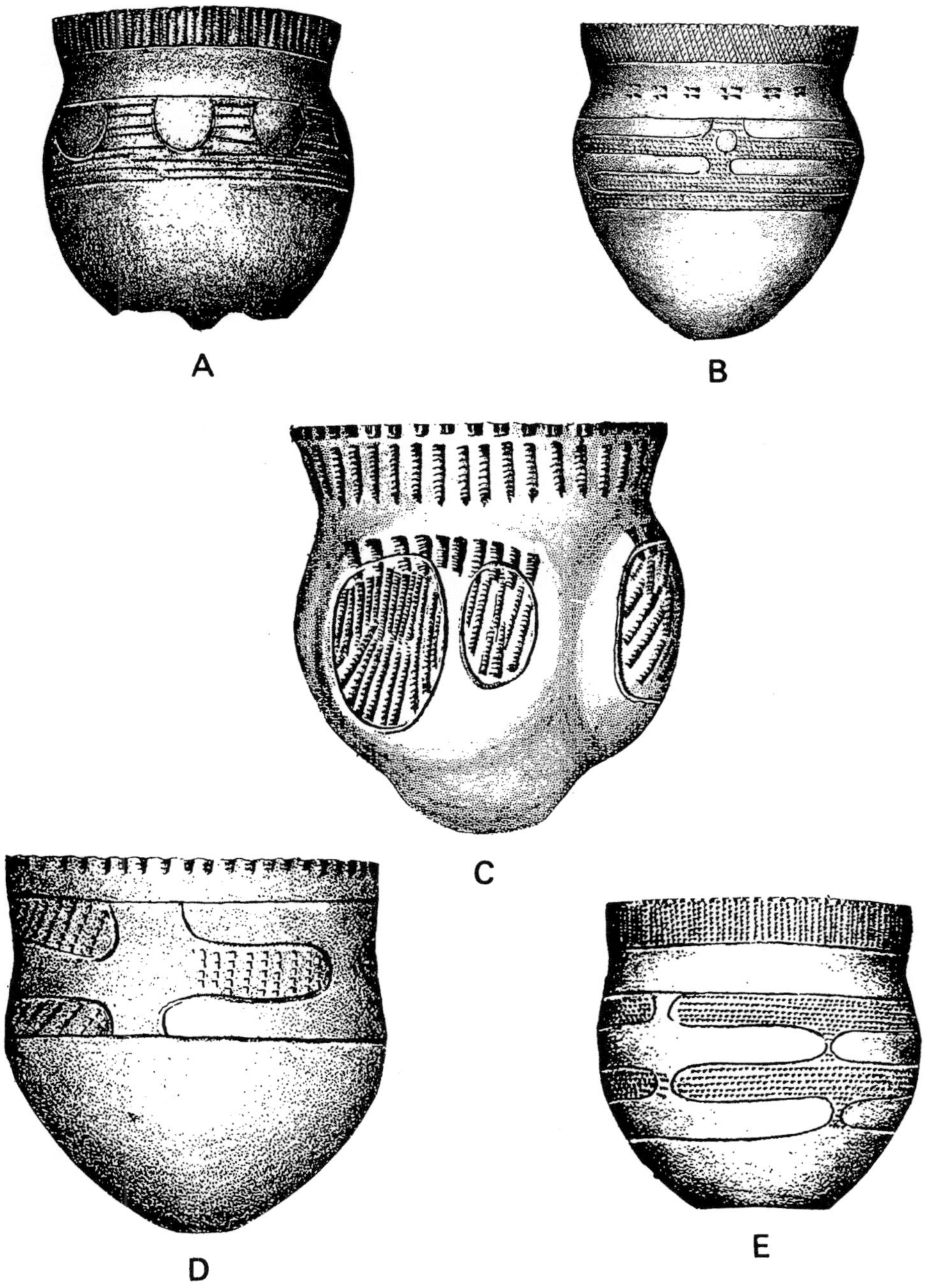

Fig. 37. *A*. Vessel M-5, Norton Zoned Dentate Stamped, height 18.5 cm. *B*. Vessel M-6, Norton Zoned Dentate Stamped, height 17.0 cm. *C*. Vessel M-8, Norton Zoned Cordwrapped Stick, height 9.5 cm. *D*. Vessel M-7, Norton Zoned Dentate Stamped, height 10.2 cm. *E*. Vessel M-9, Norton Zoned Dentate Stamped, height 12.0 cm.

sand, tends to crumble easily. Color is tan to dark grey exterior, grey interior, dark grey core.

Surface: Smoothed, somewhat uneven, some brush marks visible on exterior, both surfaces eroded.

Decoration: Lip has vertical sharp edged tool impressions. Horizontal band of hemiconical punctates made from the left around the neck. Body has oblique fine line zones 5 mm. apart filled with longitudinal single cord lines.

Form: Small concave-bottomed jar, marked shoulder and vertical rim. Lip is slightly thickened, flat to slightly rounded.

Dimensions: Height 4.9 cm., shoulder diameter 6.5 cm., rim diameter (est.) 4.5 cm., base diameter 3.0 cm., body thickness 5 mm., rim thickness 7 mm.

M-3 (Fig. 36,*C*) NORTON INCISED

Paste: Angular grit temper, color exterior orange base, upper brown to clouded grey, interior light brown to brown.

Surface: Well smoothed, some particles showing on exterior.

Decoration: Tool impressions 5 mm. apart on outer lip partly obliterated by parallel vertical rows of dentate stamp 8 mm. long, the upper rim bounded by a horizontal incised line. Neck is marked by a horizontal row of conical punctates made from the left. Body covered with six elements of three nested triangles each 3.5 cm. high.

Form: Round bottomed jar with slightly cambered rim, slightly rounded and insloped lip,

Dimensions: Height 8.2 cm., shoulder diameter 10.2 cm., rim diameter (est.) 7.6 cm., thickness 7 mm.

Similarities: This vessel is closely similar to Pot H-1 in major design elements, adding the slightly cambered rim and conical punctates.

M-4 (Fig. 36,*D*) NORTON PLAIN

Paste: Temper angular crushed granite, color light brown on both surfaces with grey firing clouds on upper half.

Surface: Smoothed, some brush marks visible on both surfaces.

Decoration: Outer lip deep tool impressions 3 to 4 mm. apart, 3 mm. long.

Form: Jar with slightly flattened semi-conoidal base, slight shoulder and vertical rim, flat to slightly rounded lip.

Dimensions: Height 14.0 cm., shoulder diameter 13.0 cm., rim diameter (est.) 12.2 cm., thickness 7 mm.

Similarities: Close in form to Vessel C-1 except tool impressions instead of dentate stamp on the rim.

M-5 (Fig. 37,*A*) NORTON ZONED DENTATE STAMPED

Paste: Temper angular crushed granite with sparse sand, light orange brown exterior with grey firing clouds near rim, dark grey core and light brown interior.

Surface: Smoothed, both surfaces badly eroded with particles showing.

Decoration: Outer lip tool impressions 4 mm. wide followed by parallel, vertical dentate stamp 1.5 cm. long. Upper rim bounded by horizontal incised line followed by plain zone 2.3 cm. wide, then another horizontal incised line with pendant semicircles 3.0 cm. wide and 3.0 cm. apart, the semicircles contained in a zone 4.0 cm. wide and filled with dentate stamp.

Form: Globular jar with marked neck, slightly cambered rim and flat insloped lip.

Dimensions: Height (est.) 18.5 cm., shoulder diameter (est.) 18.0 cm., rim diameter (est.) 16.5 cm., body thickness 7 mm., rim thickness 1.0 cm.

M-6 (Fig. 37,*B*) NORTON ZONED DENTATE STAMPED

Paste: Temper largely sand, some angular grit. Exterior brown to red brown with grey firing clouds on top half.

Surface: Smoothed, almost polished in spots, particles well covered.

Decoration: Outer lip tool impressions 5 mm. apart, rim covered by incised crosshatchings 2.2 cm. wide with lines 3 mm. apart. Rim bounded by incised line, then a plain zone 3.0 cm. wide with "rabbit track" stamps, the hind feet 5 mm. long and front feet 3 mm. long, approximately 2.0 cm. apart. Middle body has a zone 4.0 to 4.8 cm. wide with a four-lobed dentate-filled motif with one circle in upper lobe of each element. The crosshatched lines originally ran 1.5 cm. farther down onto the neck but have been cut off by the horizontal line and partially smoothed out.

Form: Globular jar with slightly flaring, slightly cambered rim. Lip is flat and insloped.

Dimensions: Height (est.) 17.0 cm., shoulder diameter 15.8 cm., rim diameter (est.) 17.5 cm., body thickness 5 mm., rim thickness 8 mm.

Similarities: The four-lobed body design is similar to Pot C-2 and the cambered rim is found in at least five other vessels in this group. The "rabbit track" stamp and crosshatched rim are unique for this group.

M-7 (Fig. 37,*D*) NORTON ZONED DENTATE STAMP

Paste: Angular grit and sand temper, both surfaces brown to gray.

Surface: Smoothed, particles well covered.

Decoration: Outer lip marked with dentate stamp (two teeth), followed by plain zone 7 mm. wide. Upper body and neck covered by zone 3.6 cm. wide enclosing cruciform lobate designs surrounded by dentate stamp.

Form: Globular jar with slightly flaring rim, slightly rounded lip.

Dimensions: Height 10.2 cm., shoulder diameter 10.2 cm., rim diameter 9.8 cm., thickness 6 mm.

Similarities: The lobed design is similar to several of the vessels from this mound and to Pot C-2.

M-8(Fig. 37,*C*) NORTON ZONED CORD-WRAPPED STICK

Paste: Angular grit and sand temper, brown to orange exterior with grey firing clouds on top half, interior light brown with ferrous stains.

Surface: Both surfaces smoothed, a few particles extruded.

Decoration: Outer lip tool impressions 5 mm. apart, followed by vertical cordwrapped stick impressions 1.3 cm. long and 2 mm. wide. Each lobe marked with two oblong zones 3.5 to 4.0 cm. long and 2.0 to 3.0 cm wide filled with vertical cordwrapped stick impression.

Form: Quadrilobate jar with flared rim, flat to slightly rounded insloped lip. Base is rounded, resembles the lobes in size and form.

Dimensions: Height 9.5 cm., maximum body diameter 10.0 cm., diameter between lobes 9.0 cm., rim diameter 9.0 cm., thickness 8 mm.

Similarities: The quadrilobate form with the fifth lobe on the base is similar to a vessel from Cook County, Iowa and to one from the Goodall site (Brown, 1964: Pl. VII,C), and one from Brangenberg Mound 3 (Griffin and Morgan, 1941: Pl. 50, No. 1).

M-9 (Fig. 37,*E*) NORTON ZONED DENTATE STAMP

Paste: Temper largely sand, some angular grit. Exterior light brown to brown, interior brown to grey.

Surface: Smoothed, no temper particles visible.

Decoration: Outer lip tool impression 5 mm. apart, rim marked with vertical dentate rows 1.8 cm. long bounded by horizontal incised line, then a plain zone 2.0 to 2.5 cm. wide. Middle body decorated with three levels of long adjoined oval zones 1.3 cm. wide, average three to a circumference, which are plain and filled with dentate stamp alternately.

Form: Jar with slightly concave base, slight shoulder and slightly cambered rim with flat, insloped lip.

Dimensions: Height 12.0 cm., shoulder diameter 12.5 cm., lip diameter 11.7, base diameter 5.0 cm., thickness 5 mm.

Similarities: General similarities to other Norton and Utica Mound vessels with ovate zones and a cambered, dentate stamped rim.

Summary of Skeletal Material

Charles Eyman did some preliminary analysis on the skeletal material from 20KT1 and Richard Wilkinson furnished additional data after the Mound M excavation, including the tables on sex and age distribution and morphological characteristics (Tables 3 and 4). We are indebted to Mr. Wilkinson for comparisons and insights into burial practices and physical characteristics adding to the body of data on Michigan Hopewell.

The tables do not indicate stage of decomposition or displacement of skeletal remains. Of the total of 35 identifiable individuals, the great majority were disarticulated bundles, often with some attempt to replace the bones in some kind of anatomical order. Only four adults, two in Mound C, one in J and one in M, were in articulatory position. It would seem that most of the individuals represent reburials and even the four adults mentioned above were disarranged enough to suggest some decomposition before final covering. A practice of multiple burials is indicated by the remains of adults in Mound H and children in Mound I. Table 3 shows a ratio of 4:1 for males over females in identifiable adults. With the exception of Mound I, males are more numerous in all mounds and three mounds have no adult females. The presence of children in the mounds including those without adult females tempts one to postulate a patri-based family system. The total number of individuals in each arbitrary age group is indicative of a mortality profile considered normal for primitive populations with the highest mortality among the younger children and the middle-aged adults, according to Richard Wilkinson.

Table 4 illustrates the distribution of various morphological characteristics observed on the skulls and post-cranial remains. Three of the traits—bifronto-occipital deformation, lambdoid deformation form and plaque removal—are cultural indicators. The presence of these traits in individuals from all mounds suggests a short temporal span in the construction of

TABLE 3

SEX AND AGE DISTRIBUTION

	Sex			Age					
Burial	M	F	?	0-5	6-10	11-15	16-25	26-40	40+
H1	X						X		
H2	X								X
H3			X		X				
H4			X	X					
H5			X					X	
H total	2	0	3	1	1	0	1	1	1
J6	X							X	
J7	X								X
J8			X					X	
J-			X		X				
J total	2	0	2	0	1	0	0	2	1
I9		X							X
I10			XX	XX					
I11			X		X				
I total	0	1	3	2	1	0	0	0	1
C13	X							X	
C14			X		X				
C15	X						X		
C16	X							X	
C17	X								X
C18			X					X	
C total	4	0	2	0	1	0	1	3	1
M1	X								X
M2	X								X
M3	X								X
M4		X				X			
M5			X	X					
M6	X						X		
M7			X		X				
M8		X					X		
M9			X		X				
M10			X	X					
M11			X	X					
M12			X		X				
M13			X	X					
M14			X	X					
M total	4	2	8	5	3	1	2	0	3
TOTAL	12	3	18	8	7	1	4	6	7

the mounds. This is especially true of the plaque removals, as they show practically no variation in their form and location. All (41.2 per cent of the Norton burials) are found on the left side of the skull immediately above the asterionic point. Neumann (1942: 309) mentions bifronto-occipital deformation at the Turner and Hopewell Sites in Ohio and at the Albany Mounds in Whiteside County, Illinois. Three of the White County, Illinois mounds, Wh°6, Wh°7 and Wh°9, have burials with simple occipital deformation (Neumann and Fowler, 1952: 247). Both Dickison mounds contain occipitally deformed skulls, in this case three out of 12 burials (Walker, 1952: Pl. 26). In the northern Illinois Valley, there are nine burials with occipital deformation in four of the Adler Mounds (Winters, 1961: 80). The plaque

TABLE 4

DISTRIBUTION OF MORPHOLOGICAL CHARACTERISTICS

Burial	Bifronto-occipital def.	Plaque Removal	Ear Exostoses	Wormian Bones	Vertical Lambdoid Flattening	Tympanic Dehiscences	Parietal Notch Bones	Caries	Abscesses	Vertebral Lipping	Septal Apertures	Neural Arch Unfused
H1	X	X	0	X	0	0	0	0	0	0	0	0
H2	0	X	X	X	0	0	0	0	X	X	X	0
J6	X	X	0	X	X	0	0	0	0	. . .	0	. . .
J7	0	. . .	X	X	0	0	0	. . .	. . .	. . .	0	. . .
I9	. . .	X	X	X	. . .	0	. . .	0	0	0	0	0
C13	. . .	. . .	. . .	. . .	. . .	. . .	. . .	. . .	. . .	0	0	0
C14	X	0	0	. . .	X	X	X	0	0	0	0	0
C15	. . .	. . .	. . .	. . .	. . .	. . .	. . .	. . .	. . .	. . .	. . .	X
C16	X	X	X	X	X	0	0	0	0	X	0	X
C17	X	X	0	0	X	X	. . .	X	X	X	0	0
M1	0	0	X	0	X	0	0	0	0	X	X	0
M2	X	0	X	X	X	0	0	0	0	X	0	X
M3	0	X	0	X	0	0	0	0	X	X	0	0
M4	0	X	0	X	X	0	. . .	0	0	0	0	0
M5	0	. . .	0	X	X	X	. . .	0	0	0	0	0
M6	X	X	0	0	X	0	0	0	0	0	0	X
M7	0	0	0	0	0	0	0	X	0	0	X	0
M8	0	. . .	0	X	0	X	0	0	0	0	X	0
M9	0	X	X	X	0	X	0	0	0	0	0	0
M12	0	X	0	X	X	0	. . .	0	0	0	0	0
Totals	7	11	7	13	10	5	1	2	3	6	4	4
Freq.	41.2	73.3	38.9	76.5	58.8	27.8	7.1	11.8	17.6	35.3	21.1	21.1

removal has only one exact parallel in terms of position, size and technique of removal, although it is seen in various forms among Late Woodland populations of southeastern Michigan and western Ontario. One other possible occurrence of this practice is found in notes attributed to A. R. Kelley of the original excavating crew by James B. Griffin concerning excavation of Mound 5A, Group 1 of the Utica Mound Group. Kelley describes a subfloor pit with three extended burials and a contracted burial "thrust" into one corner of the pit; a young adult male . . . "on the left parietal . . . close to the asterion point, a round hole occurs. . . . A preliminary examination shows no scarifying or grooving, no obvious marks of cutting, no indications of healing and growth of new bone. It does not appear to be trephined, and is more likely to be an aperture punched into the skull by a powerful blow with a blunt, rounded weapon." This passage describes very well the trait exhibited by 73 per cent of the Norton population. Close similarities exist between the Utica and Norton groups on the basis of ceramics and other artifacts and it is tempting to interpret this burial in the corner of the pit as an unfortunate visiting relative.

The biological or genetic characteristics tend to support a view of internal homogeneity, although the random nature of the inherited characteristics as compared to those determined culturally makes the former less suitable for predicting homogeneity, especially when the sample size is small. If the genetic characteristics do not demonstrate a necessary genetic relationship between the Norton population and those of Illinois, they still suggest this affinity. The presence of ear exostoses in 38.9 per cent of the Norton skulls, for example, is very similar to the frequency observed among Hopewellian burials from Illinois (Addis-Castro and Neumann, 1948). Unfused neural arches, specifically of the fifth lumbar vertebra, occur in 21.1 per cent of the Norton burials and a similar frequency was observed by Mr. Wilkinson among burials from the Knight Site in Illinois. However, the bones saved from the Knight burials were only those in near "perfect" condition or those showing gross pathologies or anomalies, so frequencies may be misleading. Mr. Wilkinson is undertaking a more comprehensive analysis dealing with metric as well as discrete characteristics, with an end to demonstrating physical similarities between Norton and other Woodland populations.

SUMMARY AND COMPARISONS

There is some evidence for an occupation of this area by people making a pottery very similar to Marion Thick. The relationship of this ware to the more easily recognized Middle Woodland wares in this area is not clear, although it is significant that this pottery is found in the lower levels of the Spoonville site, 20-0T-1, the Schultz site-in Saginaw, 20-SA-1, and at the base of at least Mound M of the Norton Group. Almost none was recovered, however, from the fill of Mound M which would mean either that it was a very light occupation or that fill dirt for the mound was carried in from some distance. The latter seems rather unlikely. It is clear that the Marion Thick occupation could have been about 500 B.C. and there is a possible hiatus of 500 years between the Marion Thick and the Havana-like materials which would allow for some build up of soil from flooding. At any rate, the total area under the mound was evidently stripped to within 0.3 feet of the gravel layer. At the same time some kind of structure was removed which was quite possibly related to the ceremonial activities of the mound construction. The first feature built in the mound area was evidently the puddled yellow silt floor which partially overlapped one wall of the rectangular structure. The trenches, poles and the bark slab at the west end were evidently included in this stage of construction. The next step was the erection of a small ramplike structure of very dark organic silt around the edges of the burial area with a small ledge next to the burial area. The next step in construction was the placement of slabs of bark, some with a section of the log intact, along the small ledge and over the face of the ramp facing the burial area. This stage, with or without the burials, was evidently left open long enough to show some washing of the dark silt on the small ramp. At the same time or subsequent to the placement of the bark slabs, the burials and burial-goods were laid on the floor and into the trenches in the floor. A part of the large loaded cap was built at this time over the top of the small ramp and bark again applied to the face, as evidenced by the double line of decomposed bark. The depression in the east side of the cap and perhaps the one in the west side may have been left open as passages during this time, and then were filled in during the construction of the large cap, leading to the "double cap" profile noted above for these two edges. The separation between the dark cap soil and the lighter sandy loam top fill is sharp and shows no evidence of weathering or water action, suggesting that the large cap and the upper fill were constructed in a single stage.

The fragmentary and incomplete nature of most of the burials was noted before as well as the scattered disposal of all but two individuals (Burials 3 and 6), and Burial 6 is the only complete one in the mound. The rest are generally lacking sternum, patellae, hand and foot bones and many lack the upper spine and ribs which were evidently not included in the bundle. The four adults are all males and although there are several fragmentary subadults and infants located near Burials 1, 2 and 3, the bulk of the grave goods and in particular the "exotic" thems were located closest to Burials 2 and 3. Burial 2 was associated with the "work kit" of antler sections, hammerstones and beaver teeth and Burial 3 had the antler points, two pottery vessels and the mussel shell claw effigies in direct association. Between the two burials and along the trench in the prepared floor were the mica sheet, the *Oliva* shell, the conch shell vessel and the eagle and falcon remains. Also close to Burial 3 was the group of Norton projectile points and the pile of turtle shell dishes. Burial 6 was the most complete and closest to articulatory position and therefore could have been the necessary cause which signalled the beginning of mound construction. However, when the distribution of artifacts in association with burials is taken into account, a more likely interpretation in this case would be that there was a particular period of time in question during which the deceased members of a group (family or several families?) were preserved until the proper time for mound construction. Burial 6 would have been the most recently deceased of this hypothetical group. The equipment that is the most characteristic of burials in the Norton group—mussel shell spoon, hornstone chips and turkey bone awls—is present in this case with Burial 6 as well as with all the other more or less complete burials. All the adults in this mound show some form of occipital or lambdoid flattening, but Burials 1 and 2 are the only adults in this mound that do not have some form of plaque removal. It is tempting to surmise that these individuals for some reason did not need this treatment, which was certainly ritualistic in some respect.

In general, the same grave goods are found in Mound M as in the other Norton mounds with the mussel shell—chert chip—turkey bone awl group, turtle shell dishes, elk bone pins, *Busycon* vessels and Havana-like pottery in evidence. Some exceptions are the *Oliva* shell and the antler points, and the lack of pipes and copper in any amount. The Norton variant points in this mound are almost identical in overall dimensions and proportions to the groups of seven in Mound C and the group of six in Mound H (Table 2). The stone used in this group of points is a light grey banded fossiliferous chert very similar to the material of points C-1 to -8. The majority of chips and flakes, particularly those with the turkey bone awls, are made from a blue to dark grey compact flint which was tentatively identified as Dongola chert in the other mounds (e.g. discoidals in Mound H). The presence of finished objects (blades and the hook-shaped artifact) and the use of both small and large primary flakes in this mound as in the others as burial associations suggests that some value was placed on this imported stone. The pottery vessels from Mound M show the same crudity as the majority of vessels from the other mounds, suggesting manufacture specifically for burial purposes. There is a marked difference between the vessels in the burial area and the Havana-like sherds from the mound fill, with the fill sherds showing a much harder surface finish and more compact paste with much less tendency to foliate or crumble than the pots in the burial. The only exact similarity in body decorative motifs is between Pots M-3 and H-1, both with a pattern of concentric incised triangles (Figs. 36,*C*; 39,*A*). Otherwise, a general pattern of dentate-filled lobed zones is found on several vessels in both M and the other Norton mounds. Four of the vessels from M show traits which did not appear in complete vessels from the other mounds. Both M-2 and M-8 have cord impressions as a decorative technique, M-8 has a quadrilobate body and M-6 shows a slightly cambered rim with incised crosshatching. All the other vessels in this mound and in the other mounds of the group with some kind of rim treatment have parallel rows of vertical dentate stamp impressions on the upper rim, with the exception of the crosshatched rim sherds from the fill of Mound J and the cap area of Mound D. The quadrilobate body and crosshatched rim are traits ordinarily associated with the classic Hopewell style, but both traits are also found in other contexts on vessels which would ordinarily be classified as Havana Ware on the basis of paste, vessel form and rim profile. The lobed form is found on a vessel from Titterington's Illinois collection (Griffin, 1941: 216) which is Havana in other characteristics and the crosshatched rim is found on two burial vessels from Mound Wh°5, White County, Illinois which have been reconstructed at The Museum, Southern Illinois University and which have the squat, flat-bottomed body with vertical rim and insloped lip characteristic of Havana burial vessels. Sherds of these two vessels are seen in Neumann and Fowler, 1952, Plate LXI, page 190. Geographically, the closest Hopewellian manifestation with similar pottery is in the Goodall area and in the Utica Mound Group in LaSalle County, Illinois. Similarities between some of the Utica vessels and pots from the other mounds have been noted above. In Mound M specifically, one Utica vessel (Griffin and Morgan 1941: Pl. 53, Fig. 2) has a flat base, lobed design and crosshatched rim like Pot M-6 and another from Utica (ibid., Pl. 55, Fig. 2) has a "cord-twig" decorative technique similar to M-8 in this mound.

The loaded burial cap and the soil stripping prior to construction are characteristic of at least the Norton and Spoonville Mounds of the Goodall focus. However, all the other Goodall mounds about which there is detailed information have some form of central subfloor burial pit as the only feature and Mound M with its "prepared floor" burial area would seem to be unique in this respect. The prepared floor burial area is widespread in both Illinois and Ohio and the material used ranges from fine sand to gumbo. A close similarity to the construction in Mound M is found in Bedford Mound 9 in southern Illinois where a log-lined crypt was surrounded by clay "ramps" like the small cap in Mound M, and with small logs laid parallel across the floor (Streuver, 1960). Other traits in common between Mound M and Bedford 9 are a large number of bone skewers (metapodial pins) in the crypt walls, bundle burials and an artifact assemblage including mica sheets, conch shells, a turtle shell container and a single copper awl. Bedford 9 also contained a limestone slab lining and an Ohio pipestone raven effigy pipe. Two of the other Bedford mounds, 10-11 and 12, had prepared yellow sand floors with artifacts contained in what are described as "pockets" in the floor, which may be similar in function to the trenches in Mound M where a good number of the artifacts were placed.

It was noted during the 1963 Norton excavations that all the definable burial pits (those not completely removed previously) with the possible exception of Mound J, when viewed through their long dimension seem to point in toward the center of the mound group, and specifically toward Mound M. The appearance is that of a central mound, or possibly three depending on the contents of Mound L and Mound N, with a series of subsidiary mounds in a semicircular pattern. The similarities in grave goods and particularly in the ceramics between Mound M and those mounds dug in 1963 were noted above, with the only marked discrepancy being the lack of copper in M. One possible interpretation of this arrangement is a large central mound with remains of members of several different families, a "community effort" perhaps, and small individual mounds around the outside which may represent individual family tombs. It should be noted again that the decorative patterns and vessel forms from Mounds C, H and I are represented in Mound M, although not necessarily in the same combinations.

The pottery vessels from the older excavations of the Norton Group include some types that were not found with burials during the University of Michigan excavations. One of these is a Hopewell Zoned Rocked Dentate vessel (Quimby, 1941:*a* Pl. 15, No. 2) which appears to be limestone tempered from the photograph. Quimby also refers to a somewhat similar vessel that should be included in this same type (ibid: 92-93). A third vessel said to be from the Norton Group would probably most closely approximate the Baehr style (ibid: Pl. 17, No. 1). If it is from the Norton group (Griffin is not certain that it is), it is the only Baehr example from the site. A fourth vessel (ibid: Pl. 17, No. 7) is grit tempered and looks like a local product copying the Hopewell style. The fifth vessel (ibid: Pl. 17, No. 9) is Norton Crosshatched and is also a locally made vessel by a potter familiar with the Hopewell style. A sixth vessel was described by Quimby (ibid: 93) but was not illustrated. It is either a Hopewell style vessel possibly brought in from the Illinois Valley or it is an unusually well made local product incorporating many features of the Hopewell style. It is unusual in the alternate zones of punctates and incised lines on the body and in the incised pattern on the lower rim which is normally left undecorated on Hopewell style pottery (Fig. 38). The design on the lower body with two parallel lines bisecting a four-sided figure is similar to a limestone tempered Hopewell Zoned Rocked Dentate vessel from the burial pit in Utica Mound 8, Group 1 (Griffin and Morgan, 1941: Pl. 57, No. 2; Henrickson, 1965: Fig. 30, A); to a jar from the

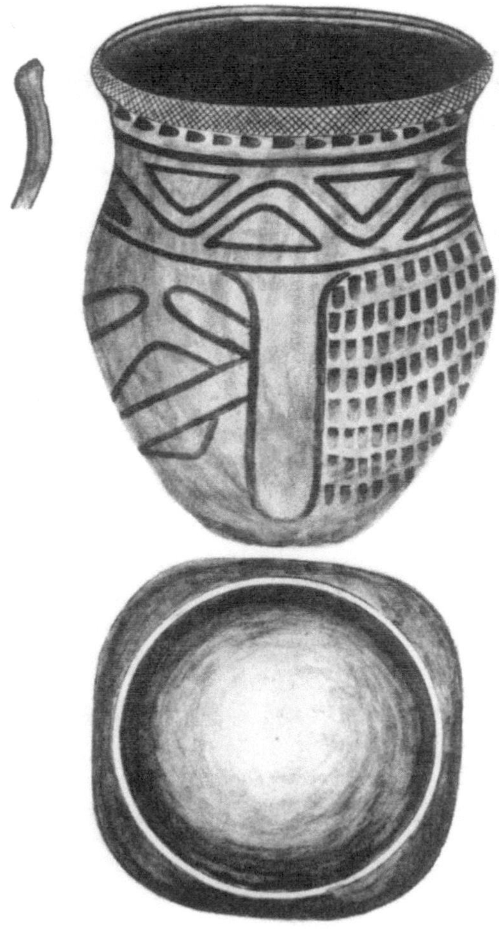

Fig. 38. Hopewell Zoned Incised-Punctate vessel from Norton Mound Group. Taken from W. S. Coffinberry manuscript.

Cook farm Mound 3 (Farquharson, 1876: Pl. VIII, No. 1), at Davenport, Iowa; to a Hopewell Zoned Dentate Stamped jar with Burial 8 in Klunk Mound 1, Calhoun County, Illinois (Perino, 1968: Fig. 9); to a vessel from the Crooks Mound in Lousiana (Ford and Willey, 1940: Fig. 32, d) and to one from El Trapiche, Vera Cruz, Mexico (García Payón, 1950: Pl. 12, Fig. 4).

Two of the vessels from the Norton Group, I-2, and M-6, have a curious pattern of punctates on the rim which are somewhat unusual. There are remarkable

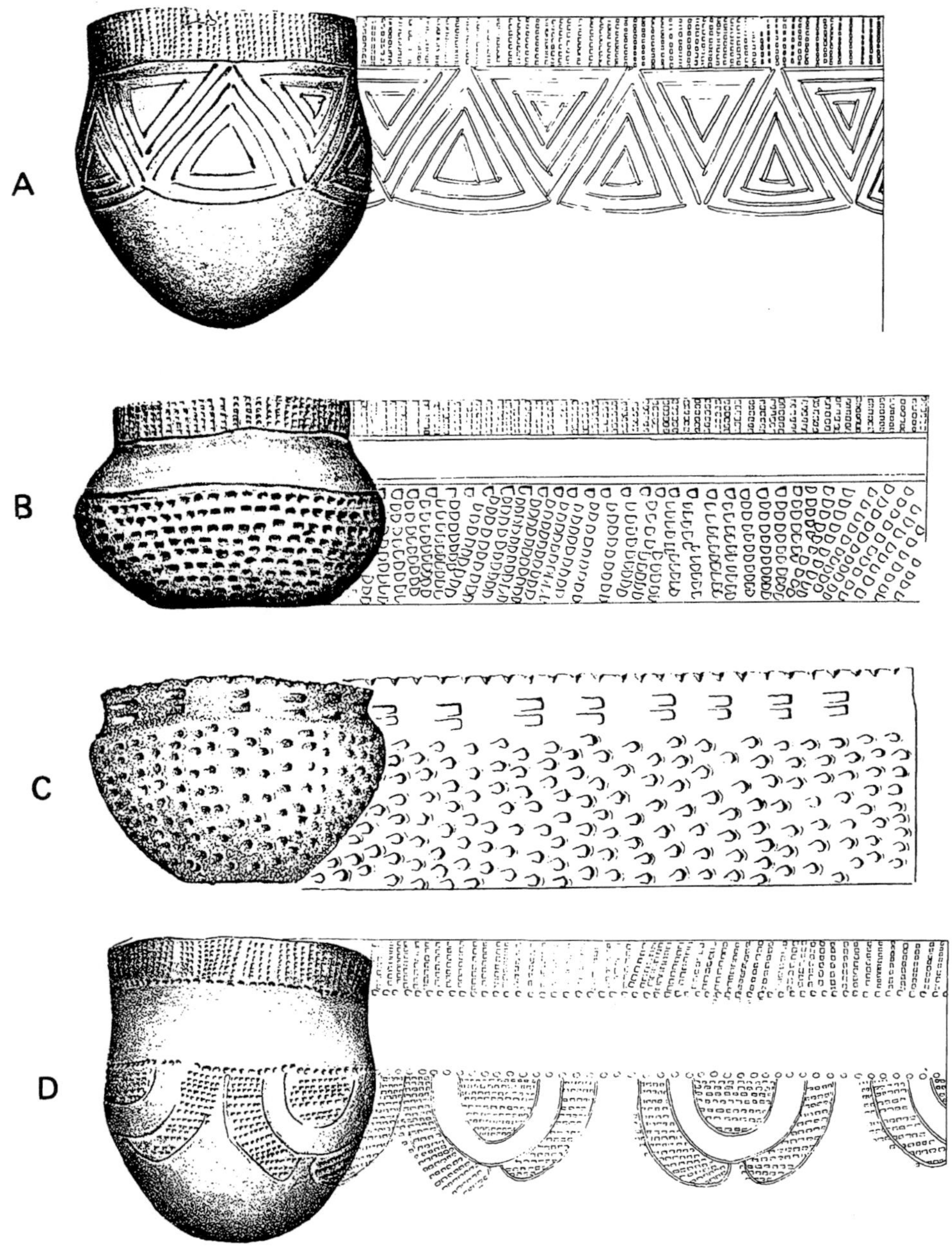

Fig. 39. *A*. Norton Zoned Incised vessel, H-1, with Group 1 of Central Burial pit, height 15.1 cm. *B*. Norton Zoned Punctate vessel H-3, with group 2 of Central Burial pit, height 7.5 cm. *C*. Norton Punctate vessel I-2, height 4.0 cm. *D*. Norton Zoned Dentate Stamp vessel I-1, height 12.5 cm.

parallels to this lower rim treatment on one of the vessels from Cook Farm Mound mentioned above and also to a zoned dentate stamped vessel from Mound 4 of the Rock River Group, Rock Island County, Illinois, according to the plate caption (Farquharson, 1876, Pl. VIII, No. 3), whereas the text on page 134 says it is from a mound in Scott County, Iowa. The point is, however, that the Hopewellian communities in the Davenport area were participating in the same art styles of the Middle Woodland period as were the potters in the Grand Rapids area. The Havana ceramic traditions have local regional expressions but the techniques of decoration and the art canons were shared over wide areas. The essential homogeneity of the Norton vessels and their connection to the Havana ceramic tradition is seen in the design layout in Figures 30, 40 and 41.

There was, unfortunately, not enough material suitable for radiocarbon dating from the burials in the Norton Group. Given the striking similarity of construction of the mounds and the burial offerings it would seem that the burial activities did not cover a very long span of time so that it is possible that radiocarbon dates would not have been precise enough to have reflected such temporal differences as may be present. A rough estimate of this time span would be of the order of about fifty years and should be closer to the date of 10 B.C. ± 120, obtained from Mound C, than to the other assays of A.D. 100 ± 125 and A.D. 160 ± 120 from Mound H, which are toward the later end of a reasonable result.

The most common trade item in the Norton Mound Group and in the related Middle Woodland Hopewellian burials in Michigan and northern Indiana is the *Busycon* shell dipper or container. In marked contrast to the Illinois Valley sites where the *Cassis* is quite common, the Goodall sites do not have that marine shell and are in this respect closer to Ohio Hopewell where the *Cassis* is also not common. The *Oliva* shell is not common anywhere in Hopewellian sites but was found at Harness and Mound City in Ross County, Ohio. It was obtained from the South Atlantic and Gulf Coast areas. The plain platform pipe from earlier excavations at Norton is believed to be of Ohio pipestone but the effigy pipes in Mounds H and C, and the plain platform pipe in Mound C were apparently locally made. The mica sheets in Mounds J and M are probably from North Carolina and their rare use in the Norton site parallels that at the Knlght site. In Mound J at Norton the mica plate was placed under the skull of No. 6 as was the case in Knight Mound 3, Burial 17. Both plates were associated with red ocher, points, knives, and awls which would appear to be personal possessions of the individual buried. The mica plate in Norton Mound M was near crania No. 11, but not in the type of direct association just described.

Some of the chert or flint at Norton appears to be the bluish grey nodular flint from Union County, Illinois but this has not been definitely established. Some of the white and mottled white blades are similar in appearance to those from Hopewellian sites in the lower Illinois Valley. If these flint specimens are indeed of Illinois origin they would increase the number of connections already established on the basis of mound construction similarities, ceramic styles and specific transported vessels between the Grand Rapids area and the Middle Woodland Hopewellian complexes in the Illinois Valley. It is not known whether the flint itself was brought in and worked into tools in western Michigan or whether the tools were brought in from Illinois. The latter is less likely to be the case but a study of available collections and excavations of village areas is needed to clarify this point. Some of the small chert chips

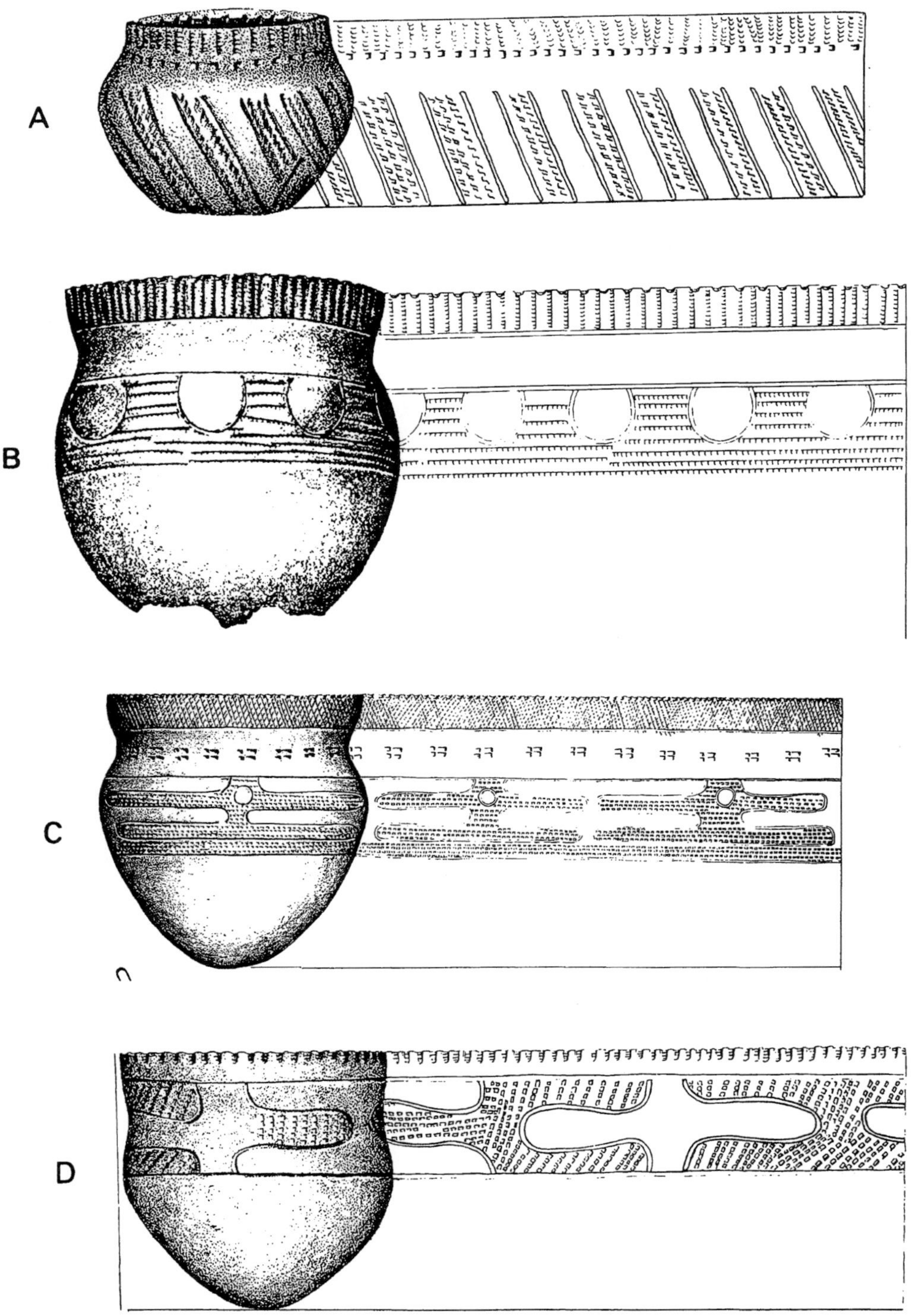

Fig. 40. *A*. Norton Zoned Corded vessel M-2, height 4.0 cm. *B*. Norton Zoned Dentate Stamped vessel M-5, height 18.5 cm. *C*. Norton Zoned Dentate Stamped vessel M-6, height 17.0 cm. *D*. Norton Zoned Dentate Stamped vessel M-7, height 12.0 cm.

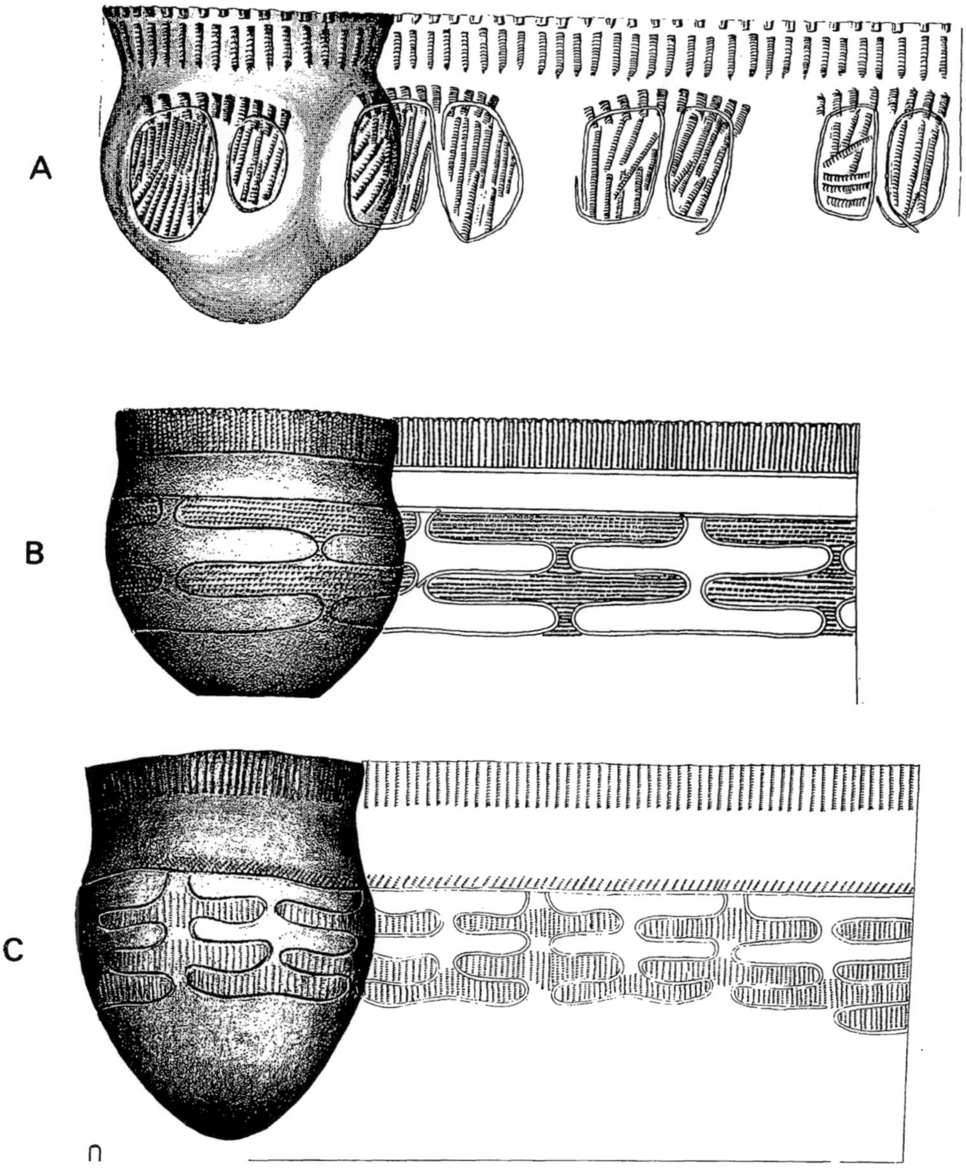

Fig. 41. *A*. Norton Zoned Cordwrapped vessel M-8, height 9.5 cm. *B*. Norton Zoned Dentate Stamp vessel M-9, height 12.0 cm. *C*. Norton Zoned Dentate Stamped vessel C-2, height 25.7 cm.

and flakes found at Norton with turkey bone awls might represent the use of chippage from the manufacture of stone tools at this site. At the Spoonville site, another western Michigan Hopewellian manifestation about 20 miles downstream from Norton, salvage work in a burial mound uncovered a light tan blade core and two blades of the same material, one of which fits on the core. The core is associated with a mica plate, copper celts and a Michigan Hopewellian pot (Flanders, 1969: 147). Ohio sources, and particularly Flint Ridge, do not seem to be represented in western Michigan.

The copper celts with Burials 16 and 17 in Norton Mound C may be trade or exchange items or may have been made locally. They were wrapped in cloth and probably in bark. The burial associations with these two burials were rather extensive for Michigan mounds and were primarily items associated with economic activities or with such supernatural beliefs as would be involved in a medicine bundle or in the needs of the individual for food and drink in the afterworld. One of the interesting facets of the western Michigan Hopewellian burials is that there are no earspools of copper, or of any other material, and this is in marked contrast to both Ohio and Illinois burials.

One of the close similarities of Norton and Knight burial practices was the inclusion of shell spoons with a burial vessel. In fact shell spoons, particularly with carved handles, first make their appearance in Middle Woodland but then continue up to the historic period. The split turkey tibiotarsus awls placed with flint blades as a tool kit perhaps associated with weaving or mat-making is one of the burial groups found in both areas and evidently regarded as of considerable importance. This distinctive bone awl was recognized by Mills as characterizing Hopewell in Ohio in contrast to the Fort Ancient type where the bone was not split. A careful examination of Ohio Hopewell materials would undoubtedly show that this artifact was more common than might be supposed (Willoughby, 1922: Pl. 7,C), and is one of the Hopewellian tool forms of economic activity incorporated into the mortuary activities in that area as well as in the Illinois area. The interest aroused by more spectacular materials has caused this important connection to be overlooked or ignored.

The blade knives of the burial kits at the Norton and Knight Mound Groups are not only an important instance of common burial concepts but they are one of the most distinct items of the Hopewellian tool kit. In two instances at Knight, the blades were freshly made and included in the mound instead of taking some of the ones available in village use. This is possibly the case for Norton Mound J and is almost certainly the same procedure that was followed in Helena, Arkansas Mound B, Burial 79 (Ford, 1963: 44) with the cache of eight lamellar blades. These latter blades are more likely to have been made from the Dongola chert of Union County Illinois, than the Harrison County, Indiana flint mentioned by Ford.

One of the most distinctive burial features at the Norton Group was the placement of a group of points or knives with certain burials. The group of seven points with male Burial 16 in Mound C were apparently placed as points without hafting while the seven points with male Burial 17 in the same mound were so aligned that they suggest placement in the grave with either shafts or handles. The six points in Norton Mound H were not made to the same rigorous conformity as in Mound C nor were they clustered into a single deposit. The group of six Norton points in Mound M were overlapped and pointed in the same direction under six nested turtle carapace dishes, suggesting placement while hafted. The antler tine point near, but not under, Skull 3 in Mound M lay at the end of a narrow dark soil discoloration, perhaps the remains of a shaft. It is possible that some of the burials in the Converse Mound Group and in the Goodall area in Indiana also had such clusters of points. The Franz-Green Mound in Porter County, Indiana had a group of seven points in a subfloor pit along with at least 17 burials and other grave goods. The points were not specifically with a burial but had a group of four placed side by side pointing in one direction, and the other three placed side by side on top of them pointing in the opposite direction (McAllister, 1932: 24-26). These points are of the Snyders to Norton Corner Notched style. Another distinctive group are the seven Gibson Corner Notched points found in Gibson Mound 4 in northeastern Calhoun County near Kampsville and six Gibson points were in the nearby Kamp Mound 9.

In Fulton County, Illinois (Walker, 1952) in Mound 478 of the Dickison Group, eight Snyders Corner Notched forms were found with the young adult male Burial No. 3. The points were found near the right ankle pointing toward the east and overlapping each other so that they may possibly have been hafted at the time they were deposited. The association of the head and talons of a predatory bird with this burial is paralleled by the placement of the lower leg of the male snowy owl with Burial 16 of Norton Mound C, and by the eagle and falcon remains near Burial 3 in Norton Mound M.

The variety of materials associated with the burials in Mound C is an interesting assemblage. It represents such practical needs in the afterworld as kits for the manufacture of flint implements and perhaps for sharpening bone awls for mats or basketry. The containers vary from the marine shells as containers for liquids possibly associated with supernatural events to the turtle carapace cups, probably for food or special burial gifts of the type that tobacco was used for in historic times. When the carapace cups were stacked the interpretations must be that it was their future use which was important and not their content at the time of placement in the grave. The jars and mussel shell spoons also would have been for food and for subsequent use. The spoon implies the preparation of some sort of soup or stew in the vessel as contrasted with the baking or steaming pit or broiling or roasting cooking techniques. The import of the points is not clear. They may have been for future use or symbolic of past success as hunter or warrior. The copper axe is certainly a symbol but its significance is not clear. It was probably part of a medicine bundle, and it might be suspected that this was also the case with the platform pipes, for smoking was an effective part of communication with the spirit world for a wide variety of activities.

References have been made to the similarity of the subfloor pit burial location of the first burials in the Norton Mounds and to those in Knight and other Illinois Hopewellian sites. As in Norton Mound M and at Knight there are Hopewellian mounds without a subfloor pit. The absence of log-tombs at Knight was a marked difference from many other Illinois mounds and the same lack of log-tombs is found not only at Utica, Adler and Norton but at most of the Michigan Hopewellian mounds. This is an important difference and cannot be because of the lack of trees available for tomb construction.

If burial in mounds is *ipso facto* because of some status position in the society it is not clear what the status was. At the Knight Group, there is no immediately apparent preference of sex or age groups in burials of either the Pike or Fox Creek phases. In the Pike phase features, bundles and skeletons in approximate anatomical position are about equally represented, with extended burial the predominant method for the "flesh" burials. In the Fox Creek features, there is a tendency for primary burials in a flexed position to predominate. There is also a tendency for Pike extended burials to have the most burial associations and it may be that the death of these individuals was the initiating cause for mound construction with the inclusion of previously deceased individuals related by social or family connections. These latter individuals are not likely to have been preserved in anatomical order. The affect of the winter season in determining burial patterns in the midwest has not often been mentioned by interpreters of these patterns. The association of such grave goods as projectile points and "artisan kits" of antler sections and hammerstones with adult males at Knight as well as other Illinois and Michigan mounds would reflect a simple division of labor, where sex is more readily apparent to those arranging the burials than to those uncovering them. At the Norton Group there is certainly a preponderance of adult male burials over adult females and a majority of all burials are secondary. Although the sample is small (three identifiable females as opposed to twelve males) articles including pipes, projectile points, artisan kits and raptorial bird and carnivore remains are associated with males or with subadults, not with females. Males, females and subadults all have the range of "containers" or marine shell, turtle carapace and pottery, perhaps for food offerings, and the ubiquitous turkey bone awls, bladelets and mussel shell spoons. As at the Knight Group, there seems to be a class of artifacts indicating simply division of labor with some emphasis on males as those concerned with supernatural affairs, perhaps through medicine bundles with pipes and raptorial bird remains for example. In neither mound group is it clearly a case of politically or socially dominant males with families and/or "retainers" buried with them. There is a current tendency to interpret Hopewellian burial practices in terms of "priestly" or even "ruling" heirarchies. Although this might apply in the case of some of the Ohio manifestations, it is not at all clear in most other Hopewell groups.

The grave goods at Norton and Knight are to some degree reflections of the status or role of the individual during life, but are at least as intimately involved with useful items for future use. All of these activities involved items which were primarily of local manufacture and were part of the general cultural behavior of the group. The basic similarity of these activities at the Norton and Knight groups is the primary item to be considered in the recognition of participation by those societies in a Hopewellian cultural pattern of the Illinois Valley area.

Little or nothing has been said about the economic base of the Knight or Norton populations. Our restraint in this is because of the absence of sound data bearing on this from the two sites and not because we are unaware that these two populations required a dependable subsistence base. The assumption may be made that the food resources of the Knight population would have been nearly identical to that of the contemporary Middle and early Late Woodland occupants of the Lower Illinois Valley. When the data is made available by the controlled studies of Streuver and his associates on this latter area we believe it will also apply to to Knight people as well. The Norton people lived in a different zone on the northern border of the Carolinian zone but in a river valley location with some analogies in food resources to those of the Illinois Valley. It is significant that Hopewellian societies did not penetrate much farther north than the lower Muskegon-Saginaw Bay line in Michigan.

In the mid-1930's when the collections of the Grand Rapids Museum were first studied by Griffin and George I. Quimby, it was immediately apparent that the material from the Grand Rapids Norton and Converse groups and the other Goodall focus materials were most closely related to the Illinois Valley Hopewellian centers rather than to the Ohio Hopewell assemblages. Quimby's published studies of this material and all subsequent excavations or reports have not only emphasized this relationship but have served to strengthen the early hypothesis that the most likely explanation for the appearance of Hopewellian societies in the Goodall focus area was by expansion of Middle Woodland people east along the Kankakee River and from there to the stream valleys in western Michigan as far north as the Muskegon, and, moving east along the Grand River Valley into the Saginaw Basin. The closest conections in terms of burial procedures and recovered grave materials and the other collections of the Goodall focus, as it was called thirty years ago, are to the Illinois Valley area.

The term "Goodall focus" should probably be abandoned for it is now known that the variations within it and the temporal span of at least 300 years is too great to conform to what a "focus" was supposed to be. This has been recognized earlier and something systemmatic should be done about it in the near future. The complex recovered by earlier excavations and by the Museum of Anthropology in 1963 and 1964 from the Norton Group appear to be early in the occupation of the western part of Michigan by Hopewellian populations. The term Norton phase is suggested to apply to the initial occupation. The materials from the Converse Mound Group as far as they are preserved seem to belong towards the latter part of the Middle Woodland period so that the term Converse phase would be appropriate.

BIBLIOGRAPHY

Abbott, R. T.
1954 American Seashells. D. Van Nostrand. New York.

Adams, William R.
1949 Archaeological Notes on Posey County. The Indiana Historical Bureau, pp. 1-81. Indianapolis.

Adis-Castro, E., and Georg K. Neumann
1948 The Incidence of Ear Exostoses in the Hopewell People of the Illinois Valley. Proceedings of the Indiana Academy of Science, Vol. 57, pp. 33-36. Indianapolis.

Adler, Kraig
1968 Turtles From Archaeological Sites in the Great Lakes Region. The Michigan Archaeologist, Vol. 14, No. 3-4, pp. 147-63. Ann Arbor.

Atwater, Caleb
1820 Description of the Antiquities Discovered in the State of Ohio. The Transactions and Collections of the American Antiquarian Society, Vol. 1, pp. 109-251. Worcester.

Baerreis, David A.
1940 Delaware County Effigy. The Oklahoma Prehistorian, Vol. III, No. 1. Tulsa.
1960 A Report on a Bluff Shelter in Northeastern Oklahoma (D1-47), Archives in Archaeology, No. 1. University of Wisconsin Press, (Microcard). Madison.

Baker, Frank Collins
1941 A Study in Ethnozoology of the Prehistoric Indians of Illinois. *In*: Contributions to the Archaeology of the Illinois River Valley, J. B. Griffin and R. G. Morgan, eds. Transactions of the American Philosophical Society, Vol. XXXII, Pt. 1, pp. 51-77. Philadelphia.

Barrett, S. A.
1911 The Dream Dance of the Chippewa and Menominee Indians of Northern Wisconsin. Bulletin of the Public Museum of the City of Milwaukee, Vol. 1, Art. IV. Milwaukee.

Bennett, John W.
1945 Archaeological Explorations in Joe Daviess County, Illinois. University of Chicago Press. Chicago.

Black, Glenn A.
1933 The Archaeology of Green County. Indiana History Bulletin, Vol. 10, No. 5. Indianapolis.

Bluhm, Elaine A. and William J. Beeson
1960 The Excavation of Three Hopewell Mounds at the Caterpillar Tractor Company. *In*: Indian Mounds and Villages in Illinois. Illinois Archaeological Survey Bulletin, No. 2, pp. 1-24. Urbana.

Brown, James A.
1964 The Northeastern Extension of the Havana Tradition. *In*: Hopewellian Studies, J. R. Caldwell and R. L. Hall, eds. Illinois State Museum Scientific Papers, Vol. 12, No. 4. Springfield.

Brown, James A., ed.
1961 The Zimmerman Site. Illinois State Museum Report of Investigations No. 9, Springfield.

Clark, Malcom Sr.
1965 Hopewell Type Figurines. Central States Archaeological Journal, Vol. 12, No. 3, pp. 120-22.

Clark, W. M.
1878 Antiquities of Tennessee. Annual Report Smithsonian Institution for 1877. Pp. 269-76. Washington.

Coe, Michael D.
1965 Archaeological Synthesis of Southern Vera Cruz and Tabasco. Handbook of Middle American Indians, Vol. 3, Part 2, pp. 519-715. University of Texas Press. Austin.

Coffinberry, W. L.
1875 Mounds and Mound Builders. Unpublished manuscript.

Cole, Fay-Cooper and Thorne Deuel
1937 Rediscovering Illinois: Archaeological Explorations in and around Fulton County. University of Chicago Press. Chicago.

Collins, Henry B.
1926 Archaeological and Anthropometrical Work in Mississippi. Explorations and Field Work of the Smithsonian Institution in 1925. Smithsonian Miscellaneous Collections, Vol. 78, No. 1. Washington.

Cooper, Leland R.
1933 Red Cedar Variant of the Wisconsin Hopewell Culture. Bulletin of the Public Museum of the City of Milwaukee. Vol. 16, No. 2. Milwaukee.

Crane, H. R.
1956 University of Michigan Radiocarbon Dates I. Science, Vol. 124, No. 3224, pp. 664-72. Ann Arbor.

Crane, H. R. and J. B. Griffin
1962 University of Michigan Radiocarbon Dates VII. Radiocarbon, Vol. 4, pp. 183-203. Yale University. New Haven.
1964 University of Michigan Radiocarbon Dates IX. Radiocarbon, Vol. 6, pp. 1-24. Yale University Press. New Haven.
1966 University of Michigan Radiocarbon Dates XI. Radiocarbon, Vol. 8, pp. 256-85. American Journal of Science. New Haven.

Cvancara, Alan M.
1963 Clines in Three Species of *Lampsilis* (Pelecypods: Unionidae). Malacologia, Vol. 1, No. 2, pp. 215-25.

Dragoo, Don W.
1963 Mounds for the Dead: An Analysis of the Adena Culture. Annals of Carnegie Museum. Vol. 37. Pittsburgh.

Drake, Daniel
1815 Picture of Cincinnati. Cincinnati.

Drucker, P.
1943 Ceramic Sequences at Tres Zapotes, Vera Cruz, Mexico. Smithsonian Institution, Bureau of American Ethnology Bulletin 141. Washington.

Epstein, Jeremiah F.
1958 Ceramics and Ceramic Artifacts in the Pool Site. *In*: The Pool and Irving Villages, by John C. McGregor. University of Illinois Press, pp. 21-63. Urbana.

Farquharson, R. J.
1876 Recent Archaeological Discoveries at Davenport, Iowa. Proceedings of the Davenport Academy of Natural Sciences. Vol. 1, pp. 117-42. Davenport.

Faulkner, Charles H.
1960 The Red Ochre Culture: An Early Burial Vomplex in Northern Indiana. The Wisconsin Archaeologist, Vol. 41, No. 2, pp. 35-49. Madison.

Fenner, Gloria J.
1961 The Bowmanville Site. Illinois Archaeological Survey Bulletin No. 3, pp. 37-56. Urbana.
1963 The Plum Island Site, La Salle County, Illinois. *In*: Reports on Illinois Prehistory. Illinois Archaeological Survey Bulletin No. 4, pp. 1-106. Urbana.

Flanders, Richard E.
1965 A Comparison of Some Middle Woodland Material from Illinois and Michigan, Ph.D. Thesis, the University of Michigan. Ann Arbor.
1969 Hopewell Materials from Crockery Creek. Michigan Academician, Vol. 1, No. 1, pp. 147-51. Ann Arbor.

Flanders, Richard E. and Charles E. Cleland
1964 The Use of Animal Remains in Hopewell Burial Mounds, Kent County, Michigan. Jack Pine Warbler, Vol. 42, No. 4, pp. 302-09. Michigan Audubon Society. Kalamazoo.

Ford, James A.
1951 Greenhouse: A Troyville-Coles Creek Period Site in Avoyelles Parish, Louisiana. Anthropological Papers of the American Museum of Natural History, Vol. 44, Pt. 1. New York.

Ford, James A.
1963 Hopewell Culture Burial Mounds Near Helena, Arkansas. Anthropological Papers of the American Museum of Natural History, Vol. 50, Pt. 1. New York.

Ford James A. and Gordon R. Willey
1940 Crooks Site, A Marksville Period Burial Mound in La Salle Parish, Louisiana. Department of Conservation, Louisiana Geological Survey, Anthropological Study No. 3. New Orleans.

Fowler, Melvin L.
1952 The Clear Lake Site: Hopewellian Occupation. *In*: Hopewellian Communities in Illinois, Thorne Deuel ed. Illinois State Museum Scientific Papers, Vol. V. Springfield.
1955 Ware Groupings and Decorations of Woodland Ceramics in Illinois. American Antiquity, Vol. 20, No. 3, pp. 213-25. Salt Lake City.
1957 Rutherford Mound, Hardin County, Illinois. Illinois State Museum, Scientific Papers, Vol. VII, No. 1, pp. 1-44. Springfield.

García Payón, J.
1950 Restos de Una Cultura Prehistórica Encontrados en la Región de Zempoala, Vera Cruz. Uni-Ver, Vol. 2, No. 15, pp. 90-130. Jalapa.

Gates, S. H.
1961 An Archaeological Survey of the Du Page River Drainage. Illinois Archaeological Survey Bulletin No. 3, pp. 1-6. Urbana.

Goggin, John M.
1952 Space and Time Perspective in Northern St. Johns Archeology, Florida. Yale University Publications in Anthropology, No. 47. Yale University Press. New Haven.

Greengo, Robert E,
1964 Issaquena: An Archaeological Phase in the Yazoo Basin of the Lower Mississippi Valley. American Antiquity, Vol. 30, No. 2, Pt. 2. Memoir No. 18. Salt Lake City.

Griffin, James B.
1941 Additional Hopewell Material from Illinois. Prehistoric Research Series, Indiana Historical Society, Vol. 2, No. 3. Indianapolis.
1946 Cultural Change and Continuity in Eastern United States Archaeology. *In*: Man in Northeastern North America, F. Johnsón, ed. Papers of the Robert S. Peabody Foundation for Archaeology, Vol. 3, pp. 37-95. Cambridge.
1947 The Spruce Run Earthworks: A Forgotten Adena Site in Delaware County, Ohio. The Ohio State Archaeological and Historical Society Quarterly, April, 1947, pp. 188-200. Columbus.
1952*a* Some Early and Middle Woodland Pottery Types in Illinois. *In*: Hopewellian Communities in Illinois. Illinois State Museum Scientific Papers, Vol. V, pp. 93-130. Springfield.
1952*b* A Preview of the Ceramic Relationships of the Snyders Site, Calhoun County, Illinois. The Greater St. Louis Archaeology Society. St. Louis, Missouri. (No date indicated, but it appeared in 1952).
1965 Hopewell and the Dark Black Glass. The Michigan Archaeologist, Vol. 11, Nos. 3-4, pp. 115-55. Ann Arbor.
1967 Eastern North American Archaeology: A Summary. Science, Vol. 156 No. 3772, pp. 175-91. Washington.
1968 Observations on Illinois Prehistory in Late Pleistocene and Early Recent Times, *In*: The Quaternary of Illinois, University of Illinois College of Agriculture Special Publication, No. 14, pp. 123-37. Urbana.

Griffin, James B., A. A. Gordus and G. A. Wright
1969 Identification of the Sources of Hopewellian Obsidian in the Middle West. American Antiquity, Vol. 34, No. 1, pp. 1-14. Salt Lake City.

Griffin, James B. and Richard G. Morgan
1941 Contributions to the Archaeology of the Illinois River Valley. Transactions of the American Philosophical Society, Vol. 32, Pt. 1. Philadelphia.

Griffin, John W.
1946 The Upper Mississippi Occupation at the Fisher Site, Will County, Illinois. Unpublished Master's Thesis. University of Chicago.

Halsey, John R.
1966 Additional Hopewell Engraved Turtle Shells from Michigan. Papers of the Michigan Academy of Science, Arts, and Letters, Vol. LI, pp. 389-98. Ann Arbor.

Henricksen, Harry C.
1965 Utica Hopewell, A Study of Early Hopewellian Occupation in the Illinois River Valley. Illinois Archaeological Survey Bulletin No. 5, pp. 1-67. Urbana.

Isikowitz, K. G.
1935 Musical and Other Sound Instruments of the Southern American Indians. Goteborgs Kugl. Vetenskapsoch Vitterkets - Samhalles Handlinger. Femfte Foljden. Ser. A, Ban 5, No. 1. Goteborg.

Johnson, Glenn
1969 Excavation of the McCarter Mound, Panola County. Newsletter of the Mississippi Archaeological Society. State College, Mississippi.

Kellar, James H., A. R. Kelly and Edward McMichael
1962 The Mandeville Site in Southwest Georgia. American Antiquity, Vol. 27, No. 3, pp. 336-55. Salt Lake City.

Langford, George
1927 The Fisher Mound. Successive Aboriginal Occupations near the Mouth of the Illinois River. American Anthropologist, Vol. 29, No. 2, pp. 152-206. Menasha.

Lewis, T.M.N. and M. Kneberg
1961 Eva: An Archaic Site. A University of Tennessee Study in Anthropology. University of Tennessee Press. Knoxville.

McAllister, J. Gilbert
1932 The Archaeology of Porter County. Indiana History Bulletin, Vol. X, No. 1. Indianapolis.

McGregor, John C.
1952 The Havana Site. *In*: Hopewellian Communities in Illinois. Illinois State Museum Scientific Papers, Vol. V, pp. 43-92. Springfield.
1958 The Pool and Irving Villages. A Study of Hopewell Occupation in the Illinois River Valley. University of Illinois. Urbana.

McKern, W. C.
1931 A Wisconsin Variant of the Hopewell Culture. Bulletin of the Public Museum of the City of Milwaukee, Vol. 10, No. 2. Milwaukee.

McKern, W, C., Paul F. Titterington and James B. Griffin
1945 Painted Pottery Figurines from Illinois. American Antiquity, Vol. 10, No. 3, pp. 295-302.

McKinney, Joe J.
1954 Hopewell Sites in the Big Bend Area of Central Missouri. The Missouri Archaeologist, Vol. 16, No. 1. Columbia.

McMichael, Edward V.
1964 Veracruz [sic], The Crystal River Complex and the Hopewellian Complex. *In*: Hopewellian Studies, J. R. Caldwell and Robert L. Hall, eds. Illinois State Museum Scientific Papers, Vol. 12, pp. 123-32. Springfield.

Magrath, Willis H.
1945 The North Benton Mounds: A Hopewell Site in Ohio. American Antiquity, Vol. XI, No. 1, pp. 40-46. Salt Lake City.

Martin, Paul S., G. I. Quimby and D. A. Collier
1947 Indians Before Columbus. University of Chicago Press. Chicago.

Maxwell, Moreau S.
1951 Woodland Cultures of Southern Illinois: Archaeological Excavations in the Carbondale Area. Logan Museum Publications in Anthropology, Bulletin No. 7. Beloit.

Mills, William C.
1916 Exploration of the Tremper Mound. Ohio Archaeological and Historical Quarterly, Vol. 25, No. 3. Columbus.

Moodie, R. L.
1923 Paleopathology. University of Illinois Press. Urbana.

Moore, C. B.
1896 Two Mounds on Murphy Island. Journal of the Academy of Natural Sciences of Philadelphia, Second Series, Vol. X, Pt. 4, pp. 503-16. Philadelphia.

1902 Certain Aboriginal Remains of the Northwest Florida Coast, Part II. Journal of the Academy of Natural Sciences of Philadelphia, Second Series, Vol. XII, Part 2, pp. 127-335. Philadelphia.

1903 Certain Aboriginal Mounds of the Florida Central West Coast. Journal of the Academy of Natural Sciences of Philadelphia, Second Series, Vol. XII, Pt. 3, pp. 359-438. Philadelphia.

1905*a* Certain Aboriginal Remains of the Lower Tombigbee River. Journal of the Academy of Natural Sciences of Philadelphia, Second Series, Vol. 13, pp. 245-78. Philadelphia.

1905*b* Certain Aboriginal Remains of Mobile Bay and Mississippi Sound. Journal of the Academy of Natural Sciences of Philadelphia, Second Series, Vol. 13, Pt. 2, pp. 279-97. Philadelphia.

Moorehead, W. K.
1922 The Hopewell Mound Group of Ohio. Field Museum of Natural History, Publication 211. Anthropological Series, Vol. 6, No. 5, pp. 75-195. Chicago.

Morrell, L. Ross
1965 The Texas Site, Carlyle Reservoir, Clinton County, Illinois. Southern Illinois University Museum Archaeological Salvage Report, No. 27. Carbondale.

Morse, Dan
1967 Two Cases of Possible Treponema Infection in Prehistoric America. Technical Series No. 7. Miscellaneous Papers in Paleopathology: I. William D. Wade, ed. Museum of Northern Arizona, pp. 48-60. Flagstaff.

Morse, Dan F.
1963 The Steuben Village and Mounds: A Multicomponent Late Hopewell Site in Illinois. University of Michigan, Museum of Anthropology, Anthropological Papers, No. 21. Ann Arbor.

Munson, Patrick J.
1966 An Archaeological Survey of the 'Wood River Terrace' and Adjacent Bottoms and Bluffs in Madison County, Illinois. Illinois State Museum Preliminary Reports, No. 8. Springfield.

Neumann, Georg K.
1942 Types of Artificial Deformation in the Eastern United States. American Antiquity, Vol. VII, No. 3, pp. 306-310. Menasha.

Neumann, Georg K, and Melvin L. Fowler
1952 Hopewell sites in the Lower Wabash Valley. *In*: Hopewellian Communities in Illinois, Thorne Deuel, ed., Illinois State Museum Scientific Papers, Vol. 5, No. 5, Springfield.

Parmalee, Paul W.
1967 The Fresh-Water Mussels of Illinois. Illinois State Museum, Popular Science Series, Vol. VIII. Springfield.

Perino, Gregory
1963 A Review of the Artifacts from Indian Mounds Park, Quincy, Illinois. Central States Archaeological Journal, Vol. 10, No. 1, pp. 4-10. The Pete Klunk Mound Group, Calhoun County, Illinois.

1968 Hopewell and Woodland Site Archaeology in Illinois, Illinois Archaeological Survey Bulletin, No. 6. Urbana.

Phillips, Philip, J. A. Ford and J. B. Griffin
1951 Archaeological Survey in the Lower Mississippi Alluvial Valley, 1940-1947. Papers of the Peabody Museum of Archaeology and Ethnology, Harvard University, Vol. XXV. Cambridge.

Powell, B. Bruce
1957 Hopewell Pottery of the Lower Illinois Valley: The Snyders Site Ceramics. Papers of the Michigan Academy of Science, Arts, and Letters, Vol. 42, pp, 219-24. Ann Arbor.

Putnam, F. W,
1882 Notes on the Copper Objects from North and South America. Contained in the Collections of the Peabody Museum. Fifth Annual Report of the Trustees of the Peabody Museum of American Archaeology and Ethnology, Vol. III, No. 2. Cambridge.

Quimby, George I.
1941*a* The Goodall Focus: An Analysis of Ten Hopewellian Components in Michigan. Indiana Historical Society, Vol. 2, No. 2. Indianapolis.

1941*b* Hopewellian Pottery Types in Michigan. Papers of the Michigan Academy of Science, Arts, and Letters, Vol. 26, pp. 543-48. Ann Arbor.

Rackerby, Frank E.
1966 Archaeological Investigations at the Boulder Site: First Season. Southern Illinois University Museum Archaeological Salvage Report, No. 27. Carbondale.

Ritchie, William A.
1965 The Archaeology of New York State. The Natural History Press. Garden City.

Roberts, Helen H.
1936 Musical Areas in Aboriginal North America. Yale University Publications in Anthropology, No. 12. Yale University Press. New Haven.

Rubey, William W.
1952 Geology and Mineral Resources of the Hardin and Brussels Quadrangles (in Illinois). United States Geological Survey Professional Paper 218. Washington.

Sargent, W.
1799 A Letter from Colonel Winthrop Sargent to Dr. Benjamin Smith Barton. Accompanying Drawings and Some Account of Certain Articles, Which were Taken out of an Ancient Tumulus, or Grave in the Western-Country. Transactions of the American Philosophical Society, Vol. IV, pp. 177-81. Philadelphia.

Schoenbeck, Ethel
1941 Cultural Objects of Clear Lake Village Site. Transactions of the Illinois Academy of Science, Vol. 34, No. 2, pp. 65-66. Springfield.
1947 A Seven-pound Copper Axe among 1946 Hopewell Discoveries. Transactions of the Illinois Academy of Science, Vol. 40, pp. 36-42. Springfield.

Sears, William H.
1962 Hopewellian Affiliations of Certain Sites on the Gulf Coast of Florida. American Antiquity, Vol. 28, No. 1, pp. 5-18. Salt Lake City.

Shelford, Victor E.
1963 The Ecology of North America. University of Illinois Press. Urbana.

Shetrone, Henry C.
1926 Exploration of the Hopewell Group of Prehistoric Earthworks. Ohio Archaeological and Historical Quarterly, Vol. 35, No. 1, pp. 1-227. Columbus.

Shetrone, Henry C. and Emerson F. Greenman
1931 Explorations of the Seip Group of Prehistoric Earthworks. Ohio Archaeological and Historical Quarterly. Vol. 40, No. 3, pp. 343-509. Columbus.

Shippee, J. M.
1967 Archaeological Remains in the Area of Kansas City. The Woodland Period, Early, Middle and Late. Missouri Archaeological Society Research Series, No. 5. Columbia.

Skinner, Alanson B.
1924 The Mascoutens or Prairie Potawatomi Indians. Bulletin of the Public Museum of the City of Milwaukee, Vol. 6, No. 1. Milwaukee.
1926 The Mascoutens or Prairie Potawatomie Indians. Part II. Notes on the Material Culture. Bulletin of the Public Museum of the City of Milwaukee, Vol. 6, No. 2. Milwaukee.

Smith, H. G.
1951 The Crable Site, Fulton County, Illinois: A Late Prehistoric Site in the Central Illinois Valley. Anthropological Papers, Museum of Anthropology, The University of Michigan, No. 7. Ann Arbor.

Smith, R. S., E. E. De Turk, F. C. Bauer and L. H. Smith
1932 Calhoun County Soils. University of Illinois, Agricultural Experiment Station, Soil Report No. 53. Urbana.

Snyder, J. F.
1898 A Group of Illinois Mounds. The American Archaeologist, Vol. II, Pt. 1, pp. 16-23. Columbus.

Speck, Frank G.
1909 Ethnology of the Yuchi Indians. University of Pennsylvania Anthropological Publications, University Museum, Vol. 1, No. 1, Philadelphia.

Starr, S. F.
1960 The Archaeology of Hamilton County, Ohio. The Journal of the Cincinnati Society of Natural History. Vol. XXIII, No. 1. Cincinnati.

Streuver, Stuart
1960 The Kamp Mound Group and a Hopewell Mortuary Complex in the Lower Illinois Valley. Masters Thesis, Northwestern University, Xerox copy.
1964 The Hopewell Interaction Sphere in Riverine-Western Great Lakes Culture History. *In*: Hopewellian Studies, J. R. Caldwell and R. L. Hall, eds. Illinois State Museum Scientific Papers, Vol. 12, No. 3, pp. 85-106. Springfield.
1965 Middle Woodland Culture History in the Great Lakes Riverine Area. American Antiquity, Vol. 31, No. 2, Pt. 1, pp. 211-23. Salt Lake City.
1968 A Re-examination of Hopewell in Eastern North America. Unpublished Ph.D. dissertation. University of Chicago. Chicago.

Taylor, William E., Jr.
1958 Ceramics of the Irving Site. *In*: The Pool and Irving Village, by John C. McGregor, University of Illinois Press, pp. 64-75. Urbana.

Titterington, Paul F.
1935 Certain Bluff Mounds of Western Jersey County, Illinois. American Antiquity, Vol. 1, No. 1, pp. 6-46. Menasha.
1942 The Jersey County, Illinois, Bluff Focus, American Antiquity, Vol. 9, No. 2, pp. 240-45. Menasha.
1950 Some Non-Pottery Sites in the St. Louis Area. Illinois State Archaeological Society, N.S., Vol. 1, No. 1, pp. 19-30. Springfield.

Turner, George
1802 Remarks on Certain Articles in an Indian Tumulus at Cincinnati, and Now Deposited in the Museum of the American Philosophical Society. Transactions of the American Philosophical Society, Vol. V, pp. 74-76. Philadelphia.

Walker, Winslow M.
1952 The Dickison Mound Group, Peoria County. *In*: Hopewellian Communities in Illinois, Thorne Deuel, ed. Illinois State Museum Scientific Papers, Vol. 5, No. 1, pp. 13-41. Springfield.

Webb, Clarence H.
1968 The Extent and Content of Poverty Point Culture. American Antiquity, Vol. 33, No. 3, pp. 297-321. Salt Lake City.

Wedel, Waldo R.
1943 Archeological Investigations in Platte and Clay Counties, Missouri. U.S. National Museum Bulletin, 183. Washington.

Weiant, C. W.
1943 An Introduction to the Ceramics of Tres Zapotes, Vera Cruz, Mexico. Smithsonian Institution Bureau of American Ethnology Bulletin 139. Washington.

White, Anta Montet
1963 Analytic Description of the Chipped Stone Industry from Snyders Site, Calhoun County, Illinois. *In*: Miscellaneous Studies in Typology and Classification. Anthropological Papers, Museum of Anthropology, the University of Michigan, No. 19, pp. 1-70. Ann Arbor.
1968 The Lithic Industries of the Illinois Valley in the Early and Middle Woodland Period. Anthropological Papers, Museum of Anthropology, The University of Michigan, No. 35. Ann Arbor.

Willey, Gordon R. and Philip Phillips
1958 Method and Theory in American Archaeology. University of Chicago Press. Chicago.

Willoughly, Charles C. and Earnest H. Hooton
1922 The Turner Group of Earthworks, Hamilton County, Ohio. Papers of the Peabody Museum of Archaeology and Ethnology, Vol. 8, No. 3. Cambridge.

Wimberly, Steve B. and Harry A. Tourtelot
1941 The McQuorquodale Mound: A Manifestation of the Hopewellian Phase in South Alabama. Geological Survey of Alabama, Museum Paper 19. University of Alabama. Tuscaloosa.

Winters, Howard D.
1961 The Adler Mound Group, Will County, Illinois. Chicago Area Archaeology. Illinois Archaeological Survey Bulletin 3, pp. 57-88. Urbana.

Wood, W. Raymond
1967 The Frestoe Burial Complex of Southwestern Missouri. The Missouri Archaeologist, Vol. 29. Columbia.

Wray, Donald E.
1952 Archeology of the Illinois Valley: 1950. *In*: Archeology of Eastern United States, James B. Griffin, ed. pp. 152-64, The University of Chicago Press, Chicago.

Wray, Donald E. and R. S. MacNeish
1961 The Hopewellian and Weaver Occupations of the Weaver Site, Fulton County, Illinois State Museum Scientific Papers, Vol. VII, No. 2. Springfield.

Young, Phillip D.
1960 The Frederick Site, Sc-11. *In*: Indian Mounds and Villages of Illinois. Archaeological Survey Bulletin No. 2, pp. 71-79. University of Illinois. Urbana.

PLATES 2-177

1
2
3
4
5
6

PLATE 2

Plate 2. Composite of Knight Mounds 1-13 on ridge to the east of the village site. UMMA Negs. 12802 to 12802D.

PLATE 3

a

b

Pl. 3 *a*. Partly cremated mass burial of C°1-2 to 6, skeletons in dark soil under burial C°1-1. The small Canteen Zoned Punctate vessel C°1-7 is on the same level as the group burial. Projectile point C°1-27 is in the northwest corner of the pit. UMMA Neg. 12803. *b*. A secondary extended male burial C°1-1, placed above group burial C°1-2 to 6. UMMA Neg. 12805.

PLATE 4

a

Pl. 4 *a*. Canteen Zoned Punctate vessel C°1-7 found three feet north of the group burial and on the same level. Height 9.5 cm. UMMA Neg. 12809. *b*. Child burial C°1-9 with pottery and two bone awls or pins. UMMA Neg. 12812.

PLATE 5

a

b

Pl. 5 *a*. Canteen Plain vessel C°1-9A associated with child burial. Height 13.6 cm. UMMA Neg. 100-4-4. *b*. Artifacts from C°1-9, 11, 17 and 18. Left: Two sections of turtle carapace C°1-9B of *Terrapene carolina*, two worked beaver incisors C°1-17, two copper fragments C°1-18, two copper awls C°1-9; lower center, turtle carapace C°1-9A of *Clemmys gutata;* lower right, turtle carapace of *Terrapene ornata*, C°1-11. UMMA Neg. 16110.

PLATE 6

a

b

c

Pl. 6 *a*. Artifacts from $C^{o}1$: long bone hairpin $C^{o}1$-9D of elk metapodial, flat bone awl from large mammal rib $C^{o}1$-9G, plano-convex scraper $C^{o}1$-30. UMMA Neg. 101-1. *b*. Knight Diagonal Notch d point $C^{o}1$-28, and Steuben Expanded Stem $C^{o}1$-29. UMMA Neg. 101-1. *c*. Burial $C^{o}1$-11 with Cante n Cordmarked ves el. UM 1A eg. 12814.

PLATE 7

a

b

Pl. 7 *a*. Canteen Cordmarked vessel C°1-11 associated with the skull of a child. Height 14.5 cm. UMMA Neg. 100-19-2. *b*. Canteen Cordmarked vessel C°1-12 associated with infant burial. Height 6.5 mm. UMMA Neg, 15662.

PLATE 8

a

b

Pl. 8 *a*. Canteen Plain vessel C°1-13 *in situ*, with two extended infant burials. UMMA Neg. 12816. *b*. Canteen Plain vess l C°1-13 a sociat d with two extended infant burials. Height 11 cm. UMMA Neg. 15663.

PLATE 9

a

b

Pl. 9 *a*. An extended adult female burial C°1-14 with Canteen Cordmarked vessel in the area of the right pelvis. UMMA Neg. 12819. *b*. Canteen Cordmarked vessel with burial C°1-14. Height 20 cm. UMMA Neg. 100-20-6.

PLATE 10

a

b

Pl. 10 *a*. Extended child burial C°1-16 with head to southeast and a small triangular knife at each hand. UMMA Neg. 12823. *b*. Triangular points or knives with C°1-16, and notched point C°1-27. UMMA Neg. 100-2-4.

PLATE 11

a

Pl. 11 *a*. Extended adult male C°1-17 with two unworked beaver incisors just below the left hand. UMMA Neg. 12824. *b*. Close view of beaver incisers at left hand of C°1-17. UMMA Neg. 12824a.

PLATE 12

a

b

Pl. 12 *a*. Extended adult male C°1-18 with three small fragments of sheet copper over the left clavicle. UMMA Neg. 12825. *b*. Extended burial of a child 7 to 8 years old, C°1-19 with a Canteen Cordmarked vessel at the left side of the skull. UMMA Neg. 12827.

PLATE 13

a

b

Pl. 13 *a*. Canteen Cordmarked vessel with child burial C°1-19. The height is 13.3 cm. UMMA Neg. 100-4-3. *b*. Partially flexed adult female on the left side, C°1-20, without grave goods. UMMA Neg. 12828.

PLATE 14

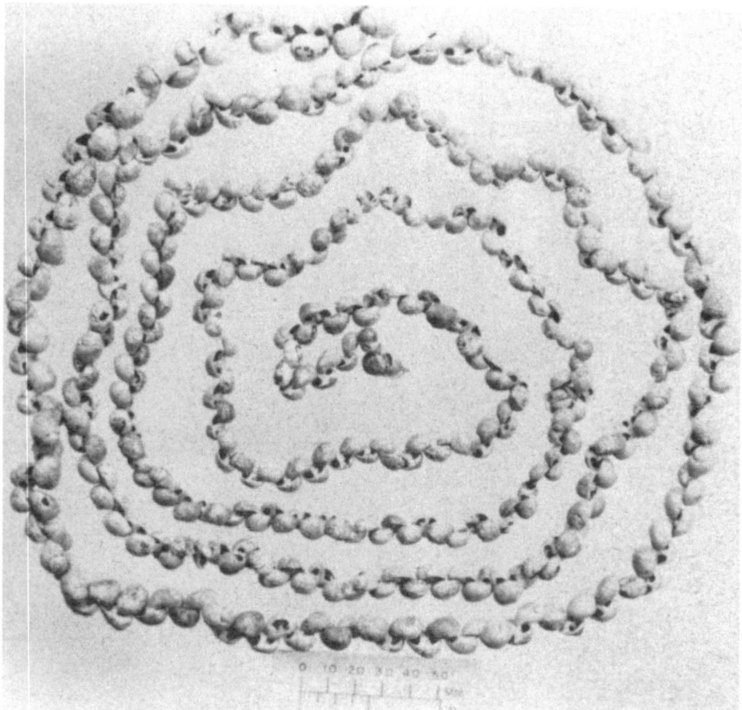

a

Pl. 14 *a*. Four hundred *Anculosa praerosa* beads found between upper flexed and lower extended burials. UMMA Neg. 16111. *b*. Canteen Plain jar, C^{o}2-11. Height 18.5 cm. UMMA Neg. 12835.

PLATE 15

a

Pl. 15 *a*. Canteen Plain jar, C°2-12. Height 13 cm. UMMA Neg. 12838. *b*. Canteen Plain jar, C°2-13. Height 12.3 cm. UMMA Neg. 12837.

PLATE 16

a

Pl. 16 *a*. Canteen Cordmarked jar, C^{o}2-14. Height 13.5 cm. UMMA Neg. 12840. *b*. Small Canteen Plain jar, C^{o}2-15, with rim area missing. UMMA Neg. 100-2-3.

PLATE 17

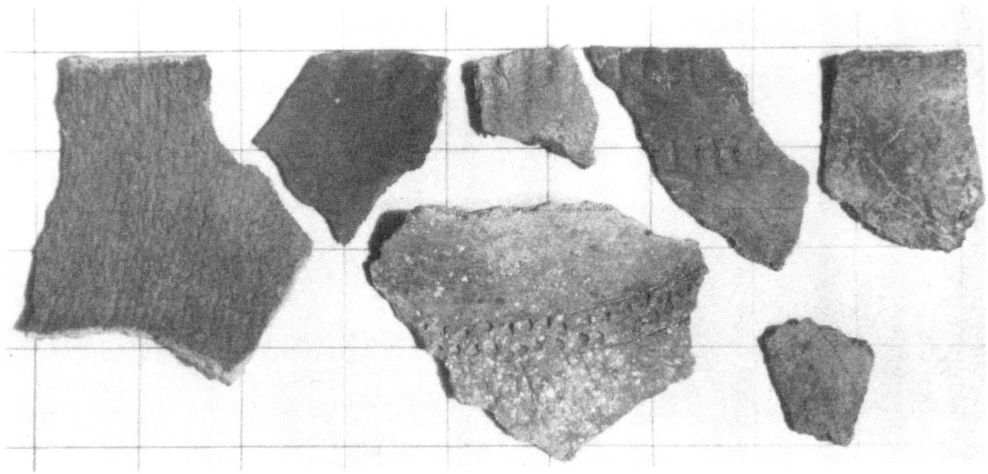

a

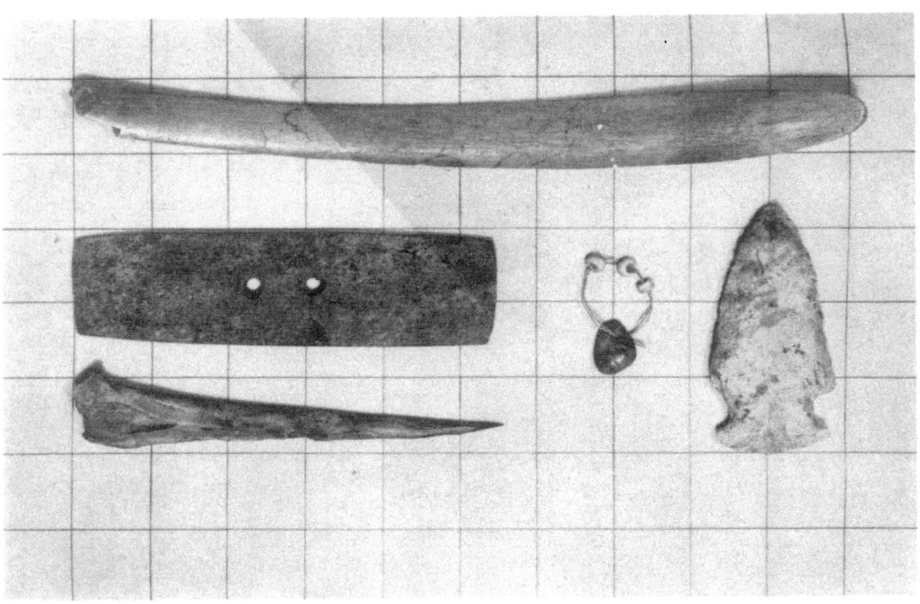

b

Pl. 17 *a*. Sherds from C°2 included in mound fill. UMMA Neg. 12843. *b*. Long spatula-like bone tool, C°2-21; slate gorget; shell beads and unidentified perforated object, C°2-21; Gibson Diagonal Notched point C°2-23; and turkey split tibiotarsal awl, C°2-22. UMMA Neg. 12845.

PLATE 18

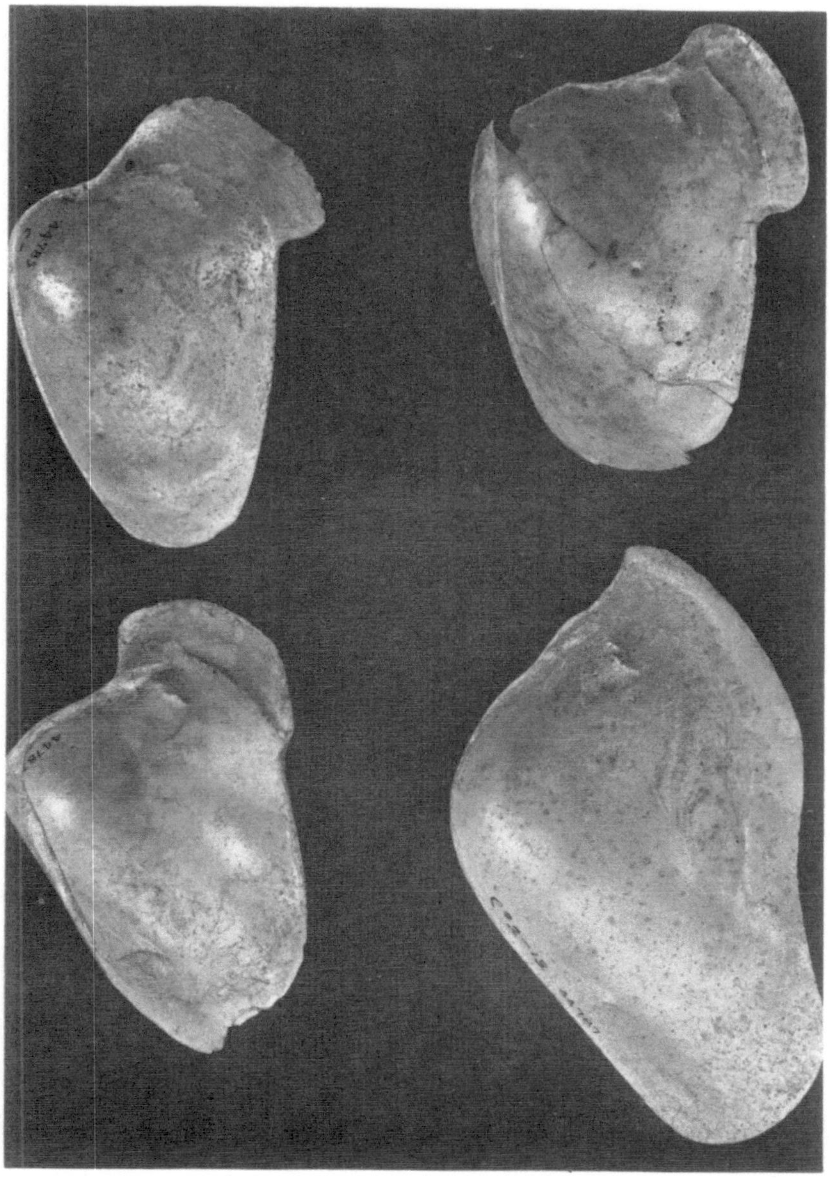

Pl. 18. Shell spoons with ves els "2-11 to 15. The first three were made from *Lampsilis ventricosa* and the fourth from *Proptera capax*. UMMA Neg. 100-1-5.

PLATE 19

a

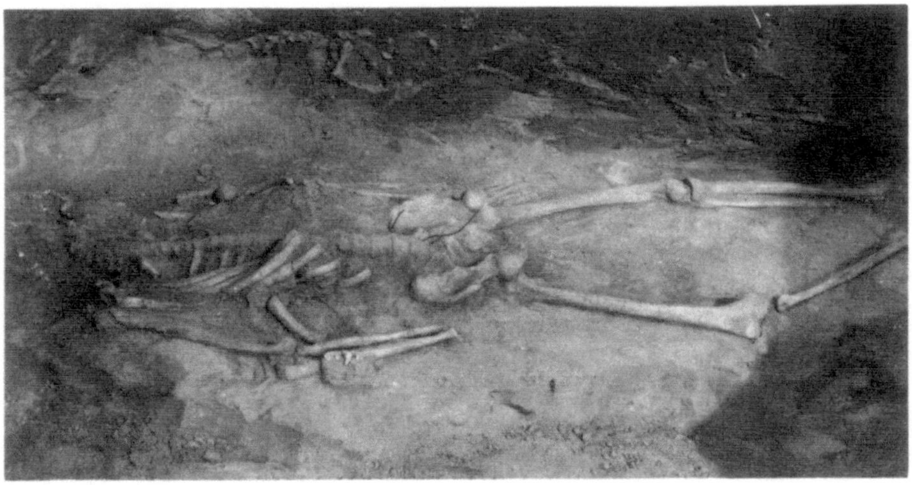

Pl. 19 *a*. Canteen Plain jar C°2-24, with notched lip. Found in the mound without known association. Height 15.5 cm. UMMA Neg. 12844. *b*. Extended adult male burial C°2-10 with cut and ground canine maxilla at right elbow and cut and polished antler section between right elbow and rib cage. UMMA Neg. 12833.

PLATE 20

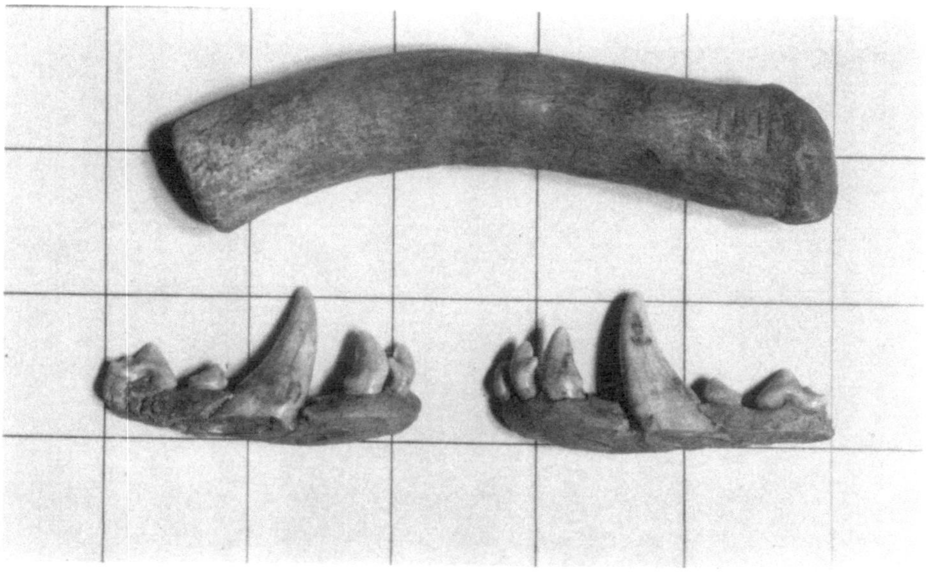

a

Plate 20 *a*. Antler section and split and ground canine maxilla with C°2-10. UMMA Neg. 12834. *b*. Canteen Plain jar C°2-25 found over the frontal bone of an adolescent extended female. UMMA Neg. 12846a.

PLATE 21

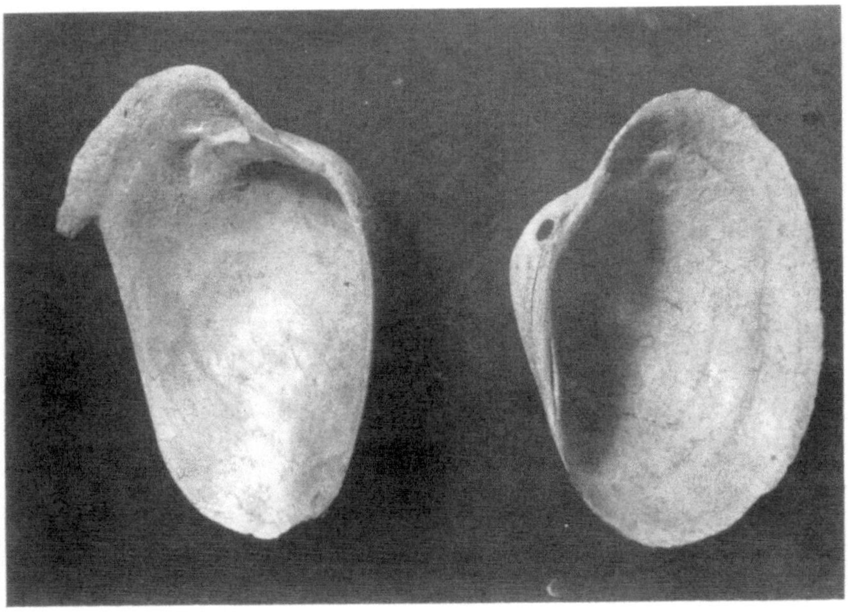

a

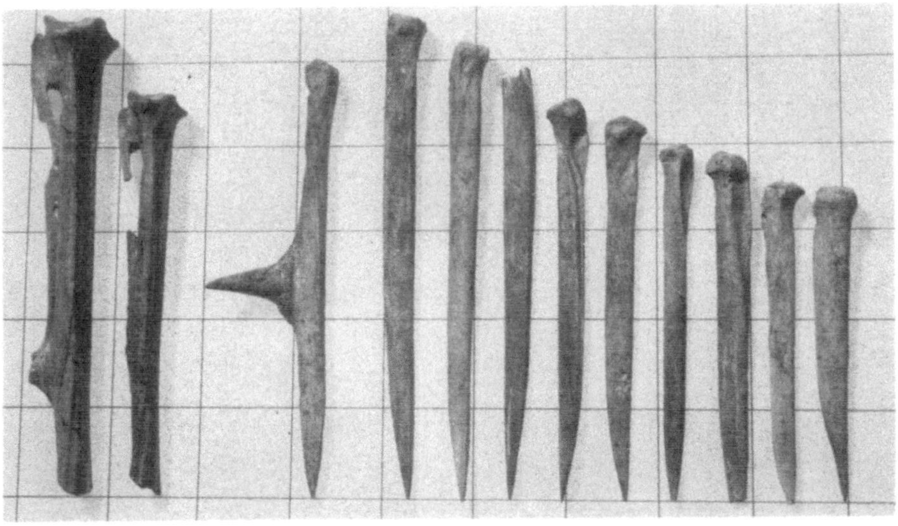

Plate 21 *a*. Mussel shell spoons C°2-26 and 27 made from *Lampsilis ventricosa* found in jar C°2-25. UMMA Neg. 12847. *b*. Worked and partially worked turkey tibiotarsal awls found over the left upper chest of C°2-25. UMMA Neg. 12848.

PLATE 22

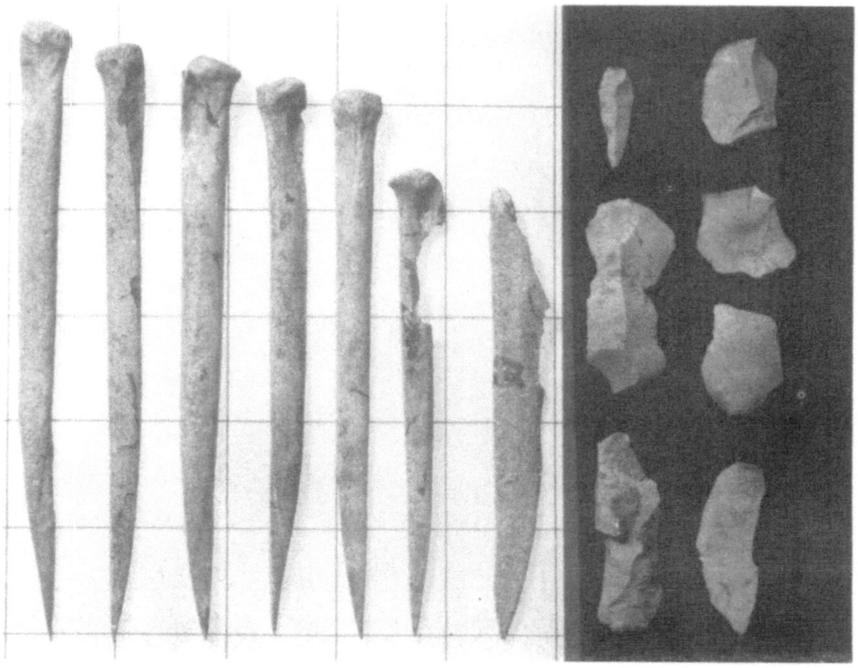

a

b

Plate 22 *a*. Six split turkey leg bone awls, an awl of flat bone and seven flake knives found in the axillary region of an adolescent extended female C°2-43. UMMA Neg. 12849. *b*. Young adult extended male burial C°2-57 with skull associated with Canteen Plain jar at the knee. UMMA Neg. 12850.

PLATE 23

a

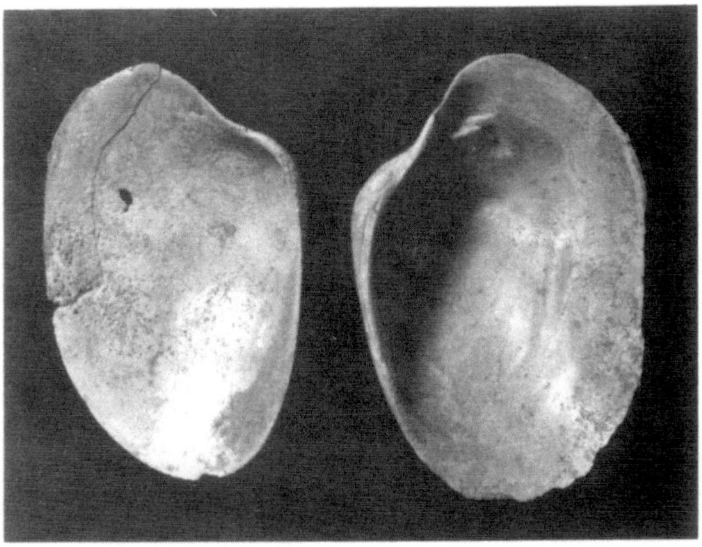

b

Plate 23 *a*. Canteen Plain jar Co2-57 found with an extended male burial. Height 22 cm., UMMA Neg. 12851. *b*. Mussel shell spoons Co2-58 and 59 made from *Lampsilis ventricosa* found in an adult male burial. They are 11.5 and 12.0 cm. long. UMMA Neg. 12852.

PLATE 24

a

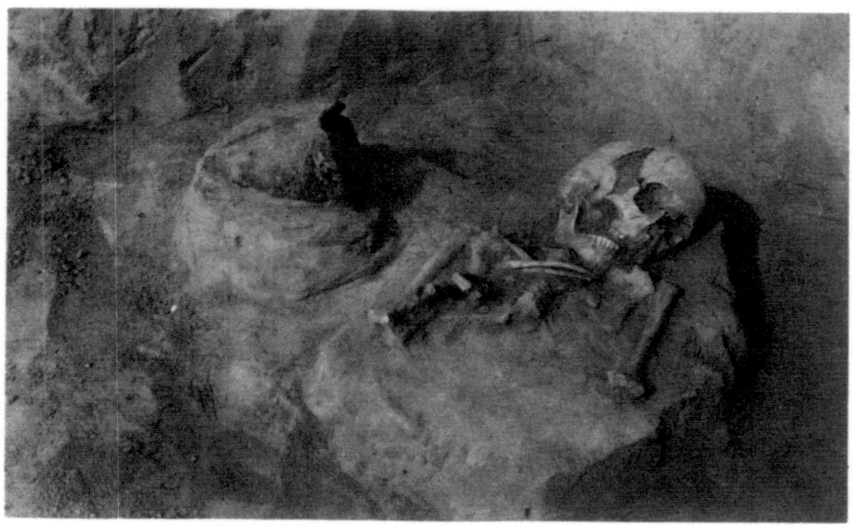

Plate 24 *a*. Artifacts from trench between C°2 and C°3. Canteen Cordmarked sherd, greyish flint lanceolate blade, flint chip and lamellar blade of mottled pink flint, stemmed scraper of Dongola flint and unworked valve of *Anodonta corpulenta*. UMMA Neg. 12853. *b*. Adolescent burial C°2-68 with Canteen Cordmarked jar near right shoulder. UMMA Neg. 12854a.

PLATE 25

a

b

Plate 25 *a*. Canteen Cordmarked jar C^{o}2-68 found with burial of an adolescent. Height 16 cm. UMMA Neg. 100-4-1. *b*. Detail view of offerings at right shoulder of Burial C^{o}2-70 (a young male adult) with a Gibson Notched point, worked and unworked bone awl and thirteen flint blades. UMMA Neg. 12857.

PLATE 26

a

Plate 26 *a*. Burial goods from Burial C^{o}2-68 and Burial C^{o}2-70. UMMA Neg. 100-29-1. *b*. Burial C^{o}2-71, a large adult male partially flexed on the right side with head to the southeast at a depth of one foot. UMMA Neg. 12858.

PLATE 27

a

Plate 27 *a*. Burial C°2-72, an adult male tightly flexed on the left side with head to the north at a depth of 16 inches. UMMA Neg. 12859. *b*. Burial C°2-74, an extended adult male with burial goods over the upper right chest, and a crude, stone bird effigy platform pipe over the left chest. UMMA Neg. 12861.

PLATE 28

a

Plate 28 *a*. Artifacts from C°2: sandstone abrader C°2-77; ten split turkey bone awls C°2-30 to 33 and 35-40; antler drift sections C°2-77; a worked beaver jaw C°2-87; and four split turkey bone awls C°2-74. UMMA Neg. 16109. *b*. Canteen Zoned Incised vessel over the feet of adult male C°2-74. Height 17.7 cm. UMMA Neg, 12864.

PLATE 29

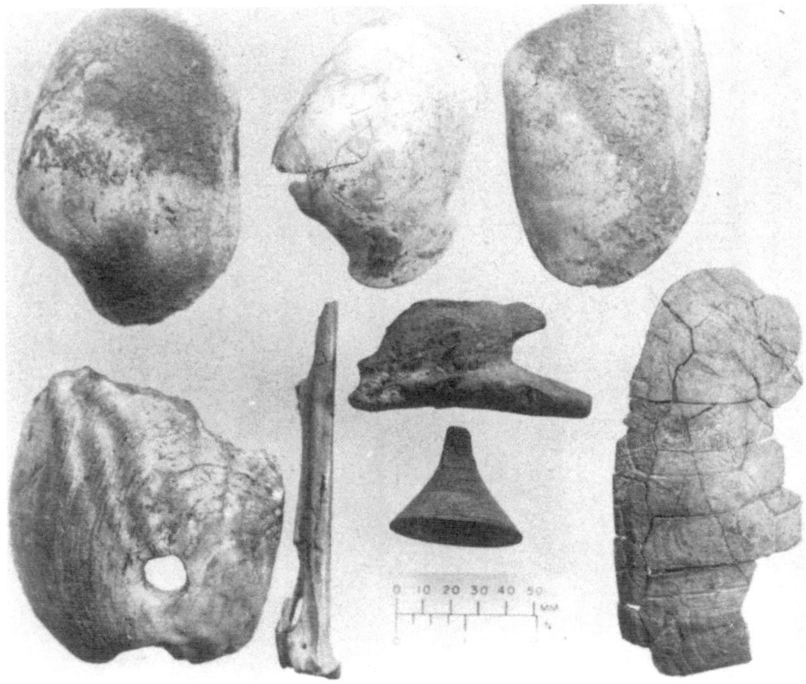

b

Plate 29 *a*. Artifacts from C^{o}2; mussel shell spoons C^{o}2-59, 14, and 58; mussel shell hoe C^{o}2-87; worked turkey leg bone C^{o}2-28; stone effigy pipe depicting bird C^{o}2-74, cone-shaped object C^{o}2-76; cup of Blandings turtle C^{o}2-74. UMMA Neg. 16112. *b*. Close up of C^{o}2-77 for location of burial offerings. UMMA Neg. 12866.

PLATE 30

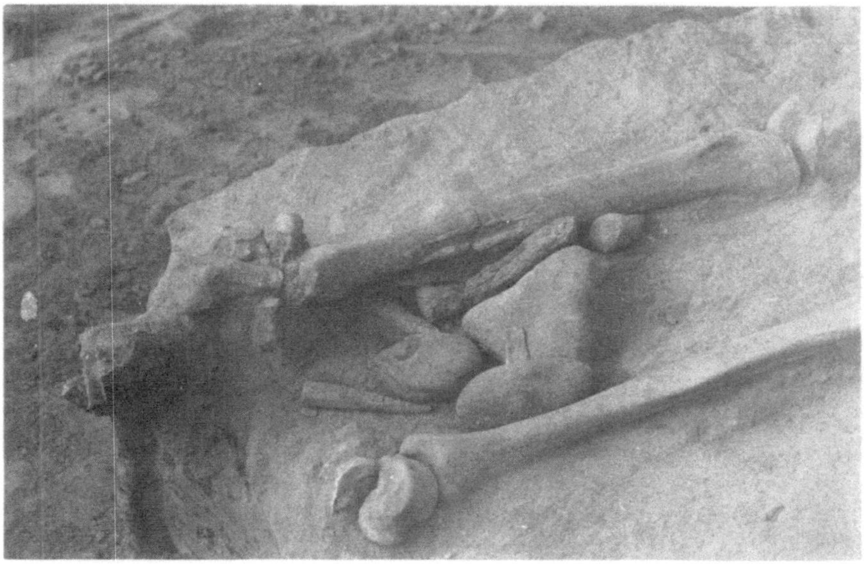

a

Plate 30 *a*. Burial goods of a flint knappers kit between the lower legs of C°2-77, consisting of a sandstone abrader, two hammerstones, portions of two antler drifts, a flint blade and a worked antler tip. UMMA Neg. 12868. *b*. Canteen Cordmarked jar, C°2-77 with extended male burial. Height 21.8 cm. UMMA Neg. 100-5-1.

PLATE 31

a

Plate 31 *a*. Canteen Zoned Punctate vessel C°2-85 with bear paw design. Height 7 cm. UMMA Neg. 15875. *b*. Small cup-shaped Canteen Cordmarked container, C°2-75, from large pit on west side of mound. Height 12 cm. UMMA Neg. 100-24-2.

PLATE 32

a

Plate 32 *a*. Canteen Plain jar, C°2-78, which contained a mussel shell spoon. Height 11 cm. UMMA Neg. 100-24-1. *b*. *Busycon* marine shell bowl with vessel C°2-78, not associated with a burial. UMMA Neg. 12870.

PLATE 33

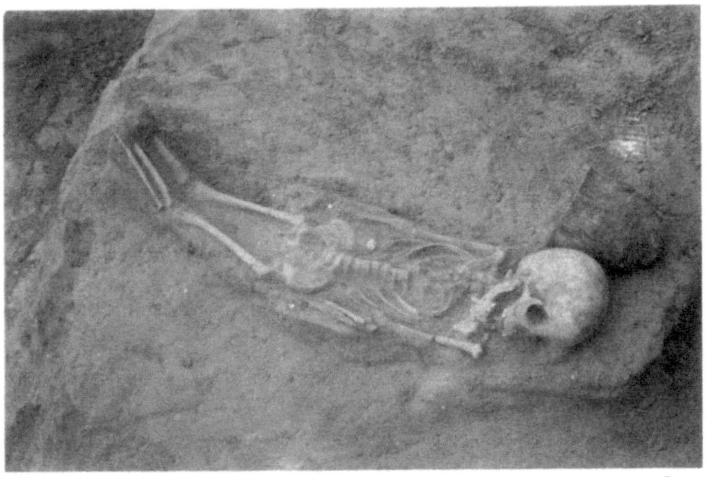

a

b

Plate 33 *a*. Extended child burial C°2-90 with Canteen Cordmarked vessel at the head. UMMA Neg. 12871B. *b*. Canteen Cordmarked jar C°2-90 with an extended child burial. Height 15 cm. UMMA Neg. 100-5-6.

PLATE 34

a

Plate 34 *a*. Burials C°3-16 to 19. Number 16 with a Canteen Plain jar is at the upper right and C°3-17 is at the lower left. Burial C°3-18 and the skull of C°3-19 are in the center of the photograph. UMMA Neg. 12887. *b*. Head area of adult male C°3-17 with Norton point at right of skull; a bone awl and mica sheet above to the left. UMMA Neg. 12890.

PLATE 35

a

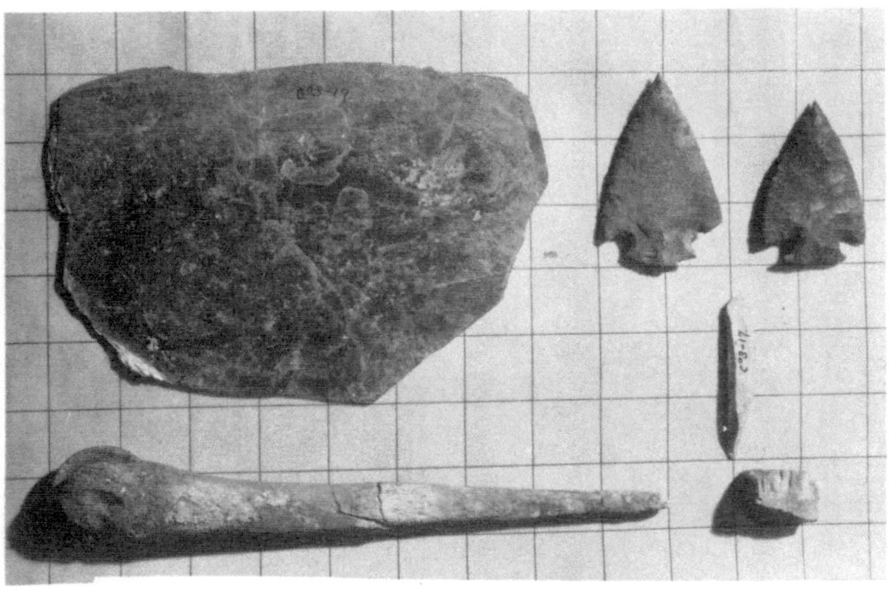

b

Plate 35 *a*. Head area of male C^{o}3-17 after removal of bone awl and mica sheet. UMMA Neg. 12891. *b*. Mica sheet, Norton points, flake knife, elk metapodial awl and a galena cube with C^{o}3-17. UMMA Neg. 12882.

PLATE 36

a

b

Plate 36 *a*. Extended burials C°3-18 to 21, two adult females, an adolescent and an adult male, without burial goods. UMMA Neg. 12889. *b*. Canteen Plain jar with adult female C°3-16 near the top of the mound. UMMA Neg. 15661.

PLATE 37

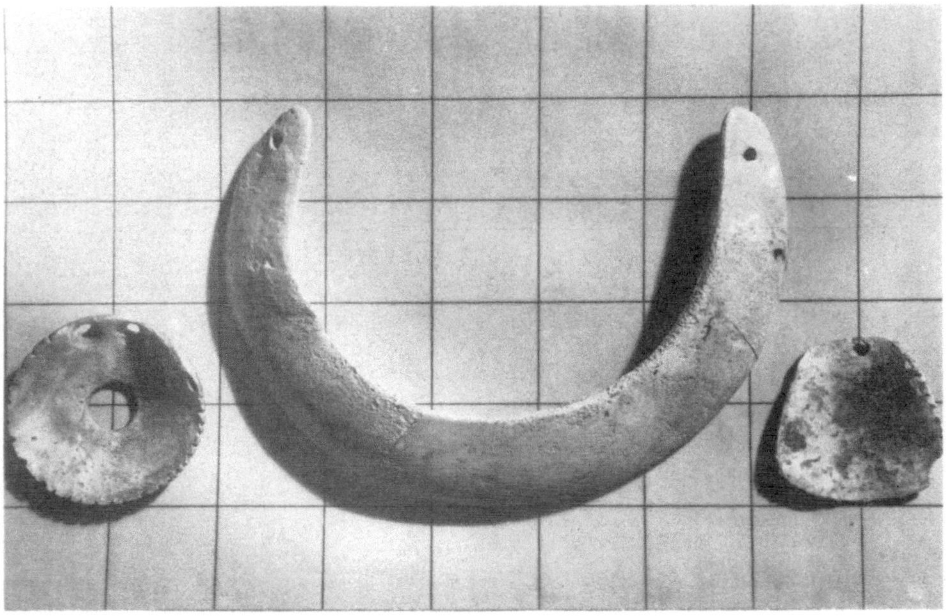

a

b

Plate 37 *a*. Shell crescent C°3-1, small shell gorget C°3-8 and shell pendant C°3-12. UMMA Neg. 12872. *b*. Canteen plain jar C°3-1 found with shell crescent gorget. Height 13.8 cm. UMMA Neg. 12873.

PLATE 38

a

Plate 38 *a*. Small, partially reconstructed Canteen Plain jar C°3-2. Height 10.5 cm. UMMA Neg. 100-4-6. *b*. Baehr Zoned Incised jar C°3-3. Height 20.5 cm. UMMA Neg. 100-5-2.

PLATE 39

a

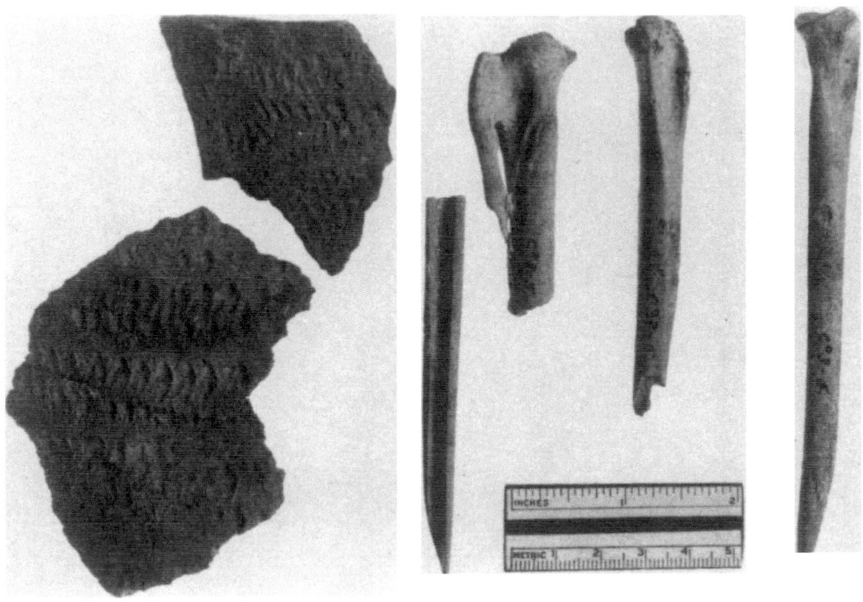

b

Plate 39 *a*. Canteen Incised jar C°3-4. Height 13 cm. UMMA Neg. 100-4-5. *b*. Specimens found at the feet of child burial C°3-5. Part of a Canteen Ware jar with horizontal rows of rocker stamped impressions and turkey leg bone awls. UMMA Neg. 12874.

PLATE 40

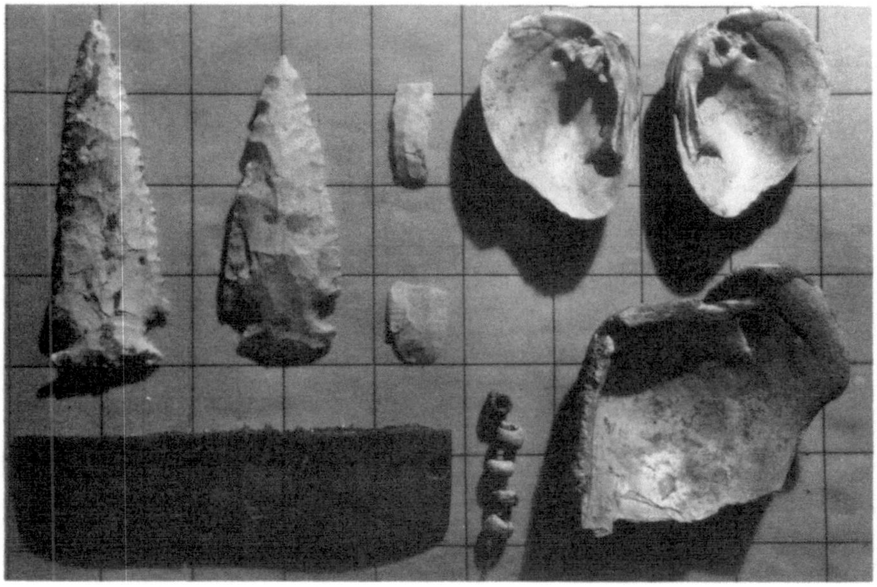

a

b

Plate 40 *a*. Specimens at th feet of child burial C°3-6. Two Gibson Notched points. 2 blades. 2 mussel shell spoons. turtle plastron. shell beads and a mussel shell hoe. UMMA Neg. 12875. *b*. Baehr Brushed jar C°3-7 at the feet of an adult female. Height 12.8 cm. UMMA Neg. 12876.

PLATE 41

a

b

Plate 41 *a*. Canteen Plain jar C^{o}3-8 found at the left shoulder of a child burial. Height 16 mm. UMMA Neg. 12877. *b*. Canteen Cordmarked jar C^{o}3-9 found at the right pelvis of a child burial. Height 16.5 cm. UMMA Neg. 100-5-4.

PLATE 42

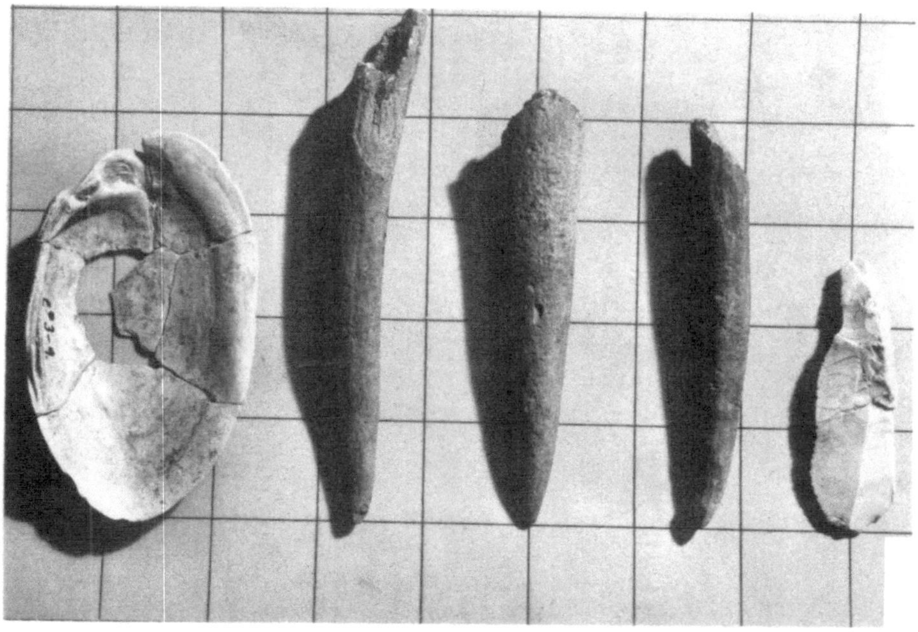

a

b

Plate 42 *a*. Specimens with C°3-9; shell spoon, three antler tips, lamellar flake blade. UMMA Neg. 12879. *b*. Specimens with adolescent burial C°3-11: Shell spoon contained the bone awl and flakes of red flint under right side of mandible, 29 globular beads at the right wrist and 10 *Marginella* beads at the left wrist. UMMA Neg. 12880.

PLATE 43

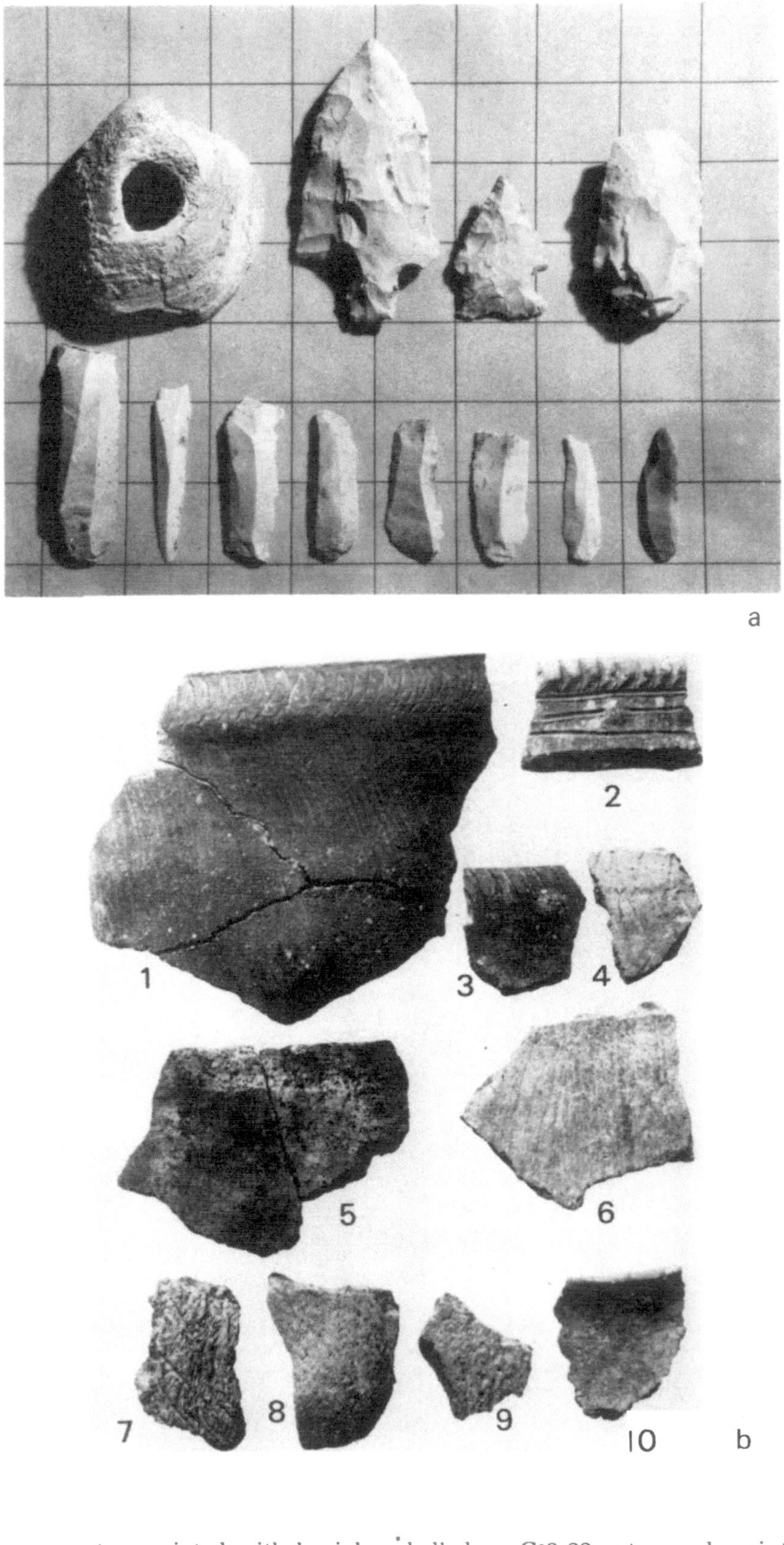

Plate 43 *a*. Specimens not associated with burials: shell hoe C^{o}3-22; stemmed point C^{o}3-31; point C^{o}3-32; scraper C^{o}3-33 and lamellar flake knives C^{o}3-24 to 30 and 34. UMMA Neg. 12883a. *b*. Sherds from Mound C^{o}3: 1 & 4, Pike Brushed; 2, Pike Incised; 3, Pike Plain; 5, Baehr Plain rim; 6, Pike Brushed body sherd; 7 & 8, Havana Cordmarked body sherd; 9, Canteen Cordmarked body sherd; 10, Canteen Plain rim. UMMA Neg. 100-2-1.

PLATE 44

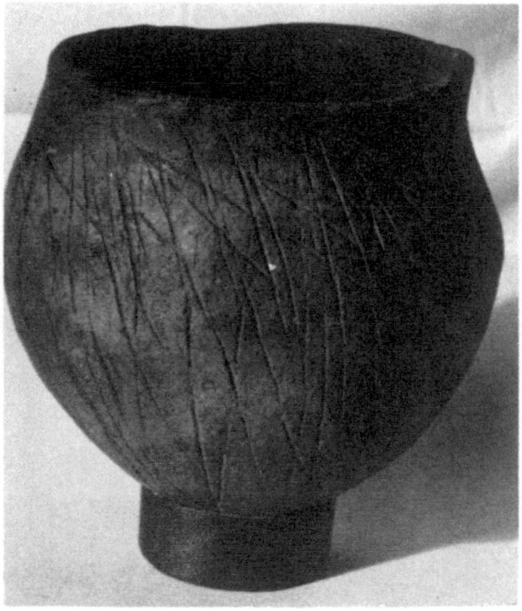

a

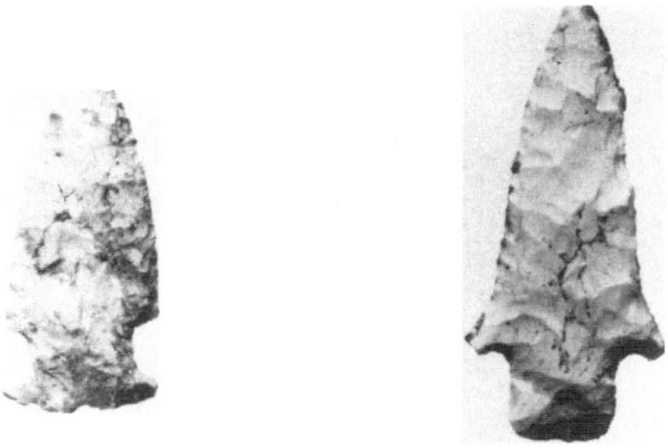

b

Plate 44 *a*. Canteen Incised jar C⁰4-1 found with an adult burial. Height 12.5 cm. UMMA Neg. 12892. *b*. Gibson Corner Notched point C⁰4-9 found at the bottom of a pit excavated in 1900, and a Marshall Barbed point C⁰4-2 found with Canteen Incised jar C⁰4-1. UMMA Neg. 100-2-4.

PLATE 45

a

Plate 45 *a*. Adult male extended burial C°4-3 with head to west, with 2 mica plates, 3 raccoon penii and a beaver incisor along lower left leg. UMMA Neg. 12894a. *b*. Close up of grave goods with C°4-3. UMMA Neg. 12895.

PLATE 46

a

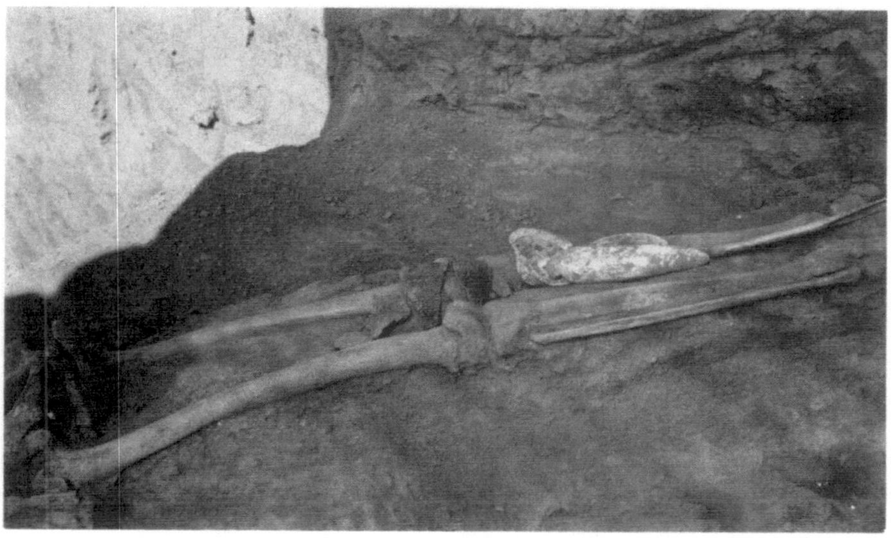

b

Plate 46 *a*. Raccoon penii, unmodified beaver incisor and mica plates with burial C°4-3. UMMA Neg. 12893. *b*. Burial cache between lower legs of an extended adolescent male C°4-8. UMMA Neg. 12899.

PLATE 47

a

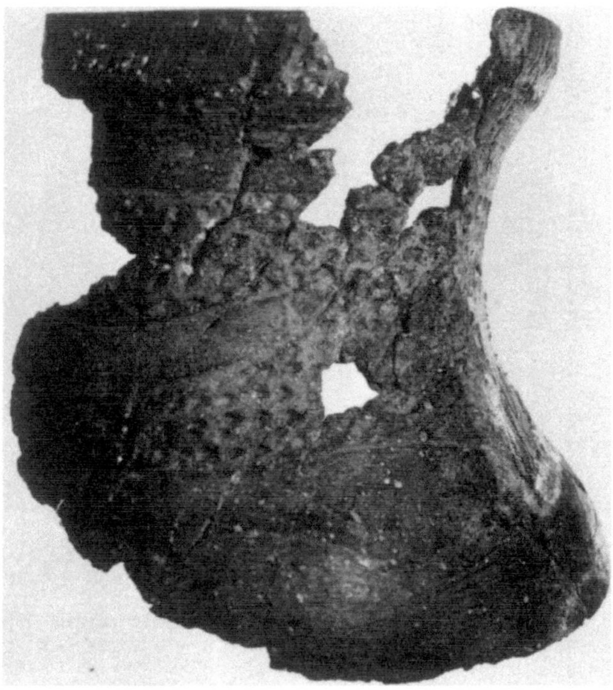

Plate 47 *a*. Cache of 2 unworked mussel shells, a shell spoon, a shell pendant, and a swan ulna awl with burial C°4-8. UMMA Neg. 12900. *b*. Fragmentary Baehr Zoned Punctate jar C°4-8. Height 11.3 cm. UMMA Neg. 12901.

PLATE 48

a

b

Plate 48 *a*. Appearance of central burial area of C°4 after seven days excavation with 4 rows of limestone slabs, three layers deep placed above burials in central pit. UMMA Neg. 12927. *b*. Thin line of disintegrated bark (?) covering burial area, and limestone slab in southwest corner of burial pit. UMMA Neg. 12902.

PLATE 49

a

Plate 49 *a*. Fragmentary remains of thirteen individuals in central portion of pit in C°4. UMMA Neg. 12914. *b*. View from southwest after mud had been removed from the central burial area of C°4. Pit in left foreground is area earlier removed by "Messers." Wadlow and Gibson. UMMA Neg. 12916.

PLATE 50

Plate 50. Owl effigy platform pipe of Ohio pipestone with burial C^{a}4-24, an adult male. Length of platform 6.1 cm. UMMA Neg. 12919 & 12921.

PLATE 51

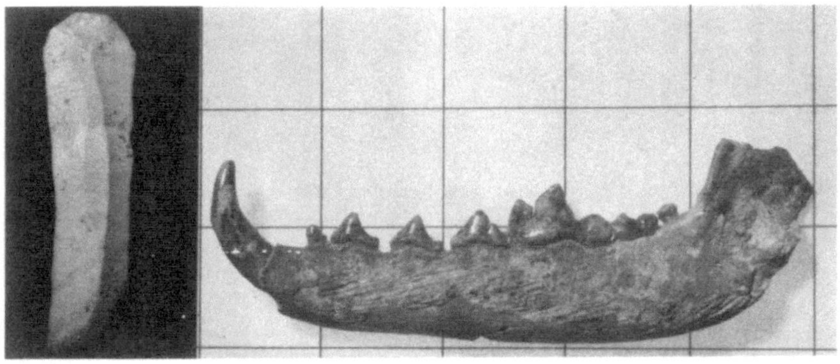

a

Plate 51 *a*. Blade and unworked left mandible of dog with adult male C°4-24. UMMA 4-24. UMMA Neg. 12918. *b*. Artifacts from fill of C°4; C°4-10 group of 161 percussion flakes; C°4-1 baroque pearl bead (in top part of tube); C°4-12 so-called antler drift 13 cm. long; C°4-9 Gibson point; C°4-17 small rose quartz pebble; C°4-16 four flake blades; C°4-14, -13, -15, three whitish flint blades resembling Sedalia points, length 15 to 12.4 cm. UMMA Neg. 12922.

PLATE 52

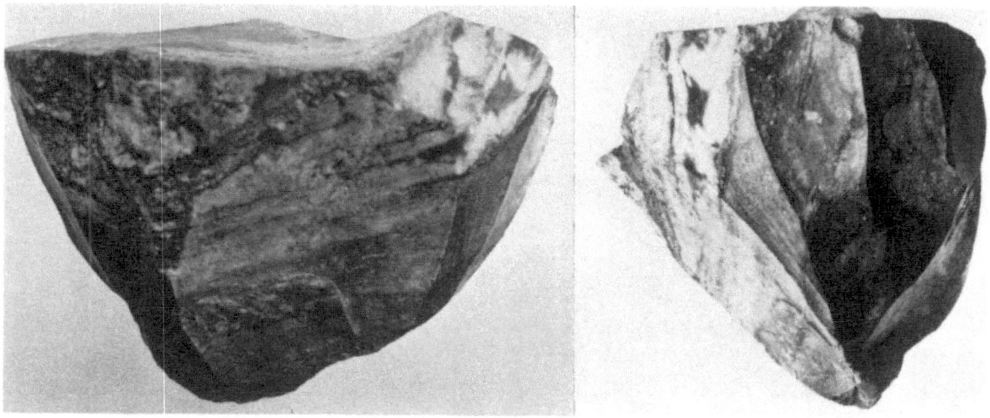

a

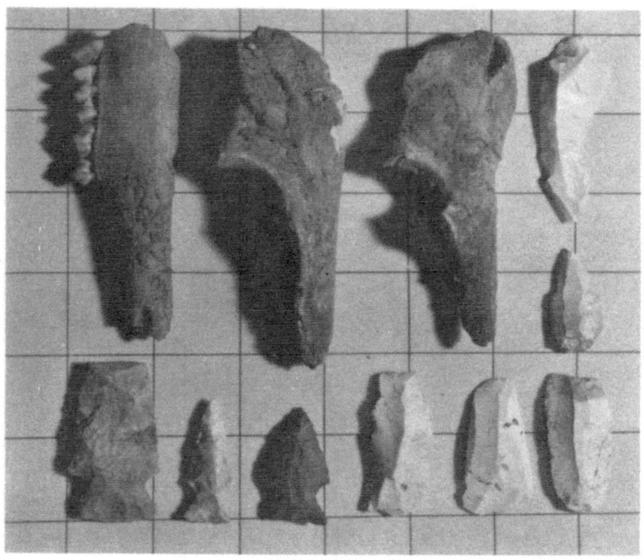

Plate 52 *a*. Large red and white mottled flint core C°4-18. Length 17.5 cm. UMMA Neg. 15666 + 100-3-2. *b*. Artifacts from refuse pit between C°4 & C°5. Deer mandible and 2 deer ulnae; 5 flake blades; fragments of a Steuben Expanding Stem point and two smaller points. UMMA Neg. 12928.

PLATE 53

a

Plate 53 *a*. Sherds from refuse pit between C^{o}4 and C^{o}5. Baehr Zoned Brushed; Montezuma Punctate; Pike Incised; Pike Rocked Dentate. UMMA Neg. 12929. *b*. Large Baehr Brushed rim from refuse pit between C^{o}4 and C^{o}5. UMMA Neg. 12930.

PLATE 54

a

Plate 54 *a*. Burial vessel C°5-2, -1A, and -1 in place in west side of mound at the 1 foot depth. UMMA Neg. 12964. *b*. Small Canteen Plain jar C°5-1. Height 11.4 cm. UMMA Neg. 12960.

PLATE 55

a

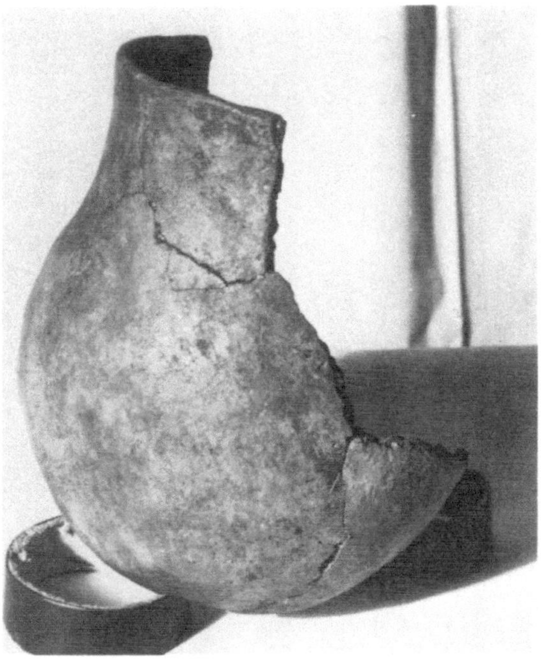

Plate 55 *a*. Canteen Incised jar C°5-1A. Height 13.8 cm. UMMA Neg. 100-19-4. *b*. Canteen Plain jar section C°5-2. Height 18 cm. UMMA Neg. 12962.

PLATE 56

a

Plate 56 *a*. Baehr Zoned Brushed-Incised jar C^{o}5-4. Height 13.5 cm. UMMA Neg. 12963. *b*. Canteen Plain jar C^{o}5-5. Height 23 cm. UMMA Neg. 12996.

PLATE 57

a

b

Plate 57 *a*. Excavation at end of second day in Knight Mound C°5 showing some of the material in top 3 feet of the mound. View is to the north. UMMA Neg. 12959. *b*. Burials 6-7-8 and 9 in C°5. UMMA Neg. 12973.

PLATE 58

a

Plate 58 *a*. Upper part of fragmentary burial C°5-10 with compressed vessel C°5-10. UMMA Neg. 12977. *b*. Badly warped Canteen Plain jar C°5-10. Height 23.5 cm. UMMA Neg. 12976.

PLATE 59

a

b

Plate 59 *a*. First stone of southwest corner marker at top of lensed area. View from south. UMMA Neg. 12939. *b*. Southwest corner marker, horizontal light color layer of decayed bark(?) over lensed basket loads of central burial area which extends to the north. View from the south. UMMA Neg. 12941.

PLATE 60

a

b

Plate 60 *a*. Northern corner markers at upper left and right of area over central burial of C°5. View from south. UMMA Neg. 12944. *b*. Top layer of central burials at depth of 10 feet, 6 inches, of 4 extended adults with heads to north. The skeletal material was in a poor state of preservation. UMMA Neg. 12947.

PLATE 61

a

Plate 61 *a*. The two mass bundle burials in C°5 at a depth of 11 feet. The burial to the left in the north end of the central tomb contained a platform pipe, bone effigy bear canine and a shell bead. UMMA Neg. 12948. *b*. Curved base platform pipe, of grey Ohio pipestone, and bone effigy bear canine with bundle burial of three to four individuals in C°5. UMMA Neg. 12950.

PLATE 62

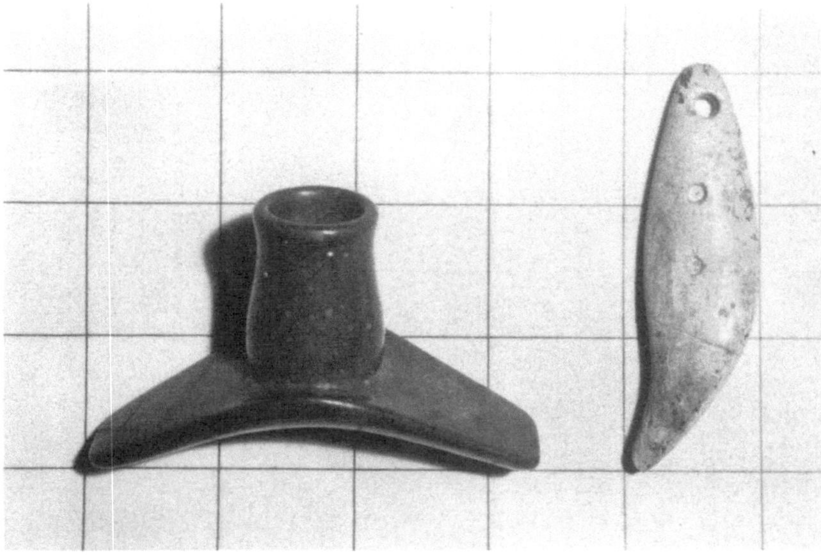

a

b

Plate 62 *a*. Curved base plain platform pipe of grey Ohio pipestone and bone effigy canine. UMMA Neg. 12933. *b*. Excavation in C°5 at end of seventh day. Corner markers of burial area, lensed layers and bundle burials. UMMA Neg. 12982.

PLATE 63

a

b

Plate 63 *a*. The north corner markers, the north mass burial extended in the flesh and the bundle burials of two individuals as seen from the south. UMMA Neg. 12953. *b*. Central burial area of C°5 with unwanted hungry visitors. UMMA Neg. 100-74-1.

PLATE 64

a

b

Plate 64 *a*. Artifacts from general area of the central burial of C°5. Top row: C°5-18, -13, -14, -11, -24. Bottom row has 3 Havana Zoned Dentate and one Havana Plain body sherd. UMMA Neg. 12932. *b*. Canteen Cordmarked and one Canteen Incised sherd from upper 3 feet of C°5. UMMA Neg. 12935.

PLATE 65

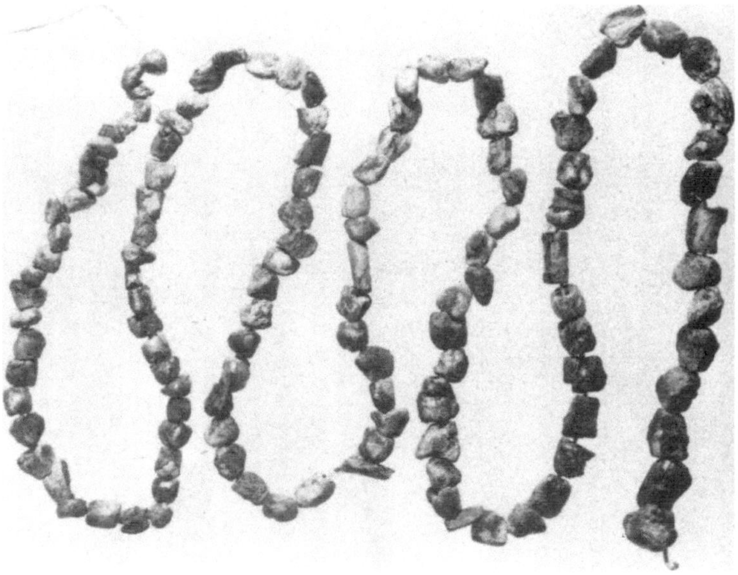

a

Plate 65 *a*. Shell and pearl beads from central burial area of C°6 around the upper arms of two burials. Length 33 inches. UMMA Neg. 100-40-1. *b*. Havana Zoned Dentate Stamped jar from central burial pit of C°6. Height 14.9 cm. UMMA Neg. 100-5-5.

PLATE 66

a

Plate 66 *a*. Baehr Plain jar with adult burial $C^{0}8$-1. Height 10.3 cm. UMMA Neg. 12987. *b*. Baehr Brushed jar with child burial $C^{0}8$-2. Height 7-8 cm. UMMA Neg. 12988.

PLATE 67

Plate 67. Baehr Zoned Brushed jar with adult male (?) burial C98-3. Height 10.5 cm. UMMA Neg. 12989-90.

PLATE 68

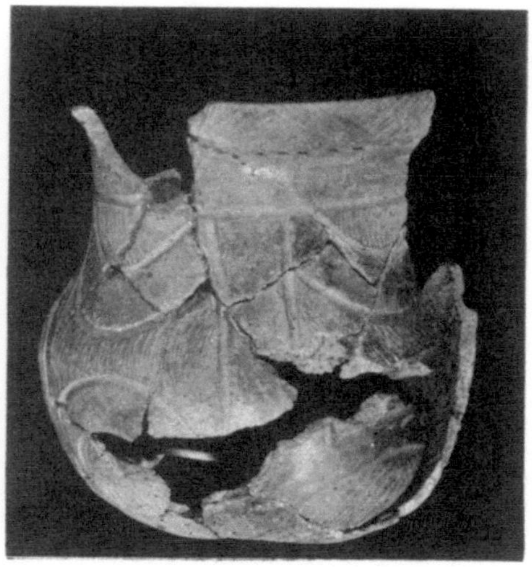

a

b

c

Plate 68 *a*. Hopewell Zoned Plain Rocker Stamped jar with child burial C⁰8-4. Height 7.8 cm. UMMA Neg. 12991. *b*. Hopewell Zoned Plain Rocker Stamped jar from Spoonville, Michigan. Height 10.2 cm. UMMA Neg. 15606. *c*. Baehr Zoned Plain Rocker Stamped jar with adult burial C⁰8-5. Height 16.5 cm. UMMA Neg. 12992.

PLATE 69

Plate 69. Male clay figurine C98-7, kneeling and holding an atlatl. Height 7.7 cm. UMMA Neg. 12999B-13002.

PLATE 70

Plate 70. Femal sitting clay figurine $C^{0}8$-6. Height 8.4 cm. UMMA Neg. 12945-12948A.

PLATE 71

Plate 71. Female clay figurine C°8-10. Height 7.9 cm. UMMA Neg. 13012-15.

PLATE 72

Plate 72. Standing female Cº8-9. Height 9.4 cm. UMMA Neg. 13007-10.

PLATE 73

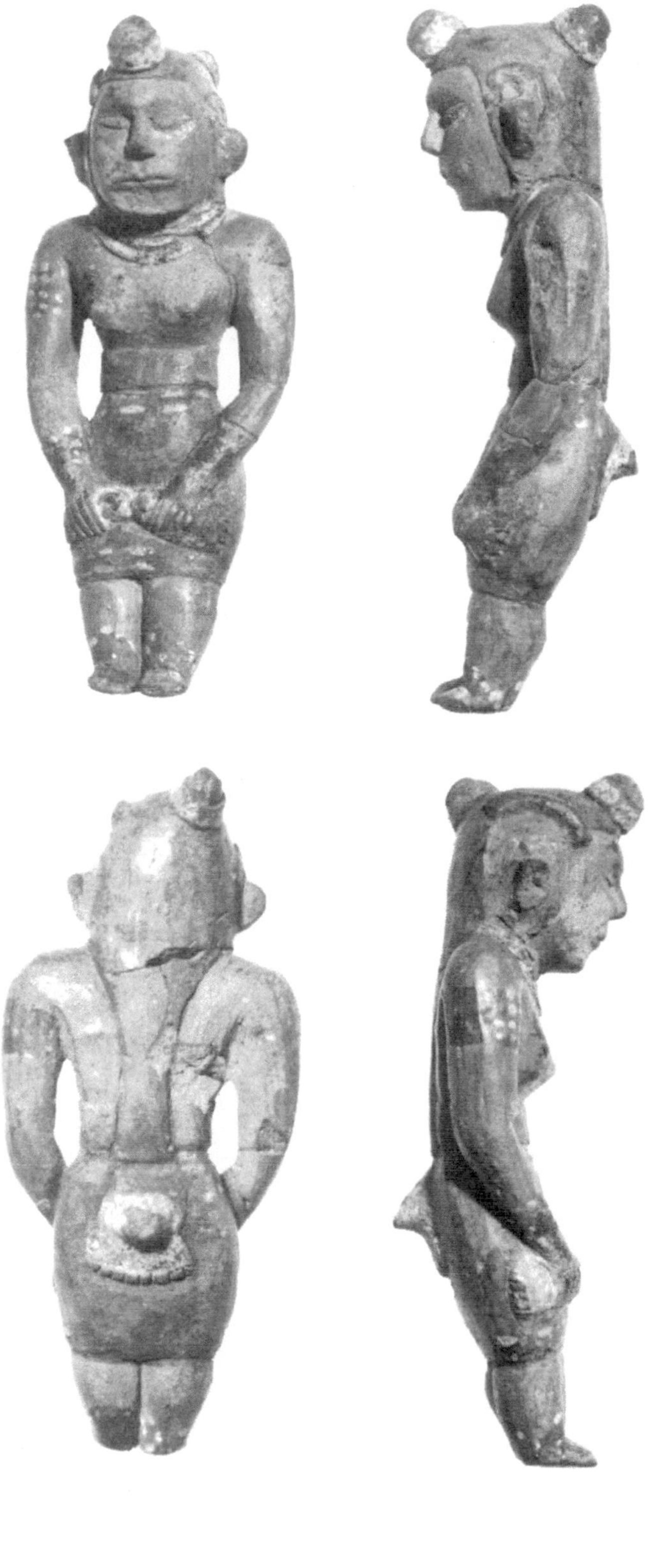

Plate 73. Standing female figurine C°8-8. Height 11.1 cm. UMMA Neg. 13003-06.

PLATE 74

a

Plate 74 *a*. Baehr Brushed-Incised jar fragments C^{o}8-32. UMMA Neg. 15664. *b*. Baehr Zoned Punctate jar C^{o}8-33. Height 17 cm. UMMA Neg. 12994.

PLATE 75

a

Plate 75 *a*. Baehr Zoned Brushed jar C°8-31 with adult burial. Height 12.4 cm. UMMA Neg. 12993 *b*. Large fragment of Baehr Incised jar C°8-54 from a depth of six feet. Estimated height 10 cm. UMMA Neg. 12986.

PLATE 76

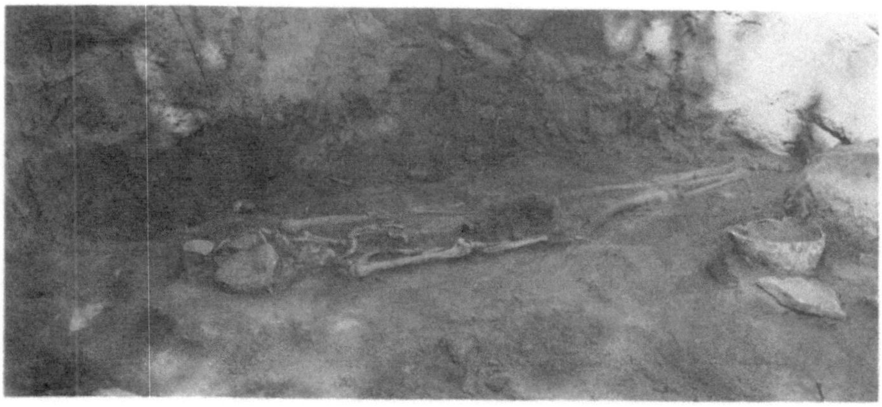

a

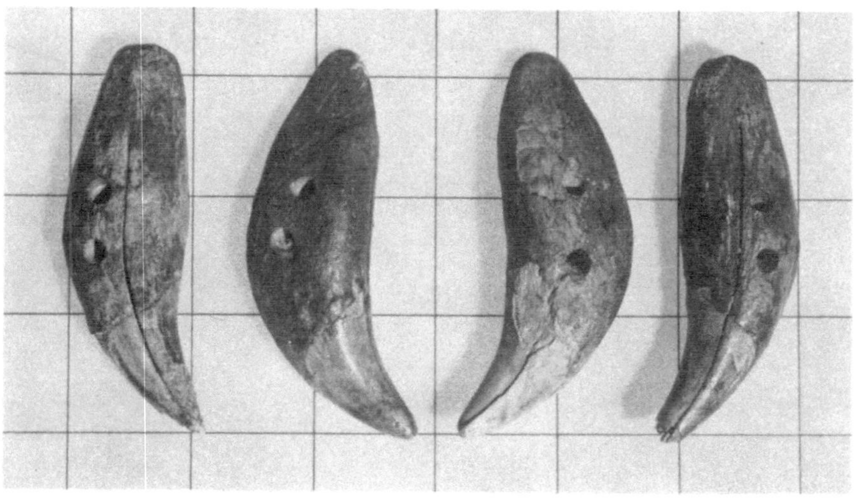

b

Plate 76 *a*. Extended adult female burial C°8-30 with *Cassis* shell vessel C°8-29 on the right. UMMA Neg. 13031. *b*. Four drilled bear canines C°8-22 to 25 with adult female burial C°8-30. Length 8.3 cm. UMMA Neg. 13018.

PLATE 77

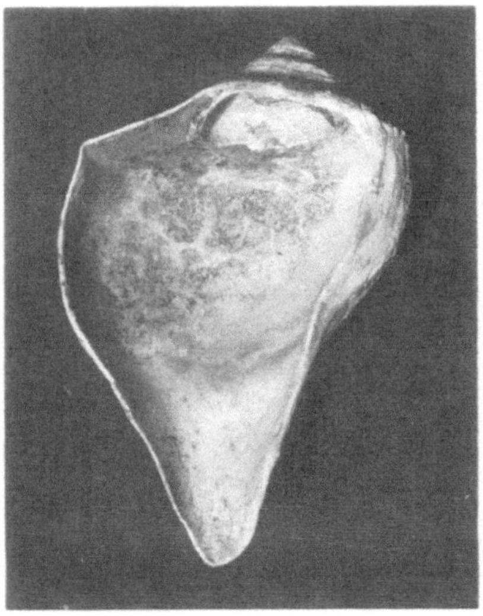

a

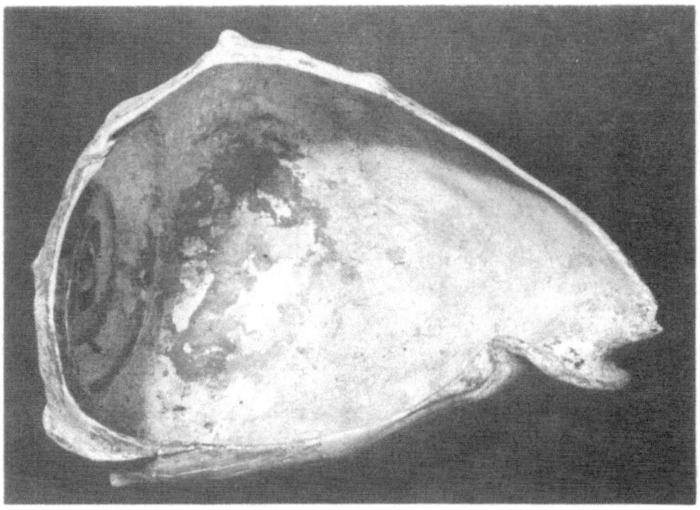

Plate 77 *a*. *Busycon* shell C°8-28 found with burial C°8-30. UMMA Neg. 13027. *b*. Worked *Cassis* shell C°8-27. UMMA Neg. 13022.

PLATE 78

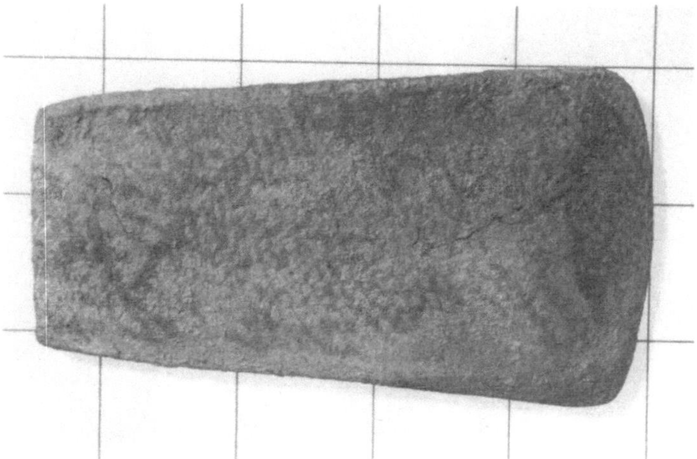

a

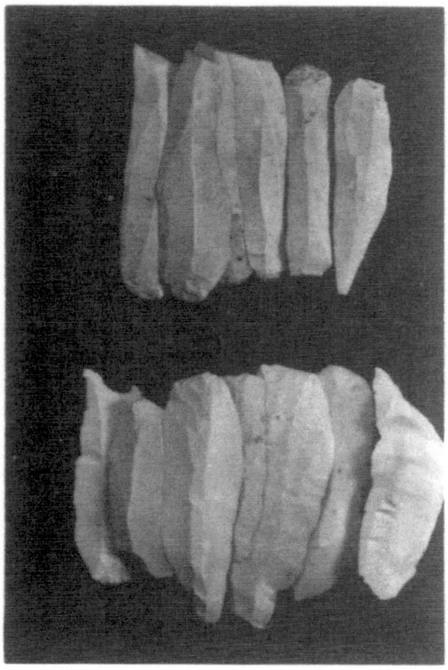

b

Plate 78 *a*. Copper adze 11.3 cm. long with Burial C°8-26. This is the flat side which has the impressions of a woven cloth. UMMA Neg. 13019. *b*. Lamellar flake knives of white flint. C°8-13 -18. found with the figurines; and C°8-30-50 from center of Mound C°8 at a depth of two and one-half feet, made from the same core. Average length of lower row 4.4 cm. UMMA Neg. 100-12-3.

PLATE 79

Plate 79. Crudely made clay figurine with burial of small child. Height two and three-fourths inches (6.9 cm.). UMMA Neg. 13035-37.

PLATE 80

Plate 80. Four views of clay figurine found in woven fiber bag with a copper celt and a small pottery vessel, from the big Baehr Mound, Brown County, Illinois. Excavated by J. F. Snyder, it is now in the St. Louis Academy of Science. Photo courtesy of Leonard Blake of St. Louis. Height, 13.5 cm.

PLATE 81

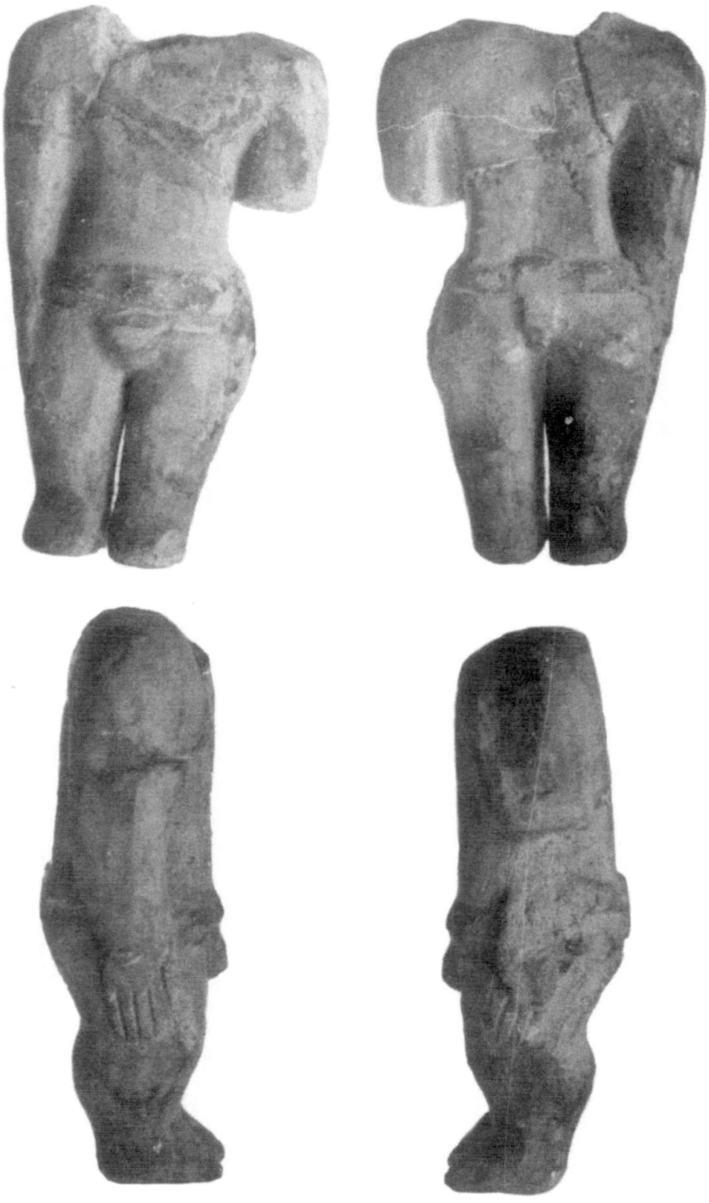

Plate 81. Four views of clay figurine which was found on a mica plate near a skull in the big Baehr Mound, Brown County, Illinois. Excavated by J. F. Snyder, the figurine is now in the St. Louis Academy of science. Photo courtesy of Leonard Blake of St. Louis. Height, 7.5 cm.

PLATE 82

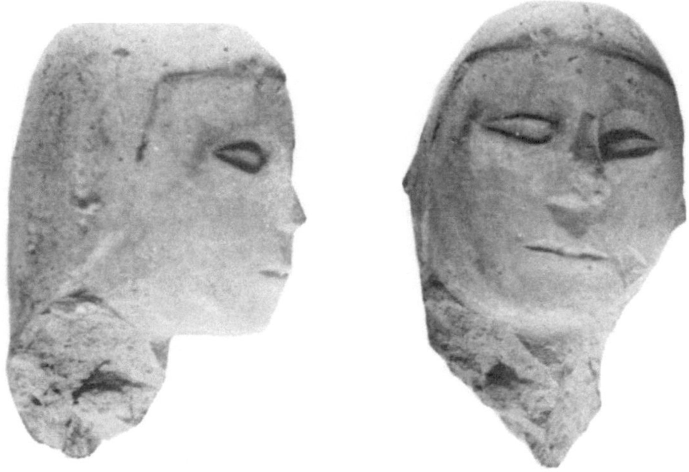

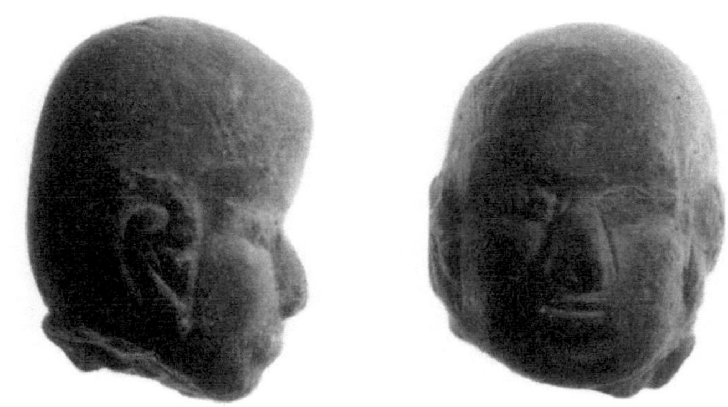

Plate 82 *a*. Figurine head from the Crable Site, Fulton County, Illinois. Dr. Dan Morse Collection. Height 3.7 cm., width 2 cm. *b*. Figurin head from the Steuben Village Site, Marshall County, Illinois. Photograph courtesy of Illinois tate Museum Height, 2.4 cm.

PLATE 83

Plate 83 *a-c*. Seated male figurine from Schuyler County, Illinois. Length 9.7 cm.; head 3.5 cm. long and 3.0 cm. wide. *d-f*. Standing male figurine from Schuyler County, Illinois. Length 12.2 cm.; head 3.5 cm. long and 2 cm. wide. Plates 83-85, courtesy of Dr. Dan Morse.

PLATE 84

Plate 84 *a-c*. Seated female figurine from Schuyler County, Illinois. Length 10.5 cm.; head 3.5 cm. long and 2.3 cm. wide. Views are not to same scale. *d-f*. "Naughty Marietta"-style female figurine from Schuyler County, Illinois. Length 7.5 cm.; head 3.0 cm. long and 1.5 cm. wide. *g-h*. Kneeling female figurine from Schuyler County, Illinois. Length 5.5 cm.; head 2.0 cm. long and 1.3 cm. wide.

PLATE 85

Plate 85 *a-b, c-d, e-f*. Three head fragments of female figurines from Schuyler County, Illinois. Each head is 3.5 cm. long and 2.5 cm. wide. *g*. Various figurine fragments from Schuyler County, Illinois. Length of lower right figure is 5.25 cm.

PLATE 86

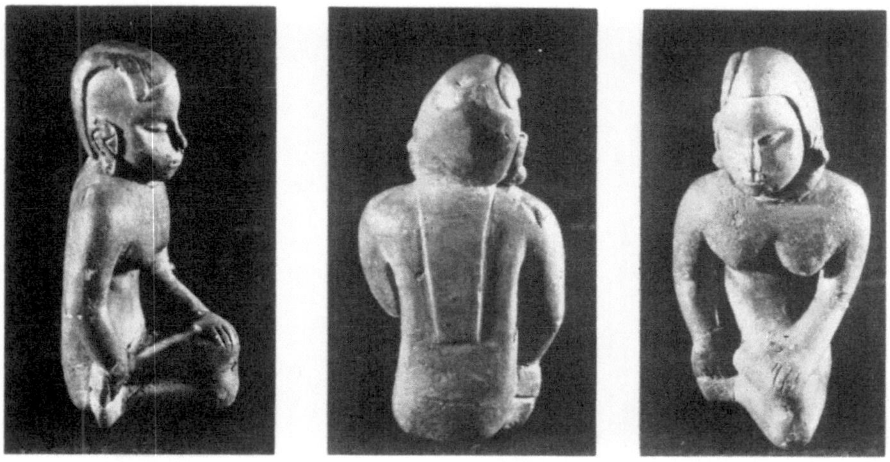

Plate 86 *a.* Seated female figurines from the Twenhofel Site, Jackson County, Illinois, Southern Illinois University Collection. Height 5.5 cm. UMMA Neg. 10656-59. *b.* Clay female figurine from Marietta, Ohio, in the Peabody Museum—Harvard University collection.

PLATE 87

Plate 87. Clay figurines from the Turner Site, Hamilton County, Ohio, in the Peabody Museum—Harvard University. Photographed from Willoughby, 1922.

PLATE 88

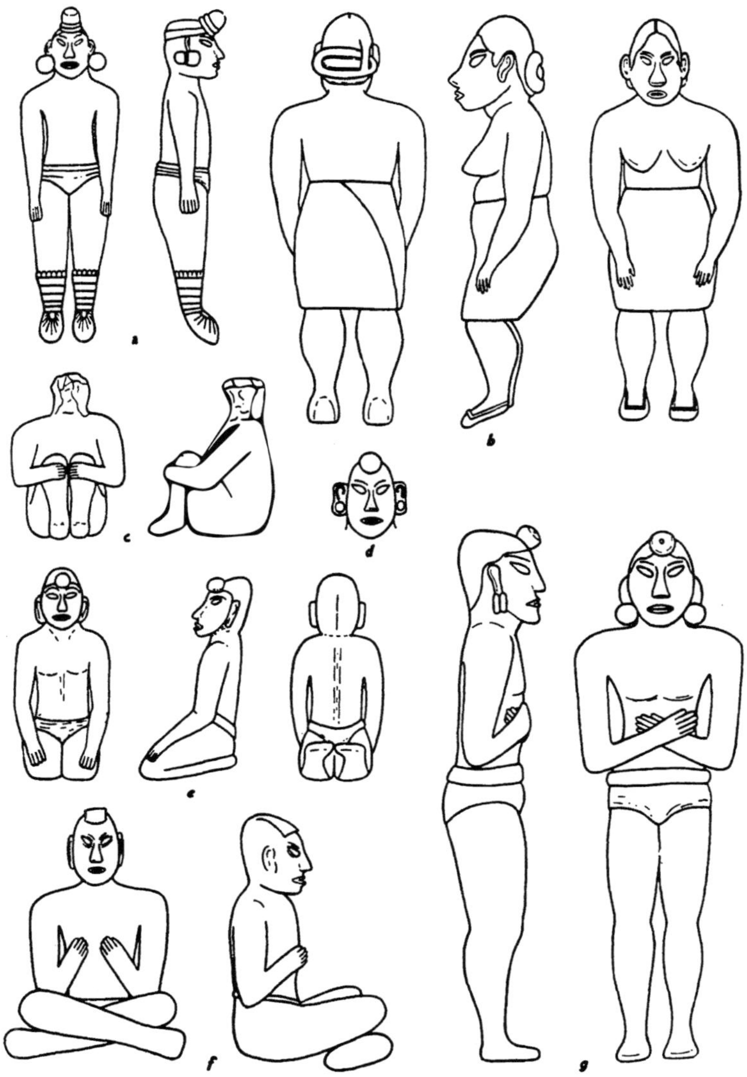

Plate 88. Projected reconstructions of clay figurines from the Turner site, Hamilton County, Ohio, in the Peabody Museum—Harvard University. Photographed from Willoughby, 1922.

PLATE 89

Plate 89. Steuben Expanding Stemmed point, a Havana Plain rim and the interior view of a Pike Plain jar rim from Knight Mound C°10. Length of point 8.7 cm. UMMA Neg. 13039.

PLATE 90

Plate 90 *a, b*. Two views of bundle burial with large, roughly rectangular block of flint, 9 feet, 2 inches deep in center of C°14. Note horizontal humus line of pre-mound period. UMMA Neg. 13042 and 13043.

PLATE 91

Plate 91. Four basally notched points C^{o}14-1 to -4 found on premound humus line, three at a depth of 9 feet 8 inches and the fourth C^{o}14-1, at a depth of 9 feet, 6 inches. The largest form is 13.1 cm. by 5.9 cm. UMMA Neg. 100-21-3.

PLATE 92

a

Plate 92. Two bifacially worked white flint choppers or adzes from a low knoll called C°15. Length of C°15-1, 10.6 cm. UMMA Neg. 100-22-1.

PLATE 93

Plate 93 *a*. Burials C°16-4 to -7 at depth of 15 feet, 3 feet south of mound center. UMMA Neg. 13046. *b*. Black clay in orbits, nasal aperture and mouth of adult male extended burial C°16-4. UMMA Neg. 13051.

PLATE 94

Plate 94 *a*. Burial C°16-6 between lower legs of C°16-4. Burial C°16-7 is skull to the left, and C°16-5 is in front of a Havana Zoned Dentate Stamped jar with the same number. UMMA Neg. 13047. *b*. Shell disc beads with burials C°16-4 and C°16-6. UMMA Neg. 100-1-3.

PLATE 95

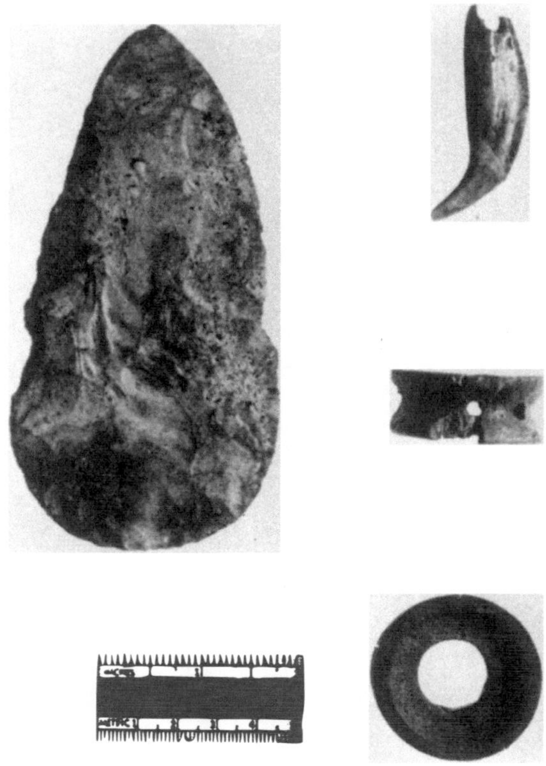

a

Plate 95 *a*. Ovate pink flint knife over rib cage of C°16-6, bear canine 5.4 cm. long with burials C°16-9 and -10, and perforated bone pulley-type earspools with C°16-8. UMMA Neg. 100-36-2. *b*. Havana Zoned Dentate jar C°16-5. Height 13 cm. UMMA Neg. 15660.

PLATE 96

a

b

Plate 96 *a*. Pit burial of adult male (?) C°16-12 overlain by 6 small limestone slabs and within a roughly rectangular four postmold pattern. UMMA Neg. 100-41-4. *b*. Relationship of rock wall to adult male extended burial C°16-16. UMMA Neg. 100-70-3.

PLATE 97

a

Plate 97 *a*. Burial C°16-16. centrally placed on floor of mound. Part of pit outline is evident above the skull. UMMA Neg. 100-37-2. *b*. Most of the artifacts *in situ* with adult male C°16-16: a *Cassis* shell container, platform pipe of reddish Ohio pipestone, and a group of turkey and whistling swan leg bones. UMMA Neg. 100-38-3.

PLATE 98

a

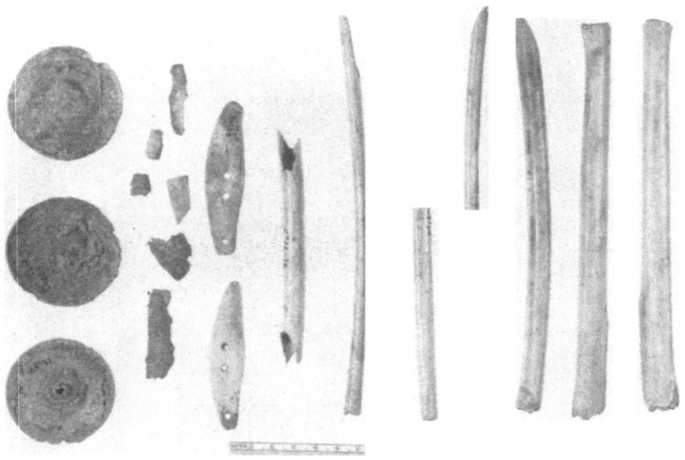

b

Plate 98 *a*. Reddish plain platform pipe of Ohio pipestone with C°16-16. Length 12 cm. UMMA Neg. 87-3-5. b. Artifacts with C°16-16. Inner surface of 4 copper ear spool discs; copper fragments probably from conjoined tubes; bone imitation bear canine ; bird bone sections of turkey and whistling swan. UMMA Neg. 15668.

PLATE 99

a

b

Plate 99 *a*. Copper pendant 3.4 cm. long with original cord found on upper chest area of C°16-16. UMMA Neg. 87-5-3. *b*. Shell and two copper beads from C°16-16 and from the mound fill of C°16. UMMA Neg. 100-26-4.

PLATE 100

a

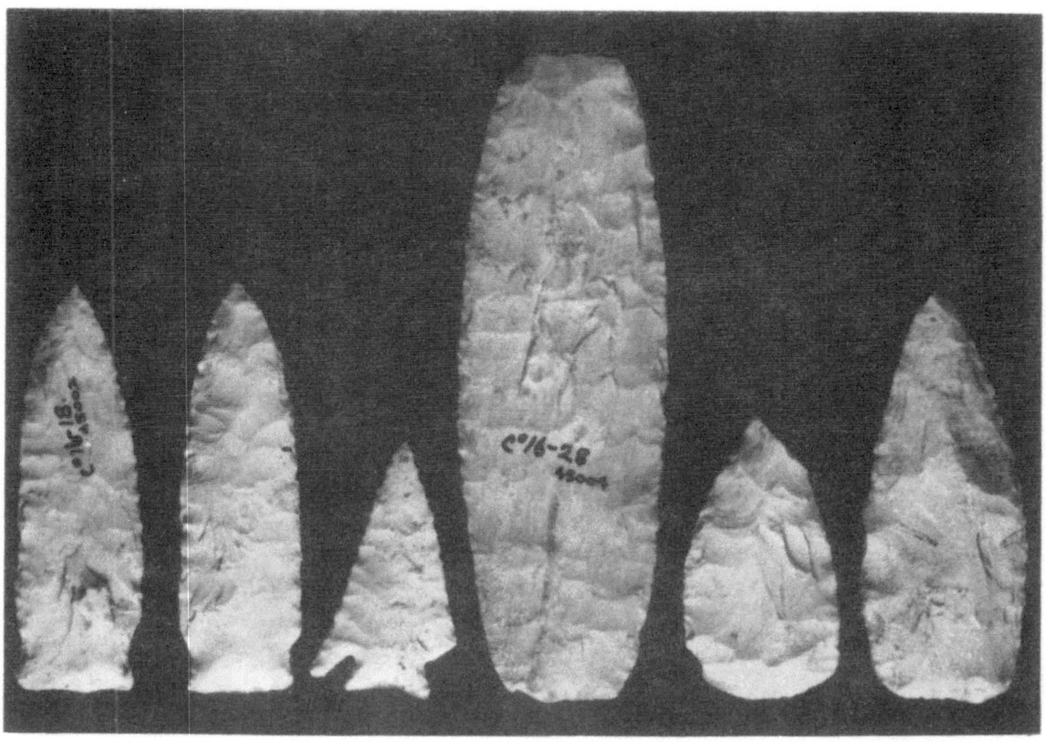

b

Plate 100 *a*. Cassis shell container with adult male burial C°16-16. UMMA Neg. 100-57-3. *b*. Two white flint Ansell Constricted Stem points with Burial C°16-18; a white flint Marshall Barbed form with a child burial C°16-19; and three flint forms not associated with burials in C°16. UMMA Neg. 100-20-3.

PLATE 101

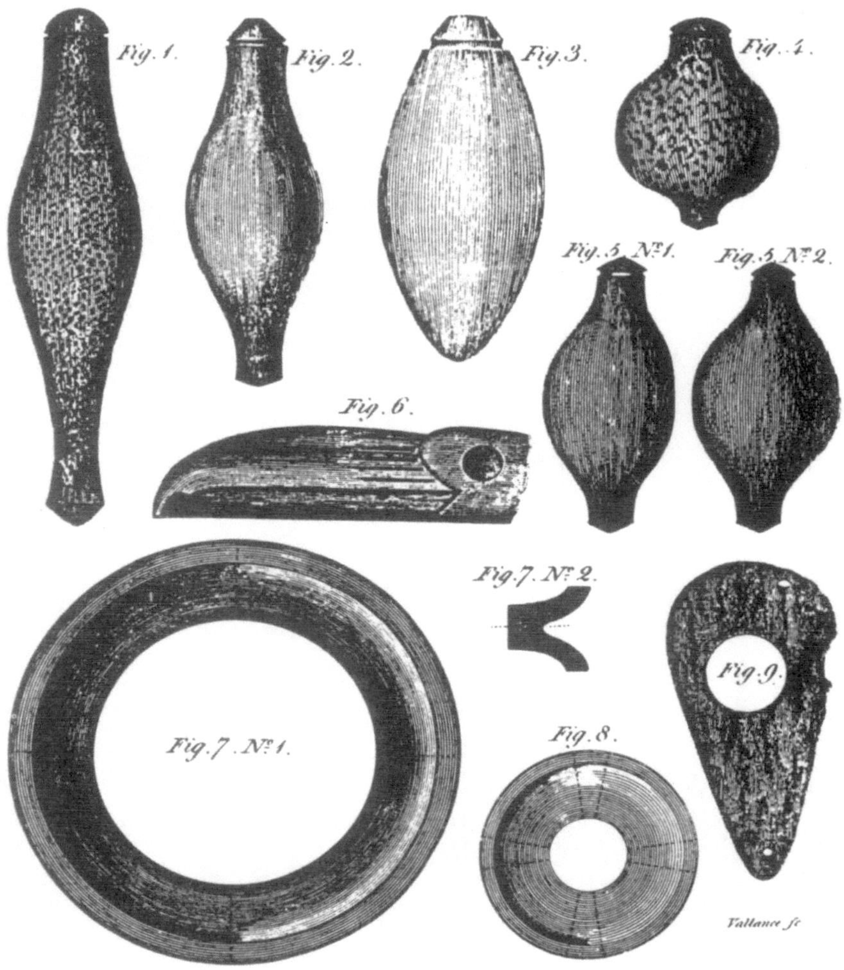

Plate 101. Reproduction of artifacts associated with copper panpipe found near a mound in downtown Cincinnati about 1794. No. 1 is a plummet of "grey porphyry." No. 2 is of "jasper marked with blood-coloured veins and spots on a green basis," No. 3 of "transparent rock crystal," No. 4 "porphyry of mixed blacks and yellow," No. 5 "a ferruginous stone and perhaps of volcanic origin," No. 6 a "rapacious bird probably of cannel coal. No. 7 an earspool of cannel coal, No. 8 an earspool of clay, No. 9 an object of copper. UMMA Neg. 100-35-3.

PLATE 102

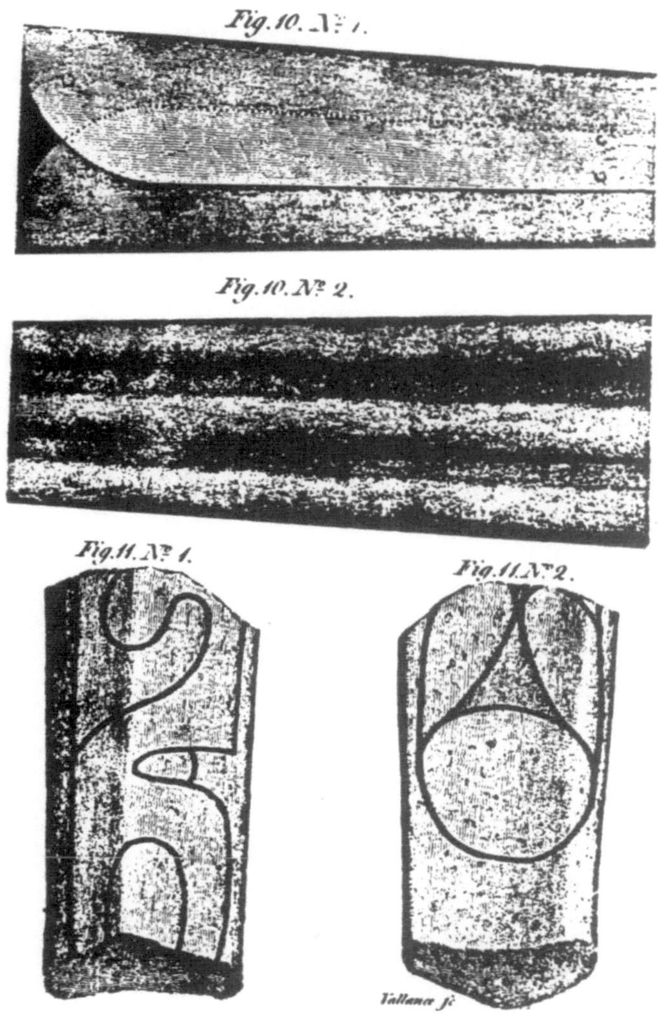

Plate 102. Reproduction of artifacts associated with copper panpipe found near a mound in downtown Cincinnati about 1794. No. 10 is a three-tube panpipe and No. 11 is a carved bone. UMMA Neg. 100-34-1.

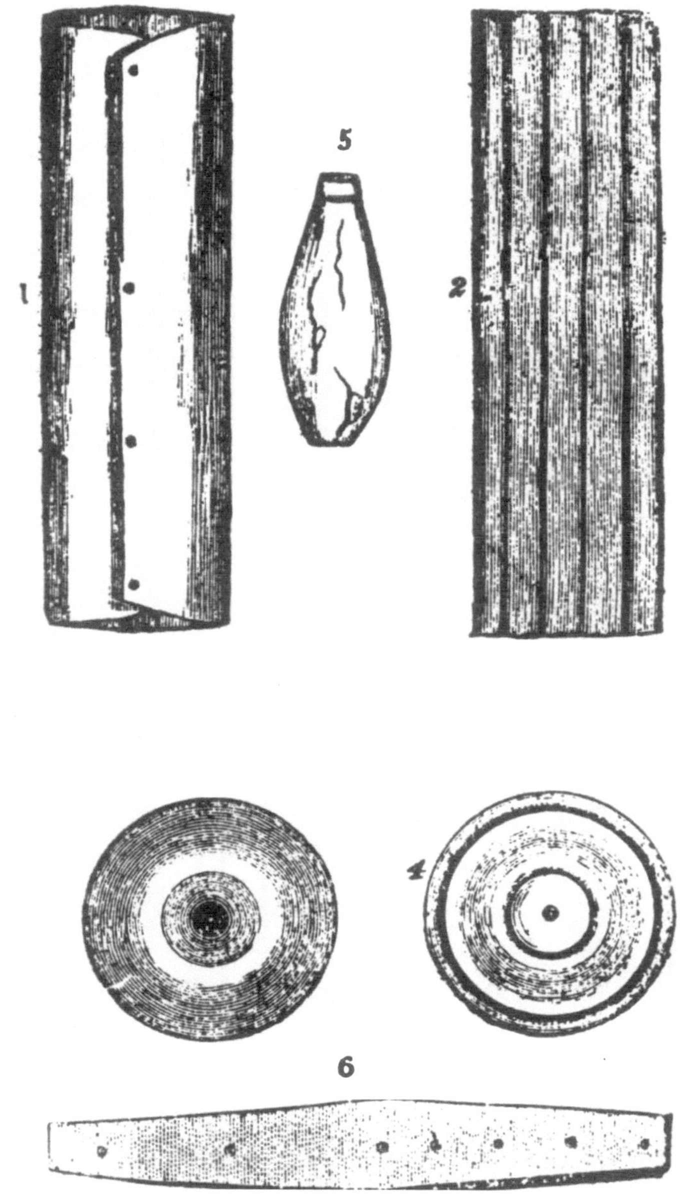

Plate 103. Reproduction of drawings of artifacts from a mound at Marietta, Ohio (Atwater, 1820). The descriptions of the silver panpipe says three ridges and is regarded as more accurate than the drawing. Three and four are copper and silver earspools. No. 5 is a copper and silver plummet, while No. 6 is a stone gorget 14 inches long from a field back of the great mound. UMMA Neg. 100-35-6.

PLATE 104

b

c

Plate 104 *c* and *d*. Two views of panpipe. *a* and *b*. Front and back views of reconstructed panpipe based on specimen from Mound 25 of the Hopewell Group, Ross County, Ohio. Negatives 91892 and 90993, courtesy of Field Museum of Natural History.

PLATE 105

Plate 105. Copper panpipe from Mallon Mound F in Newaygo County, Michigan. Length 130 cm. UMMA Neg. 16132-3.

PLATE 106

Plate 106. Copper panpipe from the Le Vesconte site in Ontario. Interior face of corrugated section with vegetal tubes. UMMA Neg. 100-27-3.

PLATE 107

Plate 107. Detail of tubes from Le Vesconte site in Ontario when in place in copper sheath. Some of the cordage used to tie the tubes can be seen. UMMA Neg. 100-27-3.

PLATE 108

a

Plate 108 *a*. Compound flexed burial of two adult males C°17-4 and -5. UMMA Neg. 13052. *b*. Burials C°21-1 to -6 in north end of mound. UMMA Neg. 13055.

PLATE 109

Plate 109. *Anculosa praerosa Say* beads found in association with burials C°21-4 to -6. UMMA Neg. 100-1-2.

PLATE 110

a

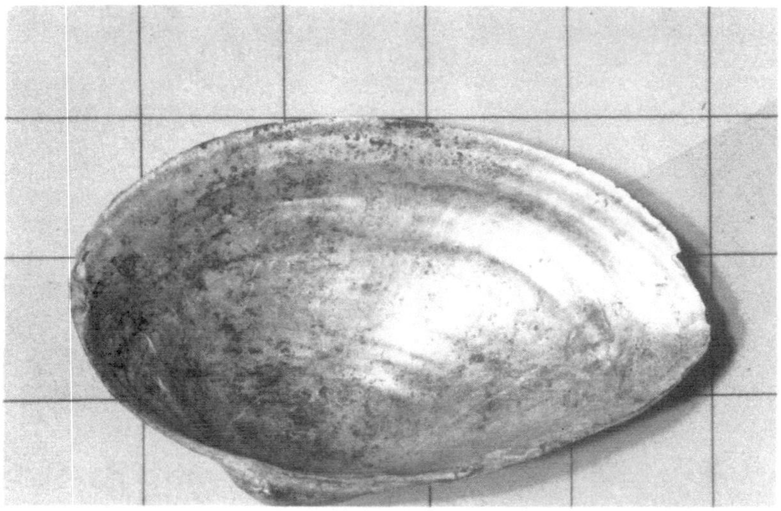

Plate 110 *a*. Canteen Cordmarked vessel with a burial in C°19. Height 23.5 cm. UMMA Neg. 13060. *b*. Left valve of *Proptera capax* mussel shell spoon found in jar C°19. UMMA Neg. 13061.

PLATE 111

a

b

Plate 111 *a*. Burials C°22-3 to -5 in upper level of mound. UMMA Neg. 13062. *b*. Adult burial C°22-10 with Baehr Brushed vessel at the skull. UMMA Neg. 13065.

a

b

Plate 112 *a*. Baehr Brushed jar C°22-10. Height 15.3 cm. UMMA Neg. 13064. *b*. Bear canine above left clavicle of Burial C°22-11. UMMA Neg. 13067.

PLATE 113

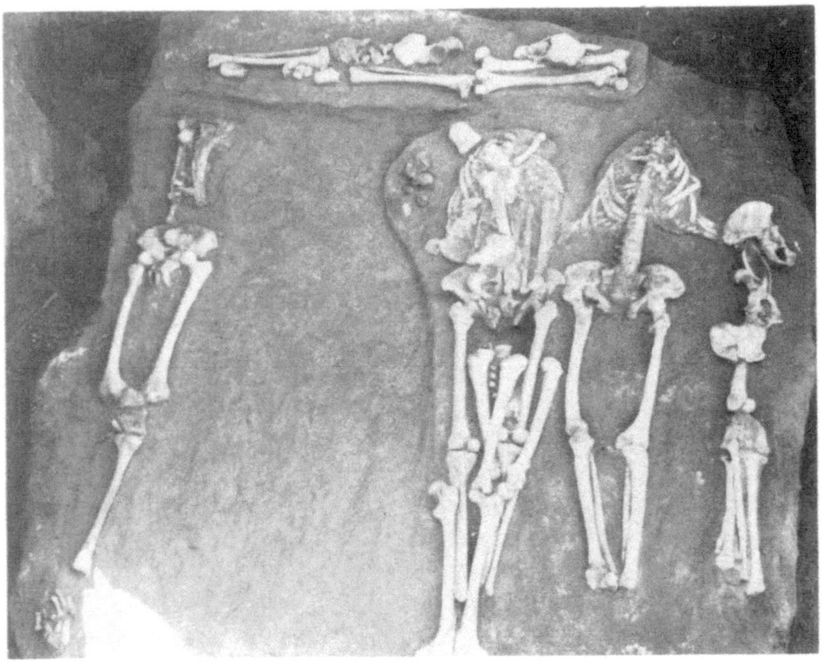

a

b

Plate 113 *a*. Burials C°22-14 to -19. Number 14 is at the extreme left; 15 is at the top; 16 is at the extreme right and 17 and 18 are in the center. UMMA Neg. 13071. *b*. Ash or niter over the area of the central burials C°22-14 to -19. UMMA Neg. 13070.

PLATE 114

a

b

Plate 114 *a*. Central burial group in C°22 containing Burials C°14 to -19 with dark area above the group. View looking east. UMMA Neg. 13072. *b*. Artifacts near right shoulder of adult Burial C°22-18, which included two standstone abraders, three antler fragments, a flake knife, a projectile point, a galena cube, two pieces of hematite and modified flake. UMMA Neg. 13077.

a

b

Plate 115 *a*. Tool kit artifacts with Burial C°22-18 on inch square scale. UMMA Neg. 13076. *b*. Clay pulley type earspool, galena cube, flake knife, and small *Obovaria subrotunda* mussel shell bracelet specimens found in the mound fill or with skeletal fragments and Baehr Brushed rim—sherd with adult female C°22-9A. UMMA Neg. 15667.

PLATE 116

a

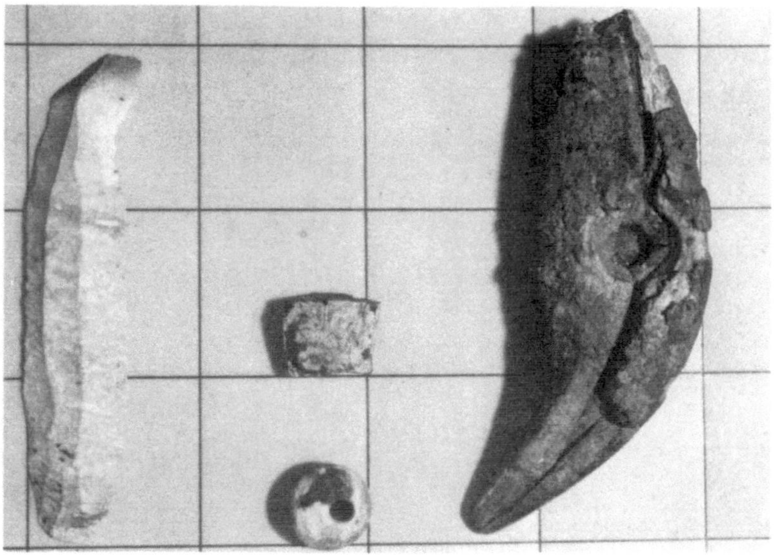

b

Plate 116 *a*. White flint projectile point C^o22-19, of the Mason-Dickson Group, not mentioned in notes. UMMA eg. 100-26-3. *b*. Artifacts from C^o22: a flint knife, a chunk of galena, a globular shell bead and a perforated bear canine. UMMA Neg. 13066.

PLATE 117

Plate 117. Norton Mound Group from the west across gravel quarry. Mound M is in the left center. Courtesy of the Grand Rapids Press.

PLATE 118

a

b

Plate 118 *a*. Norton Mound H from the north before excavation. UMMA Neg. 15619. *b*. Dark soil cap with "loading" effect beside burial pit of Norton Mound H. UMMA Neg. 15680.

PLATE 119

a

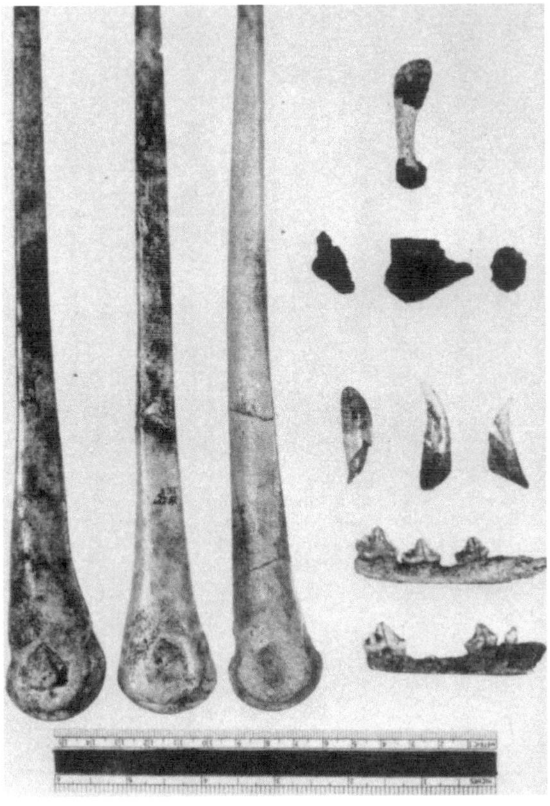

b

Plate 119 *a*. Norton Mound H central burial pit exposed to basal gravel. UMMA Neg. 16558. *b*. Elk metapodial pins, burned human phalanx, copper fragments, split bear canines and modified wolf jaws from floor area of Norton Mound H central pit. UMMA Neg. 15609.

PLATE 120

a

b

Plate 120 *a*. Norton Mound H Burial Group 1 in the northeast corner of the central pit. UMMA Neg. 15621. *b*. Discoidal blanks from Burial Group 1 of Norton Mound H central pit. Average length 7.8 cm. UMMA Neg. 15609.

PLATE 121

a

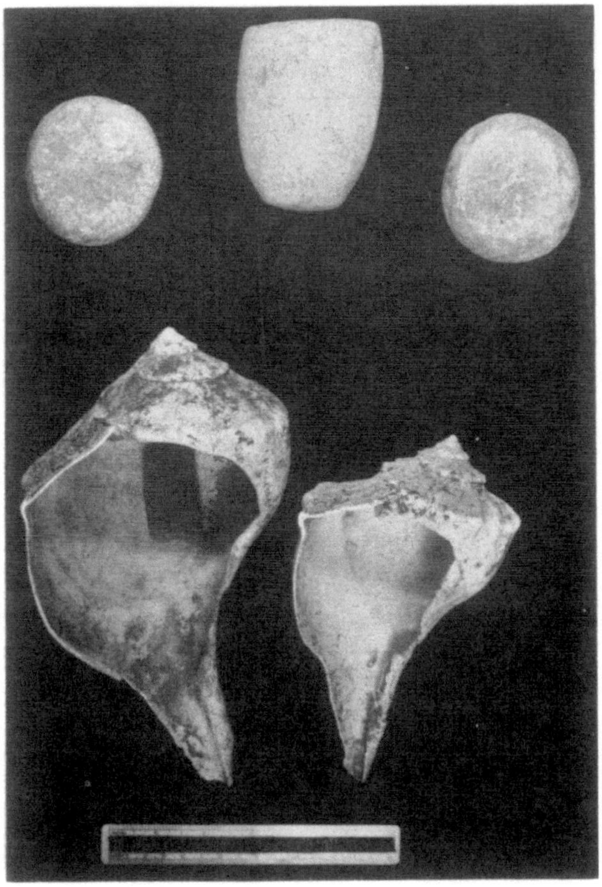

b

Plate 121 *a*. Group 1 artifacts from Norton Mound H worked beaver incisors. pyrite fragment, shell spoon with handle, flint blade, and deer antler sections. UMMA g. 87-1-5. *b*. Group 1 artifacts from Norton Mound H. Two hammerstone , and sandstone abrader top center, and 2 *Busycon contrarium* ontainers. The specimen on the right is from Group 2. MMA Neg. 15608.

PLATE 122

Plate 122 *a*. Norton Zoned Incised vessel H-1, with Group 1 central burial pit. Height 15.1 cm. UMMA Neg. 15612. *b*. Norton Zoned Punctate vessel H-3 with Group 2 of Central burial pit. Height 7.5 cm. UMMA Neg. 15612. *c*. Norton Zoned Dentate vess l. H-2. with Group 2 of Central burial pit. Height 14 m. UMMA Neg. 15612. *d*. Burial Group 2 in the northwest corner of the central pit of Norton Mound H. UMMA Neg. 15633.

PLATE 123

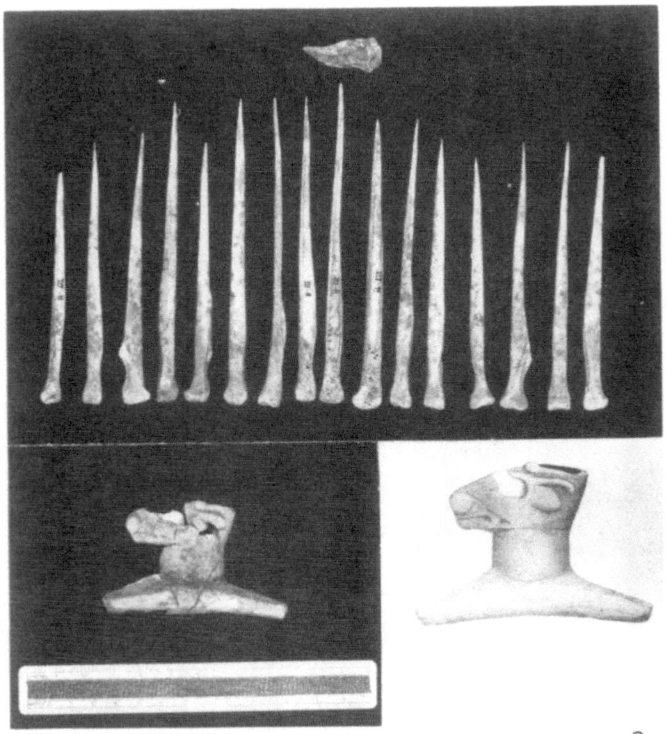

a

b

Plate 123 *a*. Split turkey leg bone awls and elk (?)effigy platform pipe of limestone and chert near Skull 1 of the central burial pit of Norton Mound H. UMMA Neg. 15611. *b*. Norton Corner Notched points from floor area of Mound H central pit. UMMA Neg. 15609.

a

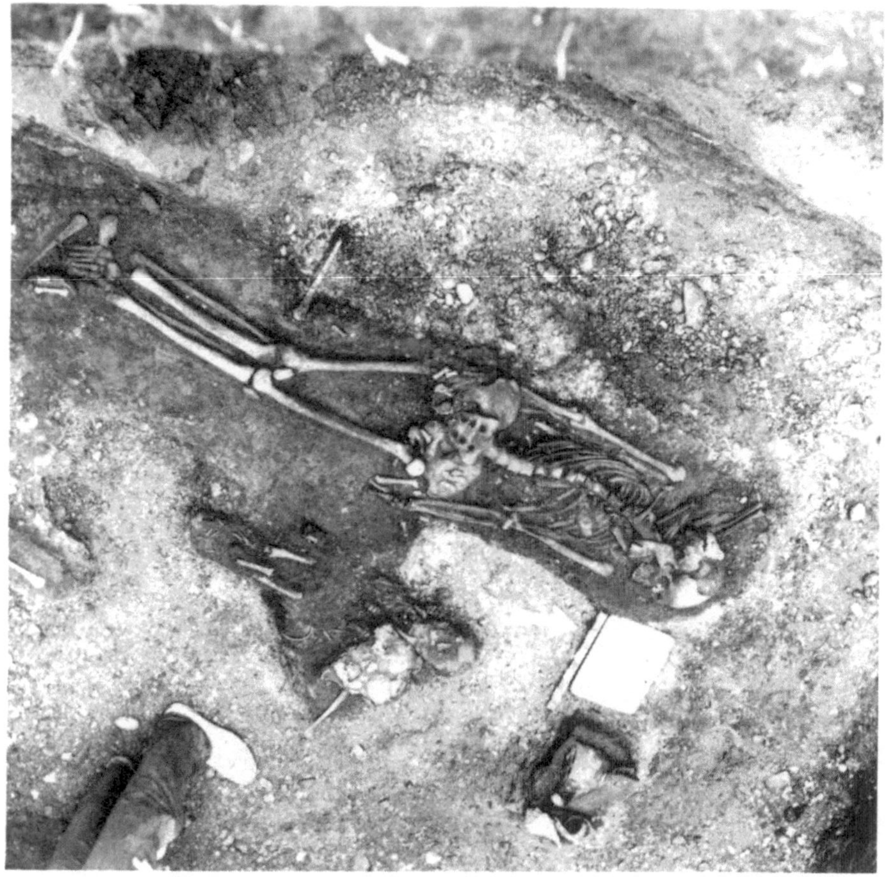

b

Plate 124 *a*. Norton Mound I upper level of central burial pit with "loaded" effect over original ground surface. UMMA Neg. 15624. *b*. Mound I central burial pit cleared to basal gravel, extended adult female, child burial and extra child's skull. UMMA Neg. 15685.

PLATE 125

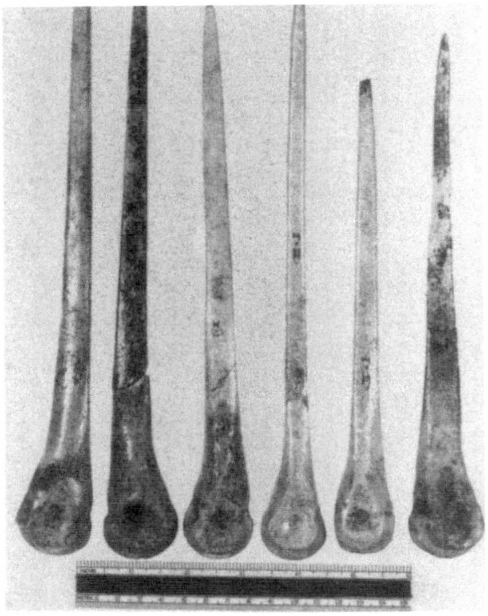

a

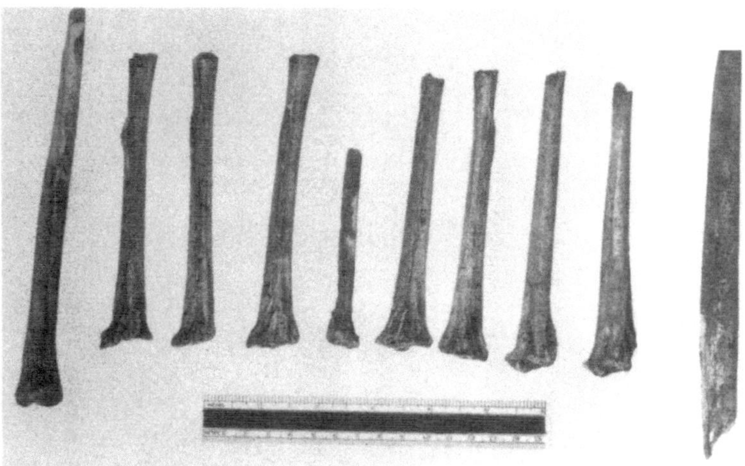

b

Plate 125 *a*. Elk metapodial bones from central pit of Norton Mound I. UMMA Neg. 98-4. *b*. Partly worked deer bone sections and eight partly worked turkey leg bones with skull 9 in central pit of Norton Mound I. UMMA Neg. 99-4-4.

PLATE 126

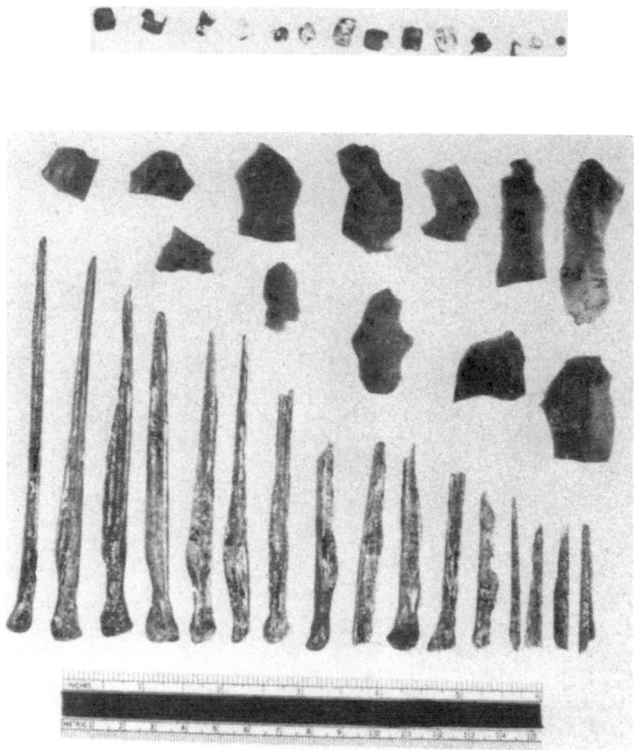

Plate 126. Shell beads, flint flakes and 16 worked turkey leg bone awls with child burial 10 in Norton Mound I central pit. UMMA Neg. 98-5.

PLATE 127

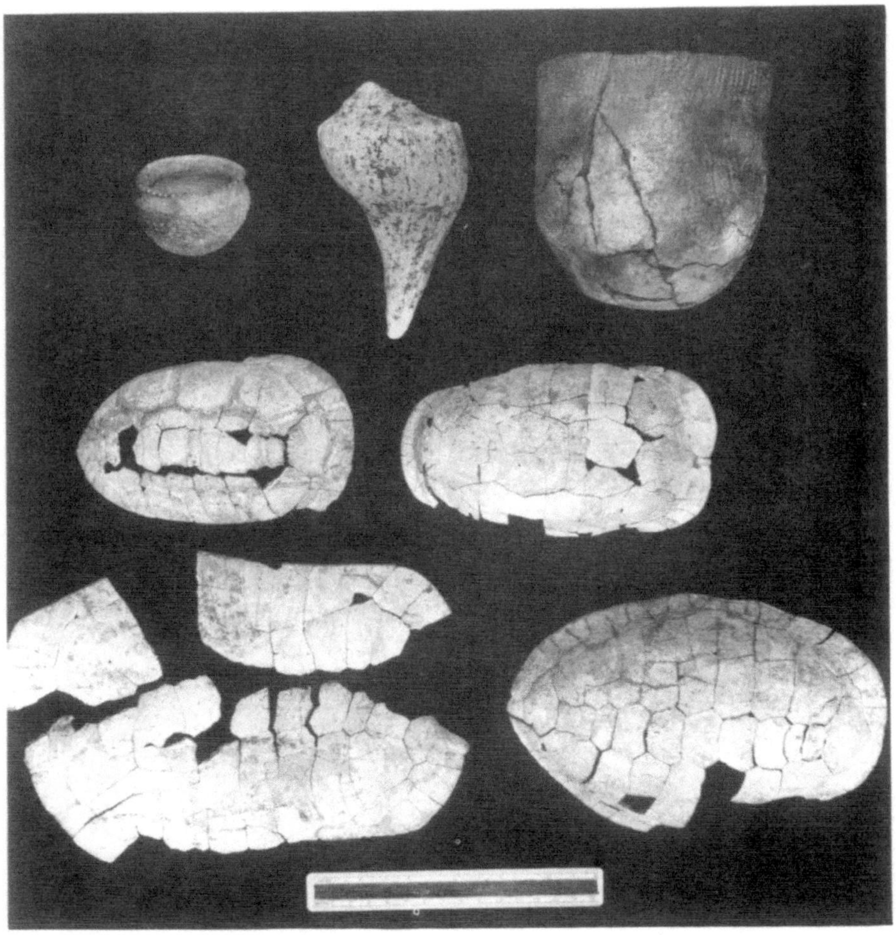

Plate 127. Burial offerings in the northeast corner of the central pit of Norton Mound I. Norton Punctate vessel I-2, small *Busycon* shell, Norton Zoned Dentate Stamp vessel I-1, and 3 engraved and 1 undecorated carapaces of Blandings turtle. UMMA Neg. 15610.

PLATE 128

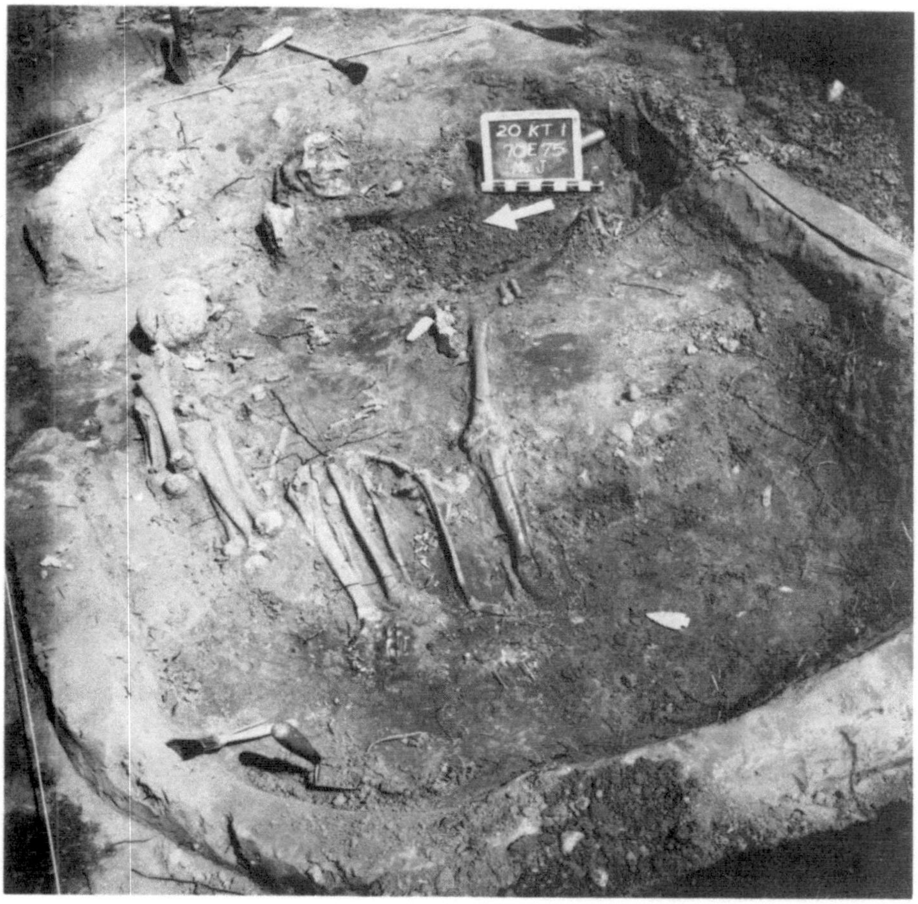

Plate 128. Central burial pit of Norton Mound J from the west. UMMA Neg. 15684.

PLATE 129

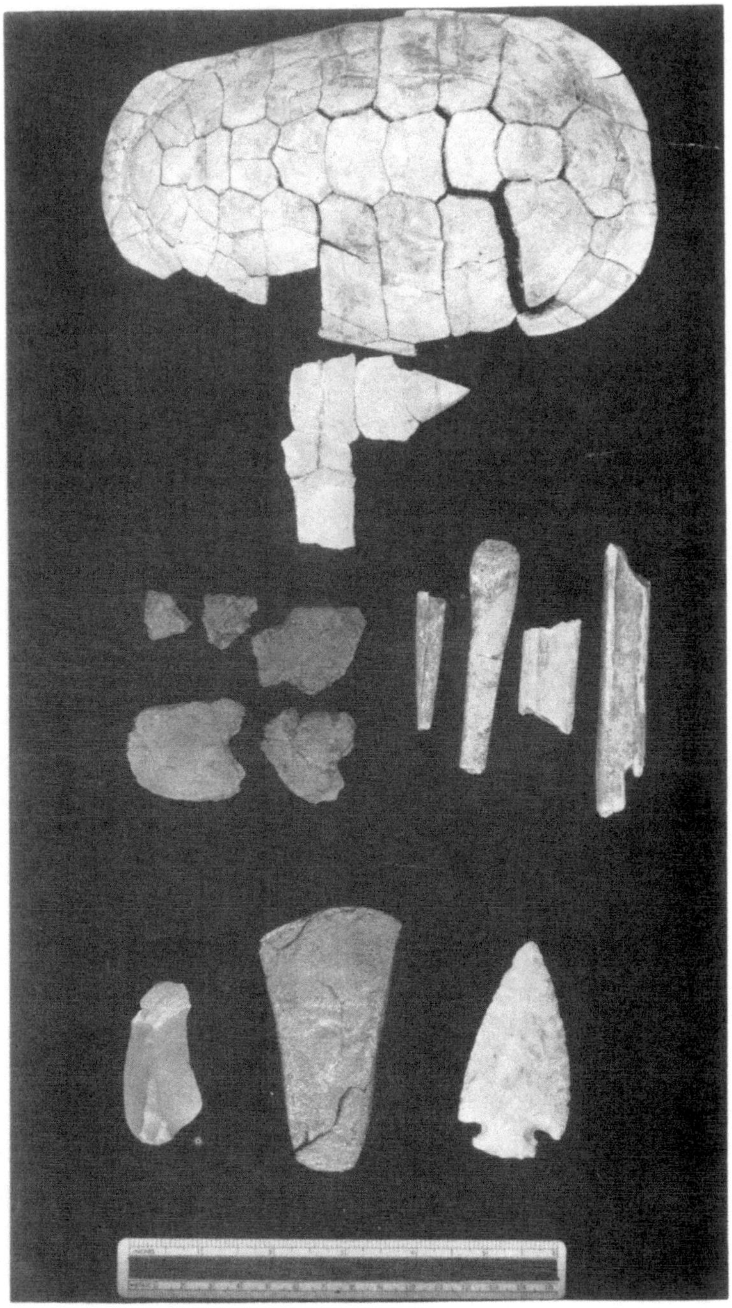

Plate 129. Artifacts from central pit of Mound J. Blandings turtle carapace cup, modified section of carapace with sharp point; 3 Norton crosshatched rims and 2 body sherds; deer metapodial pin fragments; flake of dark grey flint, copper celt and Norton Corner Notched point. UMMA Neg. 15602.

PLATE 130

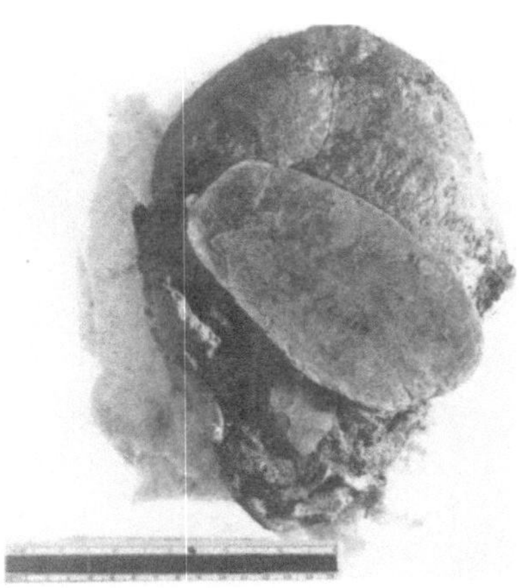

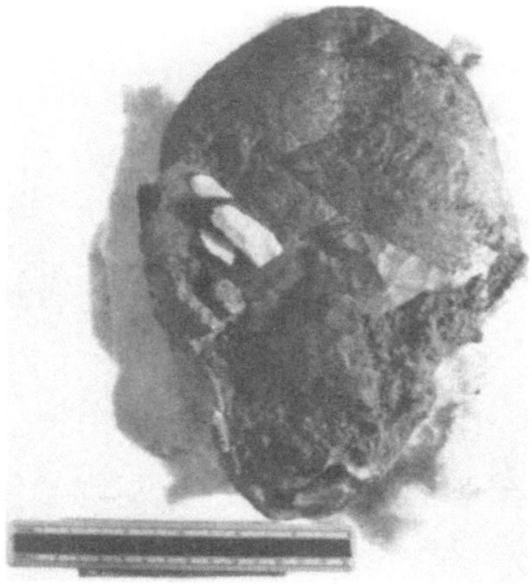

a b

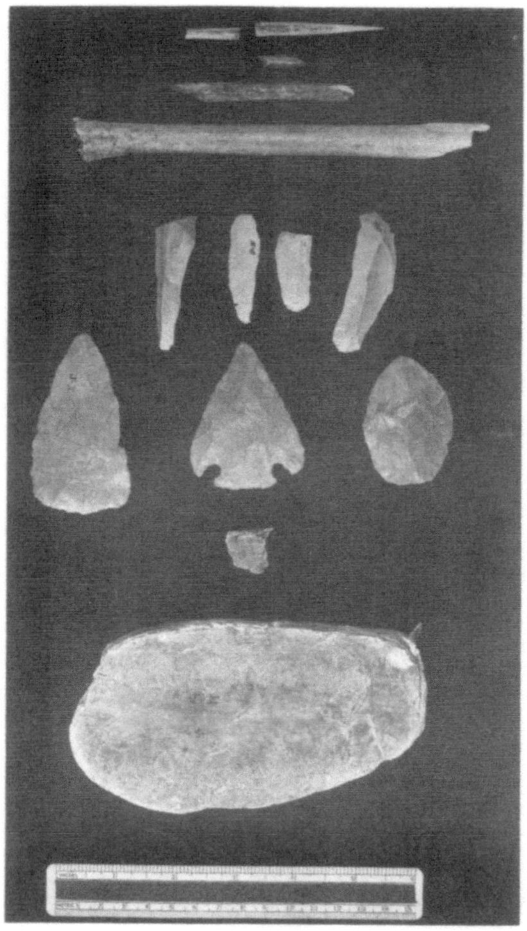

c

Plate 130 *a*. Mica plate in place beneath skull No. 6 in the central pit of Norton Mound J. UMMA Neg. 15636. *b*. Flint flakes and Norton Corner-Notched point under skull No. 6 after removal of mica plate. UMMA Neg. 15637. *c*. Artifacts placed under skull o. 6 of central pit of Norton Mound J. Turkey leg bone worked fragment . flint flakes. flint blanks. Norton Conor notched point. worked bone object and mica plate. UMMA Neg. 15607.

PLATE 131

a

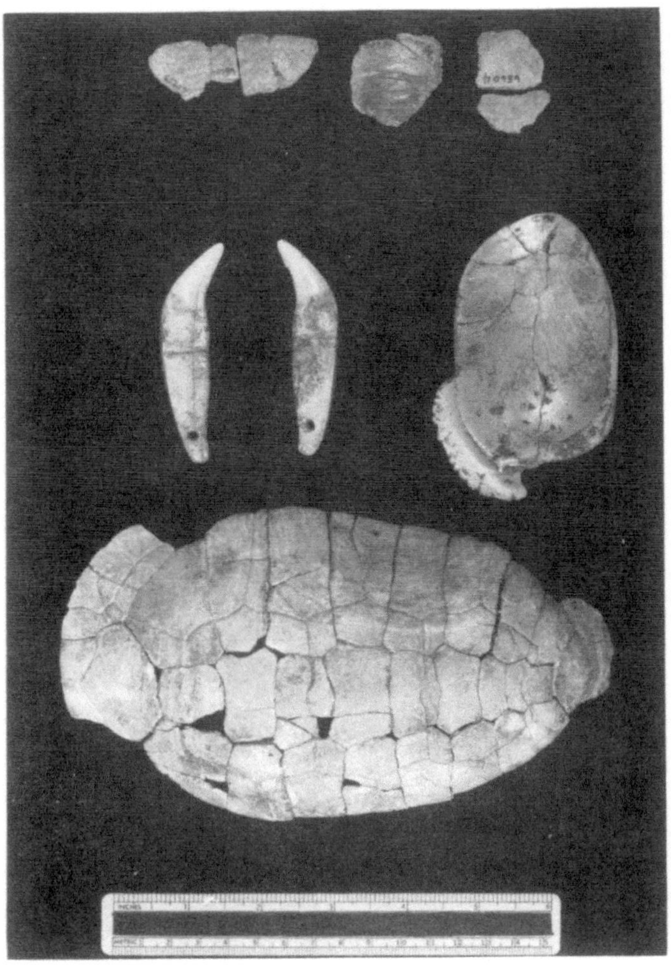

b

Plate 131 *a*. Ash cache with bear canines in cap on north side of the central pit of Norton Mound D. UMMA Neg. 16567. *b*. Artifact in ash cache of Mound D. Cro shatched rim zoned body and lower body herds of limestone and grit tempered vessel; perforated canines from a small black bear; handled *Lampsilis ventricosa* shell spoon and engraved Blandings turtle carapace. UMMA Neg. 15600,

PLATE 132

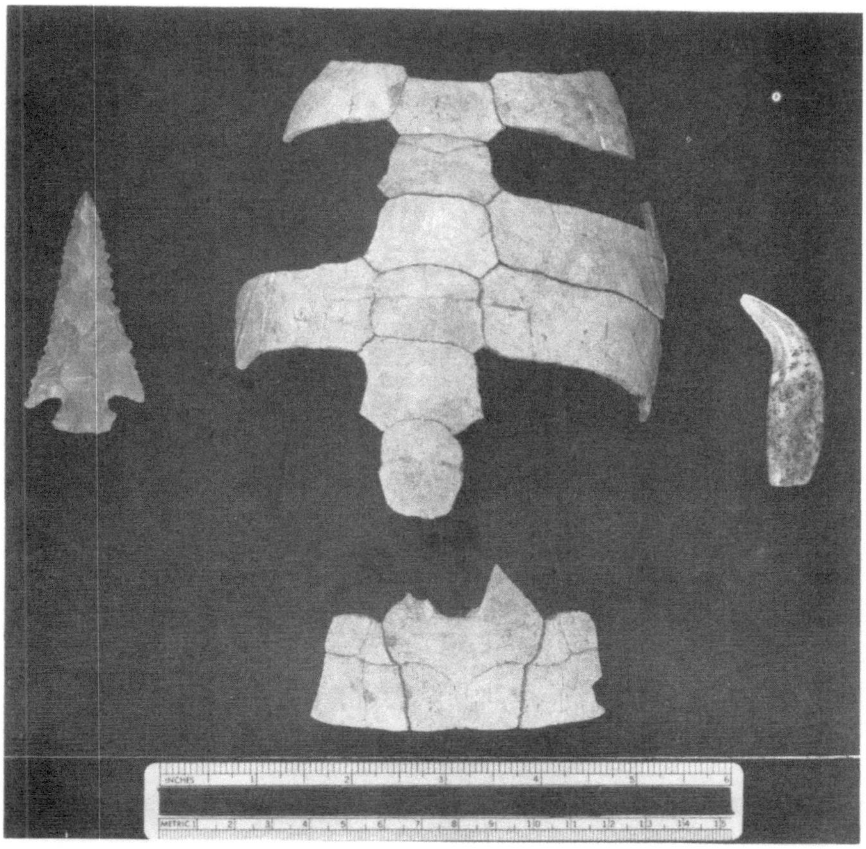

a

b

Plate 132 *a*. Artifacts remaining in the central pit of Norton Mound D after the previous violation. Norton variant point; engraved sections of Blandings turtle carapace; and bear canine. UMMA Neg. 15601. *b*. Norton Mound F before excavation. View to the south. UMMA Neg. 15642.

PLATE 133

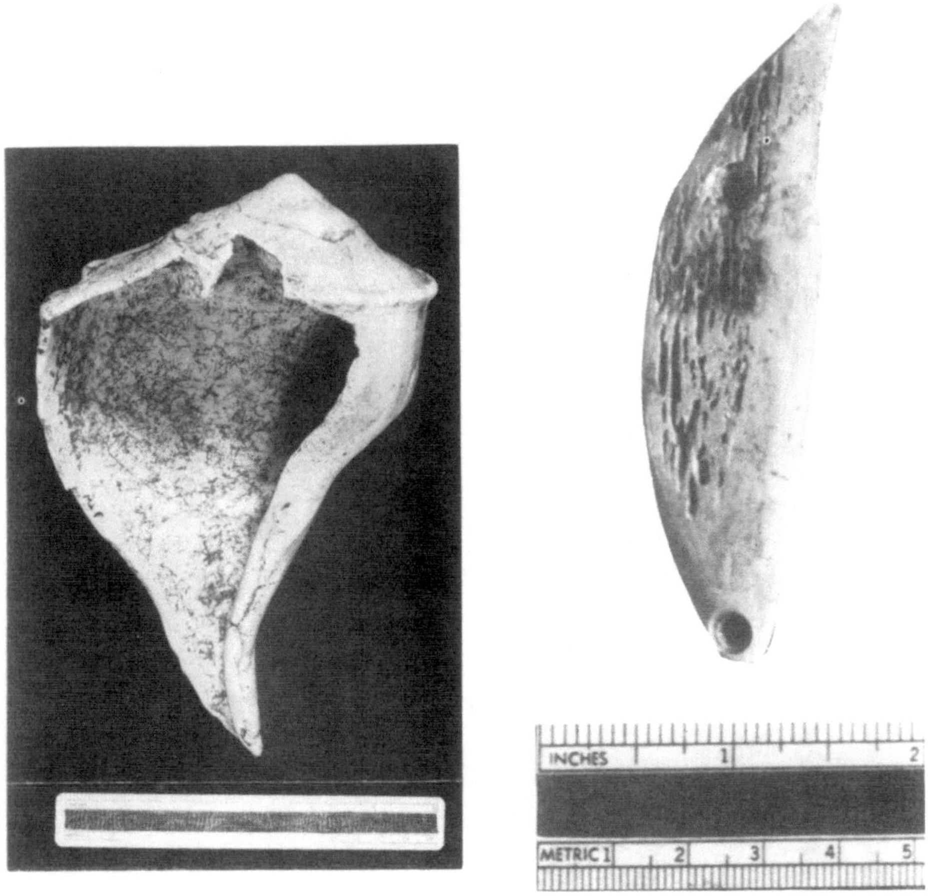

Plate 133. *Busycon contrarium* container and ground and double perforated bear canine found in back dirt of the previous excavation of Norton Mound F. UMMA Neg. 15604.

PLATE 134

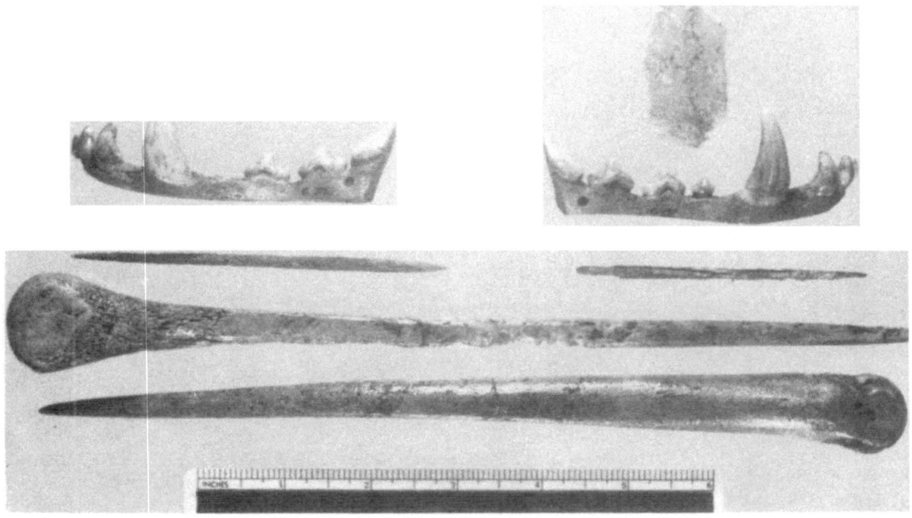

a

b

Plate 134 *a*. Artifacts from around Burial 17 of Norton Mound C: 2 flint flakes and 2 shell beads, 2 cut wolf jaws and 3 pearl beads, 2 copper awls and 2 deer metapodial pins. UMMA Neg. 87-4-5. *b*. Norton Zoned Dentate Stamped jar C-2 from near head of Burial 17. UMMA Neg. 16571 and 16572.

PLATE 135

Plate 135 Norton Mound C with supplementary burial group on the left and dark soil of center pit. UMMA Neg. 15673.

PLATE 136

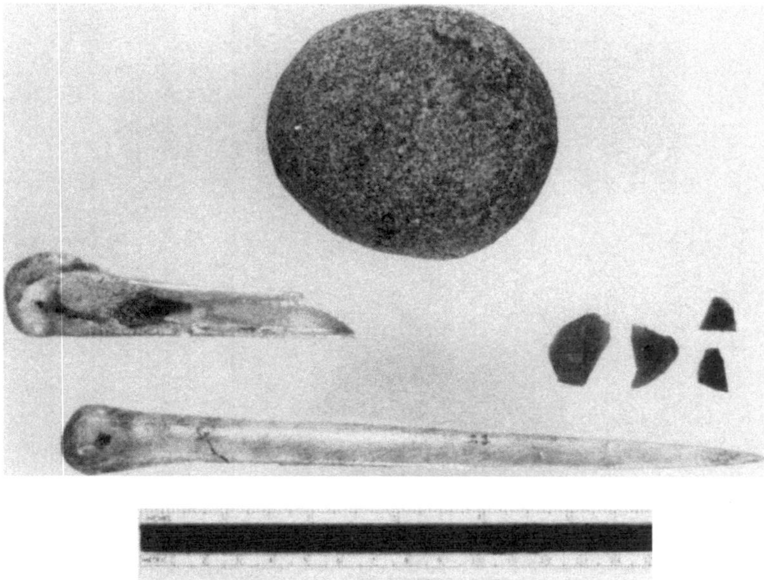

a

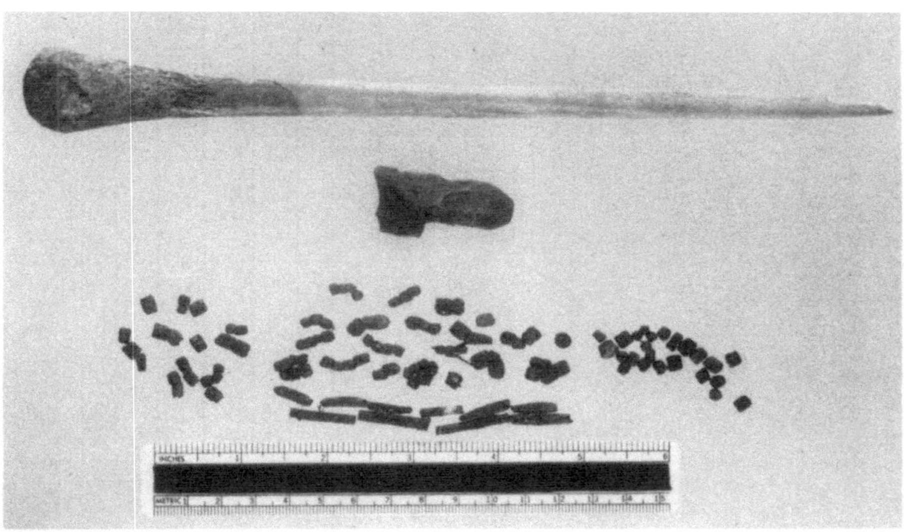

b

Plate 136 *a*. Artifacts with supplementary Burial 13 on ledge of central pit of Norton Mound C; hammerstone, deer metapodial pins and flint chips. UMMA Neg. 87-3-1. *b*. Deer metapodial pin, flint flake and copper beads with supplementary Burial 14 of Norton Mound C. UMMA Neg. 87-3-3.

PLATE 137

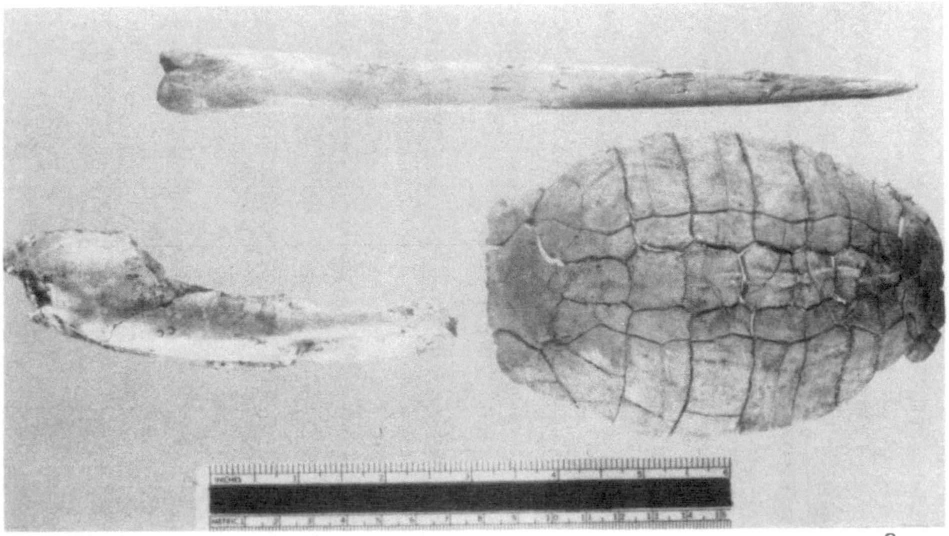

a

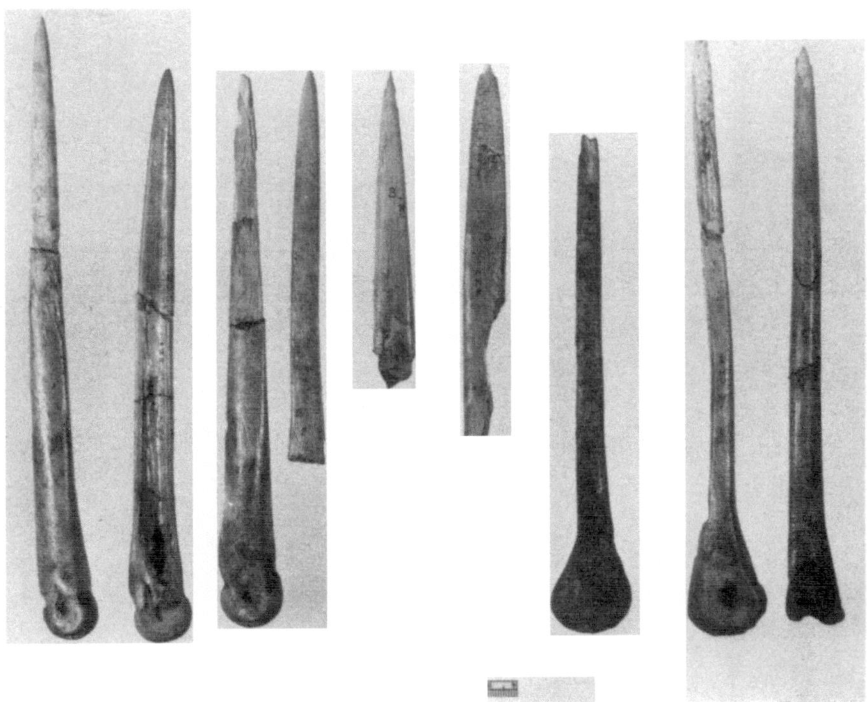

b

137 *a*. Deer metapodial pin; worked valve of *Ligumia recta latissima*, and Blandings Turtle carapace with supplementary Burial 15 of Norton Mound C. UMMA Neg. 87-5-1. *b*. Deer metapodial pins from Norton Mound C central burial pit. UMMA Neg. 15669.

a

b

Plate 138 *a*. Burial 16 left, and Burial 17. East half of central burial pit of Norton Mound C. UMMA Neg. 15623. *b*. Burial offering to the east of Burial 16 of central pit of Norton Mound C. UMMA Neg. 16570.

PLATE 139

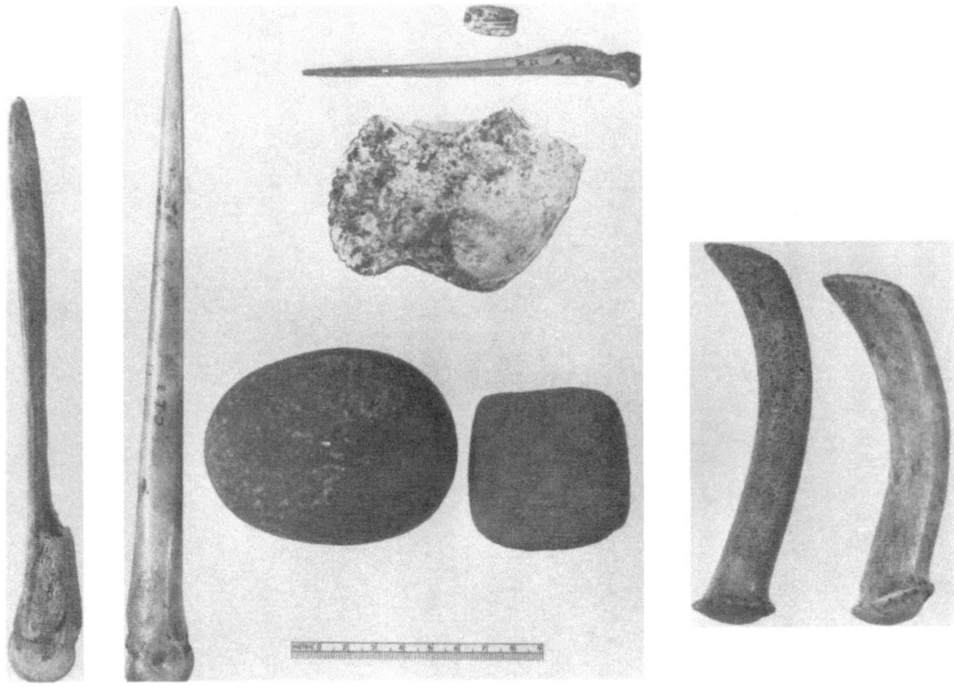

a

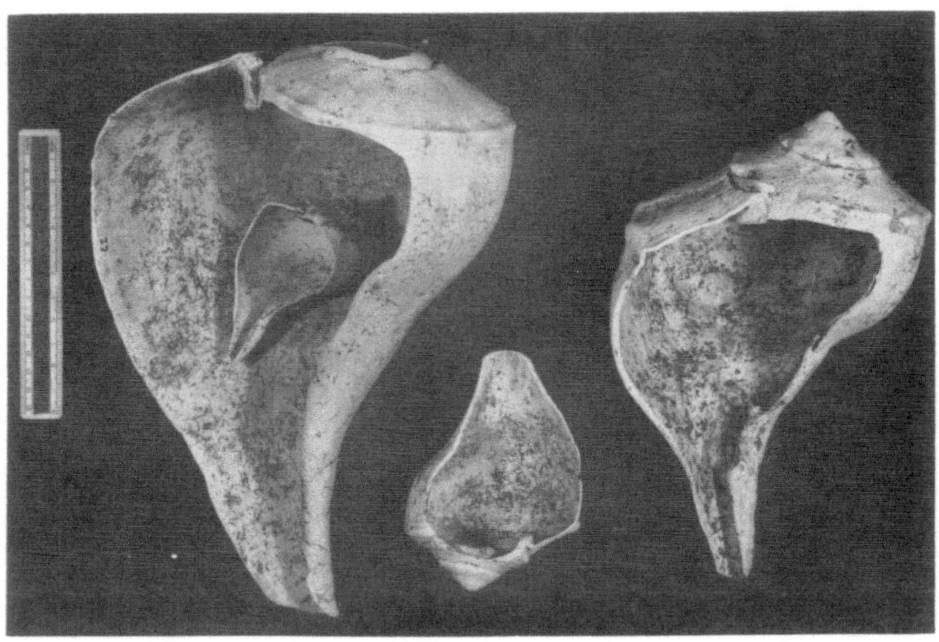

b

Plate 139 *a*. Artifacts from near skull of Burial 16: deer metapodial pins, shell beads, turkey leg bone awl, fragment of mussel shell spoon, hammerstone, standstone abrader and deer antler sections. UMMA Neg. 97-8. *b*. Three *Busycon contrarium* containers on the left near skull of Burial 16 and *Busycon* specimen from near skull of Burial 17 in the central pit of Norton Mound C. UMMA Neg. 15605.

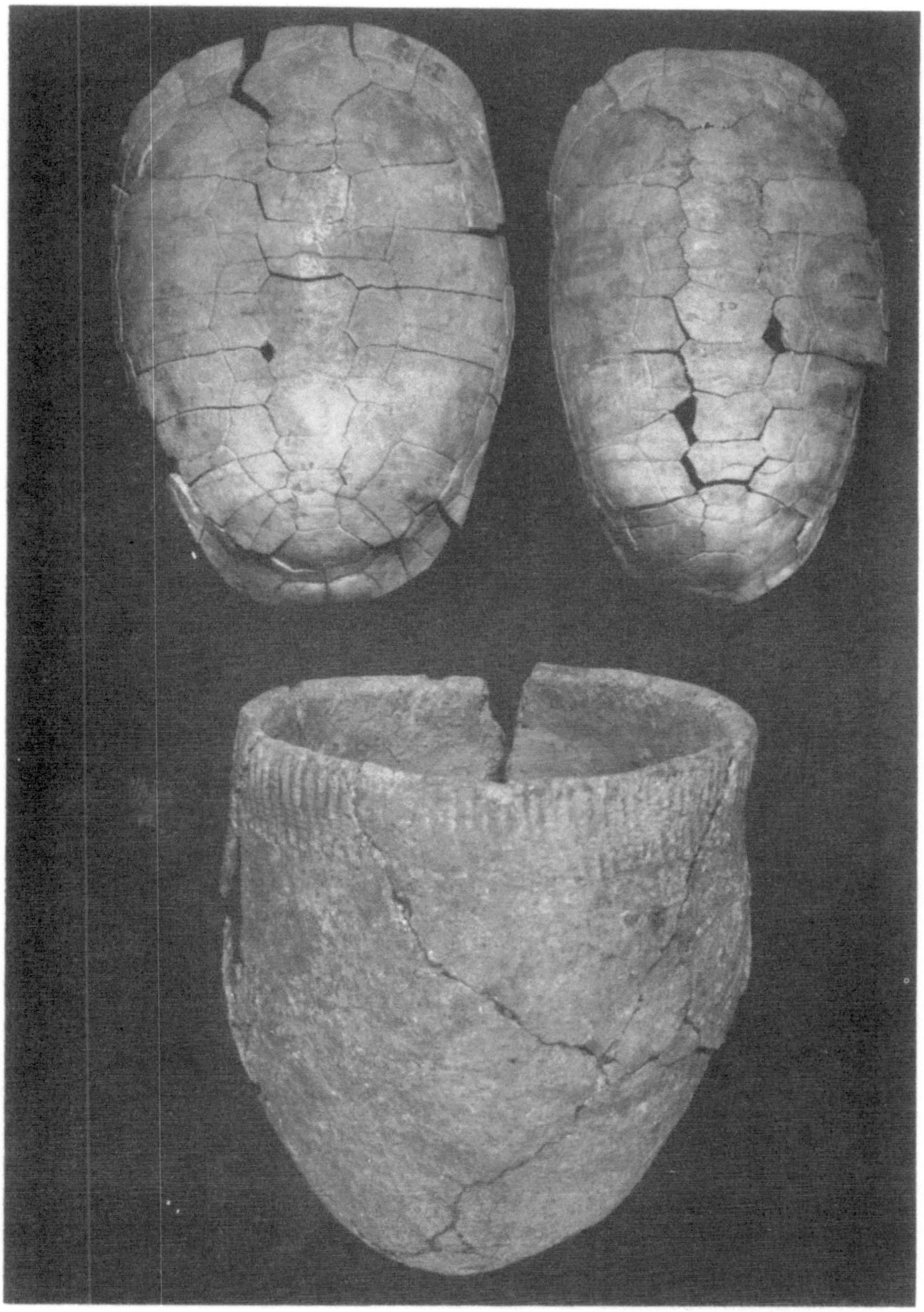

Plate 140. Two engraved Blandings turtle carapaces and Norton Dentate Stamp jar C-1 near skull of Burial 16 in the central pit of Norton Mound C. Ves el height is 16.8 cm. UMMA Neg. 15598.

PLATE 141

a

b

Plate 141 *a*. Central burial pit of Norton Mound C after excavation. UMMA Neg. 15673. *b*. Matched set of 7 Norton Corner Notched points near skull of Burial 16 in the central pit of Norton Mound C. UMMA Neg. 87-2-3.

PLATE 142

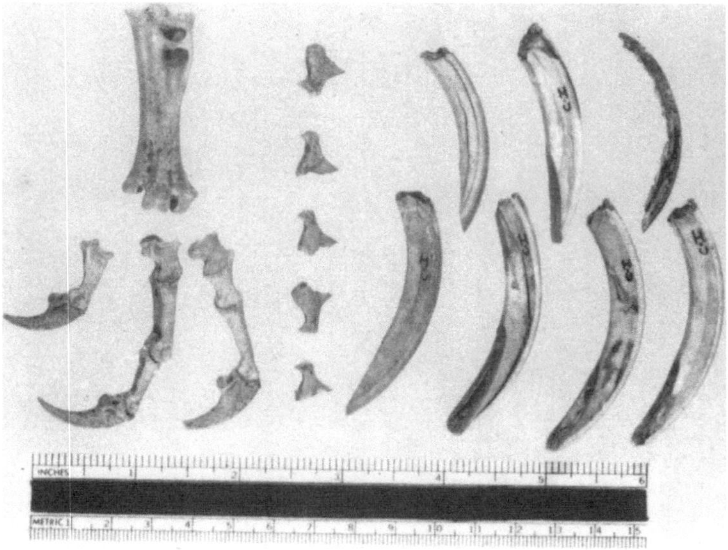

a

b

Plate 142 *a*. Snowy owl lower leg and claws, bobcat claws and worked beaver incisors near the skull of Burial 16 in Norton Mound C. UMMA Neg. 97-8. *b*. Detail of mid-section of Burial 16 with copper axe over left pelvic area and cut bear jaw under upper left femur. UMMA Neg. 15674.

PLATE 143

a

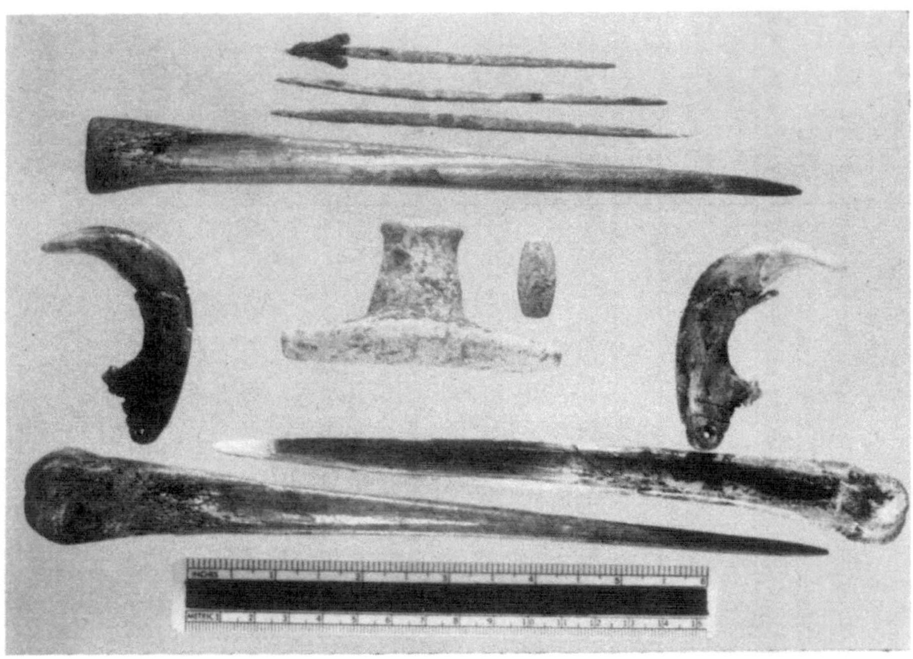

b

Plate 143 *a*. Detail of twilled twined fabric of bast fibers covering copper axe with Burial 16 of Norton Mound C. UMMA Neg. 99-1. *b*. Artifacts with Burial 16 of Norton Mound C; wood handle on copper awl, 2 copper awls, deer metapodial pin, worked bear jaws near left and right hand region, plain platform pipe of limestone near right hand, shell bead, and 2 deer metapodial pins. UMMA Neg. 87-2-5.

PLATE 144

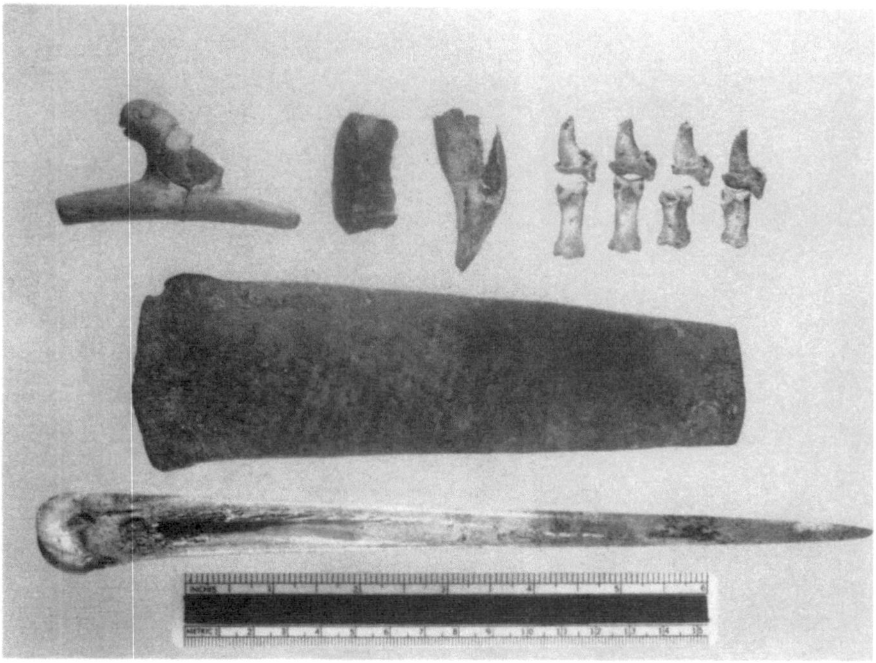

a

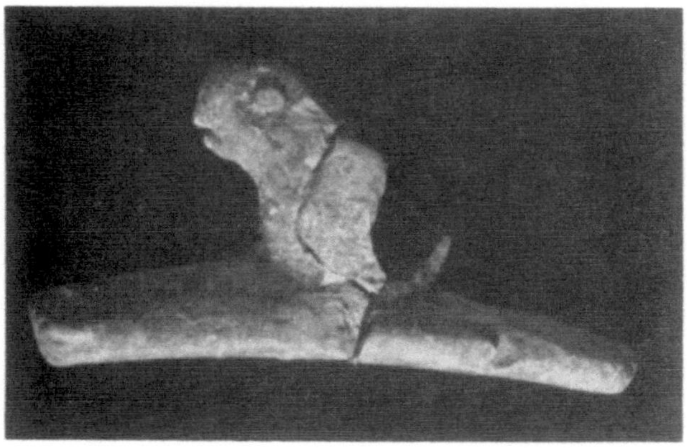

b

Plate 144 *a*. **Platform effigy** pipe of fine gray soft siltstone near head of Burial 16; flint chip, bear canine and wolf phalanges near vessel C-2, copper celt with faint fabric impressions from under left elbow and deer metapodial pin from near vessel C-2 in Norton Mound C. UMMA Neg. 87-1-3. *b*. Effigy platform pipe of soft grey siltstone, not Ohio pipestone, with Burial 17 of Norton Mound C. The length of the pipe is 6.9 cm. UMMA Neg. 100-87-1.

PLATE 145

a

b

Plate 145 *a*. Norton Mound C Burial 17 with copper axe under left elbow, effigy pipe and Norton Zoned Dentate Vessel C-2. UMMA Neg. 15676. *b*. Detail of left side of Burial 17 in Norton Mound C. Copper axe under left elbow and cache of 7 matched Norton Corner Notched points. UMMA Neg. 15677.

PLATE 146

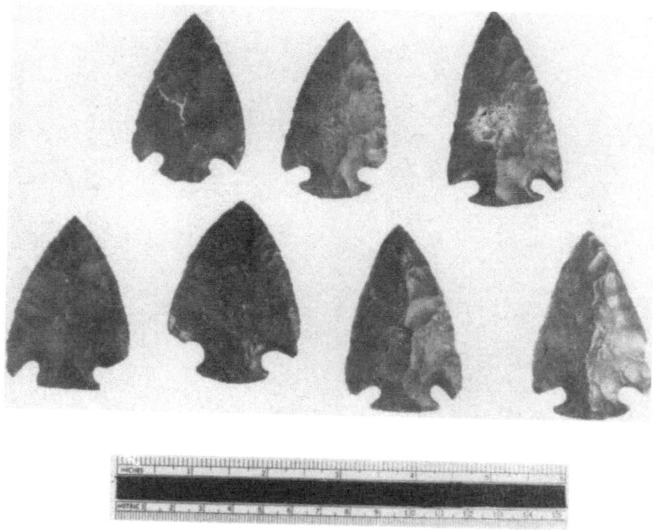

a

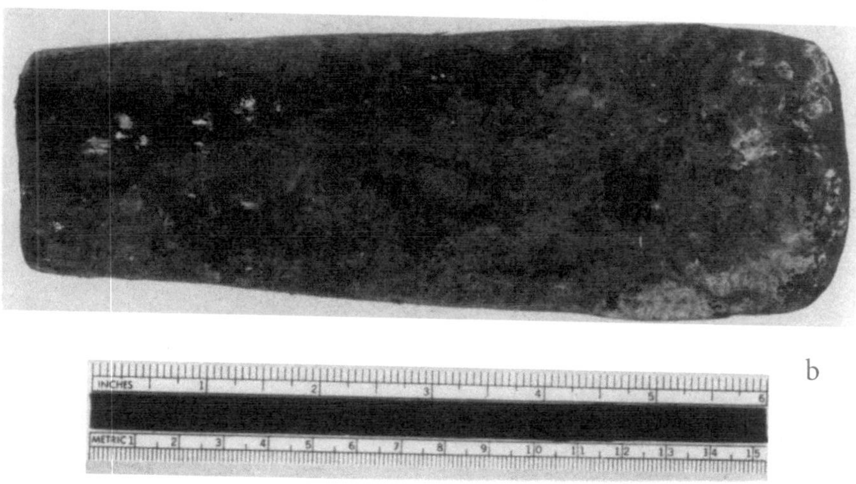

b

Plate 146 *a*. Seven matched Norton Corner Notched points near left pelvic area of Burial 17. UMMA Neg. 16572. *b*. Copper celt found in central part of the left humeru of Burial 17, Norton Mound C. UMMA Neg. 98-7-5.

PLATE 147

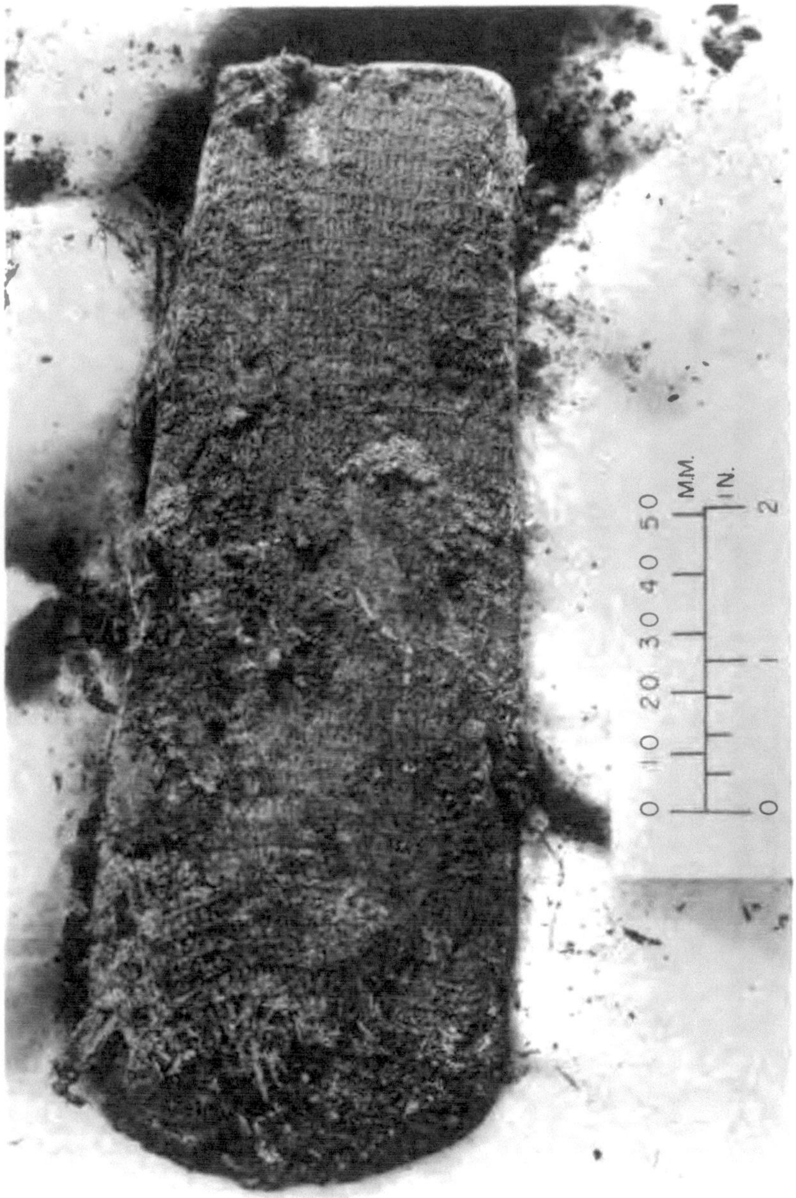

Plate 147. Copper celt with Burial 16 of Mound C. Lower face with preserved twilled twined fabric of native bast fibers. Length 19.2 cm. UMMA Neg. 15665.

PLATE 148

a

b

Plate 148 *a*. Mound M from south with photo tower and Paradome during initial excavation activities. UMMA Neg. 79-2-1. *b*. Truncated top of Mound M. UMMA Neg. 87-2-1.

PLATE 149

Plate 149. Norton Mound M. Cordmarked sherds from the top level of fill. UMMA Neg. 16487.

PLATE 150

Plate 150. Norton Mound M. Havana Ceramic Tradition sherds from above cap in fill. UMMA Neg. 16488.

PLATE 151

a

b

Plate 151 *a*. View to the north of central balk and profile trenche. UMMA Neg. 79-5-6. *b*. Norton Mound M. Profile trench at south end of mound. Note loading of cap. UMMA Neg. 99-10-3.

PLATE 152

a

b

Plate 152 *a*. View to north with western part of upper layer of basket loads of earth of Mound M. UMMA Neg. 16576. *b*. Ea t face of central balk with W. L. Coffinberry pit visible to th right of the photo board. Individual basket loads of earth are xposed in lower part of picture. UMMA Neg. 16575.

PLATE 153

a

b

Plate 153. *a*. Center balks removed and bark line appears in Mound M. View to the south. UMMA Neg. 100-69-2. *b*. Central burial area of orton Mound 1 from photo tower. Whiti h cover is niter from decomposed bark. View toward the southea t. UMMA Neg. 15701*d*.

PLATE 154

a

b

Plate 154 *a*. View of the central burial area from the south. Central pit was excavated by field crew not the builders of Mound B. UMMA Neg. 15701a. *b*. Jame B. Griffin examining northeast corner of the central burial area of Norton Mound M. UMMA Neg. 87-1-1.

PLATE 155

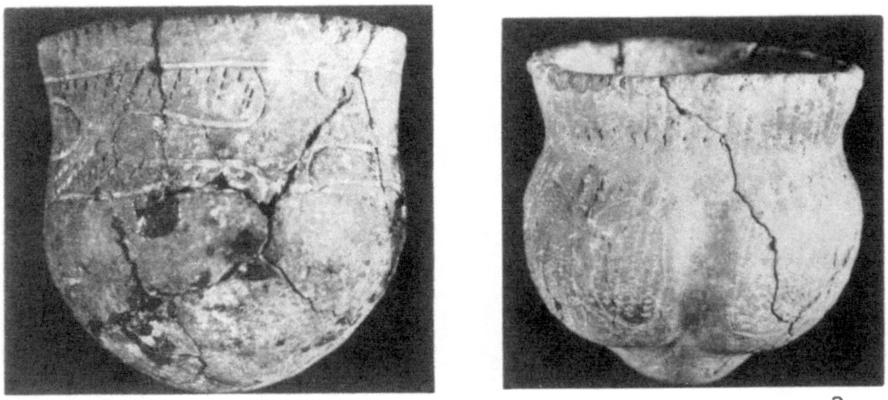

a

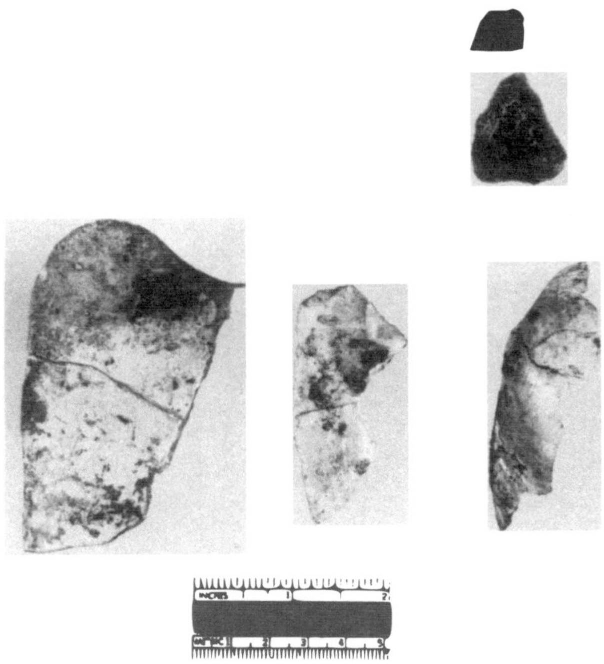

b

Plate 155 *a*. Norton Zoned Dentate Stamp vessels M-7 and Norton Zoned Cordwrapped Stick M-8. Height of M-7 102. cm. and of M-8 9.5 cm. UMMA eg. 15276. *b*. Chert chips and fragments of mussel shell spoons from Norton Mound M Burial 6. UMMA Neg. 16466.

PLATE 156

Plate 156. Norton Mound M. Turtle carapace cups with adult male Burial 1. UMMA Neg. 16494.

PLATE 157

Plate 157. Marine shell beads from Columnella of *Busycon* (?) from Burial 13, and turkey leg bone awls and chert chip from Norton Mound M, Burial 10. UMMA Neg. 16477.

PLATE 158

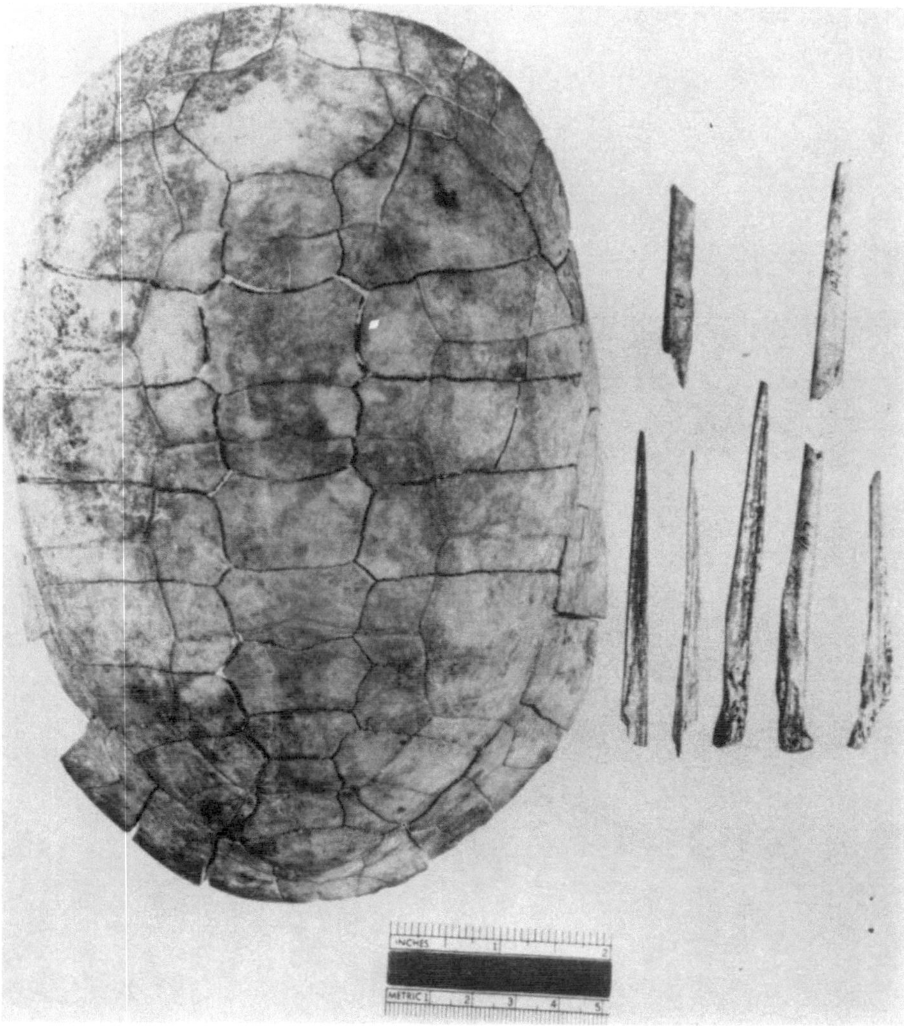

Plate 158. Carapace of Blandings turtle and 7 turkey bone awls with Burial 5, Norton Mound M. UMMA Neg. 16476.

PLATE 159

a

b

Plate 159 *a*. North section of east burial section of central pit of Norton Mound M. Norton Incised vessel M3 in upper left. UMMA Neg. 79-1-4. *b*. Detail of south portion of east burial section of the central pit of Norton Mound M. Mica plate. *Busycon* container and turtle carapaces on left. View toward the west. UMMA Neg. 79-6-4.

PLATE 160

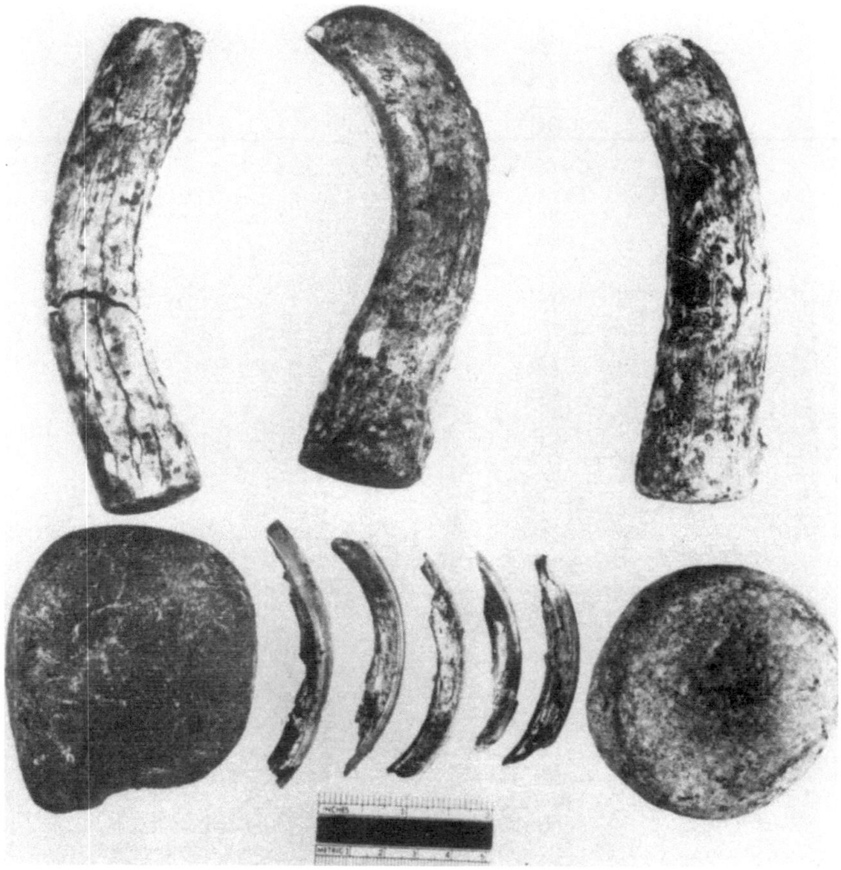

Plate 160. Elk antler sections, worked beaver incisors, grinding stone and hammerstone with Burial 2, Norton Mound M. UMMA Neg. 16492.

PLATE 161

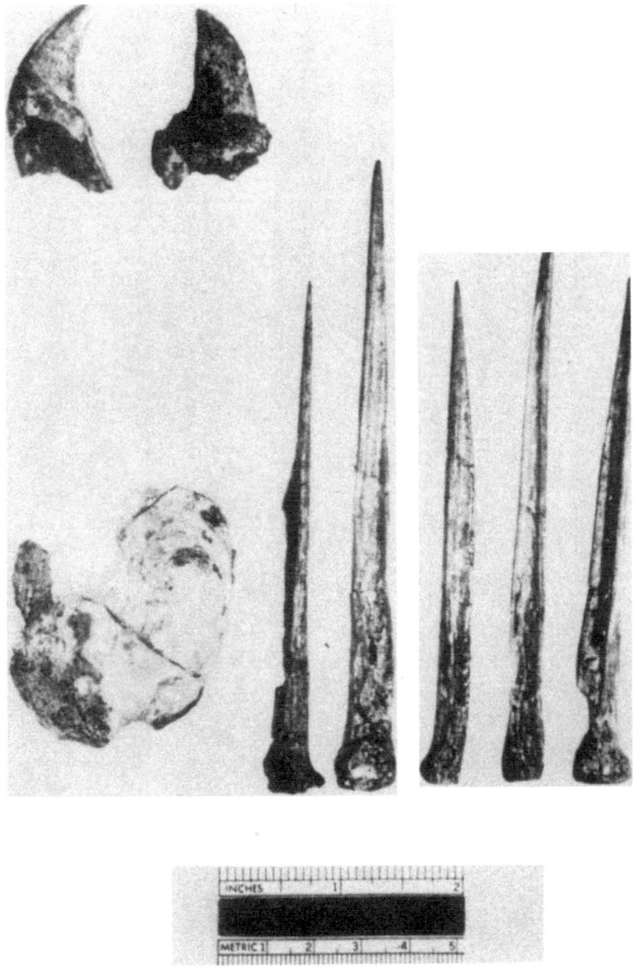

Plate 161. Norton Mound M, Burial 12 artifacts: fragment of mussel shell spoon and split turkey leg bone awls, bear canine and bear claw core. UMMA Neg. 16469.

PLATE 162

a

b

Plate 162 *a*. View from south of skull 12 of Norton Mound M with *Oliva* shell in lower left. UMMA Neg. 87-4-1. *b*. Lobed Norton Zoned Cordwrapped vessel associated with Burial 8, and *Busycon* container. The only unbroken ves el from the orton Mound Group. UMMA eg. 87-4-3.

PLATE 163

Plate 163. Mica sheet, 23.1 cm. long in trench near Burial 3. UMMA Neg. 16478.

PLATE 164

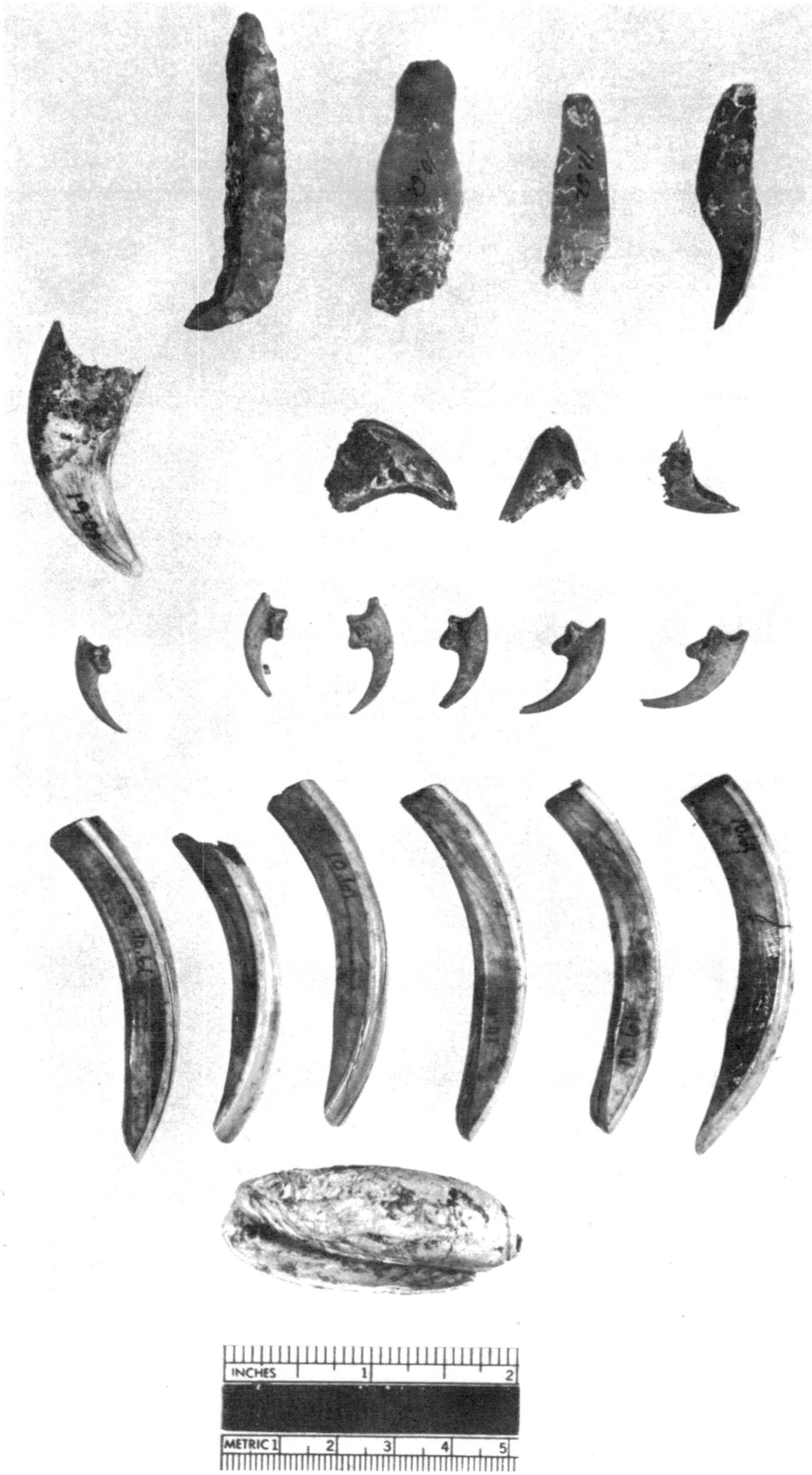

Plate 164. Norton Mound M. Trench between Buials 11 and 12 and Burial 3. Broken flint artifact perhaps a fish hook, three flint flakes, a bear canine, two Golden Eagle jaws, a falcon jaw, bird claws, modified beaver incisors, and an *Oliva* shell. UMMA Neg. 16474.

PLATE 165

Plate 165. Mussel shell spoon and *Busycon* shell container in trench near Burial 3, 11 and 12 of Norton Mound M. UMMA Neg. 16495.

PLATE 166

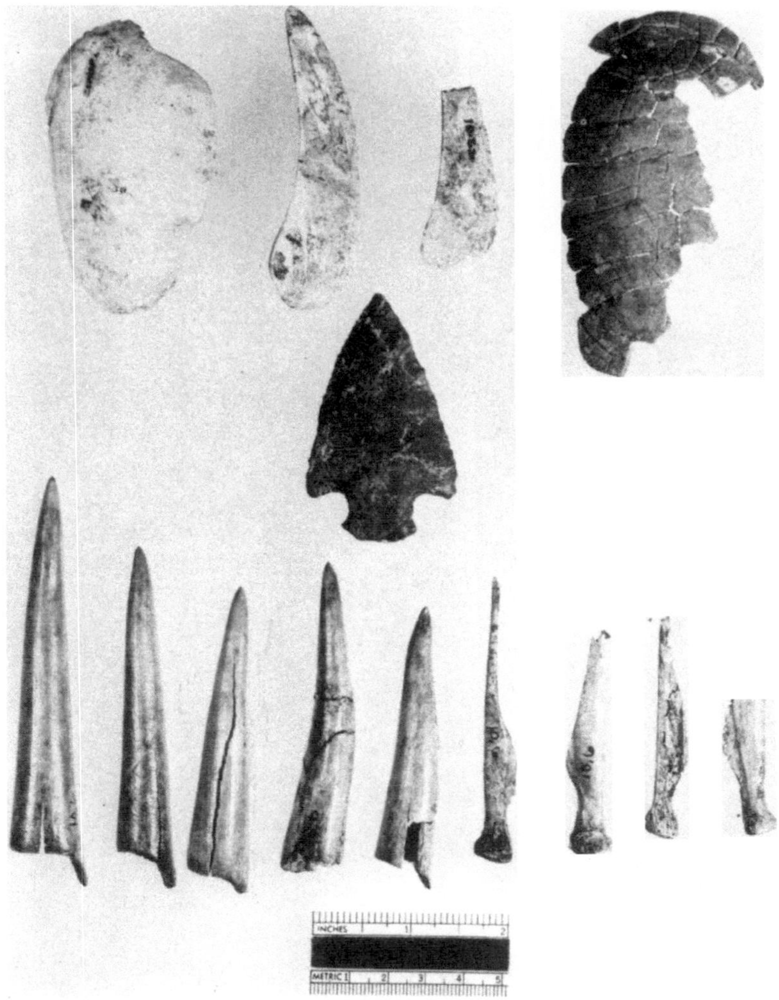

Plate 166. Artifacts with Norton Mound, Burial 3. Mussel shell spoon and 2 mussel shell claw effiges; small Norton Side Notched point; antler tine points, notched turkey bone awls. UMMA Neg. 16490.

PLATE 167

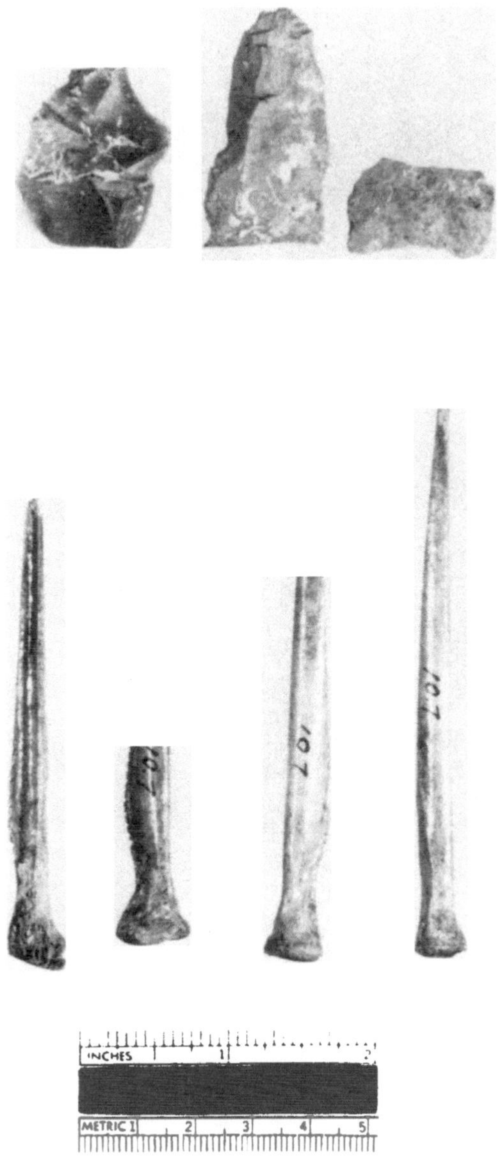

Plate 167. Turkey leg bone awls and chert chips from Burial 3 in Norton Mound M. UMMA Neg. 16468.

PLATE 168

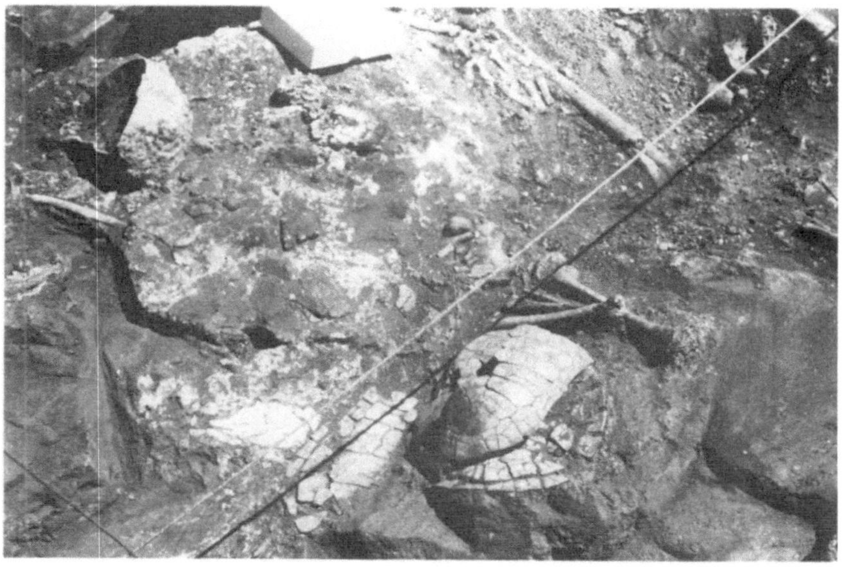

a

b

Plate 168 *a*. Close up of stocked carapaces near knees of Burial 3 in mound M. UMMA Neg. 67-1-5. *b*. Cache of 6 Norton Corner Notched points placed under the 6 carapace cups near knees of Burial 3 in Mound M. UMMA Neg. 79-7-3.

PLATE 169

Plate 169. Six Carapace containers of *Emys blandingi* associated with Burial 3 of Mound M. UMMA Neg. 16568.

PLATE 170

Plate 170. Six orton Corner Notched points with Burial 3 in Norton Mound M. These points were cover d by 6 Blandings turtle carapace cups. UMMA Neg. 16471.

PLATE 171

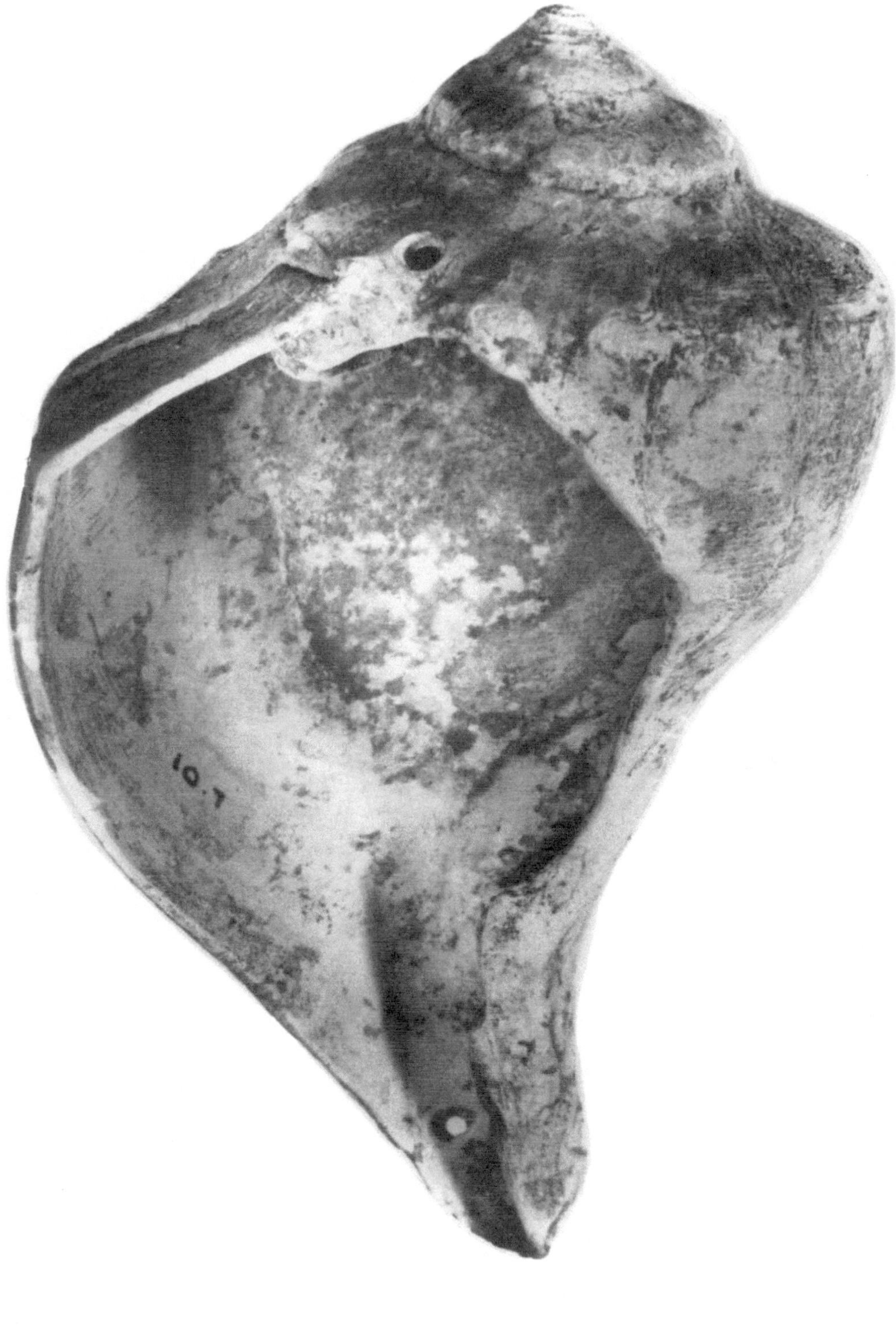

Plate 171. *Busycon contrarium* shell vessel with Burial 8 of Norton Mound M. UMMA Neg. 16472.

PLATE 172

Plate 172. Three turtle carapace dishes of Blandings turtle, and a carapace dish of the eastern box turtle (lower left) all found inside pottery vessel M-8. The Blandings turtle dishes are engraved. Small projectile point from Burial 9. The rest including the turkey leg bone awl were with Norton Mound M, Burial 9. UMMA Neg. 16484.

PLATE 173

Plate 173. orton Mound M. Burial 7: turtle carapace with repair holes on the left side. UMMA Neg. 16475.

PLATE 174

a

b

Plate 174 *a*. Northeast edge of burial area with end of Coffinberry pit indicated by ruler. Mica plate at right center. UMMA Neg. 67-3-1. *b*. Sub-mound M post mold pattern of pre-mound tructur . View to northeast. UMMA Neg. 67-3-6.

PLATE 175

Plate 175. Cordmarked and plain pottery and flint chips from the sub-mound post mold area. UMMA Neg. 16473.

PLATE 176

Plate 176. Norton Mound M. Artifacts from the floor of the mound. UMMA Neg. 16489.

PLATE 177

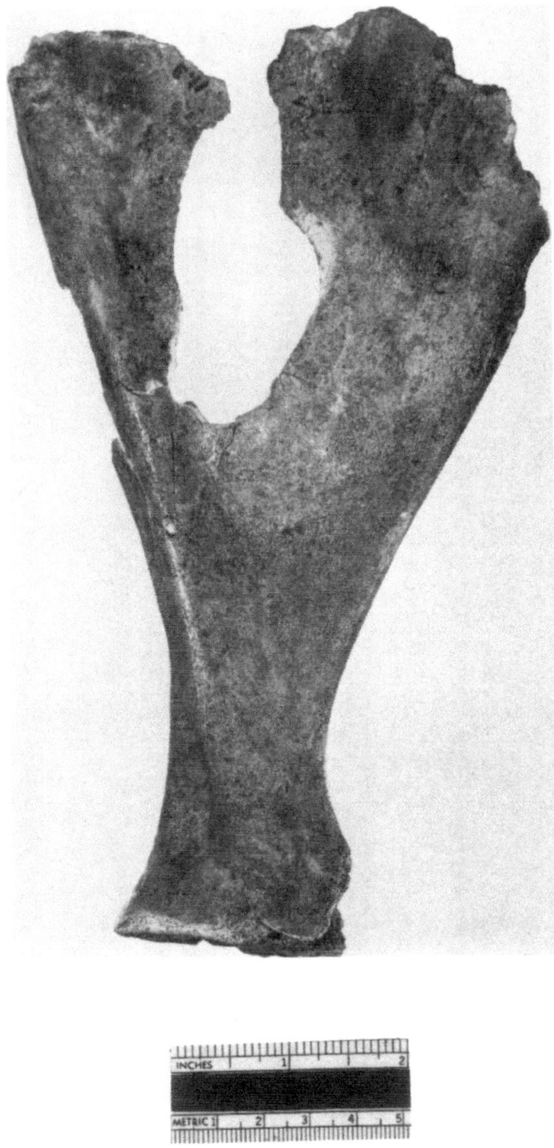

Plate 177. Elk scapula hoe or shovel from below cap of Mound M between burial area and Feature 3. UMMA Neg. 16486.